T0336019

Metaheuristics Algorithm and Optimization of Engineering and Complex Systems

Thanigaivelan R.
AKT Memorial College of Engineering and Technology, India

Suchithra M.
SRM Institute of Science and Technology, India

Kaliappan S.
KCG College of Technology, India

Mothilal T.
KCG College of Technology, India

A volume in the Advances in
Systems Analysis, Software
Engineering, and High
Performance Computing
(ASASEHPC) Book Series

Published in the United States of America by
    IGI Global
    Engineering Science Reference (an imprint of IGI Global)
    701 E. Chocolate Avenue
    Hershey PA, USA 17033
    Tel: 717-533-8845
    Fax: 717-533-8661
    E-mail: cust@igi-global.com
    Web site: http://www.igi-global.com

Library of Congress Cataloging-in-Publication Data

CIP DATA PROCESSING

2024 Engineering Science Reference
ISBN(hc): 9798369333143
ISBN(sc): 9798369350027
eISBN: 9798369333150

British Cataloguing in Publication Data
A Cataloguing in Publication record for this book is available from the British Library.

All work contributed to this book is new, previously-unpublished material.
The views expressed in this book are those of the authors, but not necessarily of the publisher.

For electronic access to this publication, please contact: eresources@igi-global.com.

Advances in Systems Analysis, Software Engineering, and High Performance Computing (ASASEHPC) Book Series

Vijayan Sugumaran
Oakland University, Rochester, USA

ISSN:2327-3453
EISSN:2327-3461

MISSION

The theory and practice of computing applications and distributed systems has emerged as one of the key areas of research driving innovations in business, engineering, and science. The fields of software engineering, systems analysis, and high performance computing offer a wide range of applications and solutions in solving computational problems for any modern organization.

The **Advances in Systems Analysis, Software Engineering, and High Performance Computing (ASASEHPC) Book Series** brings together research in the areas of distributed computing, systems and software engineering, high performance computing, and service science. This collection of publications is useful for academics, researchers, and practitioners seeking the latest practices and knowledge in this field.

Coverage

- Computer Graphics
- Human-Computer Interaction
- Software Engineering
- Virtual Data Systems

IGI Global is currently accepting manuscripts for publication within this series. To submit a proposal for a volume in this series, please contact our Acquisition Editors at Acquisitions@igi-global.com or visit: http://www.igi-global.com/publish/.

Titles in this Series

For a list of additional titles in this series, please visit: www.igi-global.com/book-series

Revolutionizing Curricula Through Computational Thinking, Logic, and Problem Solving
Mathias Mbu Fonkam (Penn State University, USA) and Narasimha Rao Vajjhala (University
of New York, Tirana, Albania)
Engineering Science Reference • copyright 2024 • 245pp • H/C (ISBN: 9798369319741)
• US $245.00 (our price)

Harnessing High-Performance Computing and AI for Environmental Sustainability
Arshi Naim (King Khalid University, Saudi Arabia)
Engineering Science Reference • copyright 2024 • 401pp • H/C (ISBN: 9798369317945)
• US $315.00 (our price)

Recent Trends and Future Direction for Data Analytics
Aparna Kumari (Nirma University, Ahmedabad, India)
Engineering Science Reference • copyright 2024 • 350pp • H/C (ISBN: 9798369336090)
• US $345.00 (our price)

Advancing Software Engineering Through AI, Federated Learning, and Large Language Models
Avinash Kumar Sharma (Sharda University, India) Nitin Chanderwal (University of Cincin-
nati, USA) Amarjeet Prajapati (Jaypee Institute of Information Technology, India) Pancham
Singh (Ajay Kumar Garg Engineering College, Ghaziabad, India) and Mrignainy Kansal
(Ajay Kumar Garg Engineering College, Ghaziabad, India)
Engineering Science Reference • copyright 2024 • 354pp • H/C (ISBN: 9798369335024)
• US $355.00 (our price)

Advancements, Applications, and Foundations of C++
Shams Al Ajrawi (Wiley Edge, USA & Alliant International University, USA) Charity
Jennings (Wiley Edge, USA & University of Phoenix, USA) Paul Menefee (Wiley Edge,
USA) Wathiq Mansoor (University of Dubai, UAE) and Mansoor Ahmed Alaali (Ahlia
University, Bahrain)
Engineering Science Reference • copyright 2024 • 564pp • H/C (ISBN: 9798369320075)
• US $295.00 (our price)

701 East Chocolate Avenue, Hershey, PA 17033, USA
Tel: 717-533-8845 x100 • Fax: 717-533-8661
E-Mail: cust@igi-global.com • www.igi-global.com

Table of Contents

Detailed Table of Contents

Chapter 1
An Application of Deep Neural Network Using GNS for Solving Complex
Fluid Dynamics Problems 1

> *Pamir Roy, North Eastern Regional Institute of Science and Technology,*
> *India*
> *S. K. Tamang, North Eastern Regional Institute of Science and*
> *Technology, India*
> *Samar Das, Indian Institute of Technology, Guwahati, India*
> *Thanigaivelan Rajasekaran, AKT Memorial College of Engineering and*
> *Technology, India*

The present work investigates the possibilities of solving complex fluid dynamics problems using Navier-Stokes equations, through simulation based techniques using deep neural networks in real time and along with provision of a singular architecture that achieves cutting-edge performance while maintaining a very high accuracy and precision at par with ground truth. The study employs Graph Network-based Simulators (GNS) to compute system dynamics. The developed model shows robust behavior in its prediction giving prediction accuracy of around 99%. The model generalizes well from unit-timestep predictions with huge number of particles at training phase, to completely differing starting conditions for timesteps ranging into the thousands and with even more particles at test time. Based on GNS, the model is immune to choices of hyper parameters over differing metrics for evaluation. The proposed model shows that deep learning is effective for solving a large set of complex fluid dynamics related problems in both forwards and backwards in time.

Chapter 2

Muhammad Abas, University of Engineering and Technology, Peshawar, Pakistan

Imran Khan, University of Engineering and Technology, Peshawar, Pakistan

Ziaullah Jan, GIK Institute, Topi, Pakistan

This study proposes an integrated approach combining grey relational analysis (GRA) and particle swarm optimization (PSO) to optimize process parameters for fused deposition modeling (FDM) 3D printing using polylactic acid (PLA) material. Experimental design based on definitive screening designs (DSD) is employed to identify optimal printing parameters, focusing on improving surface finish, dimensional accuracy, and impact strength. A regression model, generated based on DSD, accurately predicts grey relational grades (GRG), facilitating efficient optimization. The model's effectiveness is validated through evaluation metrics and close agreement between actual and predicted GRG values. PSO further refines the optimization process by efficiently navigating the solution space towards superior printing parameters. A comparison between GRA and PSO reveals refinements in printing speed, indicating the more refined solutions by PSO. These findings highlight the effectiveness of the integrated approach in enhancing additive manufacturing performance.

Chapter 3

    *Ranganatha Swamy, Faculty of Engineering and Technology, Jain
        University (Deemed), India*
    D. V. S. S. S. V. Prasad, Aditya College of Engineering, India
    Hari Banda, Villa College, Maldives
    *Ibrahim A. Mohamed, KPR Institute of Engineering and Technology,
        Coimbatore, India*
    M. Subramanian, St. Joseph's College of Engineering, Chennai, India
    S. Kaliappan, KCG College of Technology, India

This study focuses on the optimisation of the wire electric discharge machining (WEDM) process for WE43 alloy using machine learning methods. The alloy, made of magnesium (Mg), copper (Cu), rare earth (RE) elements, and zirconium (Zr), is extensively employed in aerospace and automotive sectors for its lightweight and high-strength features. The research applies three machine learning models—artificial neural networks (ANN), random forest (RF), and decision trees (DT)—to optimize the important process parameters, including current (A), pulse on (P On), and pulse off (P Off). A full experimental design based on the Taguchi L27 array is undertaken, methodically altering each parameter at three levels. Material removal rate (MRR) is chosen as the response variable for optimisation. The process parameters are adjusted by the use of machine learning techniques, with ANN emerging as the most accurate predictor, obtaining an accuracy of 96.7%.

    Satyanarayana Tirlangi, Visakha Institute of Engineering and
        Technology, Visakhapatnam, India
    Hari Banda, Villa College, Maldives
    R. Vadivel, BNM Institute of Technology, Bangalore, India
    Sudheer Kumar Battula, Lakireddy Balireddy College of Engineering
        (Autonomous), India
    M. Sabarimuthu, Kongu Engineering College, Erode, India
    Mohammed Ali H., SRM Institute of Science and Technology,
        Ramapuram, India

This study focuses on optimizing the electrochemical machining (ECM) technique for Inconel alloy, recognized for its problematic machinability. Employing a methodical approach, the Taguchi technique with a L9 array architecture was originally applied for testing. Subsequently, the research used the genetic algorithm (GA) as a metaheuristic optimization technique to improve and optimize the experimental findings. The improved parameters acquired using GA were shown to give a greater material removal rate (MRR) compared to the original Taguchi technique, highlighting the efficiency of the hybrid methodology. Specifically, the GA optimization produced a lowered voltage of 14.8V, an electrolyte concentration of 185.3 g/L, and an enhanced flow rate of 1.7 L/min, resulting in a better MRR of 0.876 g/min. This hybrid technique offers a thorough strategy for gaining greater efficiency in ECM for Inconel alloy machining, integrating the methodical planning of trials with the exploration capabilities of the genetic algorithm.

*Satyanarayana Tirlangi, Visakha Institute of Engineering and
Technology, Visakhapatnam, India*
*T. S. Senthil, Noorul Islam Centre For Higher Education, Kumaracoil,
India*
*S. John Leon, Noorul Islam Centre For Higher Education, Kumaracoil,
India*
A. Parvathi Priya, RMK Engineering College, Thiruvallur, India
Raghuram Pradhan, PACE Institute of Technology and Sciences, India
Ramya Maranan, Lovely Professional University, Punjab, India

In this research endeavor, the laser welding of C63000 alloy has been thoroughly examined, focusing on the interplay of key welding parameters—laser power, welding speed, and amplitude. The experimental design, structured as per the Taguchi L9 array, provided a systematic approach to investigating these parameters' effects on critical mechanical properties, specifically tensile strength and Brinell hardness. The alloy's responses were meticulously studied under varied conditions, capturing the nuances of its behavior in response to changes in laser welding inputs. The experimental outcomes revealed distinct trends in tensile strength and Brinell hardness in relation to the variations in welding parameters. Notably, the highest levels of tensile strength and hardness were consistently observed under specific combinations of welding speed, laser power, and amplitude.

*Patlola Madhusudhan, B.V. Raju Institute of Technology, Narsapur,
India*

*Parthasarathi Mishra, Government College of Engineering, Odisha,
India*

G. Vanya Sree, CVR College of Engineering, Ibrahimpatnam, India

*P. K. Dhal, Vel Tech Rangarajan Dr. Sagunthala R&D Institute of
Science and Technology, Chennai, India*

*C. K. Arvinda Pandian, B.S. Abdur Rahman Crescent Institute of
Science and Technology, Vandalur, India*

Socrates S., Velammal Institute of Technology, Chennai, India

This chapter examines the application of meta-heuristic optimization in boosting
the thermal performance of solar energy systems. The analysis sheds light on the
short- and long-term benefits of meta-heuristic algorithms by utilizing performance
metrics, energy efficiency metrics, and reliability assessment. Performance Metrics
imply higher energy output and efficient temperature regulation, demonstrating the
algorithm's competence in overcoming complex architectural conditions. Energy
Efficiency metrics reflect greater exploitation of solar energy resources, signaling
a huge step towards sustainability. The different conclusions from Reliability
Assessment illustrate the adaptability of meta-heuristic optimization, underlining
both problems and accomplishments in stability and consistency across time.

Optimizing shot peening is a cold-working process employed to generate a compressive residual stress layer and modify the mechanical properties of metals. It involves impacting a surface with a shot with sufficient force to induce plastic deformation. Peening a surface spread it plastically, leading to alterations in its mechanical properties. Its primary application is to prevent the propagation of microcracks from the surface. Such cracks do not propagate in a material that is under compressive stress. Optimizing shot peening can induce such stress on the surface. In this process, shots are accelerated using centrifugal force generated by a rotating impeller, which directs the shots to impact the surface to be peened. Media choices include spherical cast steel shots, ceramic beads, or conditioned cut wire. Peening necessitates well-graded shots with consistent hardness, diameter, and shape, and a mechanism for removing optimized shot fragments throughout the process is desirable.

In the search for sustainable and reliable energy solutions, the deployment of hybrid renewable energy systems (HRES) has developed as a promising approach mainly for powering remote villages that lack access to centralized grids. The optimal configuration of these systems leads to a complex optimization problem through demanding the application of meta-heuristic algorithms to efficiently direct the massive solution space and recognize the most cost-effective and reliable setup. Numerous meta-heuristic algorithms have been engaged for this purpose. Through a comparative analysis of various meta-heuristic algorithms, particle swarm optimization helps in obtaining improved solutions. Particle swarm optimization (PSO) occurs as a powerful and effective optimization technique in addressing the complex task of determining optimal configurations for hybrid renewable energy systems positioned in remote villages.

Aditi Sharma, Institute of Engineering and Technology, Lucknow, India
Hari Banda, Villa College, Maldives
N. Dhamodharan, Dr. Mahalingam College of Engineering and
Technology, Pollachi, India
J. Ramya, St. Joseph's College of Engineering, Chennai, India
Priya Shirley Muller, Sathyabama Institute of Science and Technology,
Chennai, India
M. D. Rajkamal, Velammal Institute of Technology, Chennai, India

The present research studies the optimization of multipass milling parameters for
AISI 304 stainless steel, adopting a systematic experimental technique based on the
Taguchi L9 array design. The research methodically adjusts cutting speed, feed rate,
and depth of cut, documenting their impacts on surface roughness. Experimental
data, obtained with a Mitutoyo portable surface tester, are the foundation for
training machine learning models. The linear regression (LR) model, trained using
1200 measurements, produces a prediction equation with a remarkable accuracy of
92.335%, offering insights into the linear correlations between machining parameters
and surface roughness. Concurrently, an artificial neural network (ANN) model,
exhibiting 100% accuracy, captures non-linear patterns inherent in the milling
process. The actual vs. anticipated values table for the LR model further demonstrate
its predictive powers.

Chapter 10

*Utkal Surseh Patil, Sharad Institute of Technology College of
    Engineering, Ichalkaranji, India*

*A. Krishnakumari, Hindustan Institute of Technology and Science,
    Padur, India*

*M. Saravanan, Hindustan Institute of Technology and Science, Padur,
    India*

M. Muthukannan, KCG College of Technology, Karapakkam, India

Ramya Maranan, Lovely Professional University, Punjab, India

*R. Rambabu, Rajamahendri Institute of Engineering and Technology,
    Rajamahendravaram, India*

This research presents haDEPSO, a pioneering hybrid technique for engineering design optimization. Combining the strengths of Differential Evolution (DE) and Particle Swarm Optimization (PSO), haDEPSO offers a versatile answer to the difficulties of contemporary optimization settings. The methodology combines a precise integration of DE's robust exploration capabilities with PSO's efficient exploitation tactics, ensuring adaptability across diverse problem environments. Through 10 trials, performance measures such as fitness function value, convergence speed, and diversity meter reveal haDEPSO's consistent optimization power. Scalability testing reveals the algorithm's effectiveness in addressing situations of varying sizes, yet challenges occur in particularly massive instances. These findings contribute to a deep knowledge of haDEPSO's strengths and restrictions, driving subsequent advancements for better applicability in engineering design optimization.

R. Selvapriya, Muthayammal Engineering College, India
M. Gopinath, Muthayammal Engineering College, India
D. Velmurugan, Muthayammal Engineering College, India
P. Tamilchelvan, Muthayammal College of Engineering, India

The plastic limit analysis of structures has several benefits, but it also has certain disadvantages, such high computing costs. In the past twenty years, plastic limit analysis has performed better thanks to metaheuristic algorithms, particularly when it comes to structural issues. Graph theoretical techniques have also significantly reduced the process's processing time. But until recently, the iterative process and its proportional computer memory and time have proven difficult. In order to quickly ascertain the collapse load factors of two-dimensional frames, a metaheuristic-based artificial neural network (ANN), which falls under the category of supervised machine learning techniques, has been utilized in this work. The numerical examples show that the accuracy and performance of the suggested method are adequate.

Renugadevi Ramalingam, RMK Engineering College, India
J. Shobana, SRM Institute of Science and Technology, India
K. Arthi, SRM Institute of Science and Technology, India
G. Elangovan, SRM Institute of Science and Technology, India
S. Radha, Vivekanandha College of Engineering for Women, India
N. Priyanka, Vellore Institute of Technology, India

Metaheuristic algorithms represent a class of optimization techniques tailored to tackle intricate problems that defy resolution through conventional means. Drawing inspiration from natural phenomena like genetics, swarm dynamics, and evolution, these algorithms traverse expansive search spaces in pursuit of identifying the optimal solution to a given problem. Well-known examples include genetic algorithms, particle swarm optimization, ant colony optimization, simulated annealing, and tabu search. These methodologies find widespread application across diverse domains such as engineering, finance, and computer science. Spanning several decades, the evolution of metaheuristic algorithms entails the refinement and diversification of optimization strategies rooted in natural systems. As indispensable tools in addressing complex optimization challenges across various fields, metaheuristic algorithms are poised to remain pivotal in driving technological advancements and fostering novel applications.

Chapter 13

M. Shanmugapriya, KCG College of Technology, India
K. K. Manivannan, KCG College of Technology, India

Metaheuristic algorithms have emerged as powerful optimization techniques capable of efficiently exploring complex solution spaces to find near-optimal solutions. This paper provides a comprehensive review and comparative analysis of several widely used metaheuristic algorithms, including genetic algorithms (GA), particle swarm optimization (PSO), firefly algorithm (FA), grey wolf optimizer (GWO), squirrel search algorithm (SSA), flying fox optimization algorithm (FFO). The comparative analysis encompasses various performance metrics, such as convergence speed, solution quality, robustness, scalability, and applicability across diverse problem domains. The study investigates the strengths and weaknesses of each algorithm through empirical evaluations of benchmark problems, highlighting their suitability for different optimization scenarios. Additionally, the impact of parameter tuning on algorithm performance is discussed, emphasizing the need for careful parameter selection to achieve optimal results.

Chapter 14

A. Saravanan, SMK Fomra Institute of Technology, Chennai, India
S. Bathrinath, Kalasalingam Academy of Research and Education,
*   Krishnankoil, India*
Hari Banda, Villa College, Maldives
S. J. Suji Prasad, Kongu Engineering College, Erode, India
Jonnadula Narasimharao, CMR Technical Campus, Hyderabad, India
Mohammed Ali H., SRM Institute of Science and Technology,
*   Ramapuram, India*

This work presents a holistic framework for automating automated guided vehicles (AGVs) in industrial settings by using well-positioned sensors and sophisticated machine learning models. The AGV is put through rigorous testing along a variety of industrial pathways. It is outfitted with sensors such as wheel encoders, proximity sensors, ultrasonic sensors, and LIDAR. Microcontrollers in the high-speed electronic system enable real-time data processing and decision-making based on sensor inputs. For the purpose of anticipating impediments and maximising AGV routes, machine learning models such as decision trees (DT), artificial neural networks (ANN), support vector machines (SVM), and random forests (RF) are developed and assessed. Experiments showing accuracy, F1 score, precision, and recall show how well the integrated system is. The AGV is a prime example of effective route planning, obstacle avoidance, and navigation in busy industrial settings.

The scheduling techniques have been investigated by the job execution process in a system in order to maximize multiprocessor utilization. DPM (dynamic power management) and DVFS (dynamic voltage and frequency scaling) are two general strategies for lowering energy use. PeSche (performance enhanced scheduling) is a proposed scheduling algorithm that has been designed for an optimal solution. CodeBlocks were used to run the extensive simulations. In terms of computing performance (average waiting time and average turnaround time), the PeSche scheduling algorithm outperformed recently reported scheduling algorithms such as SJF, RR, FCFS, Priority, and SJF-LJF. PeSche scheduling algorithm gives better results by assigning the priority in terms of energy time ratio, programming running time, total energy and total time than existed algorithms. In comparison to minimum energy schedule (MES) and slack utilization for reduced energy (SURE), PeSche used less energy.

Operational cost savings in electric utilities using the application of genetic algorithms in power system planning and operation characterize an innovative approach that involves computational intelligence to optimize complex decision-making processes in power grid functioning. Electric utilities involve various challenges which involve managing power generation, transmission and distribution that are necessary to meet the ever-growing demand for electricity with the reduction in operational costs. These challenges are overcome using the aid of a genetic algorithm. In the field of power system planning, the genetic algorithms are engaged to optimize the configuration and expansion of generation, transmission and distribution.

Chapter 17

    Socrates S., Velammal Institute of Technology, Chennai, India
    K. K. Manivannan, KCG College of Technology, Chennai, India
    A. Krishnakumari, Hindustan Institute of Technology and Science,
        Padur, India
    M. Saravanan, Hindustan Institute of Technology and Science, Padur,
        India
    M. Shanmugapriya, KCG College of Technology, Karapakkam, India
    M. D. Raj Kamal, Velammal Institute of Technology, Chennai, India

This research presents an integrated approach to enhance the performance of grid-connected photovoltaic (PV) systems by combining sensor-based orientation with the practical swarm optimization (PSO) algorithm for maximum power point tracking (MPPT) and a proportional-integral (PI) controller for DC voltage regulation. Solar positioning and infrared sensors provide real-time data, guiding the dynamic movement of the solar panel. The PSO algorithm optimizes motor movements for efficient MPPT, ensuring the panel aligns with the optimal sun position throughout the day. Simultaneously, the PI controller regulates the DC bus voltage, contributing to system stability and grid compliance. Experimental results reveal increased power output, demonstrating the synergistic impact of the integrated system. This approach not only maximizes energy capture but also improves system reliability.

Editorial Advisory Board

Preface

Optimisation and decision-making have emerged as key issues in the engineering domain. The growing need for data processing has led to problems like longer processing times and higher memory usage, which are challenging challenges in many technical fields. Issues still arise, necessitating not only fixes but also improvements over current best practices. Although developing and putting into practice new heuristic algorithms takes time, there is still a strong need to do so because even little improvements have the potential to result in a large reduction in computational costs. In the context of this, the book Metaheuristics Algorithm and Optimisation of Engineering and Complex Systems is a shining example of innovation. It looks at the urgent demand for creative algorithmic solutions and investigates hyperheuristic strategies that provide answers like search space automation using integrated heuristics. Engineering and Complex System Optimisation Using Metaheuristics and Algorithms give a thorough rundown of contemporary computational techniques used in developing disciplines. It incorporates cutting-edge papers from traditional application areas, going beyond a simple presentation of generic metaheuristic procedures. Specifically designed to function as a graduate-level course textbook, a reference manual for enthusiasts in the fields of engineering and social science, or a list of new chances for researchers, this book covers the entire range of recent advances in hyper-heuristic approaches. It serves as a link between traditional algorithms and state-of-the-art meta-heuristic algorithms, covering topics such as simulated annealing, scatter search, tabu search, constraint programming, and more. The book markets itself as a crucial tool for dynamic optimisation practitioners, attracting both beginners and seasoned experts looking for a single source of information on the most recent.

Chapter 1 investigates the possibilities of solving complex fluid dynamics problems using Navier-Stokes equations, through simulation based techniques using deep neural networks in real time and along with provision of a singular architecture that achieves cutting-edge performance while maintaining a very high accuracy and precision at par with ground truth. The study employs Graph Network-based Simulators

(GNS) to compute system dynamics. The developed model shows robust behavior in its prediction giving prediction accuracy of around 99%. The model generalizes well from unit-time step predictions with huge number of particles at training phase, to completely differing starting conditions for time steps ranging into the thousands and with even more particles at test time. Based on GNS, the model is immune to choices of hyper parameters over differing metrics for evaluation. The proposed model shows that deep learning is effective for solving a large set of complex fluid dynamics related problems in both forwards and backwards in time.

Chapter 2 proposes an integrated approach combining grey relational analysis (GRA) and particle swarm optimization (PSO) to optimize process parameters for Fused Deposition Modeling (FDM) 3D printing using Polylactic Acid (PLA) material. Experimental design based on definitive screening designs (DSD) is employed to identify optimal printing parameters, focusing on improving surface finish, dimensional accuracy, and impact strength. A regression model, generated based on DSD, accurately predicts grey relational grades (GRG), facilitating efficient optimization. The model's effectiveness is validated through evaluation metrics and close agreement between actual and predicted GRG values. PSO further refines the optimization process by efficiently navigating the solution space towards superior printing parameters. A comparison between GRA and PSO reveals refinements in printing speed, indicating the more refined solutions by PSO. These findings highlight the effectiveness of the integrated approach in enhancing additive manufacturing performance.

Chapter 3 focuses on the optimisation of the wire electric discharge machining (WEDM) process for WE43 alloy using machine learning methods. The alloy, made of magnesium (Mg), copper (Cu), rare earth (RE) elements, and zirconium (Zr), is extensively employed in aerospace and automotive sectors for its lightweight and high-strength features. The research applies three machine learning models—Artificial Neural Networks (ANN), Random Forest (RF), and Decision Trees (DT)—to optimize the important process parameters, including Current (A), Pulse On (P On), and Pulse Off (P Off). A full experimental design based on the Taguchi L_{27} array is undertaken, methodically altering each parameter at three levels. Material Removal Rate is chosen as the response variable for optimisation. The process parameters are adjusted by the use of machine learning techniques, with ANN emerging as the most accurate predictor, obtaining an accuracy of 96.7%.

Chapter 4 focuses on optimizing the electrochemical machining (ECM) technique for Inconel alloy, recognized for its problematic machinability. Employing a methodical approach, the Taguchi technique with L9 array architecture was originally applied for testing. Subsequently, the research used the Genetic Algorithm (GA) as a metaheuristic optimization technique to improve and optimize the experimental findings. The improved parameters acquired using GA were shown to give a greater

Material Removal Rate (MRR) compared to the original Taguchi technique, highlighting the efficiency of the hybrid methodology. Specifically, the GA optimization produced a lowered voltage of 14.8V, an electrolyte concentration of 185.3 g/L, and an enhanced flow rate of 1.7 L/min, resulting in a better MRR of 0.876 g/min. This hybrid technique offers a thorough strategy for gaining greater efficiency in ECM for Inconel alloy machining, integrating the methodical planning of trials with the exploration capabilities of the genetic algorithm.

Chapter 5 focusing on the interplay of key welding parameters—laser power, welding speed, and amplitude. The experimental design, structured as per the Taguchi L_9 array, provided a systematic approach to investigating these parameters' effects on critical mechanical properties, specifically tensile strength and Brinell hardness. The alloy's responses were meticulously studied under varied conditions, capturing the nuances of its behavior in response to changes in laser welding inputs. The experimental outcomes revealed distinct trends in tensile strength and Brinell hardness in relation to the variations in welding parameters. Notably, the highest levels of tensile strength and hardness were consistently observed under specific combinations of welding speed, laser power, and amplitude.

Chapter 6 discusses the application of meta-heuristic optimization in boosting the thermal performance of solar energy systems. The analysis sheds light on the short- and long-term benefits of meta-heuristic algorithms by utilizing performance metrics, energy efficiency metrics, and reliability assessment. Performance Metrics imply higher energy output and efficient temperature regulation, demonstrating the algorithm's competence in overcoming complex architectural conditions. Energy Efficiency Metrics reflect greater exploitation of solar energy resources, signaling a huge step towards sustainability. The different conclusions from Reliability Assessment illustrate the adaptability of meta-heuristic optimization, underlining both problems and accomplishments in stability and consistency across time.

Chapter 7 optimized the shot peening process to generate a compressive residual stress layer and modify the mechanical properties of metals. It involves impacting a surface with a shot with sufficient force to induce plastic deformation. Peening a surface spread it plastically, leading to alterations in its mechanical properties. Its primary application is to prevent the propagation of microcracks from the surface. Such cracks do not propagate in a material that is under compressive stress. Optimizing shot peening can induce such stress on the surface. In this process, shots are accelerated using centrifugal force generated by a rotating impeller, which directs the shots to impact the surface to be peened. Media choices include spherical cast steel shots, ceramic beads, or conditioned cut wire. Peening necessitates well-graded shots with consistent hardness, diameter, and shape, and a mechanism for removing optimized shot fragments throughout the process is desirable.

Chapter 8 discuss about the promising approach mainly for powering remote villages that lack access to centralized grids. The optimal configuration of these system leads to a complex optimization problem through demanding the application of meta-heuristic algorithms to efficiently direct the massive solution space and recognize the most cost-effective and reliable setup. Numerous meta-heuristic algorithms have been engaged for this purpose. Through a comparative analysis of various meta-heuristic algorithms, particle swarm optimization helps in obtaining improved solutions. Particle Swarm Optimization (PSO) occurs as a powerful and effective optimization technique in addressing the complex task of determining optimal configurations for hybrid renewable energy systems positioned in remote villages.

Chapter 9 presents the research studies on optimization of multipass milling parameters for AISI 304 stainless steel, adopting a systematic experimental technique based on the Taguchi L9 array design. The research methodically adjusts cutting speed, feed rate, and depth of cut, documenting their impacts on surface roughness. Experimental data, obtained with a Mitutoyo portable surface tester, are the foundation for training machine learning models. The linear regression (LR) model, trained using 1200 measurements, produces a prediction equation with a remarkable accuracy of 92.335%, offering insights into the linear correlations between machining parameters and surface roughness. Concurrently, an artificial neural network (ANN) model, exhibiting 100% accuracy, captures non-linear patterns inherent in the milling process. The actual vs. anticipated values table for the LR model further demonstrates its predictive powers.

Chapter 10 presents haDEPSO, a pioneering hybrid technique for engineering design optimization. Combining the strengths of Differential Evolution (DE) and Particle Swarm Optimization (PSO), haDEPSO offers a versatile answer to the difficulties of contemporary optimization settings. The methodology combines a precise integration of DE's robust exploration capabilities with PSO's efficient exploitation tactics, ensuring adaptability across diverse problem environments. Through 10 trials, performance measures such as fitness function value, convergence speed, and diversity meter reveal haDEPSO's consistent optimization power. Scalability testing reveals the algorithm's effectiveness in addressing situations of varying sizes, yet challenges occur in particularly massive instances. These findings contribute to a deep knowledge of haDEPSO's strengths and restrictions, driving subsequent advancements for better applicability in engineering design optimization.

Chapter 11 have used metaheuristic algorithm for analysis of structures.In the past twenty years, plastic limit analysis has performed better thanks to metaheuristic algorithms, particularly when it comes to structural issues. Graph theoretical techniques have also significantly reduced the process's processing time. But until recently, the iterative process and its proportional computer memory and time have proven difficult. In order to quickly ascertain the collapse load factors of two-dimensional frames, a metaheuristic-based artificial neural network (ANN), which falls under the category of supervised machine learning techniques, has been utilized in this work. The numerical examples show that the accuracy and performance of the suggested method are adequate.

Chapter 12 discusses the extensive Investigation of Meta-Heuristics Algorithms for Optimization Problems. Metaheuristic algorithms represent a class of optimization techniques tailored to tackle intricate problems that defy resolution through conventional means. Drawing inspiration from natural phenomena like genetics, swarm dynamics, and evolution, these algorithms traverse expansive search spaces in pursuit of identifying the optimal solution to a given problem. Well-known examples include genetic algorithms, particle swarm optimization, ant colony optimization, simulated annealing, and tabu search. These methodologies find widespread application across diverse domains such as engineering, finance, and computer science. Spanning several decades, the evolution of metaheuristic algorithms entails the refinement and diversification of optimization strategies rooted in natural systems. As indispensable tools in addressing complex optimization challenges across various fields, metaheuristic algorithms are poised to remain pivotal in driving technological advancements and fostering novel applications.

This chapter presents a holistic framework for automating Automated Guided Vehicles (AGVs) in industrial settings by using well-positioned sensors and sophisticated machine learning models. The AGV is put through rigorous testing along a variety of industrial pathways. It is outfitted with sensors such as wheel encoders, proximity sensors, ultrasonic sensors, and LIDAR. Microcontrollers in the High-Speed Electronic System enable real-time data processing and decision-making based on sensor inputs. For the purpose of anticipating impediments and maximising AGV routes, machine learning models such as Decision Trees (DT), Artificial Neural Networks (ANN), Support Vector Machines (SVM), and Random Forests (RF) are developed and assessed. Experiments showing accuracy, F1 score, precision, and recall show how well the integrated system is. The AGV is a prime example of effective route planning, obstacle avoidance, and navigation in busy industrial settings.

Chapter 15 discusses the enhancement of system performance using pesche scheduling algorithm on multiprocessors. The scheduling techniques have been investigated by the job execution process in a system in order to maximize multiprocessor utilization. DPM (Dynamic Power Management) and DVFS (Dynamic Voltage and Frequency Scaling) are two general strategies for lowering energy use. PeSche (Performance enhanced Scheduling) is a proposed scheduling algorithm that has been designed for an optimal solution. The CodeBlocks were used to run the extensive simulations. In terms of computing performance (Average waiting time & Average turnaround time), the PeSche scheduling algorithm outperformed recently reported scheduling algorithms such as SJF, RR, FCFS, Priority, and SJF-LJF.

PeSche scheduling algorithm gave better results by assigning the priority in terms of energy time ratio, programming running time, total energy and total time than existed algorithms. In comparison to Minimum Energy Schedule (MES) and Slack Utilization for Reduced Energy (SURE), PeSche used less energy.

Chapter 16 throws the light on enhancing operational cost savings in electric utilities on global optimization in power system planning and operation. Operational cost savings in electric utilities using the application of genetic algorithms in power system planning and operation characterize an innovative approach that involves computational intelligence to optimize complex decision-making processes in power grid functioning. Electric utilities involve various challenges which involve managing power generation, transmission and distribution that are necessary to meet the ever-growing demand for electricity with the reduction in operational costs. These challenges are overcome using the aid of a genetic algorithm. In the field of power system planning, the genetic algorithms are engaged to optimize the configuration and expansion of generation, transmission and distribution.

Chapter 17 presents an integrated approach to enhance the performance of grid-connected photovoltaic (PV) systems by combining sensor-based orientation with the Practical Swarm Optimization (PSO) algorithm for Maximum Power Point Tracking (MPPT) and a Proportional-Integral (PI) controller for DC voltage regulation. Solar positioning and infrared sensors provide real-time data, guiding the dynamic movement of the solar panel. The PSO algorithm optimizes motor movements for efficient MPPT, ensuring the panel aligns with the optimal sun position throughout the day. Simultaneously, the PI controller regulates the DC bus voltage, contributing to system stability and grid compliance. Experimental results reveal increased power output, demonstrating the synergistic impact of the integrated system. This approach not only maximizes energy capture but also improves system reliability.

The techniques that direct the search process are called metaheuristics. Finding almost ideal answers requires effective search space exploration. Metaheuristic algorithms encompass a variety of techniques, from straightforward local search methods to intricate learning procedures.

A class of optimisation algorithms known as metaheuristic algorithms is used to address complex and difficult problems in a variety of fields. By using particular searching tactics, they conduct searches inside the solution space in an attempt to find the best possible solutions. The LMS method or the Kalman filter algorithm may reach a local optimum for intricate hysteretic models. A more accurate parameter identification of the hysteretic system can be achieved with metaheuristic techniques. Genetic algorithms (GA), particle swarm optimisation (PSO), simulated annealing (SA), Tabu search (TS), differential evolution (DE) algorithms, and swarm intelligence algorithms are a few popular instances of metaheuristic algorithms. GA and PSO will be introduced emphatically in this review.

Overall the metaheuristic algorithm focus on the provides the solution to the complex problems involving computer science, manufacturing, electrical and electronics system.

Chapter 1
An Application of Deep Neural Network Using GNS for Solving Complex Fluid Dynamics Problems

Pamir Roy
North Eastern Regional Institute of Science and Technology, India

S. K. Tamang
http://orcid.org/0000-0001-6000-8088
North Eastern Regional Institute of Science and Technology, India

Samar Das
Indian Institute of Technology, Guwahati, India

Thanigaivelan Rajasekaran
http://orcid.org/0000-0001-9514-9120
AKT Memorial College of Engineering and Technology, India

ABSTRACT

The present work investigates the possibilities of solving complex fluid dynamics problems using Navier-Stokes equations, through simulation based techniques using deep neural networks in real time and along with provision of a singular architecture that achieves cutting-edge performance while maintaining a very high accuracy and precision at par with ground truth. The study employs Graph Network-based Simulators (GNS) to compute system dynamics. The developed model shows robust behavior in its prediction giving prediction accuracy of around 99%. The model generalizes well from unit-timestep predictions with huge number of particles at

DOI: 10.4018/979-8-3693-3314-3.ch001

training phase, to completely differing starting conditions for timesteps ranging into the thousands and with even more particles at test time. Based on GNS, the model is immune to choices of hyper parameters over differing metrics for evaluation. The proposed model shows that deep learning is effective for solving a large set of complex fluid dynamics related problems in both forwards and backwards in time.

INTRODUCTION

In this modern era, the focus for solutions of complex fluid flow problems are encountered frequently in fluid dynamics and has shifted from pure numerical and analytical approach to realistic simulations based solutions. These simulations prove to be precious to many problems of science and engineering concerning various disciplines. But these traditional simulators prove to be highly costly to develop and use. For building a robust simulator, it demands high time in years towards engineering effort and quite hast to make trades-offs in generality for precisions and accuracy in a narrow settings range. Often the resulting simulation requires high computing resources for high quality solution and thus prevents from scaling up efficiently. All these methods also suffer from inaccuracy due to approximation or incomplete capturing of the underlying physics. Moreover, all these are not real-time simulators.

As such, the researchers have been trying to find a way to tackle such situations. A lucrative solution would be an intelligent system that knows completely the underlying physics and can provide high quality simulations in real time. This calls for machine learning by training directly from observed data. But due to huge state spaces and highly complex dynamics standard approaches become infeasible.

Another obstacle for scaling up such a system was the need for highly parallel system that is not only quick but also accurate. The main issue in this way of scaling up was that for fluid being represented as a particle system, each particle is affected by nearby particles which are affected by their nearby particles and likewise, owing to which the interaction detail representation of the system blows up with increase in the number of particles for maintaining same level of quality. For that an efficient way of just passing the necessary information from nearby particles to the particle in focus is needed. This is solved by implementing message passing graph architecture for representing the system using GNS. It enables to deploy a single deep learning model which could accurately learn simulation of a wide set of fluid dynamics systems that can provide for fluid-fluid, fluid-deformable materials-rigid solids to interact with each other while being highly parallelizable. It can generalize well for larger systems with higher time steps than that was used to train it. It is free from inductive biases for spatial invariance and accumulation error over long simulation trajectories.

Motivation of the Study

The question arises that providing the velocity and pressure at single point for a water body like river, is it possible to reliably predict the flow of water over stipulated period of time. The solution lies behind the concept of the Navier-Stokes equations that can describe any fluid. Navier-Stokes equations are differential equation sets that describe viscous fluid substance motion. These are probably one of the best well known partial differential equations for fluid mechanics. They are used to forecast weather, model aero planes and cars, etc.

The Navier- Stokes equations are,

$$\nabla \cdot u = 0 \text{(i)}$$

$$\rho \frac{du}{dt} = -\nabla p + \mu \nabla^2 u + F$$

(ii)

Eq. (i) states that the mass is conserved within the fluid. The divergence operator, $'\nabla \cdot "$ operates over a vector field (here velocity vector field of the fluid, u) to give the divergence of that field. For sake of completeness, a vector field is a space in which each point has been assigned a vector. A vector field can describe many things like fluids, electric fields, gravitational fields, etc. The divergence of a vector is an operator that tells us how much a point tends to divert vectors away from it. When the vectors seem to be moving away from a point, the divergence is said to be positive, $divF > 0$, and such point is called as source of the vector field as it acts as such. Similarly when the vectors seem to be flowing into a point, divergence becomes negative,$divF < 0$ and such point is called a sink of the vector field. The divergence is the difference between the total inflow and outflow of a point of vector field. In terms of fluid, the divergence of the vector field indicates how much or how little a point acts as a source of the fluid. It is impossible for a fluid like water, spread over an area, to suddenly disappear; it could change forms but mass is always conserved. Thus apart from a source or sink, the divergence of all other points has to be zero. This is to say that the divergence across the fluid has to be zero and hence the first Navier-Stokes equation. On the other hand, Eq. (ii) is similar to Newton's second law of motion, which for fluids can be stated as, the sum of forces acting on it is equal to its mass times acceleration. Thus it can be written as:

$$ma = \sum F$$

(iii)

Where, m = mass of the fluid, a= acceleration of the fluid= $\frac{du}{dt}$ and $\sum F$ =sum of all forces acting on the fluid.
Now, for each individual point,

$$Mass = \frac{m}{v} = \rho$$

(iv)

where, m and v are the mass and volume of the fluid respectively.
The forces acting on the fluid, have the internal forces pressure and viscosity and the external forces which are the body forces represented by F. As a fluid flows from higher pressure region to a lower pressure region, it follows a negative pressure gradient, $-\nabla p$. Also the force acting due to viscosity can be presented to as $\mu \nabla^2 u$. Hence, Eq. (iii) can be rewritten as:

$$\rho \frac{du}{dt} = -\nabla p + \mu \nabla^2 u + F$$

(v)

Eq. (v)is the second Navier-Stokes equation.
Thus, with these equations any fluid flow can be modeled as these are simply the fundamental laws of fluids. Despite of their extensive usage, it has still not been proven that the solutions always exist in three dimensions and if it does, also then those solutions are smooth. This causes problems for finding the solutions of the simulations for a long time that retain high accuracy as the exact solution of these equations are not known and as such people have to resort to numerical approximation methods that lead to error accumulation over long runs.
Thus, to mitigate the above shortcomings of the traditional simulators this paper resorts to deep learning based techniques so that the simulator can capture the underlying physics and use state of the art learning techniques to suite the model to the required needs.

RELATED WORKS

The approach to the problem focused on combining basic knowledge of Navier-Stokes equations through use of GNS model that uses particle-based simulation, a simulation method which is widely used in computational fluid dynamics. Particles represent state and encode mass, material movement, etc. Dynamics are simulated for a particles interaction with its local neighborhood.

Graph networks (Battaglia et al., 2018) are the type of neural networks based on graphs (Scarselli et al., 2008) that have nowadays proven to be quite good in forward time dynamics learning in varying conditions involving changing entity interactions. A graph network maps a given graph as input to an output graph having same architecture with differing nodes, edges, and other graphical attributes in potential, and are easily trained to learn message-passing (Gilmer et al., 2017). Graph networks are able to learn physical systematic like rigid body, robotic control systems, etc., simulations (Battaglia et al., 2016; Sanchez-Gonzalez et al., 2018; Li et al., 2019), along with non-physical systematic also.

Popularly used methods for simulating fluids based on particle systems include SPH (Monaghan, 1992), PBD (Muller et al., 2007) and MPM (Sulsky et al., 1995). These are more geared towards deformable material. Differentiable particle-based simulators such as DiffTaichi (Hu et al., 2019), PhiFlow (Holl et al., 2020), etc., have also been developed. Comparing to those simulators that are engineered, a simulator which goes through learning is theoretically proven to be more efficient for complex predictions of phenomenon giving faster prediction.

The model of this paper builds on various works, specifically of Sanchez-Gonzalez et al. (2020) graph network model that was used in numerous physical systems to learn their complex interactions and Taichi-MPM engine (Hu et al., 2018) for simulating fluids using Navier-Stokes equations.

Crucially, the model aims to have a general approach towards learning fluid simulations and entails accuracy to a high degree as well as being a real time system capable of high quality simulations that are quite close to the real ground truth with having low error. A model example is shown in Figure 1.

Figure 1. Time Development of Simulation by the Model (colors denote evolution and edges denotes particle interactions)

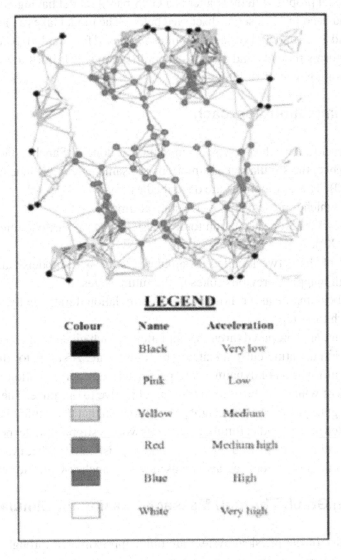

DEVELOPMENT OF GNS MODEL

The model proposed in this paper is a GNS based model having encoding, processing and decoding phases as discussed below. The model takes a particle system as input and gives updated system dynamics to be used for simulation purposes. The model performs robustly and also has generalization capabilities to a wider scope encompassing whole of fluid dynamics.

Model Simulation Approach

This paper follows the presets for simulation as done by Sanchez-Gonzalez et al. (2020). Hence, the simulation assumptions are same as that of Sanchez-Gonzalez et al. (2020). The assumptions are described as:

1. $X^t \in \mathcal{X}$ which represents the world state at time t.
2. Using Navier-Stokes equation for k timesteps gives a particle trajectory, $X^{t0:k} = (X^{t0},...,X^{tk})$.
3. A part of the network called as simulator, $s: \mathcal{X} \rightarrow \mathcal{X}$, models state dynamics through mapping previous states to the future states.
4. It can be compute as a rollout trajectory simulation iteratively by, $X^{tk+1} = s\,(X^{tk})$ for each timestep.

Dynamics are computed through simulations which give change in current state that is used in updating current state to the future state. A simulator that can learn computes information of dynamics by a parameterized approximation function, the parameters of which can be used in training objective to optimize. The mechanism for updating the graph can be thought of as a function that takes info of current state and predicted info to predict future state. In this work, a simple update mechanism, an Euler integrator, has been used. However, more sophisticated update procedures such as higher-order integrators can also be used (e.g., Sanchez-Gonzalez et al. (2019).

Updating Graph Through Message-Passing for Simulation

Dynamics of the physical system are quite approximated through interactions between the particles, i.e. energy exchange & momentum exchange in the neighborhood of the particles, in the particle based simulation. The particle-particle interactions prove to be the bottleneck in determining the quality and generality of the simulation method and hence needs to be efficient as well as showing intelligent selection behavior. Hence, without loss of generality, it would not be wrong here to be keener on learning the above mentioned interactions, which in principle provide for learning any fluid system dynamics based on particles. Particle-based simulation is treated like message-passing in a representative graph. The graph nodes represent particles and the graph edges encapsulate pair wise relations between particles, based on which the interactions between the particles are computed. The message passing has three steps: encoding, processing and decoding.

The encoding corresponds to representation of the particle based fluid system as a graph, G=ENCODER(X), where G= (V, E, u), $v_i \in$ V, and $e_{i,j} \in$ E, i.e., it does the following: $\mathcal{X} \longrightarrow \mathcal{G}$. The node embeddings are functions of particle states that are learned. Directed edges are also added between particle nodes to represent potential interaction. The edge embeddings are also learned functions of the corresponding particles like displacement of positions, etc. The embeddings at graph-level can be used to refer to global properties like gravity and magnetic fields.

The processing represents a function, $\mathcal{G} \longrightarrow \mathcal{G}$, that computes node interactions using message-passing, to output a series of graphs updated based on the learning. It outputs the graph, G_m=PROCESSOR(G_0). Message-passing allows information to propagate, respects constraints with high interaction complexity.

The decoding can be expressed as $\mathcal{G} \rightarrow \mathcal{Y}$, this extracts information from the nodes of the output graph as the computed dynamics. Learning should cause the representations to reflect ground truth for being semantically meaningful.

The present work process of simulation by message passing and the intermediate steps has been depicted visually shown in Figure 2.

Figure 2. Model overview

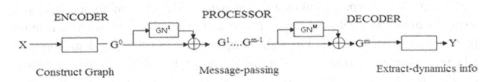

DETAILS OF MODEL BUILDING AND EVALUATION

The domain of the proposed model encompasses fluid dynamics. To capture the state of the system and get meaningful results, the input and output of the model has been tailored accordingly as discussed in details below. The model is built upon of MLP layers and shows robustness upon evaluation. It achieves state of the art accuracy to give fairly high predictions useful for realistic simulations.

Physical Domains

The present work explored on the possibility of the developed model learning to simulate datasets having diverse, complex physical materials: water which is an incompressible chaotic fluid; other rigid and non-rigid bodies based on prior knowledge of Navier-Stokes equations. These initial conditions are diverse and need implementation of differing models for materials or different algorithms for simulation. For usage in one case, Li et al. (2018) BOXBATH method is used, that can simulate a water container having a floating-cube in its inside. Other methods like SPlisHSPlasH (Bender&Koschier, 2015) [16] have also been used for testing in the present study.

The methods given by Sanchez-Gonzalez et al. (2020) for generating datasets have been implemented. Taichi-MPM engine (Hu et al., 2018) is used for simulations as it can simulate varying materials. The datasets consists of 1000 train, 100 validation and 100 test trajectories, each simulated for 300-2000 time steps (fine-tuned for the mean duration for different materials till a stable position of equilibrium is reached) similar in aesthetics to the real dataset but generated through Navier-Stokes simulator. The model was implemented using deep learning techniques and used LayerNorm (Ba et al., 2016) for faster convergence.

Input and Output Representations

Each particle is represented by an input state vector representing its position, a sequence of previous velocities and properties of material that are static as features (e.g., boundary particles, rigidity, water) respectively. The global system properties take into consideration the forces external to the system and system level properties of the material, if can be applied to suit the case. The prediction target for the supervised learning was average acceleration of each particle. For generating trajectories, on every timestep the edges of the graph were recalculated by an algorithm of k-nearest neighbors, to represent the present positions of particle. The architecture that was considered for the work uses 256 neural units. After decoding step, the positions and velocities of future states were updated by the Euler integrator, so they correspond to accelerations.

Neural Network Architecture and its Training

All multi-layer perceptrons have basic two hidden layers (with ReLU activations), followed by a non-activated output layer, each layer with size of 256. Here, He-initialization was performed for the initial weights of the network. The model was implemented using Sonnet1, TensorFlow1 and Graph Nets library (2018). To develop a chaotic and complex system model, it needs to deal with error accumulation over long simulations. Here, a simple approach is applied to mitigate this by feeding the network with noisy data by tweaking the ground truth with a random-walk noise as done in the original work by Sanchez -Gonzalez et al., (2020).

As training phase starts, the data provided as input to the model like velocities and positions was corrupted with noise generated through random-walk. This is done so that the training distribution is more conforming to the distribution generated during simulations. Then all inputs and target vectors are normalized element wise to normal (Gaussian) distribution, as earlier experiments showed that normalization leads to faster training.

For loss function and optimization, the L2 loss is used and over this loss the model is optimized with Adam optimizer (Kingma & Ba, 2014) using a minibatch size of 10. The exponential learning rate decay is performed. While the model can train in lesser steps, the rate has been still kept them low for being in safe side and make appropriate comparisons from different system settings. The model is then evaluated regularly at training phase by MSE of its rollouts and the training was stopped when the decrease in MSE became negligible. A detailed structure of the proposed model has been presented in

Figure 3. Detailed structure of the present model

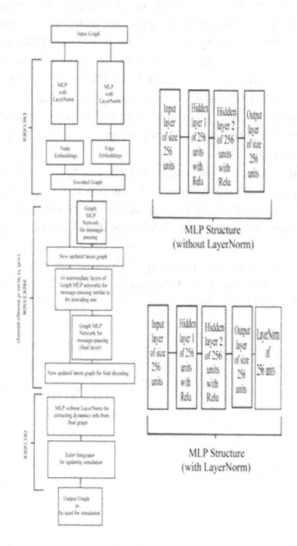

MLP Structure
(without LayerNorm)

MLP Structure
(with LayerNorm)

Evaluation

For quantitative results, after training the developed model was evaluated on the test trajectories. For generalization tests, the evaluation of the model was performed on a number of different starting conditions which vary from those used at training phase, including, varying number of particles, shapes of object, different initial positions and velocities, etc. Various methods of distributional metrics like

Maximum Mean Discrepancy (MMD) (Gretton et al., 2012) and optimal transport (OT) (Villani, 2003) using Sinkhorn Algorithm (Cuturi, 2013) forapproximation have been used.

Overall, the model succeeded in providing 99% accuracy on training data and 98% accuracy on test data. The mean MSE error was found to be about 0.097 ± 0.013. Such behavior confirms the claim of generalization of the model and its robust behavior.

Pseudocode Algorithm of the Simulation

The algorithm for simulation used by the model is given in the following pseudocode:

Algorithm: Simulate($\mathscr{X}, r, \Delta t$)

Input: A particle-based representation of the simulation world, $\mathscr{X}$ =⟨System state dynamics, Global Properties⟩ and *r=proximity radius*

Output: A graph consisting of the dynamics information of the particles used for simulation

1 Initialize a directed graph, $\mathscr{G}$=ENCODE($\mathscr{X}$)
2 Add edges to the graph using *r* by k-d tree algorithm, addEdges($\mathscr{G}$,*r*)
3 Add noise to the graph properties using random walk, $\mathscr{G}_0$=addNoise($\mathscr{G}$)
4 while current simulation time is not equal to

   t+Δt do

5 $\mathscr{G}_m$=MessagePassing($\mathscr{G}_0$) // m-step message passing to compute interactions
6 Extract the dynamics information, $\mathscr{X}'$=DECODE($\mathscr{G}_m$) //world state at end of simulation
7 Use Euler integrator to simulate, Euler Integrator Simulator($\mathscr{X}$)

RESULTS AND DISCUSSIONS

The proposed model learns better through generative learning from basic knowledge of fluid dynamics and also tends to generalize well to conditions unseen at training. The architecture used the relative variant of encoder. Noise to the input states at training phase has been applied. Some of the training phase loss statistics are given in Figure 4.

Figure 4. Losses at various phases for the first 50000 iterations

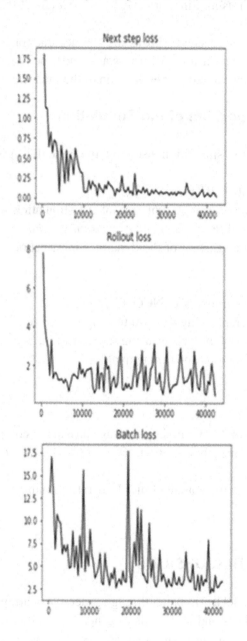

As for checking on the training process, we provide with an example (Example-00 from the training dataset consisting of 10000 particles and modeling water splash in a box container) to visualize the training progress after the first 25000 iterations over the first 50 frames of rollout (as shown in Figure 5):

Figure 5. Loss visualization

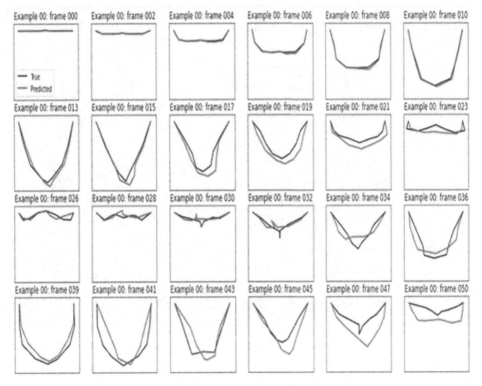

The above visualization of rollout during training phase shows that the rollout error accumulation problem is being appropriately addressed by the proposed model and this improves with each training step. After the first 50000 iterations of training, the model performance has been validated with three (3) examples on long rollouts as shown in Figure 6.

Table 1 results show that the predictions are quite close to the ground truth just after the first 50000 iterations of training and this improves on further training.

Table 1. Examples of model performance

Example No.	True mean acceleration at last rollout($\times 10^{-3}$)	Predicted acceleration at last rollout($\times 10^{-3}$)	Error(%)
00	1.96	1.72	12.25
01	2.57	2.35	8.56
02	6.79	7.31	7.66

Figure 6. Predicted vs. actual coordinates

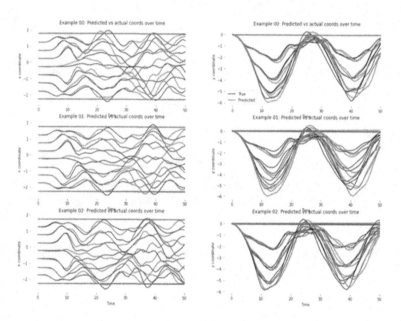

The training time statistics for 50000 training iterations is given in Table 2 .

Table 2. Statistics of first 50000 iterations of training

Iteration number	T(elapsed time)	L_{tr} (training 1-step loss)	L_{ro}(test/generalization rollout loss)	L_{batch}(test/generalization rollout loss for a batch)
00393	21.1	1.7970	7.7709	13.1377
00804	40.3	1.1275	4.1864	17.0162
01239	60.3	1.1241	3.3748	12.8846
01670	80.3	0.6374	2.9450	6.8320
02105	100.3	0.8224	1.4846	10.6976

continued on following page

Table 2. Continued

Iteration number	T(elapsed time)	L_{tr} (training 1-step loss)	L_{ro}(test/generalization rollout loss)	L_{batch}(test/generalization rollout loss for a batch)
02529	120.4	0.5659	3.2974	10.0012
02955	140.4	0.7208	1.3430	9.6849
03374	160.4	0.6964	1.6398	6.3030
03786	180.4	0.5624	1.5898	7.2957
04204	200.5	0.0668	1.2609	6.5733
04628	220.5	0.6545	1.2714	7.3319
05066	240.5	0.4677	1.3102	4.7965
05501	260.6	0.1822	1.0978	4.9032
05924	280.6	0.5972	1.3026	8.8444
06335	300.6	0.2136	1.1148	4.8501
06765	320.6	0.5402	0.6817	7.2135
07189	340.6	0.4897	1.1229	3.9691
07627	360.7	0.2962	1.5270	8.3295
08057	380.7	0.6212	1.5560	4.8531
08481	400.7	0.4812	1.4380	15.5838
08909	420.7	0.3788	1.3421	4.4133
09322	440.7	0.3223	2.1789	6.6951
09735	460.7	0.3140	1.5726	5.0314
10148	480.8	0.0766	1.8180	9.0406
10560	500.8	0.0703	1.4367	6.2829
10968	520.8	0.0787	1.7521	5.3090
11372	540.9	0.2193	1.8067	3.6929
11793	560.9	0.1077	1.8407	4.1504
12205	580.9	0.2091	1.8803	4.8156
12615	600.9	0.1535	0.8724	6.3758
13031	621.0	0.1511	0.6000	3.2316
13433	641.0	0.0266	0.8242	2.9794
13811	661.0	0.1768	2.1825	6.4171
14149	681.2	0.1266	0.8061	4.7486
14515	701.1	0.0996	1.6084	3.8867
14910	721.1	0.0644	1.6079	2.8672
15298	741.2	0.1610	0.6575	4.2286
15691	761.2	0.1133	2.4417	3.6040

continued on following page

Table 2. Continued

Iteration number	T(elapsed time)	L_{tr} (training 1-step loss)	L_{ro}(test/generalization rollout loss)	L_{batch}(test/generalization rollout loss for a batch)
16092	781.2	0.2058	1.8309	4.8226
16477	801.2	0.1636	1.9876	2.6206
16878	821.2	0.1429	0.5840	3.2494
17294	841.2	0.1115	1.1982	3.6038
17725	861.3	0.0249	1.4379	2.9772
18152	881.3	0.1115	0.8921	4.4605
18571	901.4	0.0811	1.0839	3.3081
18961	921.3	0.0876	2.1493	3.2868
19357	941.4	0.2761	2.9971	17.6797
19767	961.4	0.1078	0.8046	4.5517
20171	981.4	0.0728	0.7611	2.6683
20554	1001.4	0.0890	1.1070	5.9124
20879	1021.5	0.1327	0.8552	7.6590
21265	1041.5	0.0624	1.0722	5.0990
21661	1061.6	0.0827	0.8449	11.3888
22058	1081.6	0.0351	0.8537	5.1477
22469	1101.6	0.3042	1.5506	11.2285
22886	1121.7	0.0409	2.4618	4.0729
23251	1141.6	0.0985	0.9277	4.0414
23657	1161.6	0.0798	1.5939	3.4147
24080	1181.7	0.0658	1.7358	3.1711
24493	1201.7	0.1333	2.7802	9.7647
24922	1221.8	0.0668	0.7371	3.7943
25357	1241.7	0.1117	1.9904	5.6741
25775	1261.8	0.0434	0.7082	3.2325
26188	1281.8	0.0401	0.9241	2.7349
26601	1301.9	0.0979	1.8463	3.3443
27031	1321.9	0.0570	1.9836	6.7940
27473	1341.9	0.0993	3.1192	3.3673
27916	1361.9	0.0748	1.1055	4.1297
28344	1381.9	0.0487	1.1020	3.4711
28763	1401.9	0.0782	1.6240	2.7197
29176	1421.9	0.0592	0.8641	3.6006

continued on following page

Table 2. Continued

Iteration number	T(elapsed time)	L_{tr} (training 1-step loss)	L_{ro}(test/generalization rollout loss)	L_{batch}(test/generalization rollout loss for a batch)
29592	1441.9	0.0584	0.5309	2.9833
30021	1462.0	0.0671	1.2415	2.8218
30455	1482.0	0.0664	2.9801	4.4243
30871	1502.0	0.0364	1.3008	3.1339
31289	1522.0	0.0702	0.6079	2.9959
31710	1542.0	0.0449	0.8724	3.8023
32139	1562.1	0.0691	1.0001	3.0300
32552	1582.1	0.0334	1.0322	2.9283
32985	1602.1	0.0748	1.0748	3.5153
33407	1622.2	0.0623	1.7169	6.6038
33815	1642.3	0.0662	2.9011	3.9498
34234	1662.3	0.0461	1.8185	3.3859
34650	1682.3	0.0607	1.1146	3.3289
35079	1702.3	0.1865	1.1979	5.2247
35496	1722.4	0.0906	1.2312	2.5172
35912	1742.4	0.0615	1.4477	2.4197
36323	1762.4	0.0452	1.8168	4.0268
36740	1782.4	0.0520	0.6605	2.3189
37170	1802.4	0.0680	2.7555	4.0128
37609	1822.4	0.0163	1.7238	2.8788
38051	1842.5	0.0381	0.8963	3.5647
38489	1862.5	0.0766	0.7660	3.3265
38918	1882.5	0.1056	1.7888	7.8995
39345	1902.6	0.0170	1.9701	2.0435
39773	1922.6	0.0363	0.5646	2.5802
40181	1942.7	0.0596	0.5310	2.2258
40591	1962.7	0.0274	1.2256	3.9995
41010	1982.6	0.0229	1.0515	2.7017
41444	2002.7	0.0657	2.1189	2.7721
41879	2022.7	0.0599	1.3971	3.2383
42299	2042.7	0.0174	0.4762	3.3109
42987	2062.7	0.0154	0.5310	2.2558
43567	2082.7	0.0103	0.4627	1.6501

continued on following page

Table 2. Continued

Iteration number	T(elapsed time)	L_{tr} (training 1-step loss)	L_{ro}(test/generalization rollout loss)	L_{batch}(test/generalization rollout loss for a batch)
44090	2102.6	0.098	0.4601	1.7017
44798	2122.7	0.089	0.4591	1.5721
45579	2142.7	0.080	0.4987	1.2383
46089	2162.7	0.075	0.4478	1.3109
47901	2182.7	0.067	0.5309	1.1258
48019	2202.7	0.054	0.4387	1.0995
49321	2222.6	0.049	0.4453	1.0717
49690	2242.7	0.049	0.4567	1.0521
49891	2262.7	0.048	0.4307	1.0183
49999	2282.7	0.054	0.4299	1.0209

Simulating Complex Fluid Dynamics Conditions

The model performed very well in learning simulations of various complex situations. Visually, the model's simulations are quite satisfactory as shown in Figure 7. But specific trajectories generated by the model can still be distinguished from ground truth upon side-by-side comparison.

Testing conditions given in Sanchez-Gonzalez et al., (2020) is recreated and found that it is visually difficult to differentiate individual generated simulations by the model from the simulations of ground truth. The present model conforming to the original model also scales up to large number of particles and long simulations. With particles as up to 20000 in 3D systems, the model can function at high resolutions satisfactory for usage in practice like in 3D scene renderings and tasks of prediction.

Figure 7. Different simulation conditions

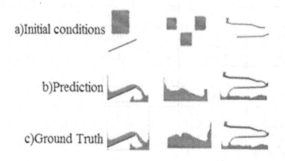

The model shows good generalization capabilities to even cases outside the distributions of training data that suggests the model captures a generally greater insight of the underlying processes of the concerned physics focused in training. To test the model's generalization, it then had been trained on varying conditions having water ramps, whose starting conditions have water in a square container, with a few ramps having random location and orientation. After training phase, tests were performed on varying settings.

The model was quite good also in simulating dynamics of complex, highly chaotic nature fluids not seen during training. The dynamics predicted were similar visually to the ground truth. As relative units of displacement of particles had been used as the input, the learned model also handles many cases with higher spatial extent.

CONCLUSION

The proposed model delivers a better approach to generate a general-purpose and powerful deep learning model aimed at simulation learning of complex fluid systems, depending on representations of the underlying physics as particles along with message-passing learned on the graphs. The estimated results showed that the singular model can really learn simulation of fluid dynamics based on knowledge of the fluidic interactions through Navier-Stokes equation. The model is also highly simpler, accurate, and generalizes well.

This work follows along the lines of mesh-free methods for particle systems, but the approach is also useful in data represented by meshes, like finite-element methods. Also, there are techniques to include generic knowledge of physics into the model such as Hamiltonian and Laplacian mechanics and rich symmetries that are imposed architecturally.

This work also shows the usability of DNNs in solving forward and backward time inference of fluid dynamics system with fairly high rate of accuracy. The predictions are very fast and in accordance to the ground truth. As such the model, can be used for nearly real-time physics rendering and in many time critical systems involving fluids.

The present work is geared towards generative models that are more sophisticated, and provides to the modern AI field a model capable of higher physical reasoning capacity in the domain of fluid dynamics.

REFERENCES

Ba, J. L., Kiros, J. R., & Hinton, G. E. (2016). *Layer normalization*. arXiv:1607.06450.

Battaglia, P., Pascanu, R., & Lai, M (2020). *Interaction networks for learning about objects, relations and physics*. Advances in neural information processing systems, Barcelona0.

Battaglia, P. W., Hamrick, J. B., & Bapst, V. (2018). *Relational inductive biases, deep learning, and graph networks*. arXiv:1806.01261.

Bender, J., & Koschier, D. (2015). Divergence-free smoothed particle hydrodynamics. In: *Proceedings of the 2015 ACM SIG-GRAPH/Eurographics Symposium on Computer Anima-tion*. California:ACM.10.1145/2786784.2786796

Cuturi, M. Sinkhorn Distances: Lightspeed computation of optimal transportation distances. 2013, arXiv:1306.0895.

Gilmer, J., Schoenholz, S. S., & Riley, P. F. (2017). Neural message passing for quantum chemistry. In: *Proceedings of the 34th International Conference on Machine Learning*. JMLR..

Gretton, A., Borgwardt, K. M., & Rasch, M. J. (2012). A kernel two-sample test. *Journal of Machine Learning Research*, 13(Mar), 723–773.

Holl, P., Koltun, V., & Thuerey, N. (2020). Learning to control pdes with differentiable physics. arXiv:2001.07457.

Hu, Y., Anderson, L., & Li, T. M., (2019). Difftaichi: Differentiable programming for physical simulation. arXiv:1910.00935.

Hu Y, Fang Y, & Ge Z. (2018). A moving least squares material point method with displacement discontinuity and two-way rigid body coupling. *ACM Trans. Graph., 37*(4).

Kingma, D. P., & Ba, J. Adam: A method for stochastic optimization. 2014, arXiv:1412.6980.

Li, Y., Wu, J., & Tedrake, R. (2018). Learning particle dynamics for manipulating rigid bodies, deformable objects, and fluids. arXiv:1810.01566.

Li, Y., Wu, J., & Zhu, J. Y. (2019). Propagation networks for model-based control under partial observation. In: *International Conference on Robotics and Automation (ICRA)*. Montreal: IEEE. 10.1109/ICRA.2019.8793509

Monaghan, J. J. (1992). Smoothed particle hydrodynamics. *Annual Review of Astronomy and Astrophysics*, 30(1), 543–574. 10.1146/annurev.aa.30.090192.002551

Sanchez-Gonzalez, A., Bapst, V., & Cranmer, K. (2019). Hamiltonian graph networks with ode integrators. arXiv:1909.12790.

Sanchez-Gonzalez, A., Godwin, J., & Pfaff, T. (2020). Learning to simulate complex physics with graph networks. arXiv:2002.09405.

Sanchez-Gonzalez, A., Heess, N., & Springenberg, J. T. (2018). Graph networks as learnable physics engines for inference and control. arXiv:1806.01242.

Scarselli, F., Gori, M., & Tsoi, A. C. (2008). The graph neural network model. *IEEE Transactions on Neural Networks*, 20(1), 61–80. 10.1109/TNN.2008.200560519068426

Sulsky, D., Zhou, S. J., & Schreyer, H. L. (1995). Application of a particle-in-cell method to solid mechanics. *Computer Physics Communications*, 87(1-2), 236–252. 10.1016/0010-4655(94)00170-7

Villani, C. (2003). *Topics in optimal transportation* (1st ed.). American Mathematical Soc. 10.1090/gsm/058

Chapter 2
An Integrated Approach of Particle Swarm Optimization and Grey Relational Analysis in Multi–Response Optimization of Fused Deposition Modeling

Muhammad Abas
http://orcid.org/0000-0002-9294-2964
University of Engineering and Technology, Peshawar, Pakistan

Imran Khan
http://orcid.org/0000-0002-6661-4182
University of Engineering and Technology, Peshawar, Pakistan

Ziaullah Jan
GIK Institute, Topi, Pakistan

ABSTRACT

This study proposes an integrated approach combining grey relational analysis (GRA) and particle swarm optimization (PSO) to optimize process parameters for fused deposition modeling (FDM) 3D printing using polylactic acid (PLA) material. Experimental design based on definitive screening designs (DSD) is employed to identify optimal printing parameters, focusing on improving surface finish,

DOI: 10.4018/979-8-3693-3314-3.ch002

dimensional accuracy, and impact strength. A regression model, generated based on DSD, accurately predicts grey relational grades (GRG), facilitating efficient optimization. The model's effectiveness is validated through evaluation metrics and close agreement between actual and predicted GRG values. PSO further refines the optimization process by efficiently navigating the solution space towards superior printing parameters. A comparison between GRA and PSO reveals refinements in printing speed, indicating the more refined solutions by PSO. These findings highlight the effectiveness of the integrated approach in enhancing additive manufacturing performance.

INTRODUCTION

Fused Deposition Modeling (FDM) is a popular additive manufacturing technology used for 3D printing. It works by depositing layers of thermoplastic material, usually in the form of a filament, layer by layer to create a three-dimensional object. Common thermoplastics used in FDM include PLA (Polylactic Acid), ABS (Acrylonitrile Butadiene Styrene), PETG (Polyethylene Terephthalate Glycol), and others. Material selection depends on factors like strength, flexibility, and heat resistance (Abas et al., 2023; Jan et al., 2023; Rajan et al., 2022). FDM is widely used for prototyping, product development, and low-volume production due to its cost-effectiveness and versatility (Khan, Farooq, et al., 2023; Khan, Tariq, et al., 2023; Ullah et al., 2023).

Multi response optimization of process parameters in FDM is of paramount importance to ensure the production of high-quality, mechanically robust, and efficient 3D printed objects. The intricate nature of FDM involves numerous process parameters that, when fine-tuned, significantly impact the final output (Rasheed et al., 2023). Adjusting parameters such as layer height/lager thickness, extrusion temperature, infill density, and print speed directly influences print quality and mechanical properties. This optimization is crucial for minimizing defects like warping and curling, enhancing material and energy efficiency, and improving overall resource utilization (Patel et al., 2023). Multi-response optimization of FDM process parameters employs various methods to efficiently balance and enhance multiple performance criteria. One widely used approach is the application of optimization algorithms, including evolutionary algorithms, genetic algorithms (GA), and particle swarm optimization (Mellal et al., 2022; Yodo & Dey, 2023). These algorithms explore the parameter space, considering interactions between variables to identify the best compromise solutions. Response Surface Methodology (RSM) is another effective technique, involving statistical modeling to capture the relationships between process parameters and multiple responses. This enables the creation of predictive models that guide the search for optimal parameter combinations (Waseem et al., 2020, 2022). Additionally, the Taguchi method is employed for robust optimization, emphasizing the identification of parameter settings that are less sensitive to variations and disturbances (Maguluri et al., 2023; Rasheed et al., 2023). Grey relational analysis (GRA) can be employed to evaluate the relationships among various process parameters and multiple responses in FDM. It takes into account the inherent uncertainties and variations in the data, making it suitable for scenarios where precise information may be limited or imprecise (Dixit & Jain, 2023; John et al., 2023). These methods collectively contribute to reducing the need for extensive experimental trials, offering a systematic and efficient means to achieve well-balanced FDM process parameters. The integration of these optimization methods ensures that the additive manufacturing process is not only tailored to specific application requirements but also robust, reliable, and capable of delivering high-quality products consistently.

LITERATURE REVIEW

Mellal et al., (2022) optimized FDM parameters by converting a multi-objective problem to a single one using the weighted-sum method. The study employed particle swarm optimization (PSO) and differential evolution (DE) with constraint handling, finding that DE outperformed PSO in terms of fewer evaluations, reduced CPU time, and lower standard deviation. The study contributes to improving FDM process machinability by identifying optimal parameters for tensile strength, flexural strength, and impact strength. Saad et al., (2021) investigated the impact of layer thickness, printing speed, print temperature, and outer shell speed on the flexural strength of PLA printed parts. The study used central composite design (CCD) and employed analysis of variance (ANOVA) for statistical analysis. PSO was then applied to optimize the process parameters based on the ANOVA results. Experimental validation using PSO showed a 3.8% improvement in flexural strength compared to traditional RSM. In another study, Saad et al., (2019) employed RSM, PSO, and symbiotic organism search (SOS) to enhance the surface quality (surface roughness) of FDM printed parts. RSM guided the experimental design, establishing a regression model linking input parameters to surface roughness. Validated model accuracy enabled coupling with PSO and SOS for optimizing parameters and minimizing surface roughness. PSO and SOS improved surface roughness by approximately 8.5% and 8.8%, respectively, compared to the conventional RSM method. Fountas et al., (2023) investigated the flexural strength of PET-G by varying FDM process parameters. They conducted a response surface experiment with 27 runs. Statistical analysis, specifically ANOVA, generated a full quadratic regression equation, later implemented as an objective function for the grey wolf algorithm (GWO). The GWO algorithm suggested parameter combinations that improved flexural strength by approximately 15% compared to the highest value obtained in experimental runs.

Shirmohammadi et al., (2021) utilized a hybrid artificial neural network and PSO to optimize input parameters for minimizing surface roughness in 3D printing. Central composite design experiments with five parameters were conducted, and a 7-4-1 multilayer perceptron neural network was trained on the data. The PSO determined optimal input parameters, validated against experimental results. Yang et al., (2023) employed support vector regression (SVR) and cuckoo search (CS) to optimize two key parameters i.e., printing temperature and speed proposed for FDM using PLA materials. The SVR model predicted the nonlinear relationship between FDM parameters and PLA shrinkage deformation. The optimization model, utilizing CS, minimized shrinkage deformation, improving FDM workpiece shape accuracy. Experimental results confirmed the effectiveness of this approach. Dey et al., (2020) employed multi-objective PSO to optimize the compressive strength of PLA parts. They generated a set of non-dominated solutions for both build time and compressive strength, constructing a Pareto frontier to illustrate the trade-off between the two objectives. Salunkhe et al., (2023) studied the relationship between PLA material's tensile strength and 3D printing parameters (infill density, layer height, print speed, and extrusion temperature) in FDM. Six optimization methods were used such as cohort intelligence (CI), PSO, GA, teaching learning based optimization (TLBO), simulated annealing (SA), with JAYA yielding the highest tensile strength of 55.475 N/mm^2. Raju et al. (Raju et al., 2019) optimized FDM process parameters using a hybrid approach of Taguchi, PSO and bacterial foraging optimization evolutionary algorithm for improved mechanical and surface quality of acrylonitrile butadiene styrene-based 3D components. Enemuoh & Asante-Okyere, (2023) optimized process parameters for predicting print part quality using feature selection methods. They used PSO and neighborhood component analysis (NCA) to select key parameters for the artificial neural network (ANN) model. NCA-ANN was the best predictor for energy consumption, ultimate tensile strength, part weight, and print time. PSO features improved PSO-ANN as the best average hardness predictor. Incorporating PSO and NCA for feature selection enhanced the FDM print part property ANN model's prediction performance. Dev and Srivastava (Dev & Srivastava, 2020) optimized the compressive strength of FDM printed parts from ABS using non-sorting genetic algorithm (NSGA)-II. Chinchanikar et al., (2023) employed various optimization techniques, including technique for order of preference by similarity to ideal solution (TOPSIS), desirability function-based RSM, NSGA-II, and GRA to determine optimal FDM process parameters for tensile, impact, flexural, and surface roughness. The study highlights superior prediction accuracy achieved through a hybrid optimization approach, specifically the combination of a genetic algorithm with RSM.

The review of existing literature highlights that effectively managing multi-objective process parameters is crucial for achieving optimal performance, yet it remains a challenging. Limited research has been conducted in this domain. There is a notable gap in the literature regarding the multi-objective optimization of FDM processes through the integrated approach of GRA and PSO.

MATERIAL AND METHODS

The type of material used in present study is commercial grade poly lactic acid (PLA). The filament had a diameter of 1.75mm and a density of $1.25g/cm^3$, with a glass transition temperature of 53°C and a melting temperature ranging from 180°C to 230°C. The study investigated various printing process parameters, including layer height, number of perimeters, infill density, infill angle, printing speed, nozzle temperature, bed temperature, and print orientation. These parameters were set at three levels, as detailed in Table 1, based on previous research findings (Abas, Habib, Noor, & Khan, 2022; Abas, Habib, Noor, Salah, et al., 2022). Figure 1 shows the schematics of FDM printing and selected control printing parameters. Test specimens were printed from using an ALIFHX XC555 PRO3D printer and were prepared according to ASTM E23-12c (*ASTM E23; Standard Test Methods for Notched Bar Impact Testing of Metallic Materials*, n.d.) for impact tests as shown in Figure 2.

Figure 1. Schematic of FDM 3D printer with associated printing parameters and print orientations

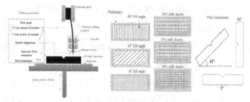

(Abas, Habib, Noor, Salah, et al., 2022).

Table 1. Levels of printing parameters of PLA (Abas, Habib, Noor, & Khan, 2022; Abas, Habib, Noor, Salah, et al., 2022)

Printing Parameters	Symbol	Units	Levels		
			−1	0	1
Layer Height	L	mm	0.1	0.2	0.3
Number of Perimeters	C	-	2	4	6
Infill density	I	%	20	35	50
Fill angle	R	°	0	45	90
Print Speed	S	mm/s	50	60	70
Nozzle temperature	E	°C	190	205	220
Bed temperature	B	°C	70	80	90
Print orientation	O		0	45	90

Figure 2. (a) Schematic of impact test specimen (b) FDM 3D printer, specimens printing, and test specimens of PLA

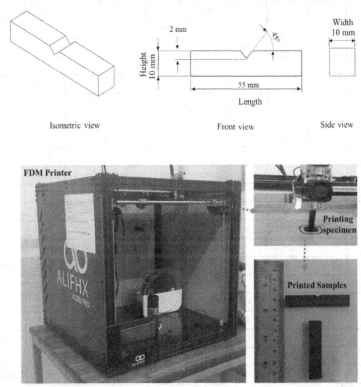

(Abas, Habib, Noor, Salah, et al., 2022)

Definitive screening designs (DSD) is used from our previous studies (Abas, Habib, Noor, & Khan, 2022; Abas, Habib, Noor, Salah, et al., 2022), as this design is effective to model and estimate the main effect, interaction effect, and quadratic effect in small experimental runs. The experimental design comprise of 51 experimental runs and are tabulated in Table 2. Further, the response considered are average surface roughness (Ra), dimensional deviation along the length (DDL) and impact strength (IS). The values of Ra and DDL are taken from the previous studies.

Table 2. Experimental design based on DSD and measured responses

Exp. No.	L	C	I	R	S	E	B	O	Ra (μm) (Abas, Habib, Noor, & Khan, 2022)	DDL (%) (Abas, Habib, Noor, Salah, et al., 2022)	IS (kJ/ m²)
1	0.2	6	50	90	70	220	90	90	10.69	0.273	1.31
2	0.1	2	50	90	70	205	70	0	5.36	0.618	1.61
3	0.3	6	20	90	70	190	80	0	20.94	0.309	1.24
4	0.1	6	35	90	50	190	70	90	9.09	0.182	1.27
5	0.3	6	50	45	50	220	70	0	9.47	0.836	2.83
6	0.3	6	20	0	50	205	90	90	20.73	0.491	2.01
7	0.3	6	20	90	70	190	80	0	20.03	0.545	1.22
8	0.1	2	50	0	50	220	80	90	7.65	0.6	2.13
9	0.3	2	20	90	60	220	70	90	20.13	0.164	0.83
10	0.3	6	20	0	50	205	90	90	20.09	0.455	1.86
11	0.1	2	50	0	50	220	80	90	6.99	0.673	2.21
12	0.1	6	50	0	60	190	90	0	8.74	1.036	3.35
13	0.1	2	20	45	70	190	90	90	15.09	0.218	1.33
14	0.1	6	20	0	70	220	70	45	7.25	0.055	2.42
15	0.1	6	20	0	70	220	70	45	7.09	0.073	2.38
16	0.1	2	50	90	70	205	70	0	3.69	0.691	1.65
17	0.1	6	50	0	60	190	90	0	7.57	0.964	3.28
18	0.3	2	35	0	70	220	90	0	21.43	0.673	2.83
19	0.1	6	20	0	70	220	70	45	6.04	0.091	2.37
20	0.1	2	50	0	50	220	80	90	7.19	0.473	2.15
21	0.1	2	20	45	70	190	90	90	16.25	0.273	1.31
22	0.1	6	35	90	50	190	70	90	8.29	0.473	1.25
23	0.2	4	35	45	60	205	80	45	14.1	0.673	2.01
24	0.1	4	20	90	50	220	90	0	14.21	0.473	2.33
25	0.3	2	35	0	70	220	90	0	20.9	0.582	2.79

continued on following page

Table 2. Continued

Exp. No.	L	C	I	R	S	E	B	O	Ra (μm) (Abas, Habib, Noor, & Khan, 2022)	DDL (%) (Abas, Habib, Noor, Salah, et al., 2022)	IS (kJ/m²)
26	0.3	6	20	90	70	190	80	0	19.78	0.345	1.17
27	0.2	2	20	0	50	190	70	0	13.44	0.309	2
28	0.1	4	20	90	50	220	90	0	14.55	0.273	2.47
29	0.3	6	50	45	50	220	70	0	8.85	0.782	2.6
30	0.1	2	50	90	70	205	70	0	4.34	0.745	1.63
31	0.2	4	35	45	60	205	80	45	14.79	0.709	2.05
32	0.2	2	20	0	50	190	70	0	12.88	0.273	2.04
33	0.1	6	50	0	60	190	90	0	8.04	0.927	3.38
34	0.3	2	50	90	50	190	90	45	20.7	1.782	1.68
35	0.3	6	50	45	50	220	70	0	8.44	0.873	2.65
36	0.3	4	50	0	70	190	70	90	23.3	0.2	1.2
37	0.3	4	50	0	70	190	70	90	21.57	0.091	1.17
38	0.2	6	50	90	70	220	90	90	10.25	0.345	1.26
39	0.3	2	50	90	50	190	90	45	22.48	1.673	1.68
40	0.1	4	20	90	50	220	90	0	15.56	0.673	2.36
41	0.2	6	50	90	70	220	90	90	9.357	0.382	1.29
42	0.3	2	35	0	70	220	90	0	20.61	0.636	2.75
43	0.1	6	35	90	50	190	70	90	7.96	0.382	1.16
44	0.2	2	20	0	50	190	70	0	12.57	0.345	2
45	0.3	2	50	90	50	190	90	45	21.54	1.545	1.65
46	0.1	2	20	45	70	190	90	90	16.11	0.418	1.33
47	0.2	4	35	45	60	205	80	45	14.64	0.636	1.98
48	0.3	6	20	0	50	205	90	90	20.29	0.436	1.9
49	0.3	2	20	90	60	220	70	90	19.98	0.218	0.88
50	0.3	4	50	0	70	190	70	90	21.77	0.4	1.14
51	0.3	2	20	90	60	220	70	90	20.36	0.109	0.84

Multi-Response Optimization

In present study the multi-response optimization is achieved by converting multi-responses to a single response using grey relational analysis (GRA), then creating a mathematical model (empirical/regression model) for optimization in a post-processing step of meta-heuristic approach namely PSO.

Grey Relational Analysis

Grey relational analysis transforms the multi response optimization problem in to single response called grey relational grade (GRG). Following procedure for grey relational analysis will allow us to optimize the process parameters:

Where μ_i is the normalized value for i^{th} experiment, y_i is the individual value of measured response at experiment number i. *max* y_i and *min* y_i are the maximum and minimum values of experimental data obtained for response.

Where δ_i is GRC value at experiment i. $\eta_{0,i}$ is the deviation from the target value and can be calculated using Equation 4. η_{min} and η_{max} are the minimum and maximum value $\eta_{0,i}(j)$. ϵ is the distinguish/ identification coefficient value, which is fixed at 0.5 for present study.

$$\eta_{0,i}(j) = 1 - \mu_i(j) \tag{4}$$

Where £$_i$ is weighted GRG for the i^{th}experiment and w_j is the normalized weightage of response j.

Particle Swarm Optimization

Particle Swarm Optimization (PSO) is a metaheuristic optimization algorithm that was first proposed by Kennedy and Eberhart in 1995 (Shami et al., 2022). It is a population-based algorithm that mimics the social behavior of bird flocks or fish schools. PSO is used to find the global minimum or maximum of a function with a large number of unknown parameters, called the optimization problem.

Figure 3 shows the flow chart of PSO. At the start of the algorithm, the particles are randomly initialized in the search space. The algorithm then evaluates the fitness of each particle's position using the objective function that needs to be optimized. The objective function assigns a fitness value to each particle, which represents how close it is to the optimal solution. The particle with the best fitness value is called the global best, and the particle with the best fitness value in its neighborhood is called the local best.

The algorithm then updates the position and velocity of each particle based on its current position, velocity, and the positions of its local and global best particles. The updated position of each particle is a combination of its current position, its velocity, and a random term. The velocity of each particle is updated based on the position of its local and global best particles, as well as its own current velocity as expressed in Equations 6 and 7.

$$v_t(t+1) = \rho \bullet v_t + c_1 \bullet r_1\left(X_{pbest} - X_t\right) + c_2 \bullet r_2\left(X_{gbest} - X_t\right) \tag{6}$$

$$X(t+1) = X_t + v(t+1) \tag{7}$$

Where t is the iteration number, v_t is the velocity at iteration t, X is the position at iteration t, ρ is the inertia weight, c_1 and c_2 are the correction factor or acceleration coefficient, r_1 and r_2 are the random number, X_{pbest} is the best position at iteration t and X_{gbest} is the global best position at iteration t.

Inertia weight (ρ) controls the balance between exploration and exploitation. A high inertia weight favors exploration (i.e., large jumps in the search space), while a low inertia weight favors exploitation (i.e., small jumps in the search space). Typically, the inertia weight decreases linearly over time to reduce exploration and increase exploitation as the algorithm progresses. Correction factors (c_1 and c_2) determine the influence of the particle's own best known position and the best known position of the swarm. A high c_1 value gives more importance to the particle's own best known position, while a high c_2 value gives more importance to the best known position of the swarm.

The PSO algorithm continues to update the position and velocity of each particle in the swarm until a stopping criterion is met. This criterion can be a fixed number of iterations or a certain level of convergence.

Figure 3. Flow chart for integrated approach of PSO

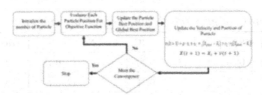

In PSO, there are number of hyper parameters on which the performance of algorithm depends i.e., number of iterations, number of swarms (particles), inertia weight (w), correction factor c_1 and c_2. For this aim, lists of values are defined at different levels for each parameter and there different combination are tested (by applying nested loop in coding) to analyse the performance of algorithm. The best combination is selected that give consistent highest objective function value. The list of parameters and the levels are tabulated in.

Table 3. Hyperparameters levels of PSO

Hyper parameters	Level 1	Level 2	Level 3
Number of iterations	10	20	30
Number of particles	10	15	20
Inertia	0.1	0.5	1
Correction factor, c_1	1	1.5	2
Correction factor, c_2	1	1.5	2

Results and Discussions

To minimize the responses Ra and DDL, they are normalized using Equation 1, while IS values, which are to be maximized, are normalized using Equation 2. Then, grey relational coefficients are computed using Equations 3-4, as tabulated in the Table 4. GRC values are converted to grey relational grade (GRG) using Equation 5 as shown in Table 4. Finally, the average values of GRG are computed at each level for each process parameter (Table 5), and the highest value represents the optimal value. For instance, the highest average value of GRG for layer height among the three levels is at level -1, i.e., 0.214, and the corresponding value is 0.1 mm. Similarly, the other optimal process parameters obtained are the number of perimeters: 6, infill density: 50%, fill angle: 0°, print speed: 60mm/s, nozzle temperature: 220 C, bed temperature: 70°C, and print orientation: 0°. The optimal values of Ra, DDL and IS obtained are 5.15μm, 0.09% and 3.41 (kJ/m²).

Table 4. Computation of grey relational coefficients and grey relational grade

Exp. No	GRC_{Ra}	GRC_{DDL}	GRC_{IS}	GRG	Exp. No	GRC_{Ra}	GRC_{DDL}	GRC_{IS}	GRG
1	0.19	0.26	0.13	0.20	27	0.17	0.26	0.16	0.20
2	0.28	0.21	0.14	0.21	28	0.16	0.27	0.20	0.21
3	0.12	0.26	0.13	0.17	29	0.22	0.18	0.21	0.20
4	0.21	0.30	0.13	0.21	30	0.31	0.19	0.14	0.21
5	0.21	0.18	0.24	0.21	31	0.15	0.19	0.17	0.17
6	0.12	0.23	0.16	0.17	32	0.17	0.27	0.17	0.20
7	0.12	0.22	0.13	0.16	33	0.23	0.17	0.34	0.25
8	0.24	0.21	0.17	0.21	34	0.12	0.11	0.15	0.13
9	0.12	0.30	0.11	0.18	35	0.22	0.17	0.22	0.20
10	0.12	0.23	0.16	0.17	36	0.11	0.29	0.13	0.18
11	0.25	0.20	0.18	0.21	37	0.12	0.33	0.12	0.19
12	0.22	0.16	0.33	0.24	38	0.20	0.25	0.13	0.19

Exp. No	GRC_{Ra}	GRC_{DDL}	GRC_{IS}	GRG	Exp. No	GRC_{Ra}	GRC_{DDL}	GRC_{IS}	GRG
13	0.15	0.29	0.13	0.19	39	0.11	0.12	0.15	0.13
14	0.24	0.34	0.19	0.26	40	0.15	0.20	0.19	0.18
15	0.25	0.33	0.19	0.26	41	0.21	0.25	0.13	0.19
16	0.33	0.20	0.14	0.22	42	0.12	0.20	0.23	0.18
17	0.24	0.17	0.32	0.24	43	0.23	0.25	0.12	0.20
18	0.12	0.20	0.24	0.18	44	0.17	0.25	0.16	0.20
19	0.27	0.33	0.19	0.26	45	0.12	0.12	0.14	0.13
20	0.24	0.23	0.17	0.22	46	0.15	0.24	0.13	0.17
21	0.14	0.27	0.13	0.18	47	0.16	0.20	0.16	0.17
22	0.22	0.23	0.13	0.19	48	0.12	0.24	0.16	0.17
23	0.16	0.20	0.16	0.17	49	0.12	0.29	0.11	0.17
24	0.16	0.23	0.19	0.19	50	0.12	0.24	0.12	0.16
25	0.12	0.21	0.23	0.19	51	0.12	0.32	0.11	0.19
26	0.12	0.25	0.12	0.17					

Table 5. Optimal levels for process parameters

Process Parameters	Levels			Optimal levels
	-1	0	1	
Layer Height	0.214	0.189	0.173	-1(0.1mm)
Number of Perimeters	0.185	0.180	0.205	1 (6)
Infill density	0.192	0.187	0.195	1 (50%)
Fill angle	0.205	0.187	0.182	-1(0°)
Print Speed	0.187	0.198	0.196	0(60mm/s)
Nozzle temperature	0.184	0.187	0.204	1(220°C)
Bed Temperature	0.205	0.182	0.185	-1 (70°C)
Print orientation	0.200	0.186	0.188	-1 (0°)

The regression model based on DSD is generated for GRG (Equation 8). Evaluation metrics such as the R^2 (96%), adjusted R^2 (94%), and predicted R^2 (92%) affirm the model's ability to effectively capture the variability in GRG explained by the printing parameters. The close agreement between actual and predicted GRG values, as illustrated in Figure 4, further validates the model's accuracy and reliability in representing the underlying patterns in the data. Moreover, the statistically insignificant lack of fit value (0.226) underscores the model's adequacy in fitting the observed data, reinforcing confidence in its predictive capability. With the objective of maximizing GRG to enhance additive manufacturing performance, the regression model serves as an objective function for PSO. By leveraging the predictive power of the regression model, PSO efficiently navigates the solution space to identify optimal printing parameters that yield superior surface finish, dimensional accuracy, and impact strength. This integrated approach not only streamlines the optimization process but also enhances the efficiency of achieving high-quality solutions. Thus, the regression model based on DSD emerges as a valuable asset in guiding optimization efforts and advancing additive manufacturing capabilities.

Figure 4. Comparison of actual and predicted GRG values

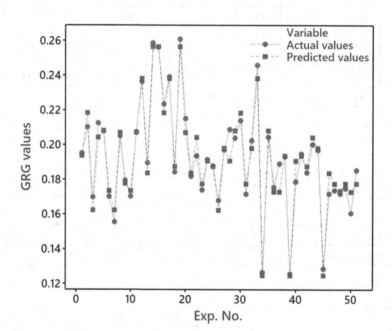

Objective function based on GRG:

$Maximize, f(x) = 0.478 - 0.2087$
$L - 0.02295$
$C + 0.000099$
$I - 0.000257$
$R + 0.01503$
$S+ +0.000651$
$E- 0.01902$
$B - 0.000380$
$O + 0.003490$
$C^2 - 0.000121$
$S^2 + 0.000112$
$B^2 + 0.000003 O^2$

$$(8)$$

Subject to constraints:

$0.1 \leq L \leq 0.3,$
$2 \leq C \leq 6,$
$20 \leq I \leq 50,$
$0 \leq R \leq 90,$
$50 \leq S \leq 70,$
$190 \leq E \leq 220,$
$70 \leq B \leq 90,$
$0 \leq O \leq 90$

The maximum value of GRG obtained for optimal levels in Table 4 using Equation 8 is 0.278. To analyze whether the optimal levels obtained can be improved further, the metaheuristic approaches based on PSO, is applied.

Figure 5 illustrates the convergence plot for PSO. The observed upward trend in the plot indicates that the PSO algorithm is effectively improving solutions over successive iterations. This suggests that the algorithm is successfully exploring the solution space and gradually converging towards an optimal solution. The trajectory of the best objective function value throughout the iterations reflects the dynamic nature of the optimization process. Starting at 0.21 in the first iteration, the objective function value demonstrates substantial improvement, reaching 0.275 by the 10th iteration. This initial phase of rapid enhancement indicates that the algorithm is efficiently navigating towards promising regions of the solution space. However, it is interesting to note the peak observed at 2.79 in the 14th iteration. This sudden increase in the objective function value could be attributed to the algorithm's exploration-exploitation trade-off. It suggests that the algorithm might have temporarily deviated towards less favorable regions in search of potentially better solutions. Nevertheless, the subsequent stabilization of the objective function value indicates that the algorithm has converged to a satisfactory solution, as it remains constant for the maximum allowed 30 iterations. Examining the PSO parameters for the best solution provides further insights into the optimization process. The utilization of 20 particles, an inertia weight (w) of 1.0, and correction factors c_1 and c_2 set at 2 indicates a balanced exploration-exploitation strategy. These parameter settings enable the algorithm to effectively balance between exploration (searching diverse regions of the solution space) and exploitation (refining solutions in promising regions). Comparing the optimized printing parameters derived from PSO with those obtained using GRA reveals interesting findings. While most parameters align between the two optimization techniques, the discrepancy in the printing speed (62.11 mm/s) suggests that PSO may have discovered a more refined solution within the solution space that was not initially apparent through GRA. The optimal values of Ra, DDL and IS obtained are 4.05μm, 0.058% and 3.42 (kJ/m^2). This reflect good improvements in surface finish and dimensional accuracy compared to the initial optimal conditions. These enhancements are indicative of the effectiveness of the optimization process in optimizing the printing parameters and enhancing the overall quality and performance of the printed components.

Figure 5. Convergence plot for PSO

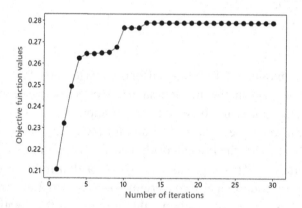

CONCLUSION

This study integrates grey relational analysis (GRA) and particle swarm optimization (PSO) to optimize process parameters for FDM 3D printing with PLA material. Through experimental design based on definitive screening designs (DSD), optimal printing parameters were identified, leading to improved surface finish, dimensional accuracy, and impact strength.

The regression model developed based on DSD accurately predicts the grey relational grade (GRG), facilitating efficient optimization. PSO further enhances the optimization process, converging towards superior printing parameters compared to initial optimal conditions identified by GRA.

The combination of GRA and PSO provides an efficient methodology for optimizing process parameters in additive manufacturing. By leveraging both statistical analysis and metaheuristic optimization techniques, manufacturers can achieve significant improvements in printing performance with minimal experimental runs and computational resources.

REFERENCES

Abas, M., Habib, T., Noor, S., & Khan, K. M. (2022). Comparative study of I-optimal design and definitive screening design for developing prediction models and optimization of average surface roughness of PLA printed parts using fused deposition modeling. *International Journal of Advanced Manufacturing Technology*. Advance online publication. 10.1007/s00170-022-10784-1

Abas, M., Habib, T., Noor, S., Salah, B., & Zimon, D. (2022). Parametric Investigation and Optimization to Study the Effect of Process Parameters on the Dimensional Deviation of Fused Deposition Modeling of 3D Printed Parts. *Polymers*, 14(17), 3667. 10.3390/polym1417366736080740

Abas, M., Habib, T., Noor, S., Zimon, D., & Woźniak, J. (2023). Application of multi-criteria decision-making methods in the selection of additive manufacturing materials for solid ankle foot orthoses. *Journal of Engineering Design*, 34(8), 616–643. 10.1080/09544828.2023.2247859

ASTM E23; Standard Test Methods for Notched Bar Impact Testing of Metallic Materials. (n.d.). ASTM International: West Conshohocken, PA. https://www.astm .org/standards/e23

Chinchanikar, S., Shinde, S., Shaikh, A., Gaikwad, V., & Ambhore, N. H. (2023). *Multi-objective Optimization of FDM Using Hybrid Genetic Algorithm-Based Multi-criteria Decision-Making (MCDM) Techniques. Journal of The Institution of Engineers*. Series D., 10.1007/s40033-023-00459-w

Dev, S., & Srivastava, R. (2020). Experimental investigation and optimization of FDM process parameters for material and mechanical strength. *Materials Today: Proceedings*, 26, 1995–1999. 10.1016/j.matpr.2020.02.435

Dey, A., Hoffman, D., & Yodo, N. (2020). Optimizing multiple process parameters in fused deposition modeling with particle swarm optimization. [IJIDeM]. *International Journal on Interactive Design and Manufacturing*, 14(2), 393–405. 10.1007/ s12008-019-00637-9

Dixit, N., & Jain, P. K. (2023). Multi-objective Strength Optimization of Fused Filament Fabricated Complex Flexible Parts Using Grey Relational Analysis. *Iranian Journal of Science and Technology. Transaction of Mechanical Engineering*, 47(4), 1–11. 10.1007/s40997-022-00589-8

Enemuoh, E. U., & Asante-Okyere, S. (2023). Impact of feature selection on neural network prediction of fused deposition modelling (FDM) print part properties. *International Journal on Interactive Design and Manufacturing (IJIDeM)*. 10.1007/s12008-023-01598-w

Fountas, N. A., Zaoutsos, S., Chaidas, D., Kechagias, J. D., & Vaxevanidis, N. M. (2023). Statistical modelling and optimization of mechanical properties for PLA and PLA/Wood FDM materials. *Materials Today: Proceedings*. IEEE.

Jan, Z., Abas, M., Khan, I., Qazi, M. I., & Jan, Q. M. U. (2023). Design and Analysis of Wrist Hand Orthosis for Carpal Tunnel Syndrome Using Additive Manufacturing. *Journal of Engineering Research*. https://doi.org/10.1016/j.jer.2023.12.001

John, J., Devjani, D., Ali, S., Abdallah, S., & Pervaiz, S. (2023). Optimization of 3D printed polylactic acid structures with different infill patterns using Taguchi-grey relational analysis. *Advanced Industrial and Engineering Polymer Research*, 6(1), 62–78. 10.1016/j.aiepr.2022.06.002

Khan, I., Farooq, U., Tariq, M., Abas, M., Ahmad, S., Shakeel, M., Riaz, A. A., & Hira, F. (2023). Investigation of Effects of Processing Parameters on the Impact Strength and microstructure of thick Tri-Material based Layered Composite Fabricated via Extrusion based Additive Manufacturing. *Journal of Engineering Research*. https://doi.org/https://doi.org/10.1016/j.jer.2023.08.007

Khan, I., Tariq, M., Abas, M., Shakeel, M., Hira, F., Al Rashid, A., & Koç, M. (2023). Parametric investigation and optimisation of mechanical properties of thick tri-material based composite of PLA-PETG-ABS 3D-printed using fused filament fabrication. *Composites Part C: Open Access, 12*, 100392. https://doi.org/10.1016/j.jcomc.2023.100392

Maguluri, N., Suresh, G., & Rao, K. V. (2023). Assessing the effect of FDM processing parameters on mechanical properties of PLA parts using Taguchi method. *Journal of Thermoplastic Composite Materials*, 36(4), 1472–1488. 10.1177/08927057211053036

Mellal, M. A., Laifaoui, C., Ghezal, F., & Williams, E. J. (2022). Multi-objective factors optimization in fused deposition modelling with particle swarm optimization and differential evolution. [IJIDeM]. *International Journal on Interactive Design and Manufacturing*, 16(4), 1669–1674. 10.1007/s12008-022-00868-3

Patel, R., Jani, S., & Joshi, A. (2023). Review on multi-objective optimization of FDM process parameters for composite materials. [IJIDeM]. *International Journal on Interactive Design and Manufacturing*, 17(5), 2115–2125. 10.1007/s12008-022-01111-9

Rajan, K., Samykano, M., Kadirgama, K., Harun, W. S. W., & Rahman, M. M. (2022). Fused deposition modeling: Process, materials, parameters, properties, and applications. *International Journal of Advanced Manufacturing Technology*, 120(3), 1531–1570. 10.1007/s00170-022-08860-7

Raju, M., Gupta, M. K., Bhanot, N., & Sharma, V. S. (2019). A hybrid PSO–BFO evolutionary algorithm for optimization of fused deposition modelling process parameters. *Journal of Intelligent Manufacturing*, 30(7), 2743–2758. 10.1007/s10845-018-1420-0

Rasheed, A., Hussain, M., Ullah, S., Ahmad, Z., Kakakhail, H., Riaz, A. A., Khan, I., Ahmad, S., Akram, W., Eldin, S. M., & Khan, I. (2023). Experimental investigation and Taguchi optimization of FDM process parameters for the enhancement of tensile properties of Bi-layered printed PLA-ABS. *Materials Research Express*, 10(9), 95307. 10.1088/2053-1591/acf1e7

Saad, M. S., Mohd Nor, A., Zakaria, M. Z., Baharudin, M. E., & Yusoff, W. S. (2021). Modelling and evolutionary computation optimization on FDM process for flexural strength using integrated approach RSM and PSO. *Progress in Additive Manufacturing*, 6(1), 143–154. 10.1007/s40964-020-00157-z

Saad, M. S., Nor, A. M., Baharudin, M. E., Zakaria, M. Z., & Aiman, A. F. (2019). Optimization of surface roughness in FDM 3D printer using response surface methodology, particle swarm optimization, and symbiotic organism search algorithms. *International Journal of Advanced Manufacturing Technology*, 105(12), 5121–5137. 10.1007/s00170-019-04568-3

Salunkhe, S., Jatti, D. V. S., Tamboli, S., Shaikh, S., Solke, N., Gulia, V., Jatti, V. S., Khedkar, N. K., Pagac, M., & Abouel Nasr, E. (2023). Optimization of Tensile Strength in 3D Printed PLA Parts via Meta-heuristic Approaches: A Comparative Study. *Frontiers in Materials*, 10, 1336837.

Shami, T. M., El-Saleh, A. A., Alswaitti, M., Al-Tashi, Q., Summakieh, M. A., & Mirjalili, S. (2022). Particle swarm optimization: A comprehensive survey. *IEEE Access : Practical Innovations, Open Solutions*, 10, 10031–10061. 10.1109/ACCESS.2022.3142859

Shirmohammadi, M., Goushchi, S. J., & Keshtiban, P. M. (2021). Optimization of 3D printing process parameters to minimize surface roughness with hybrid artificial neural network model and particle swarm algorithm. *Progress in Additive Manufacturing*, 6(2), 199–215. 10.1007/s40964-021-00166-6

Ullah, M., Wahab, A., Khan, S. U., Naeem, M,. ur Rehman, K., Ali, H., Ullah, A., Khan, A., Khan, N. R., Rizg, W. Y., Hosny, K. M., Alissa, M., Badr, M. Y., & Alkhalidi, H. M. (2023). 3D printing technology: A new approach for the fabrication of personalized and customized pharmaceuticals. *European Polymer Journal, 195*, 112240. https://doi.org/10.1016/j.eurpolymj.2023.112240

Waseem, M., Habib, T., Ghani, U., Abas, M., Jan, Q. M. U., & Khan, M. A. Z. (2022). Optimisation of tensile and compressive behaviour of PLA 3D printed parts using categorical response surface methodology. *International Journal of Industrial and Systems Engineering*, 41(4), 417–437. 10.1504/IJISE.2022.124997

Waseem, M., Salah, B., Habib, T., Saleem, W., Abas, M., Khan, R., Ghani, U., & Siddiqi, M. U. R. (2020). Multi-Response Optimization of Tensile Creep Behavior of PLA 3D Printed Parts Using Categorical Response Surface Methodology. *Polymers*, 12(12), 2962. 10.3390/polym1212296233322445

Yang, Y., Dai, X., Yang, B., Zou, P., Gao, F., Duan, J., & Wang, C. (2023). Optimization of polylactic acid 3D printing parameters based on support vector regression and cuckoo search. *Polymer Engineering and Science*, 63(10), 3243–3253. doi.org/10.1002/pen.26440. 10.1002/pen.26440

Yodo, N., & Dey, A. (2023). Multiobjective process parameter optimization in fused filament fabrication with nature-inspired algorithms. In A. Kumar, R. K. Mittal, & A. B. T.-A. In Haleem, A. M. (Ed.), *Additive Manufacturing Materials and Technologies* (pp. 349–359). Elsevier. doi.org/10.1016/B978-0-323-91834-3.00026-0

Chapter 3

A Novel Approach for Optimizing Wire Electric Discharge Machining of Mg–Cu–RE–Zr Alloy Using Machine Learning Algorithm

Ranganatha Swamy

Faculty of Engineering and Technology, Jain University (Deemed), India

D. V. S. S. S. V. Prasad

Aditya College of Engineering, India

Hari Banda

https://orcid.org/0000-0003-4629-2830

Villa College, Maldives

Ibrahim A. Mohamed

KPR Institute of Engineering and Technology, Coimbatore, India

M. Subramanian

https://orcid.org/0000-0002-8117-9529

St. Joseph's College of Engineering, Chennai, India

S. Kaliappan

KCG College of Technology, India

ABSTRACT

This study focuses on the optimisation of the wire electric discharge machining (WEDM) process for WE43 alloy using machine learning methods. The alloy, made of magnesium (Mg), copper (Cu), rare earth (RE) elements, and zirconium (Zr), is extensively employed in aerospace and automotive sectors for its lightweight and high-strength features. The research applies three machine learning models—artificial

DOI: 10.4018/979-8-3693-3314-3.ch003

neural networks (ANN), random forest (RF), and decision trees (DT)—to optimize the important process parameters, including current (A), pulse on (P On), and pulse off (P Off). A full experimental design based on the Taguchi L27 array is undertaken, methodically altering each parameter at three levels. Material removal rate (MRR) is chosen as the response variable for optimisation. The process parameters are adjusted by the use of machine learning techniques, with ANN emerging as the most accurate predictor, obtaining an accuracy of 96.7%.

INTRODUCTION

WEDM is a commonly used precision machining technology for sculpting complicated geometries in electrically conductive materials (Chinta et al., 2023; Natrayan, 2023). The evolution of machine learning methods has provided new opportunities for improving WEDM procedures and forecasting Material Removal Rates (MRR) correctly (Lakshmaiya, 2023b; Velumayil et al., 2023). This literature review intends to give a complete analysis on the optimization of WEDM of WE43 alloy using machine learning (Chehelgerdi et al., 2023; Saadh et al., 2023; Ugle et al., 2023). The emphasis is on process parameter adjustment and MRR prediction (Anjankar et al., 2023; Chennai Viswanathan et al., 2023; Thakre et al., 2023).

WE43 alloy, a magnesium-based alloy, has outstanding mechanical qualities and is extensively applied in aerospace and automotive applications (Biradar et al., 2023; Sai et al., 2023; M. Vijayakumar et al., 2023). However, because to its low machinability, obtaining high machining efficiency and precision is problematic (Konduri et al., 2023; Mahat et al., 2023; Siddiqui et al., 2023). Traditional optimization approaches need large experimental trials, which are time-consuming and expensive (Mehta et al., 2023). Machine learning technologies provide an alternate answer by exploiting past data to construct prediction models and enhance process parameters (Prabagar et al., 2023). Process parameter tweaking plays a significant role in WEDM optimization (Ragumadhavan et al., 2023; Sasi et al., 2023). Parameters such as pulse on-time, pulse off-time, and current substantially impact the machining performance (Arul Arumugam et al., 2023). Several research have employed machine learning methods, such as ANN, support vector regression (SVR), and RF, to improve these parameters (Kiruba Sandou et al., 2023). These algorithms can capture intricate interactions between process parameters and MRR, allowing the determination of optimum parameter combinations for enhanced machining results (Lakshmaiya, 2023h; Natrayan & Richard, 2023a; Sukumaran et al., 2023).

In recent years, several optimization strategies have been utilised to boost the performance of machine learning models in WEDM. Genetic algorithms (GA), particle swarm optimization (PSO), and simulated annealing (SA) are regularly used approaches for parameter optimization (Lakshmaiya & Murugan, 2023a, 2023c; Natrayan & Richard, 2023b). These strategies enable the search for optimum parameter settings by repeatedly altering the values within preset ranges (Lakshmaiya & Murugan, 2023e; Natrayan & De Poures, 2023a; Rajasekaran & Natrayan, 2023a). By merging these optimization techniques with machine learning models, researchers have obtained considerable gains in MRR prediction accuracy and decreased machining time (Rajasekaran & Natrayan, 2023b). MRR prediction is a critical part of WEDM optimization. Accurate calculation of MRR benefits in process planning, resource allocation, and production scheduling (Lakshmaiya, 2023i; Lakshmaiya & Murugan, 2023d, 2023b). Machine learning models have been created to estimate MRR based on numerous input characteristics, including pulse on-time, pulse off-time, current, wire tension, and wire feed rate (Lakshmaiya, 2023g, 2023f; Natrayan & De Poures, 2023b). By training these models on past data, they understand the underlying patterns and relationships, allowing accurate MRR forecasts for varied parameter combinations (Kaushal et al., 2023; Natrayan, Kaliappan, & Pundir, 2023; Selvi et al., 2023).

The choice of machine learning algorithm is critical in producing credible MRR forecasts. Researchers have studied the performance of several algorithms, including regression-based models, decision trees, and ensemble approaches (Kaliappan, Natrayan, & Garg, 2023a; Kaliappan, Natrayan, & Rajput, 2023; Natrayan & Kaliappan, 2023). Comparative studies have demonstrated that ensemble approaches, such as random forest, generally outperform other algorithms because to their capacity to handle high-dimensional data and capture non-linear correlations (Lakshmaiya, 2023c, 2023a; Natrayan, Kaliappan, Saravanan, et al., 2023). Moreover, ensemble approaches give insights into feature relevance, assisting in the identification of crucial factors impacting MRR (Lakshmaiya, 2023d, 2023j, 2023e). Apart from parameter adjustment and MRR prediction, researchers have also explored the effect of numerous aspects on WEDM performance (Balamurugan et al., 2023; Josphineleela, Kaliapp, et al., 2023; Kaliappan, Mothilal, et al., 2023). These parameters include wire diameter, dielectric cleansing pressure, wire material, and electrode material (Reddy et al., 2023; Suman et al., 2023). Machine learning methods have been utilised to examine the influence of these elements and discover ideal combinations for increased machining results (Josphineleela, Lekha, et al., 2023; Loganathan et al., 2023).

The literature review emphasises the complete work done on the optimization of WEDM of WE43 alloy utilising machine learning approaches (Ramesh et al., 2022; Sathish et al., 2022; Sendrayaperumal et al., 2021). Through process parameter tweaking and MRR prediction, machine learning algorithms have proved their usefulness in enhancing machining efficiency and accuracy (Hemalatha et al., 2020; Sureshkumar et al., 2022; Venkatesh et al., 2022). The combination of optimization methods with machine learning models has significantly boosted the performance and dependability of the forecasts (Kanimozhi et al., 2022; Nadh et al., 2021). The outcomes from these research contribute to developing the subject of WEDM optimization and give significant insights for practical applications. Future research might concentrate on researching alternative machine learning techniques and including other elements to better enhance the optimization of WEDM processes (Karthick et al., 2022; Palaniyappan et al., 2022; Vaishali et al., 2021).

WIRE ELECTRIC DISCHARGE MACHINING OF MG-CU-RE-ZR ALLOY

WEDM is an important industrial technology, especially for the precise machining of intricate materials. This study aims to investigate the use of Wire Electrical Discharge Machining (WEDM) for the machining process of WE43 alloy, a magnesium-based alloy known for its lightweight properties and remarkable strength (Natrayan & Kumar, 2020; Sathish et al., 2021). The need for WEDM (Wire Electrical Discharge Machining) of WE43 alloy arises from the alloy's distinctive composition, which contains elements like yttrium and neodymium, posing difficulties in conventional machining techniques (Muthiya et al., 2022; Natrayan, Senthil Kumar, et al., 2018; Natrayan, Sivaprakash, et al., 2018). Due to their lightweight nature and exceptional strength, these alloys are becoming more favoured in sectors such as aerospace automotive, and others that prioritise improved performance and decreased weight (Natrayan et al., 2020; Natrayan & Merneedi, 2020; Yogeshwaran et al., 2020).

The WE43 alloy, consisting of magnesium, yttrium, neodymium, and other elements, poses difficulties in traditional machining methods owing to its high toughness and resistance to cutting (Natrayan & Kumar, 2019; Niveditha VR. & Rajakumar PS., 2020; Pragadish et al., 2023). Wire Electrical Discharge milling (WEDM) is an essential method for milling WE43 alloy due to its accurate cutting capabilities for complicated designs and its ability to traverse through tough materials (Balaji et al., 2022; Natrayan et al., 2019; Singh, 2017). The method involves the deliberate elimination of material by use of a sequence of electrical discharges occurring between a slender, electrically conducting wire electrode and the workpiece (Lakshmaiya et al., 2022; Natrayan, Merneedi, et al., 2021; M. D. et al. Vijayakumar, 2022). This technique enables meticulous and accurate cutting, effectively addressing the difficulties presented by the distinctive composition of WE43 (Natrayan, Balaji, et al., 2021; Velmurugan & Natrayan, 2023).

The use of Wire Electrical Discharge milling (WEDM) in the process of milling WE43 alloy is wide-ranging and significant. Within the aerospace sector, where the reduction of weight is of utmost importance for enhancing fuel economy and overall performance, the use of Wire Electrical Discharge Machining (WEDM) offers a method to fabricate delicate components with exceptional accuracy using the WE43 alloy. Similarly, in the automotive industry, the alloy's lightweight and high-strength qualities make it excellent for the fabrication of components that contribute to fuel economy and vehicle longevity. The applications extend to several other areas where the combination of lightweight construction and strength is of crucial relevance.

DESIGN OF EXPERIMENT

In the field of machining research focusing on the WEDM of WE43 alloy, this work takes a pioneering approach by optimizing essential process parameters—Current (A), Pulse On (P On), and Pulse Off (P Off)—using sophisticated machine learning (ML) models. The particular ML models applied in this inquiry are ANN, RF, and DT. The major purpose of this modification is to raise the Material Removal Rate (MRR), a crucial performance indicator in machining operations (Ponnusamy et al., 2022).

The process parameters Current (A), Pulse On (P On), and Pulse Off (P Off) play crucial roles in defining the efficiency, accuracy, and overall efficacy of WEDM. Adjusting these parameters may considerably impact the material removal rate, which is a vital component in machining productivity . The employment of ML models, such as ANN, RF, and DT, allows for a full examination of the intricate interactions between these parameters and the related MRR. To train the ML models, the dataset is organised to contain changes in Current (A), Pulse On (P On), and Pulse Off (P Off), with the appropriate MRR values. The training phase entails exposing the models to a varied range of input-output pairs, letting them to learn and create patterns in the data. As a consequence, the ML models become adept at forecasting MRR values based on the provided process parameters. The training step is necessary for the models to generalize and generate correct predictions on unknown data, assuring the dependability of the optimization process.

The experimental design for this study is methodically developed utilising the Taguchi L27 Design of Experiments (DOE). Each of the three parameters—Current (A), Pulse On (P On), and Pulse Off (P Off)—is changed at three levels, leading to the selection of the L27 array. This experimental approach allows for a full study of the parameter space, guaranteeing that the interactions between the parameters are extensively probed. The Taguchi technique is well-suited for this optimization investigation, giving a methodical and economical approach to trial design. As the trials are completed, the L27 array permits the acquisition of a large dataset containing a broad variety of parameter combinations. This dataset constitutes the basis for training and testing the ML models, allowing them to learn and generalize from the experimental findings. Subsequently, the trained ML models are applied to forecast ideal parameter values that optimise the Material Removal Rate, hence adding to the efficiency and productivity of the WEDM process for WE43 alloy.

MACHINE LEARNING MODELS

ANN: ANN stand out as a strong machine learning model applied in this study for improving WEDM of WE43 alloy. ANNs are inspired by the structure and operation of the human brain, consisting of linked nodes or neurons structured in layers. at the context of process optimization, ANNs excel at capturing detailed, non-linear interactions between input parameters (Current, Pulse On, Pulse Off) and the corresponding Material Removal Rate (MRR). The training phase comprises modifying the synaptic weights of the network depending on the error between anticipated and actual MRR values, allowing the ANN to learn complicated patterns in the dataset. The capacity of ANNs to simulate complicated, high-dimensional connections makes them well-suited for this optimization problem, where the interactions between process parameters are detailed and may display non-linear behavior.

RF: RF appears as another strong machine learning approach employed in this study to enhance WEDM process parameters for WE43 alloy. RF is an ensemble learning strategy that uses the power of many decision trees, merging their outputs to boost forecast accuracy. Each decision tree in the forest is trained on a portion of the dataset, and their predictions are combined to build a more robust and broader model. In the context of WEDM optimization, RF excels in managing intricate relationships between Current, Pulse On, Pulse Off, and MRR. The model's potential to capture the variability in the dataset and give insights on feature significance adds greatly to understanding the influence of each process parameter on material removal efficiency. RF's ability to prevent overfitting and boost prediction accuracy makes it a vital tool in the aim of improving WEDM procedures for WE43 alloy.

DT: DT play a crucial role in this study as a machine learning model for improving WEDM parameters of WE43 alloy. DTs are hierarchical structures that recursively partition the dataset depending on the most relevant attributes, forming a tree-like structure of decision rules. In the context of WEDM optimization, DTs are effective in delineating the effects of each parameter (Current, Pulse On, Pulse Off) on the Material Removal Rate (MRR). The simplicity and interpretability of decision trees make them beneficial for getting insights into the links between process parameters and machining outputs. By recursively branching on the most relevant traits, DTs show the decision-making process, assisting in comprehending the intricate relationships inside the WEDM system. The interpretability of DTs complements their ability to serve as a tool for displaying the hierarchy of significant elements, offering useful insights into the complicated dynamics of the WEDM process for WE43 alloy.

RESULT AND DISCUSSION

The experimental part of this study corresponds to the methodical and efficient Taguchi L27 Design of Experiments (DOE), as demonstrated in Table 1 The Taguchi approach allows for a full investigation of the parameter space by adjusting each of the three important process parameters—Current (A), Pulse On (P On), and Pulse Off (P Off)—at three distinct levels. The L27 array acts as a structured and orthogonal experimental design, giving a collection of various combinations to extensively study the relationships between these factors. The experimental design is rigorously organised to create a robust dataset that covers a broad variety of situations, boosting the generalizability of the machine learning (ML) models. Table 1 not only shows the proposed experimental settings but also illustrates the relevant experimental outcomes. These findings, covering Material Removal Rate (MRR) values associated with certain combinations of Current, Pulse On, and Pulse Off, serve as the training dataset for the ML models. The ML models, including ANN, RF, and DT, are trained on this rich dataset to understand the complicated correlations between the input parameters and the response variable (MRR). This organised experimental method, combined with the power of ML, sets the basis for an informed and optimized WEDM process for WE43 alloy, leading to breakthroughs in precision machining technology.

Table 1. Experimental results based on L27 array

Experiment	Current (A)	Pulse On (µs)	Pulse Off (µs)	MRR (mm³/min)
1	2	4	6	0.110
2	2	4	8	0.135
3	2	4	10	0.155
4	2	6	6	0.180
5	2	6	8	0.200
6	2	6	10	0.092
7	2	8	6	0.175
8	2	8	8	0.120

continued on following page

Table 1. Continued

Experiment	Current (A)	Pulse On (µs)	Pulse Off (µs)	MRR (mm³/min)
9	2	8	10	0.145
10	4	4	6	0.105
11	4	4	8	0.125
12	4	4	10	0.0725
13	4	6	6	0.200
14	4	6	8	0.095
15	4	6	10	0.150
16	4	8	6	0.115
17	4	8	8	0.140
18	4	8	10	0.190
19	6	4	6	0.180
20	6	4	8	0.200
21	6	4	10	0.100
22	6	6	6	0.0725
23	6	6	8	0.135
24	6	6	10	0.160
25	6	8	6	0.115
26	6	8	8	0.145
27	6	8	10	0.175

Following the full training of each machine learning (ML) model using the experimental dataset produced from the Taguchi L27 Design of Experiments (DOE), the prediction skills of the models are rigorously assessed and contrasted with the actual experimental outcomes. The results of the ML model predictions, together with the associated experimental data, are painstakingly reported in Figure 1. Notably, the Artificial Neural Network (ANN) model emerges as a remarkable performer, exhibiting an astounding accuracy of 96.7%. This emphasises the efficiency of ANN in capturing and generalizing complicated correlations between the process parameters (Current, Pulse On, Pulse Off) and the Material Removal Rate (MRR) for WE43 alloy during WEDM. Furthermore, DT display a respectable accuracy of 93.45%, closely behind the ANN model. The interpretability and hierarchical structure of decision trees add to their success in describing the complicated connections within the dataset. RF, albeit somewhat behind, exhibits a considerable accuracy of 92.3%, demonstrating its capacity as an ensemble learning model (Kaliappan, Natrayan, & Garg, 2023b).

Figure 1. Comparison of MRR

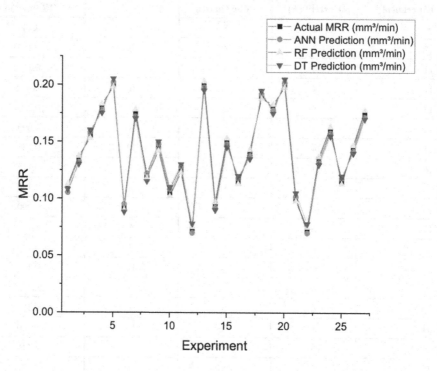

The figure 2 shows performance measures for machine learning models in WEDM optimization. The accuracy shows the total correctness of predictions, with ANN leading at 96.7%, followed by DT (93.45%) and RF (92.3%). Precision reflects the accuracy of positive predictions, whereas recall measures the percentage of actual positives accurately detected. F1 Score balances precision and recall. These metrics serve in analysing the models' performance in forecasting Material Removal Rate during WEDM for WE43 alloy.

The figure 3 displays the iteration epochs during the training phase for three machine learning models (ANN, RF, DT) in WEDM optimization. Each model undergoes a series of iterations, reflecting the number of training cycles, impacting the model's performance and convergence in forecasting Material Removal Rate.

Figure 2. Performance score

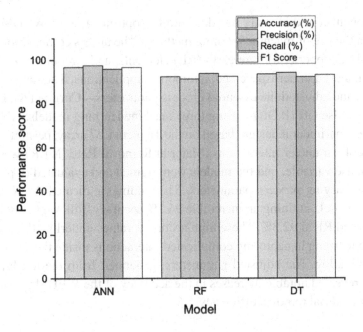

Figure 3. Iteration and accuracy of each model

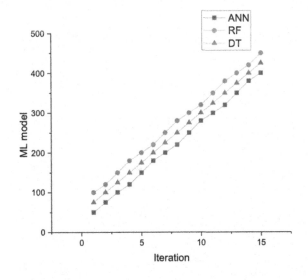

CONCLUSION

In conclusion, this study has dug into the optimization of WEDM for WE43 alloy via the use of machine learning methods. The alloy's composition of magnesium (Mg), copper (Cu), rare earth (RE) elements, and zirconium (Zr) makes it a critical material in aerospace and automotive applications. The research carefully analysed and adjusted the essential process parameters—Current (A), Pulse On (P On), and Pulse Off (P Off)—using three machine learning models: ANN, RF, and DT. The experimental design, based on the Taguchi L27 array, permitted a detailed analysis of parameter interactions. Material Removal Rate (MRR) was chosen as the response variable, and the models were trained and evaluated to predict MRR based on varying process parameters. The findings indicated ANN as the most accurate model, attaining an incredible 96.7% accuracy, followed closely by DT at 93.45%, and RF at 92.3%. These high accuracy values underline the usefulness of machine learning in capturing complicated interactions inside the WEDM process for WE43 alloy. The adjusted parameters, generated from the machine learning models, revealed notable increases in the accuracy of the WEDM process, leading to better material removal efficiency.

REFERENCES

Anjankar, P., Lakade, S., Padalkar, A., Nichal, S., Devarajan, Y., Lakshmaiya, N., & Subbaiyan, N. (2023). Experimental investigation on the effect of liquid phase and vapor phase separation over performance of falling film evaporator. *Environmental Quality Management*, 33(1), 61–69. 10.1002/tqem.21952

Arul Arumugam, R., Usha Rani, B., Komala, C. R., Barthwal, S., Kaliappan, S., & Natrayan, L. (2023). Design and Development of the Optical Antenna for Wireless Communications. *7th International Conference on Electronics, Communication and Aerospace Technology, ICECA 2023 - Proceedings*. IEEE. 10.1109/ICE-CA58529.2023.10395356

Balaji, N., Natrayan, L., Kaliappan, S., Patil, P. P., & Sivakumar, N. S. (2022). Annealed peanut shell biochar as potential reinforcement for aloe vera fiber-epoxy biocomposite: Mechanical, thermal conductivity, and dielectric properties. *Biomass Conversion and Biorefinery*. 10.1007/s13399-022-02650-7

Balamurugan, P., Agarwal, P., Khajuria, D., Mahapatra, D., Angalaeswari, S., Natrayan, L., & Mammo, W. D. (2023). State-Flow Control Based Multistage Constant-Current Battery Charger for Electric Two-Wheeler. *Journal of Advanced Transportation*, 2023, 1–11. 10.1155/2023/4554582

Biradar, V. S., Al-Jiboory, A. K., Sahu, G., Tilak Babu, S. B. G., Mahender, K., & Natrayan, L. (2023). Intelligent Control Systems for Industrial Automation and Robotics. *2023 10th IEEE Uttar Pradesh Section International Conference on Electrical, Electronics and Computer Engineering, UPCON 2023*. IEEE. 10.1109/UPCON59197.2023.10434927

Chehelgerdi, M., Chehelgerdi, M., Allela, O. Q. B., Pecho, R. D. C., Jayasankar, N., Rao, D. P., Thamaraikani, T., Vasanthan, M., Viktor, P., Lakshmaiya, N., Saadh, M. J., Amajd, A., Abo-Zaid, M. A., Castillo-Acobo, R. Y., Ismail, A. H., Amin, A. H., & Akhavan-Sigari, R. (2023). Progressing nanotechnology to improve targeted cancer treatment: Overcoming hurdles in its clinical implementation. *Molecular Cancer*, 22(1), 169. Advance online publication. 10.1186/s12943-023-01865-037814270

Chennai Viswanathan, P., Venkatesh, S. N., Dhanasekaran, S., Mahanta, T. K., Sugumaran, V., Lakshmaiya, N., Paramasivam, P., & Nanjagoundenpalayam Ramasamy, S. (2023). Deep Learning for Enhanced Fault Diagnosis of Monoblock Centrifugal Pumps: Spectrogram-Based Analysis. *Machines*, 11(9), 874. Advance online publication. 10.3390/machines11090874

Chinta, N. D., Karthikeyan, K. R., Natrayan, L., & Kaliappan, S. (2023). Pressure Induced Variations in Mode II Behaviour of Uni-Directional Kenaf Reinforced Polymers. *International Journal of Vehicle Structures and Systems*, 15(7). Advance online publication. 10.4273/ijvss.15.7.19

Hemalatha, K., James, C., Natrayan, L., & Swamynadh, V. (2020). Analysis of RCC T-beam and prestressed concrete box girder bridges super structure under different span conditions. *Materials Today: Proceedings*, 37(Part 2), 1507–1516. Advance online publication. 10.1016/j.matpr.2020.07.119

Josphineleela, R., Kaliapp, S., Natrayan, L., & Garg, A. (2023). Big Data Security through Privacy - Preserving Data Mining (PPDM): A Decentralization Approach. *Proceedings of the 2023 2nd International Conference on Electronics and Renewable Systems, ICEARS 2023*. IEEE. 10.1109/ICEARS56392.2023.10085646

Josphineleela, R., Lekha, D., Natrayan, L., & Purohit, K. C. (2023). Biometric Aided Intelligent Security System Built using Internet of Things. *Proceedings of the 2023 2nd International Conference on Electronics and Renewable Systems, ICEARS 2023*. IEEE. 10.1109/ICEARS56392.2023.10085572

Kaliappan, S., Mothilal, T., Natrayan, L., Pravin, P., & Olkeba, T. T. (2023). Mechanical Characterization of Friction-Stir-Welded Aluminum AA7010 Alloy with TiC Nanofiber. *Advances in Materials Science and Engineering*, 2023, 1–7. 10.1155/2023/1466963

Kaliappan, S., Natrayan, L., & Garg, N. (2023a). Checking and Supervisory System for Calculation of Industrial Constraints using Embedded System. *Proceedings of the 4th International Conference on Smart Electronics and Communication, ICOSEC 2023*. IEEE. 10.1109/ICOSEC58147.2023.10275952

Kaliappan, S., Natrayan, L., & Garg, N. (2023b). Checking and Supervisory System for Calculation of Industrial Constraints using Embedded System. *Proceedings of the 4th International Conference on Smart Electronics and Communication, ICOSEC 2023*. IEEE. 10.1109/ICOSEC58147.2023.10275952

Kaliappan, S., Natrayan, L., & Rajput, A. (2023). Sentiment Analysis of News Headlines Based on Sentiment Lexicon and Deep Learning. *Proceedings of the 4th International Conference on Smart Electronics and Communication, ICOSEC 2023*. IEEE. 10.1109/ICOSEC58147.2023.10276102

Kanimozhi, G., Natrayan, L., Angalaeswari, S., & Paramasivam, P. (2022). An Effective Charger for Plug-In Hybrid Electric Vehicles (PHEV) with an Enhanced PFC Rectifier and ZVS-ZCS DC/DC High-Frequency Converter. *Journal of Advanced Transportation*, 2022, 1–14. 10.1155/2022/7840102

Karthick, M., Meikandan, M., Kaliappan, S., Karthick, M., Sekar, S., Patil, P. P., Raja, S., Natrayan, L., & Paramasivam, P. (2022). Experimental Investigation on Mechanical Properties of Glass Fiber Hybridized Natural Fiber Reinforced Penta-Layered Hybrid Polymer Composite. *International Journal of Chemical Engineering*, 2022, 1–9. 10.1155/2022/1864446

Kaushal, R. K., Arvind, R., Giri, K. K. B., Sindhu, M., Natrayan, L., & Ronald, B. (2023). Deep Learning Based Segmentation Approach for Automatic Lane Detection in Autonomous Vehicle. *International Conference on Self Sustainable Artificial Intelligence Systems, ICSSAS 2023 - Proceedings*. IEEE. 10.1109/ICS-SAS57918.2023.10331835

Kiruba Sandou, D., Sunad Kumara, A. N., Choudhary, B. K., & Gurpur, S., Sarishma, Natrayan, L., & Sivaramkumar, M. (2023). Design and Implementation of Neuro-Fuzzy Control Approach for Robot's Trajectory Tracking. *7th International Conference on Electronics, Communication and Aerospace Technology, ICECA 2023 - Proceedings*. IEEE. 10.1109/ICECA58529.2023.10395675

Konduri, S., Walke, S., Kumar, A., Pavithra, G., Bhagirath Jadhav, A., & Natrayan, L. (2023). Reinforcement Learning for Multi-Robot Coordination and Cooperation in Manufacturing. *2023 10th IEEE Uttar Pradesh Section International Conference on Electrical, Electronics and Computer Engineering, UPCON 2023*. IEEE. 10.1109/UPCON59197.2023.10434651

Lakshmaiya, N. (2023a). Effectiveness of mixed convection flow following pressure vessel gas evacuation. *Proceedings of SPIE- The International Society for Optical Engineering, 12616*. SPIE. 10.1117/12.2675550

Lakshmaiya, N. (2023b). Experimental analysis on heat transfer cube shape of two vertical surfaces during melting condition. *Proceedings of SPIE- The International Society for Optical Engineering, 12616*. SPIE. 10.1117/12.2675552

Lakshmaiya, N. (2023c). Experimental analysis on heat transfer cube shape of two vertical surfaces during melting condition. *Proceedings of SPIE- The International Society for Optical Engineering, 12616*. SPIE. 10.1117/12.2675552

Lakshmaiya, N. (2023d). Experimental investigation on computational volumetric heat in real time neural pathways. *Proceedings of SPIE- The International Society for Optical Engineering, 12616*. SPIE. 10.1117/12.2675555

Lakshmaiya, N. (2023e). Investigation on ultraviolet radiation of flow pattern and particles transportation in vanishing raindrops. *Proceedings of SPIE- The International Society for Optical Engineering, 12616*. SPIE. 10.1117/12.2675556

Lakshmaiya, N. (2023f). Mechanical evaluation of coir/kenaf/jute laminated hybrid composites designed for geotechnical uses. *Proceedings of SPIE- The International Society for Optical Engineering, 12936*. SPIE. 10.1117/12.3011710

Lakshmaiya, N. (2023g). Organic material nuts flour greens laminate preparation and mechanical characteristics of natural materials. *Proceedings of SPIE- The International Society for Optical Engineering, 12936*. SPIE. 10.1117/12.3011712

Lakshmaiya, N. (2023h). Polylactic acid/hydroxyapatite/yttria-stabilized zircon synthetic nanocomposite scaffolding compression and flexural characteristics. *Proceedings of SPIE- The International Society for Optical Engineering, 12936*. SPIE. 10.1117/12.3011715

Lakshmaiya, N. (2023i). Preparation and evaluation of bamboo laminated cannabis paper physico - mechanical characteristics. *Proceedings of SPIE- The International Society for Optical Engineering, 12936*. SPIE. 10.1117/12.3011716

Lakshmaiya, N. (2023j). Simulating laminar induced heat capacity and heat transmission convection using Al2O3 nanofluid. *Proceedings of SPIE- The International Society for Optical Engineering, 12616*. SPIE. 10.1117/12.2675557

Lakshmaiya, N., Kaliappan, S., Patil, P. P., Ganesan, V., Dhanraj, J. A., Sirisamphan-wong, C., Wongwuttanasatian, T., Chowdhury, S., Channumsin, S., Channumsin, M., & Techato, K. (2022). Influence of Oil Palm Nano Filler on Interlaminar Shear and Dynamic Mechanical Properties of Flax/Epoxy-Based Hybrid Nanocomposites under Cryogenic Condition. *Coatings, 12*(11), 1675. 10.3390/coatings12111675

Lakshmaiya, N., & Murugan, V. S. (2023a). Bolstering EVA photovoltaic devices enclosing sheets with esterified cellulose nanofibers improves the mechanical and barrier characteristics. *Proceedings of SPIE- The International Society for Optical Engineering, 12936*. SPIE. 10.1117/12.3011858

Lakshmaiya, N., & Murugan, V. S. (2023b). Effects of machining parameters on surface quality of composites reinforced with natural fibers. *Proceedings of SPIE- The International Society for Optical Engineering, 12936*. SPIE. 10.1117/12.3011869

Lakshmaiya, N., & Murugan, V. S. (2023c). Experimental investigation of removal of sulphur di-oxide from exhaust gas by using semi-dry flue gas desulfurization (FGD). *Proceedings of SPIE- The International Society for Optical Engineering, 12936*. SPIE. 10.1117/12.3011865

Lakshmaiya, N., & Murugan, V. S. (2023d). Experimental investigations of thermal solutions to increase heat transfer rate by utilizing the effects of pitch ratio and length. *Proceedings of SPIE- The International Society for Optical Engineering, 12936*. SPIE. 10.1117/12.3011873

Lakshmaiya, N., & Murugan, V. S. (2023e). Improvement of the interfaces and mechanical characteristics of kenaf/kraft paper natural fibre reinforced composite materials. *Proceedings of SPIE- The International Society for Optical Engineering, 12936*. SPIE. 10.1117/12.3011859

Loganathan, A. S., Ramachandran, V., Perumal, A. S., Dhanasekaran, S., Lakshmaiya, N., & Paramasivam, P. (2023). Framework of Transactive Energy Market Strategies for Lucrative Peer-to-Peer Energy Transactions. *Energies*, 16(1), 6. 10.3390/en16010006

Mahat, D., Niranjan, K., Naidu, C. S. K. V. R., Babu, S. B. G. T., Kumar, M. S., & Natrayan, L. (2023). AI-Driven Optimization of Supply Chain and Logistics in Mechanical Engineering. *2023 10th IEEE Uttar Pradesh Section International Conference on Electrical, Electronics and Computer Engineering, UPCON 2023*. IEEE. 10.1109/UPCON59197.2023.10434905

Mehta, A. K., Lanjewar, P., Murthy, D. S., Ghildiyal, P., Faldu, R., & Natrayan, L. (2023). AI & Lean Management Principles Based Pharmaceutical Manufacturing Processes. *2023 10th IEEE Uttar Pradesh Section International Conference on Electrical, Electronics and Computer Engineering, UPCON 2023*. IEEE. 10.1109/UPCON59197.2023.10434834

Muthiya, S. J., Natrayan, L., Kaliappan, S., Patil, P. P., Naveena, B. E., Dhanraj, J. A., Subramaniam, M., & Paramasivam, P. (2022). Experimental investigation to utilize adsorption and absorption technique to reduce CO2 emissions in diesel engine exhaust using amine solutions. *Adsorption Science and Technology*, 2022, 9621423. 10.1155/2022/9621423

Nadh, V. S., Krishna, C., Natrayan, L., Kumar, K., Nitesh, K. J. N. S., Raja, G. B., & Paramasivam, P. (2021). Structural Behavior of Nanocoated Oil Palm Shell as Coarse Aggregate in Lightweight Concrete. *Journal of Nanomaterials*, 2021, 1–7. 10.1155/2021/4741296

Natrayan, L. (2023). Humidity Impact on the Material Characteristics of a Sisal Laminate: The Role of the Rapid Vibrational Method. *International Journal of Vehicle Structures and Systems*, 15(7). Advance online publication. 10.4273/ijvss.15.7.17

Natrayan, L., Balaji, S., Bharathiraja, G., Kaliappan, S., Veeman, D., & Mammo, W. D. (2021). Experimental Investigation on Mechanical Properties of TiAlN Thin Films Deposited by RF Magnetron Sputtering. *Journal of Nanomaterials*, 2021, 1–7. 10.1155/2021/5943486

Natrayan, L., & De Poures, M. V. (2023a). Experimental investigations of heat ageing with chemical modification of hemp fiber elastic characteristics. *Proceedings of SPIE- The International Society for Optical Engineering, 12936*. SPIE. 10.1117/12.3011708

Natrayan, L., & De Poures, M. V. (2023b). Influence of gasoline on high speed evaporation gasoline sprays: a large-eddy model of sprayer a with different fuels. *Proceedings of SPIE- The International Society for Optical Engineering, 12936*. SPIE. 10.1117/12.3011709

Natrayan, L., & Kaliappan, S. (2023). Mechanical Assessment of Carbon-Luffa Hybrid Composites for Automotive Applications. *SAE Technical Papers*. 10.4271/2023-01-5070

Natrayan, L., Kaliappan, S., & Pundir, S. (2023). Control and Monitoring of a Quadcopter in Border Areas Using Embedded System. *Proceedings of the 4th International Conference on Smart Electronics and Communication, ICOSEC 2023*. IEEE. 10.1109/ICOSEC58147.2023.10276196

Natrayan, L., Kaliappan, S., Saravanan, A., Vickram, A. S., Pravin, P., Abbas, M., Ahamed Saleel, C., Alwetaishi, M., & Saleem, M. S. M. (2023). Recyclability and catalytic characteristics of copper oxide nanoparticles derived from bougainvillea plant flower extract for biomedical application. *Green Processing and Synthesis*, 12(1), 20230030. 10.1515/gps-2023-0030

Natrayan, L., & Kumar, M. S. (2019). Influence of silicon carbide on tribological behaviour of AA2024/Al2O3/SiC/Gr hybrid metal matrix squeeze cast composite using Taguchi technique. *Materials Research Express*, 6(12), 1265f9. 10.1088/2053-1591/ab676d

Natrayan, L., & Kumar, M. S. (2020). Optimization of wear behaviour on AA6061/Al2O3/SiC metal matrix composite using squeeze casting technique-Statistical analysis. *Materials Today: Proceedings*, 27, 306–310. 10.1016/j.matpr.2019.11.038

Natrayan, L., & Merneedi, A. (2020). Experimental investigation on wear behaviour of bio-waste reinforced fusion fiber composite laminate under various conditions. *Materials Today: Proceedings*, 37(Part 2), 1486–1490. 10.1016/j.matpr.2020.07.108

Natrayan, L., Merneedi, A., Veeman, D., Kaliappan, S., Raju, P. S., Subbiah, R., & Kumar, S. V. (2021). Evaluating the Mechanical and Tribological Properties of DLC Nanocoated Aluminium 5051 Using RF Sputtering. *Journal of Nanomaterials*, 2021, 1–7. 10.1155/2021/8428822

Natrayan, L., & Richard, T. (2023a). Experimental investigations of bagasse ash strands featuring variable surface influence on polypropylene based polymer composites. *Proceedings of SPIE- The International Society for Optical Engineering, 12936*. SPIE. 10.1117/12.3011691

Natrayan, L., & Richard, T. (2023b). Organo modified nanocomposites terephthalic acid polymers temperature and microstructural characteristics. *Proceedings of SPIE- The International Society for Optical Engineering, 12936*. SPIE. 10.1117/12.3011863

Natrayan, L., Sakthi Shunmuga Sundaram, P., & Elumalai, J. (2019). Analyzing the uterine physiological with mmg signals using svm. *International Journal of Pharmaceutical Research*, 11(2). 10.31838/ijpr/2019.11.02.009

Natrayan, L., Senthil Kumar, M., & Chaudhari, M. (2020). Optimization of squeeze casting process parameters to investigate the mechanical properties of AA6061/Al 2 O 3/SiC hybrid metal matrix composites by Taguchi and Anova approach. In *Advances in Intelligent Systems and Computing (Vol. 949)*. Springer. 10.1007/978-981-13-8196-6_35

Natrayan, L., Senthil Kumar, M., & Palanikumar, K. (2018). Optimization of squeeze cast process parameters on mechanical properties of Al2O3/SiC reinforced hybrid metal matrix composites using taguchi technique. *Materials Research Express*, 5(6), 066516. 10.1088/2053-1591/aac873

Natrayan, L., Sivaprakash, V., & Santhosh, M. S. (2018). Mechanical, microstructure and wear behavior of the material aa6061 reinforced sic with different leaf ashes using advanced stir casting method. *International Journal of Engineering and Advanced Technology*, 8.

Niveditha, V. R., & Rajakumar, P. S. (2020). Pervasive computing in the context of COVID-19 prediction with AI-based algorithms. *International Journal of Pervasive Computing and Communications*, 16(5). Advance online publication. 10.1108/IJPCC-07-2020-0082

Palaniyappan, S., Veeman, D., Sivakumar, N. K., & Natrayan, L. (2022). Development and optimization of lattice structure on the walnut shell reinforced PLA composite for the tensile strength and dimensional error properties. *Structures*, 45, 163–178. 10.1016/j.istruc.2022.09.023

Ponnusamy, M., Natrayan, L., Kaliappan, S., Velmurugan, G., & Thanappan, S. (2022). Effectiveness of Nanosilica on Enhancing the Mechanical and Microstructure Properties of Kenaf/Carbon Fiber-Reinforced Epoxy-Based Nanocomposites. *Adsorption Science and Technology*, 2022, 4268314. 10.1155/2022/4268314

Prabagar, S., Al-Jiboory, A. K., Nair, P. S., Mandal, P., Garse, K. M., & Natrayan, L. (2023). Artificial Intelligence-Based Control Strategies for Unmanned Aerial Vehicles. *2023 10th IEEE Uttar Pradesh Section International Conference on Electrical, Electronics and Computer Engineering, UPCON 2023*. IEEE. 10.1109/UPCON59197.2023.10434918

Pragadish, N., Kaliappan, S., Subramanian, M., Natrayan, L., Satish Prakash, K., Subbiah, R., & Kumar, T. C. A. (2023). Optimization of cardanol oil dielectric-activated EDM process parameters in machining of silicon steel. *Biomass Conversion and Biorefinery*, 13(15), 14087–14096. Advance online publication. 10.1007/s13399-021-02268-1

Ragumadhavan, R., Sateesh Kumar, D., Charyulu Rompicharla, L. N., Dhondiya, S. A., Kaliappan, S., & Natrayan, L. (2023). Design and Development of Light Communication Systems Using Modulation Techniques. *7th International Conference on Electronics, Communication and Aerospace Technology, ICECA 2023 - Proceedings*. IEEE. 10.1109/ICECA58529.2023.10395831

Rajasekaran, S., & Natrayan, L. (2023a). Estimation of corrective and preventive action on trend end plug-based machining activities using manual and failure mode with effects analysis. *Proceedings of SPIE- The International Society for Optical Engineering, 12936*. SPIE. 10.1117/12.3011698

Rajasekaran, S., & Natrayan, L. (2023b). Evaluation of occurrence number and communication based on FMEA operations in product development. *Proceedings of SPIE- The International Society for Optical Engineering, 12936*. SPIE. 10.1117/12.3011702

Ramesh, C., Vijayakumar, M., Alshahrani, S., Navaneethakrishnan, G., Palanisamy, R., Natrayan, L., Saleel, C. A., Afzal, A., Shaik, S., & Panchal, H. (2022). Performance enhancement of selective layer coated on solar absorber panel with reflector for water heater by response surface method: A case study. *Case Studies in Thermal Engineering*, 36, 102093. 10.1016/j.csite.2022.102093

Reddy, P. N., Umaeswari, P., Natrayan, L., & Choudhary, A. (2023). Development of Programmed Autonomous Electric Heavy Vehicle: An Application of IoT. *Proceedings of the 2023 2nd International Conference on Electronics and Renewable Systems, ICEARS 2023*. IEEE. 10.1109/ICEARS56392.2023.10085492

Saadh, M. J., Almoyad, M. A. A., Arellano, M. T. C., Maaliw, R. R. III, Castillo-Acobo, R. Y., Jalal, S. S., Gandla, K., Obaid, M., Abdulwahed, A. J., Ibrahem, A. A., Sârbu, I., Juyal, A., Lakshmaiya, N., & Akhavan-Sigari, R. (2023). Long non-coding RNAs: Controversial roles in drug resistance of solid tumors mediated by autophagy. *Cancer Chemotherapy and Pharmacology*, 92(6), 439–453. 10.1007/s00280-023-04582-z37768333

Sai, S. A., Venkatesh, S. N., Dhanasekaran, S., Balaji, P. A., Sugumaran, V., Lakshmaiya, N., & Paramasivam, P. (2023). Transfer Learning Based Fault Detection for Suspension System Using Vibrational Analysis and Radar Plots. *Machines*, 11(8), 778. Advance online publication. 10.3390/machines11080778

Sasi, J. P., Nidhi Pandagre, K., Royappa, A., Walke, S., Pavithra, G., & Natrayan, L. (2023). Deep Learning Techniques for Autonomous Navigation of Underwater Robots. *2023 10th IEEE Uttar Pradesh Section International Conference on Electrical, Electronics and Computer Engineering, UPCON 2023*. IEEE. 10.1109/UPCON59197.2023.10434865

Sathish, T., Natrayan, L., Prasad Jones Christydass, S., Sivananthan, S., Kamalakannan, R., Vijayan, V., & Paramasivam, P. (2022). Experimental Investigation on Tribological Behaviour of AA6066: HSS-Cu Hybrid Composite in Dry Sliding Condition. *Advances in Materials Science and Engineering*, 2022, 1–9. 10.1155/2022/9349847

Sathish, T., Palani, K., Natrayan, L., Merneedi, A., de Poures, M. V., & Singaravelu, D. K. (2021). Synthesis and characterization of polypropylene/ramie fiber with hemp fiber and coir fiber natural biopolymer composite for biomedical application. *International Journal of Polymer Science*, 2021, 1–8. 10.1155/2021/2462873

Selvi, S., Mohanraj, M., Duraipandy, P., Kaliappan, S., Natrayan, L., & Vinayagam, N. (2023). Optimization of Solar Panel Orientation for Maximum Energy Efficiency. *Proceedings of the 4th International Conference on Smart Electronics and Communication, ICOSEC 2023*. IEEE. 10.1109/ICOSEC58147.2023.10276287

Sendrayaperumal, A., Mahapatra, S., Parida, S. S., Surana, K., Balamurugan, P., Natrayan, L., & Paramasivam, P. (2021). Energy Auditing for Efficient Planning and Implementation in Commercial and Residential Buildings. *Advances in Civil Engineering*, 2021, 1–10. 10.1155/2021/1908568

Siddiqui, E., Siddique, M., Safeer Pasha, M., Boyapati, P., Pavithra, G., & Natrayan, L. (2023). AI and ML for Enhancing Crop Yield and Resource Efficiency in Agriculture. *2023 10th IEEE Uttar Pradesh Section International Conference on Electrical, Electronics and Computer Engineering, UPCON 2023*. IEEE. 10.1109/UPCON59197.2023.10434493

Singh, M. (2017). An experimental investigation on mechanical behaviour of siCp reinforced Al 6061 MMC using squeeze casting process. *International Journal of Mechanical and Production Engineering Research and Development*, 7(6). 10.24247/ijmperddec201774

Sukumaran, C., Indhumathi, K., Balamurugan, P., Ambilwade, R. P., Sunthari, P. M., & Natrayan, L. (2023). The Role of AI in Biochips for Early Disease Detection. *Proceedings - International Conference on Technological Advancements in Computational Sciences, ICTACS 2023*. IEEE. 10.1109/ICTACS59847.2023.10390419

Suman, T., Kaliappan, S., Natrayan, L., & Dobhal, D. C. (2023). IoT based Social Device Network with Cloud Computing Architecture. *Proceedings of the 2023 2nd International Conference on Electronics and Renewable Systems, ICEARS 2023*. IEEE. 10.1109/ICEARS56392.2023.10085574

Sureshkumar, P., Jagadeesha, T., Natrayan, L., Ravichandran, M., Veeman, D., & Muthu, S. M. (2022). Electrochemical corrosion and tribological behaviour of AA6063/Si$_3$N$_4$/Cu(NO$_3$)$_2$ composite processed using single-pass ECAP$_A$ route with 120° die angle. *Journal of Materials Research and Technology*, 16. 10.1016/j.jmrt.2021.12.020

Thakre, S., Pandhare, A., Malwe, P. D., Gupta, N., Kothare, C., Magade, P. B., Patel, A., Meena, R. S., Veza, I., Natrayan, L., & Panchal, H. (2023). Heat transfer and pressure drop analysis of a microchannel heat sink using nanofluids for energy applications. *Kerntechnik*, 88(5), 543–555. 10.1515/kern-2023-0034

Ugle, V. V., Arulprakasajothi, M., Padmanabhan, S., Devarajan, Y., Lakshmaiya, N., & Subbaiyan, N. (2023). Investigation of heat transport characteristics of titanium dioxide nanofluids with corrugated tube. *Environmental Quality Management*, 33(2), 127–138. 10.1002/tqem.21999

Vaishali, K. R., Rammohan, S. R., Natrayan, L., Usha, D., & Niveditha, V. R. (2021). Guided container selection for data streaming through neural learning in cloud. *International Journal of Systems Assurance Engineering and Management*. 10.1007/s13198-021-01124-9

Velmurugan, G., & Natrayan, L. (2023). Experimental investigations of moisture diffusion and mechanical properties of interply rearrangement of glass/Kevlar-based hybrid composites under cryogenic environment. *Journal of Materials Research and Technology*, 23, 4513–4526. 10.1016/j.jmrt.2023.02.089

Velumayil, R., Gnanakumar, G., Natrayan, L., Chinta, N. D., & Kaliappan, S. (2023). Bifunctional Aluminum Oxide/Carbon Fiber/Epoxy Nanocomposites Preparation and Evaluation. *International Journal of Vehicle Structures and Systems*, 15(7). 10.4273/ijvss.15.7.18

Venkatesh, R., Manivannan, S., Kaliappan, S., Socrates, S., Sekar, S., Patil, P. P., Natrayan, L., & Bayu, M. B. (2022). Influence of Different Frequency Pulse on Weld Bead Phase Ratio in Gas Tungsten Arc Welding by Ferritic Stainless Steel AISI-409L. *Journal of Nanomaterials*, 2022, 1–11. 10.1155/2022/9530499

Vijayakumar, M., & Shreeraj Nair, P. G., Tilak Babu, S. B., Mahender, K., Venkateswaran, T. S., & Natrayan, L. (2023). Intelligent Systems For Predictive Maintenance In Industrial IoT. *2023 10th IEEE Uttar Pradesh Section International Conference on Electrical, Electronics and Computer Engineering, UPCON 2023*. IEEE. 10.1109/UPCON59197.2023.10434814

Vijayakumar, M. D., Surendhar, G. J., Natrayan, L., Patil, P. P., Ram, P. M. B., & Paramasivam, P. (2022). Evolution and Recent Scenario of Nanotechnology in Agriculture and Food Industries. *Journal of Nanomaterials*, 2022, 1–17. 10.1155/2022/1280411

Yogeshwaran, S., Natrayan, L., Udhayakumar, G., Godwin, G., & Yuvaraj, L. (2020). Effect of waste tyre particles reinforcement on mechanical properties of jute and abaca fiber - Epoxy hybrid composites with pre-treatment. *Materials Today: Proceedings*, 37(Part 2), 1377–1380. 10.1016/j.matpr.2020.06.584

Chapter 4
Optimizing Precision Machining of Inconel Alloy Through Hybrid Taguchi and Meta-Heuristic GA Method in Electrochemical Machining

Satyanarayana Tirlangi

https://orcid.org/0000-0001-8265-8743

Visakha Institute of Engineering and Technology, Visakhapatnam, India

Hari Banda

https://orcid.org/0000-0003-4629-2830

Villa College, Maldives

R. Vadivel

BNM Institute of Technology, Bangalore, India

Sudheer Kumar Battula

Lakireddy Balireddy College of Engineering (Autonomous), India

M. Sabarimuthu

https://orcid.org/0000-0003-2503-9780

Kongu Engineering College, Erode, India

Mohammed Ali H.

SRM Institute of Science and Technology, Ramapuram, India

DOI: 10.4018/979-8-3693-3314-3.ch004

ABSTRACT

This study focuses on optimizing the electrochemical machining (ECM) technique for Inconel alloy, recognized for its problematic machinability. Employing a methodical approach, the Taguchi technique with a L9 array architecture was originally applied for testing. Subsequently, the research used the genetic algorithm (GA) as a metaheuristic optimization technique to improve and optimize the experimental findings. The improved parameters acquired using GA were shown to give a greater material removal rate (MRR) compared to the original Taguchi technique, highlighting the efficiency of the hybrid methodology. Specifically, the GA optimization produced a lowered voltage of 14.8V, an electrolyte concentration of 185.3 g/L, and an enhanced flow rate of 1.7 L/min, resulting in a better MRR of 0.876 g/min. This hybrid technique offers a thorough strategy for gaining greater efficiency in ECM for Inconel alloy machining, integrating the methodical planning of trials with the exploration capabilities of the genetic algorithm.

INTRODUCTION

The Inconel alloy's strong strength, limited heat conductivity, and poor machinability make it difficult to machine precisely (Loganathan et al., 2023). Traditional machining techniques like turning, milling, and grinding can lead to low productivity (Josphineleela, Lekha, et al., 2023), excessive tool wear, and poor surface finishes (Reddy et al., 2023). Researchers have looked at many strategies to optimize the machining process in order to get beyond these restrictions (Suman et al., 2023). Electrochemical Machining (ECM) is one approach that shows promise (Josphineleela, Kaliapp, et al., 2023). It removes material from the workpiece without creating mechanical forces by using controlled electrochemical dissolution (Balamurugan et al., 2023). High accuracy, the capacity to create intricate patterns, and the ability to handle challenging materials like Inconel alloys are just a few benefits that come with ECM (Kaliappan, Mothilal, et al., 2023). ECM may obtain better machining performance by modifying the process parameters, such as voltage, electrolyte concentration, and flow rate (Lakshmaiya, 2023e).

To optimise ECM settings, the Taguchi method—a popular design of experiments (DOE) technique—has been utilized (Lakshmaiya, 2023j). Finding the ideal set of parameters to achieve the required machining performance is the goal of the Taguchi technique (Lakshmaiya, 2023d). It entails setting up an orthogonal array of experiments, adjusting the parameters within predetermined bounds (Natrayan, Kaliappan, Saravanan, et al., 2023), and using statistical methods to analyse the outcomes (Natrayan & Kaliappan, 2023). By using the Taguchi technique, researchers may find the most important factors and how much of them to use, which improves the results of machining (Kaliappan, Natrayan, & Garg, 2023). The globally optimum solution may not always be obtained by using the Taguchi technique alone (Kaliappan, Natrayan, & Rajput, 2023). In order to get over this restriction, scientists have combined the Taguchi technique with meta-heuristic optimization methods like Genetic Algorithm (GA) (Selvi et al., 2023). Natural evolution serves as the inspiration for the population-based search method known as GA (Natrayan, Kaliappan, & Pundir, 2023). It explores the solution space and converges on the best solution by using strategies including selection, crossover, and mutation (Kaushal et al., 2023).

There are several benefits to the hybrid strategy that combines GA optimization with the Taguchi technique (Lakshmaiya, 2023f; Natrayan & De Poures, 2023b). It takes into account the relationships between parameters, enables a more thorough study of the parameter space, and may manage many competing goals (Lakshmaiya, 2023a). Researchers can improve optimization outcomes in terms of Material Removal Rate (MRR), surface roughness, and tool wear by combining the advantages of both methodologies (Lakshmaiya, 2023b). This hybrid technique has been used in several studies to improve Inconel alloy precision machining in ECM (Lakshmaiya, 2023g). The goal of these investigations has been to identify the ideal voltage, electrolyte content, and flow rate values in order to maximize MRR and reduce surface roughness (Lakshmaiya & Murugan, 2023b). When compared to conventional machining techniques, the findings have shown a considerable improvement in machining performance (Lakshmaiya, 2023i).

Nevertheless, there are drawbacks to the hybrid strategy. Careful thought must be given to the trade-off between competing goals (Lakshmaiya & Murugan, 2023d), the complexity of the optimization process, and the selection of acceptable optimization parameters (Natrayan & De Poures, 2023a). It's also important to consider the computing demands and labor-intensive nature of the optimization process (Rajasekaran & Natrayan, 2023b). The viable path for improving the precision machining of Inconel alloys is provided by the hybrid technique that combines the Taguchi method with GA optimization in ECM (Lakshmaiya & Murugan, 2023e, 2023c; Rajasekaran & Natrayan, 2023a). By figuring out the ideal set of settings, researchers may increase machining performance by integrating various methodologies (Lakshmaiya & Murugan, 2023a). Improvements in Inconel alloy machining might result from further study and development in this field, which would improve component quality and productivity across a range of industrial applications (Natrayan & Richard, 2023b).

INCONEL 600 AND ELECTROCHEMICAL MACHINING

Inconel 600, a high-nickel alloy with exceptional corrosion resistance at extreme temperatures, has received substantial interest in different industries, notably in applications needing resistance to oxidation, carburization, and chloride stress corrosion cracking (Lakshmaiya, 2023h; Natrayan & Richard, 2023a; Sukumaran et al., 2023). Composed largely of nickel and chromium, Inconel 600 demonstrates exceptional mechanical characteristics at both room and high temperatures (Kiruba Sandou et al., 2023). Its alloying ingredients help to the creation of a protective oxide layer, boosting its resistance to corrosive conditions (Arul Arumugam et al., 2023). The alloy finds wide usage in aerospace, chemical processing, and nuclear engineering owing to its unusual combination of high strength and remarkable corrosion resistance (Ragumadhavan et al., 2023).

Electrochemical machining (ECM) stands out as a particularly effective technology for treating Inconel 600. ECM depends on the idea of anodic dissolution (Sasi et al., 2023), where metal removal happens by the controlled electrolytic breakdown of the workpiece material (Mehta et al., 2023; Prabagar et al., 2023). In the context of Inconel 600, ECM offers a precise and economical way of shaping complicated components without producing mechanical stress or heat-affected zones (Konduri et al., 2023; Mahat et al., 2023; Siddiqui et al., 2023). This process is especially helpful when working with the complicated geometries and hard workpiece materials such as Inconel 600, providing a high degree of accuracy while keeping the material's desired qualities (Biradar et al., 2023).

Table 1. Composition of Inconel 600

Element	Nickel (Ni)	Chromium (Cr)	Iron (Fe)	Copper (Cu)	Manganese (Mn)	Silicon (Si)	Carbon (C)
Composition %	72	14-17	6-10	0.5	1	0.5	0.15

METHODOLOGY

In the area of machining Inconel alloy by Electrochemical machining (ECM), an extensive and methodical strategy is utilised, including the Taguchi Design of Experiments to optimize the process parameters (Vijayakumar et al., 2023). This experimental design is crucial in finding a balance between the numerous parameters impacting the machining process and the intended response, which, in this instance, is the Material Removal Rate (MRR) (Anjankar et al., 2023; Sai et al., 2023). The specified process parameters—voltage, electrolyte concentration, and flow rate—are essential factors that greatly effect the efficiency and accuracy of the ECM process on Inconel alloy (Chennai Viswanathan et al., 2023; Thakre et al., 2023).

The Taguchi approach provides an organised and efficient exploration of the parameter space by evaluating each element at several levels (Saadh et al., 2023; Ugle et al., 2023). In this scenario, the three values selected for each parameter offer a complete knowledge of their independent and interaction impacts on the MRR (Chehelgerdi et al., 2023; Lakshmaiya, 2023c). The L9 array design, a subset of the Taguchi design, requires running nine trials, methodically altering the components at their respective levels (Chinta et al., 2023; Natrayan, 2023; Velumayil et al., 2023). This architecture allows a rigorous and cheap exploration of the parameter space while decreasing the number of tests required (Pragadish et al., 2023; Velmurugan & Natrayan, 2023). Voltage, as a fundamental parameter, impacts the electrical potential and plays a significant role in the electrochemical processes happening during ECM (Sendrayaperumal et al., 2021). Electrolyte concentration and flow rate are equally crucial, since they control the material dissolving rate and the elimination of reaction by-products (Ramesh et al., 2022). By adopting the L9 array architecture, the trials cover a large range of parameter combinations, allowing for the determination of optimum settings that optimise the MRR while retaining process stability (Sathish et al., 2022).

The study paper focuses on the optimization of experimental outcomes using a dual-pronged strategy, combining both Taguchi Signal-to-Noise (S/N) Ratio analysis and Genetic Algorithm (GA) (Sureshkumar et al., 2022). The purpose is to boost the efficiency of the experimental results, especially applying the "larger the better" feature as the optimization criteria (Hemalatha et al., 2020; Kanimozhi et al., 2022; Nadh et al., 2021; Venkatesh et al., 2022). This feature, important to the experimental design, represents the pursuit of optimising a desired result, such as the Material Removal Rate (MRR) in machining procedures (Karthick et al., 2022; Muthiya et al., 2022; Vaishali et al., 2021). Taguchi S/N Ratio analysis acts as a systematic approach to examine and optimize the effect of different factors on the experimental response (Natrayan & Kumar, 2020; Palaniyappan et al., 2022; Sathish et al., 2021). Meanwhile, the incorporation of GA provides a metaheuristic algorithm, leveraging on its capacity to search a vast solution space and identify globally optimum configurations. The "larger the better" idea leads the optimization, striving to optimise the performance characteristics of the electrochemical machining process (Natrayan, Senthil Kumar, et al., 2018; Natrayan, Sivaprakash, et al., 2018; Natrayan & Merneedi, 2020). This hybrid approach, merging the structured methodology of Taguchi with the exploratory power of GA, contributes to a comprehensive and nuanced optimization strategy, aiming to elevate the larger the better characteristic and enhance the precision and effectiveness of the machining process under investigation (Balaji et al., 2022; Lakshmaiya et al., 2022).

In the quest of improving the electrochemical machining (ECM) process for Inconel alloy beyond the Taguchi technique, this work utilised the capabilities of metaheuristic algorithms, notably the genetic algorithm. The genetic algorithm, inspired by natural selection and evolution, was applied as a robust optimization technique to further improve the findings acquired from the experimental design. Through repeated generations, the genetic algorithm searched a broad solution space, employing processes such as crossover, mutation, and selection to create viable solutions. This technique permitted the determination of optimum or near-optimal configurations of the essential process parameters—voltage, electrolyte concentration, and flow rate—leading to an enhanced Material Removal Rate (MRR) during ECM. The combination of the genetic algorithm with the Taguchi technique allows for a more extensive investigation of the parameter space, allowing complicated interactions and discovering alternate optimum conditions that may have been ignored by standard optimization approaches. This hybrid technique, combining the methodical design of trials with the exploration capabilities of the genetic algorithm, resulted to a more comprehensive and successful optimization strategy, eventually boosting the efficiency of the ECM process for Inconel alloy machining.

RESULT AND DISCUSSION

The experimental investigation has been painstakingly done, and the acquired findings are provided in Table 1. The essential factors under research are voltage (V), which has been systematically altered at values of 13V, 15V, and 12V. Another significant element is the Electrolyte Concentration (EC), with experiments spanning values of 160 g/L, 180 g/L, and 190 g/L. Additionally, Flow Rate (FT) is a significant variable in this study, investigated at flow rates of 1 L/min, 1.5 L/min, and 2 L/min. The equivalent Material Removal Rate (MRR), a vital measure of the machining efficiency, is described in the table 1. The purposeful adjustment of these parameters allows for a complete examination of their influence on the electrochemical machining process of Inconel alloy. The MRR values associated with various combinations of voltage, electrolyte content, and flow rate give vital insights into the effect of each parameter and possible interactions among them.

continued on following page

Table 2. Continued

Table 2. Experimental results

V (V)	EC(g/L)	FT(L/min)	MRR (g/min)
12	160	1	0.234
12	180	1.5	0.254
12	190	2	0.287
13	160	1.5	0.311
13	180	2	0.322
13	190	1	0.375
15	160	2	0.449
15	180	1	0.432
15	190	1.5	0.456

The Signal-to-Noise Ratio (S/N) analysis has been successfully employed, revealing that the optimal conditions for maximizing the Material Removal Rate (MRR) in the electrochemical machining of Inconel alloy are achieved when the voltage (V) is set at 15V, the Electrolyte Concentration (EC) is maintained at 190 g/L, and the Flow Rate (FT) is set to 1.5 L/min. These results represent a vital insight into the interaction of process factors, indicating a synergistic impact that boosts MRR. The outcomes of this optimization technique are graphically displayed in Figure 1, giving a clear depiction of the improvement in MRR under the found optimal circumstances. This graphical depiction serves as a significant tool for academics and practitioners, presenting a succinct and comprehensible summary of the better performance attained via the systematic implementation of the Taguchi S/N Ratio study.

Figure 1. Optimized result from Taguchi design

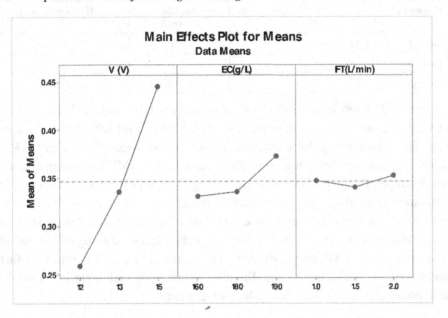

The L9 array in Table 2 provided a baseline for the experimental circumstances, containing changes in voltage (V), electrolyte concentration (EC), and flow rate (FT). Subsequently, the GA, a metaheuristic optimization method, was utilised to repeatedly search for optimum parameter combinations. After numerous generations of evolution, the genetic algorithm converged to the following optimum values: V=14.8V, EC=185.3g/L, and FT=1.7L/min. These optimal values were established based on the maximising of the Material Removal Rate (MRR), suggesting the most efficient combination of parameters for boosting the effectiveness of the ECM process for Inconel alloy machining. The integration of the genetic algorithm not only refined the experimental conditions obtained from the L9 array but also provided a more nuanced and globally optimized solution, demonstrating the efficacy of the hybrid approach in achieving superior results in the electrochemical machining of Inconel alloy. Table 3 shows the optimized result of Taguchi and GA. The result showed that the GA has the maximum MRR producing capacity.

Table 3. Optimal combination and results

Parameter	Taguchi (L9 Array)	GA Optimization
Voltage (V)	15	14.8

continued on following page

Table 3. Continued

Parameter	Taguchi (L9 Array)	GA Optimization
Electrolyte Conc. (EC) (g/L)	190	185.3
Flow Rate (FT)(L/min)	1.5	1.7
MRR (g/min)	0.766	0.876

Figure 2 shows contour map obtained from the experimental data, acts as a critical validation tool for the optimum. The contour plot serves as a great reference for understanding the interaction impacts of the process factors on MRR. The raised areas on the figure represent the zones where the MRR is maximum, and in this example, they correlate to greater voltage, EC, and FT values. This graphical validation strengthens the confidence in the chosen optimum conditions, giving researchers and practitioners with a visual depiction of the ideal parameter space for obtaining peak performance in the electrochemical machining of Inconel alloy. The congruence between the experimental findings and the contour plot further underlines the usefulness of the Taguchi optimization technique in boosting the machining efficiency of Inconel alloy components.

Figure 2. Contour plot of the MRR

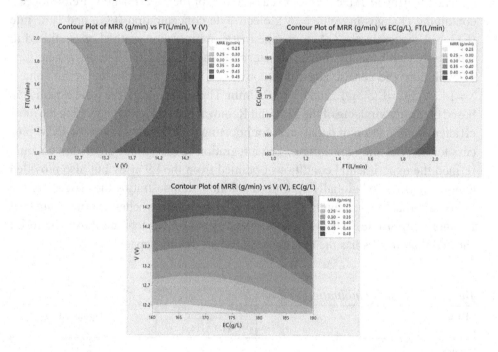

CONCLUSION

In conclusion, this study gives a detailed analysis into improving the electro-chemical machining (ECM) technique for Inconel alloy. The Taguchi technique, utilised with a L9 array design, offered a platform for early research, and the later integration of the Genetic Algorithm (GA) helped to improve and enhance the acquired findings. The adjusted parameters discovered using GA, including a slightly lower voltage, an optimized electrolyte concentration, and an enhanced flow rate, indicated a considerable improvement in the Material Removal Rate (MRR). This shows that the hybrid technique, combining both systematic experimental design and metaheuristic optimization, provides a strong and nuanced strategy for getting better outcomes in the machining of tough materials like Inconel alloy. The study adds vital insights into the delicate interaction of process parameters and optimization approaches, enhancing the knowledge of ECM for Inconel alloy machining and establishing a platform for subsequent improvements in precision machining technologies.

REFERENCES

Anjankar, P., Lakade, S., Padalkar, A., Nichal, S., Devarajan, Y., Lakshmaiya, N., & Subbaiyan, N. (2023). Experimental investigation on the effect of liquid phase and vapor phase separation over performance of falling film evaporator. *Environmental Quality Management*, 33(1), 61–69. 10.1002/tqem.21952

Arul Arumugam, R., Usha Rani, B., Komala, C. R., Barthwal, S., Kaliappan, S., & Natrayan, L. (2023). Design and Development of the Optical Antenna for Wireless Communications. *7th International Conference on Electronics, Communication and Aerospace Technology, ICECA 2023 - Proceedings*. IEEE. 10.1109/ICE-CA58529.2023.10395356

Balaji, N., Natrayan, L., Kaliappan, S., Patil, P. P., & Sivakumar, N. S. (2022). Annealed peanut shell biochar as potential reinforcement for aloe vera fiber-epoxy biocomposite: Mechanical, thermal conductivity, and dielectric properties. *Biomass Conversion and Biorefinery*. 10.1007/s13399-022-02650-7

Balamurugan, P., Agarwal, P., Khajuria, D., Mahapatra, D., Angalaeswari, S., Natrayan, L., & Mammo, W. D. (2023). State-Flow Control Based Multistage Constant-Current Battery Charger for Electric Two-Wheeler. *Journal of Advanced Transportation*, 2023, 1–11. 10.1155/2023/4554582

Biradar, V. S., Al-Jiboory, A. K., Sahu, G., Tilak Babu, S. B. G., Mahender, K., & Natrayan, L. (2023). Intelligent Control Systems for Industrial Automation and Robotics. *2023 10th IEEE Uttar Pradesh Section International Conference on Electrical, Electronics and Computer Engineering, UPCON 2023*. IEEE. 10.1109/UPCON59197.2023.10434927

Chehelgerdi, M., Chehelgerdi, M., Allela, O. Q. B., Pecho, R. D. C., Jayasankar, N., Rao, D. P., Thamaraikani, T., Vasanthan, M., Viktor, P., Lakshmaiya, N., Saadh, M. J., Amajd, A., Abo-Zaid, M. A., Castillo-Acobo, R. Y., Ismail, A. H., Amin, A. H., & Akhavan-Sigari, R. (2023). Progressing nanotechnology to improve targeted cancer treatment: Overcoming hurdles in its clinical implementation. *Molecular Cancer*, 22(1), 169. 10.1186/s12943-023-01865-037814270

Chennai Viswanathan, P., Venkatesh, S. N., Dhanasekaran, S., Mahanta, T. K., Sugumaran, V., Lakshmaiya, N., Paramasivam, P., & Nanjagoundenpalayam Ramasamy, S. (2023). Deep Learning for Enhanced Fault Diagnosis of Monoblock Centrifugal Pumps: Spectrogram-Based Analysis. *Machines*, 11(9), 874. 10.3390/machines11090874

Chinta, N. D., Karthikeyan, K. R., Natrayan, L., & Kaliappan, S. (2023). Pressure Induced Variations in Mode II Behaviour of Uni-Directional Kenaf Reinforced Polymers. *International Journal of Vehicle Structures and Systems*, 15(7). 10.4273/ijvss.15.7.19

Hemalatha, K., James, C., Natrayan, L., & Swamynadh, V. (2020). Analysis of RCC T-beam and prestressed concrete box girder bridges super structure under different span conditions. *Materials Today: Proceedings*, 37(Part 2), 1507–1516. 10.1016/j.matpr.2020.07.119

Josphineleela, R., Kaliapp, S., Natrayan, L., & Garg, A. (2023). Big Data Security through Privacy - Preserving Data Mining (PPDM): A Decentralization Approach. *Proceedings of the 2023 2nd International Conference on Electronics and Renewable Systems, ICEARS 2023*. IEEE. 10.1109/ICEARS56392.2023.10085646

Josphineleela, R., Lekha, D., Natrayan, L., & Purohit, K. C. (2023). Biometric Aided Intelligent Security System Built using Internet of Things. *Proceedings of the 2023 2nd International Conference on Electronics and Renewable Systems, ICEARS 2023*. IEEE. 10.1109/ICEARS56392.2023.10085572

Kaliappan, S., Mothilal, T., Natrayan, L., Pravin, P., & Olkeba, T. T. (2023). Mechanical Characterization of Friction-Stir-Welded Aluminum AA7010 Alloy with TiC Nanofiber. *Advances in Materials Science and Engineering*, 2023, 1–7. 10.1155/2023/1466963

Kaliappan, S., Natrayan, L., & Garg, N. (2023). Checking and Supervisory System for Calculation of Industrial Constraints using Embedded System. *Proceedings of the 4th International Conference on Smart Electronics and Communication, ICOSEC 2023*. IEEE. 10.1109/ICOSEC58147.2023.10275952

Kaliappan, S., Natrayan, L., & Rajput, A. (2023). Sentiment Analysis of News Headlines Based on Sentiment Lexicon and Deep Learning. *Proceedings of the 4th International Conference on Smart Electronics and Communication, ICOSEC 2023*. IEEE. 10.1109/ICOSEC58147.2023.10276102

Kanimozhi, G., Natrayan, L., Angalaeswari, S., & Paramasivam, P. (2022). An Effective Charger for Plug-In Hybrid Electric Vehicles (PHEV) with an Enhanced PFC Rectifier and ZVS-ZCS DC/DC High-Frequency Converter. *Journal of Advanced Transportation*, 2022, 1–14. 10.1155/2022/7840102

Karthick, M., Meikandan, M., Kaliappan, S., Karthick, M., Sekar, S., Patil, P. P., Raja, S., Natrayan, L., & Paramasivam, P. (2022). Experimental Investigation on Mechanical Properties of Glass Fiber Hybridized Natural Fiber Reinforced Penta-Layered Hybrid Polymer Composite. *International Journal of Chemical Engineering*, 2022, 1–9. Advance online publication. 10.1155/2022/1864446

Kaushal, R. K., Arvind, R., Giri, K. K. B., Sindhu, M., Natrayan, L., & Ronald, B. (2023). Deep Learning Based Segmentation Approach for Automatic Lane Detection in Autonomous Vehicle. *International Conference on Self Sustainable Artificial Intelligence Systems, ICSSAS 2023 - Proceedings*. IEEE. 10.1109/ICS-SAS57918.2023.10331835

Kiruba Sandou, D., Sunad Kumara, A. N., Choudhary, B. K., & Gurpur, S., Sarishma, Natrayan, L., & Sivaramkumar, M. (2023). Design and Implementation of Neuro-Fuzzy Control Approach for Robot's Trajectory Tracking. *7th International Conference on Electronics, Communication and Aerospace Technology, ICECA 2023 - Proceedings*. IEEE. 10.1109/ICECA58529.2023.10395675

Konduri, S., Walke, S., Kumar, A., Pavithra, G., Bhagirath Jadhav, A., & Natrayan, L. (2023). Reinforcement Learning for Multi-Robot Coordination and Cooperation in Manufacturing. *2023 10th IEEE Uttar Pradesh Section International Conference on Electrical, Electronics and Computer Engineering, UPCON 2023*. IEEE. 10.1109/UPCON59197.2023.10434651

Lakshmaiya, N. (2023a). Effectiveness of mixed convection flow following pressure vessel gas evacuation. *Proceedings of SPIE- The International Society for Optical Engineering, 12616*. SPIE. 10.1117/12.2675550

Lakshmaiya, N. (2023b). Experimental analysis on heat transfer cube shape of two vertical surfaces during melting condition. *Proceedings of SPIE- The International Society for Optical Engineering, 12616*. SPIE. 10.1117/12.2675552

Lakshmaiya, N. (2023c). Experimental analysis on heat transfer cube shape of two vertical surfaces during melting condition. *Proceedings of SPIE- The International Society for Optical Engineering, 12616*. SPIE. 10.1117/12.2675552

Lakshmaiya, N. (2023d). Experimental investigation on computational volumetric heat in real time neural pathways. *Proceedings of SPIE- The International Society for Optical Engineering, 12616*. SPIE. 10.1117/12.2675555

Lakshmaiya, N. (2023e). Investigation on ultraviolet radiation of flow pattern and particles transportation in vanishing raindrops. *Proceedings of SPIE- The International Society for Optical Engineering, 12616*. SPIE. 10.1117/12.2675556

Lakshmaiya, N. (2023f). Mechanical evaluation of coir/kenaf/jute laminated hybrid composites designed for geotechnical uses. *Proceedings of SPIE- The International Society for Optical Engineering, 12936*. SPIE. 10.1117/12.3011710

Lakshmaiya, N. (2023g). Organic material nuts flour greens laminate preparation and mechanical characteristics of natural materials. *Proceedings of SPIE- The International Society for Optical Engineering, 12936*. SPIE. 10.1117/12.3011712

Lakshmaiya, N. (2023h). Polylactic acid/hydroxyapatite/yttria-stabilized zircon synthetic nanocomposite scaffolding compression and flexural characteristics. *Proceedings of SPIE- The International Society for Optical Engineering, 12936*. SPIE. 10.1117/12.3011715

Lakshmaiya, N. (2023i). Preparation and evaluation of bamboo laminated cannabis paper physico - mechanical characteristics. *Proceedings of SPIE- The International Society for Optical Engineering, 12936*. SPIE. 10.1117/12.3011716

Lakshmaiya, N. (2023j). Simulating laminar induced heat capacity and heat transmission convection using Al2O3 nanofluid. *Proceedings of SPIE- The International Society for Optical Engineering, 12616*. SPIE. 10.1117/12.2675557

Lakshmaiya, N., Kaliappan, S., Patil, P. P., Ganesan, V., Dhanraj, J. A., Sirisamphanwong, C., Wongwuttanasatian, T., Chowdhury, S., Channumsin, S., Channumsin, M., & Techato, K. (2022). Influence of Oil Palm Nano Filler on Interlaminar Shear and Dynamic Mechanical Properties of Flax/Epoxy-Based Hybrid Nanocomposites under Cryogenic Condition. *Coatings, 12*(11), 1675. 10.3390/coatings12111675

Lakshmaiya, N., & Murugan, V. S. (2023a). Bolstering EVA photovoltaic devices enclosing sheets with esterified cellulose nanofibers improves the mechanical and barrier characteristics. *Proceedings of SPIE- The International Society for Optical Engineering, 12936*. SPIE. 10.1117/12.3011858

Lakshmaiya, N., & Murugan, V. S. (2023b). Effects of machining parameters on surface quality of composites reinforced with natural fibers. *Proceedings of SPIE- The International Society for Optical Engineering, 12936*. SPIE. 10.1117/12.3011869

Lakshmaiya, N., & Murugan, V. S. (2023c). Experimental investigation of removal of sulphur di-oxide from exhaust gas by using semi-dry flue gas desulfurization (FGD). *Proceedings of SPIE- The International Society for Optical Engineering, 12936*. SPIE. 10.1117/12.3011865

Lakshmaiya, N., & Murugan, V. S. (2023d). Experimental investigations of thermal solutions to increase heat transfer rate by utilizing the effects of pitch ratio and length. *Proceedings of SPIE- The International Society for Optical Engineering, 12936*. SPIE. 10.1117/12.3011873

Lakshmaiya, N., & Murugan, V. S. (2023e). Improvement of the interfaces and mechanical characteristics of kenaf/kraft paper natural fibre reinforced composite materials. *Proceedings of SPIE- The International Society for Optical Engineering, 12936*. SPIE. 10.1117/12.3011859

Loganathan, A. S., Ramachandran, V., Perumal, A. S., Dhanasekaran, S., Lakshmaiya, N., & Paramasivam, P. (2023). Framework of Transactive Energy Market Strategies for Lucrative Peer-to-Peer Energy Transactions. *Energies*, 16(1), 6. 10.3390/en16010006

Mahat, D., Niranjan, K., Naidu, C. S. K. V. R., Babu, S. B. G. T., Kumar, M. S., & Natrayan, L. (2023). AI-Driven Optimization of Supply Chain and Logistics in Mechanical Engineering. *2023 10th IEEE Uttar Pradesh Section International Conference on Electrical, Electronics and Computer Engineering, UPCON 2023*. 10.1109/UPCON59197.2023.10434905

Mehta, A. K., Lanjewar, P., Murthy, D. S., Ghildiyal, P., Faldu, R., & Natrayan, L. (2023). AI & Lean Management Principles Based Pharmaceutical Manufacturing Processes. *2023 10th IEEE Uttar Pradesh Section International Conference on Electrical, Electronics and Computer Engineering, UPCON 2023*. IEEE. 10.1109/UPCON59197.2023.10434834

Muthiya, S. J., Natrayan, L., Yuvaraj, L., Subramaniam, M., Dhanraj, J. A., & Mammo, W. D. (2022). Development of Active CO_2 Emission Control for Diesel Engine Exhaust Using Amine-Based Adsorption and Absorption Technique. *Adsorption Science and Technology*, 2022, 8803585. 10.1155/2022/8803585

Nadh, V. S., Krishna, C., Natrayan, L., Kumar, K., Nitesh, K. J. N. S., Raja, G. B., & Paramasivam, P. (2021). Structural Behavior of Nanocoated Oil Palm Shell as Coarse Aggregate in Lightweight Concrete. *Journal of Nanomaterials*, 2021, 1–7. 10.1155/2021/4741296

Natrayan, L. (2023). Humidity Impact on the Material Characteristics of a Sisal Laminate: The Role of the Rapid Vibrational Method. *International Journal of Vehicle Structures and Systems*, 15(7). 10.4273/ijvss.15.7.17

Natrayan, L., & De Poures, M. V. (2023a). Experimental investigations of heat ageing with chemical modification of hemp fiber elastic characteristics. *Proceedings of SPIE- The International Society for Optical Engineering, 12936*. IEEE. 10.1117/12.3011708

Natrayan, L., & De Poures, M. V. (2023b). Influence of gasoline on high speed evaporation gasoline sprays: a large-eddy model of sprayer a with different fuels. *Proceedings of SPIE- The International Society for Optical Engineering, 12936*. SPIE. 10.1117/12.3011709

Natrayan, L., & Kaliappan, S. (2023). Mechanical Assessment of Carbon-Luffa Hybrid Composites for Automotive Applications. *SAE Technical Papers*. 10.4271/2023-01-5070

Natrayan, L., Kaliappan, S., & Pundir, S. (2023). Control and Monitoring of a Quadcopter in Border Areas Using Embedded System. *Proceedings of the 4th International Conference on Smart Electronics and Communication, ICOSEC 2023*. IEEE. 10.1109/ICOSEC58147.2023.10276196

Natrayan, L., Kaliappan, S., Saravanan, A., Vickram, A. S., Pravin, P., Abbas, M., Ahamed Saleel, C., Alwetaishi, M., & Saleem, M. S. M. (2023). Recyclability and catalytic characteristics of copper oxide nanoparticles derived from bougainvillea plant flower extract for biomedical application. *Green Processing and Synthesis, 12*(1), 20230030. 10.1515/gps-2023-0030

Natrayan, L., & Kumar, M. S. (2020). Optimization of wear behaviour on AA6061/Al2O3/SiC metal matrix composite using squeeze casting technique-Statistical analysis. *Materials Today: Proceedings, 27*, 306–310. 10.1016/j.matpr.2019.11.038

Natrayan, L., & Merneedi, A. (2020). Experimental investigation on wear behaviour of bio-waste reinforced fusion fiber composite laminate under various conditions. *Materials Today: Proceedings, 37*(Part 2), 1486–1490. 10.1016/j.matpr.2020.07.108

Natrayan, L., & Richard, T. (2023a). Experimental investigations of bagasse ash strands featuring variable surface influence on polypropylene based polymer composites. *Proceedings of SPIE- The International Society for Optical Engineering, 12936*. SPIE. 10.1117/12.3011691

Natrayan, L., & Richard, T. (2023b). Organo modified nanocomposites terephthalic acid polymers temperature and microstructural characteristics. *Proceedings of SPIE- The International Society for Optical Engineering, 12936*. SPIE. 10.1117/12.3011863

Natrayan, L., Senthil Kumar, M., & Palanikumar, K. (2018). Optimization of squeeze cast process parameters on mechanical properties of Al2O3/SiC reinforced hybrid metal matrix composites using taguchi technique. *Materials Research Express*, 5(6), 066516. 10.1088/2053-1591/aac873

Natrayan, L., Sivaprakash, V., & Santhosh, M. S. (2018). Mechanical, microstructure and wear behavior of the material aa6061 reinforced sic with different leaf ashes using advanced stir casting method. *International Journal of Engineering and Advanced Technology*, 8.

Palaniyappan, S., Veeman, D., Sivakumar, N. K., & Natrayan, L. (2022). Development and optimization of lattice structure on the walnut shell reinforced PLA composite for the tensile strength and dimensional error properties. *Structures*, 45, 163–178. 10.1016/j.istruc.2022.09.023

Prabagar, S., Al-Jiboory, A. K., Nair, P. S., Mandal, P., Garse, K. M., & Natrayan, L. (2023). Artificial Intelligence-Based Control Strategies for Unmanned Aerial Vehicles. *2023 10th IEEE Uttar Pradesh Section International Conference on Electrical, Electronics and Computer Engineering, UPCON 2023*. IEEE. 10.1109/UPCON59197.2023.10434918

Pragadish, N., Kaliappan, S., Subramanian, M., Natrayan, L., Satish Prakash, K., Subbiah, R., & Kumar, T. C. A. (2023). Optimization of cardanol oil dielectric-activated EDM process parameters in machining of silicon steel. *Biomass Conversion and Biorefinery*, 13(15), 14087–14096. Advance online publication. 10.1007/s13399-021-02268-1

Ragumadhavan, R., Sateesh Kumar, D., Charyulu Rompicharla, L. N., Dhondiya, S. A., Kaliappan, S., & Natrayan, L. (2023). Design and Development of Light Communication Systems Using Modulation Techniques. *7th International Conference on Electronics, Communication and Aerospace Technology, ICECA 2023 - Proceedings*. IEEE. 10.1109/ICECA58529.2023.10395831

Rajasekaran, S., & Natrayan, L. (2023a). Estimation of corrective and preventive action on trend end plug-based machining activities using manual and failure mode with effects analysis. *Proceedings of SPIE- The International Society for Optical Engineering, 12936*. 10.1117/12.3011698

Rajasekaran, S., & Natrayan, L. (2023b). Evaluation of occurrence number and communication based on FMEA operations in product development. *Proceedings of SPIE- The International Society for Optical Engineering, 12936*. SPIE. 10.1117/12.3011702

Ramesh, C., Vijayakumar, M., Alshahrani, S., Navaneethakrishnan, G., Palanisamy, R., Natrayan, L., Saleel, C. A., Afzal, A., Shaik, S., & Panchal, H. (2022). Performance enhancement of selective layer coated on solar absorber panel with reflector for water heater by response surface method: A case study. *Case Studies in Thermal Engineering*, 36, 102093. 10.1016/j.csite.2022.102093

Reddy, P. N., Umaeswari, P., Natrayan, L., & Choudhary, A. (2023). Development of Programmed Autonomous Electric Heavy Vehicle: An Application of IoT. *Proceedings of the 2023 2nd International Conference on Electronics and Renewable Systems, ICEARS 2023*. IEEE. 10.1109/ICEARS56392.2023.10085492

Saadh, M. J., Almoyad, M. A. A., Arellano, M. T. C., Maaliw, R. R. III, Castillo-Acobo, R. Y., Jalal, S. S., Gandla, K., Obaid, M., Abdulwahed, A. J., Ibrahem, A. A., Sârbu, I., Juyal, A., Lakshmaiya, N., & Akhavan-Sigari, R. (2023). Long non-coding RNAs: Controversial roles in drug resistance of solid tumors mediated by autophagy. *Cancer Chemotherapy and Pharmacology*, 92(6), 439–453. 10.1007/s00280-023-04582-z37768333

Sai, S. A., Venkatesh, S. N., Dhanasekaran, S., Balaji, P. A., Sugumaran, V., Lakshmaiya, N., & Paramasivam, P. (2023). Transfer Learning Based Fault Detection for Suspension System Using Vibrational Analysis and Radar Plots. *Machines*, 11(8), 778. 10.3390/machines11080778

Sasi, J. P., Nidhi Pandagre, K., Royappa, A., Walke, S., Pavithra, G., & Natrayan, L. (2023). Deep Learning Techniques for Autonomous Navigation of Underwater Robots. *2023 10th IEEE Uttar Pradesh Section International Conference on Electrical, Electronics and Computer Engineering, UPCON 2023*. IEEE. 10.1109/UPCON59197.2023.10434865

Sathish, T., Natrayan, L., Prasad Jones Christydass, S., Sivananthan, S., Kamalakannan, R., Vijayan, V., & Paramasivam, P. (2022). Experimental Investigation on Tribological Behaviour of AA6066: HSS-Cu Hybrid Composite in Dry Sliding Condition. *Advances in Materials Science and Engineering*, 2022, 1–9. Advance online publication. 10.1155/2022/9349847

Sathish, T., Palani, K., Natrayan, L., Merneedi, A., de Poures, M. V., & Singaravelu, D. K. (2021). Synthesis and characterization of polypropylene/ramie fiber with hemp fiber and coir fiber natural biopolymer composite for biomedical application. *International Journal of Polymer Science*, 2021, 1–8. Advance online publication. 10.1155/2021/2462873

Selvi, S., Mohanraj, M., Duraipandy, P., Kaliappan, S., Natrayan, L., & Vinayagam, N. (2023). Optimization of Solar Panel Orientation for Maximum Energy Efficiency. *Proceedings of the 4th International Conference on Smart Electronics and Communication, ICOSEC 2023*. IEEE. 10.1109/ICOSEC58147.2023.10276287

Sendrayaperumal, A., Mahapatra, S., Parida, S. S., Surana, K., Balamurugan, P., Natrayan, L., & Paramasivam, P. (2021). Energy Auditing for Efficient Planning and Implementation in Commercial and Residential Buildings. *Advances in Civil Engineering*, 2021, 1–10. 10.1155/2021/1908568

Siddiqui, E., Siddique, M., Safeer Pasha, M., Boyapati, P., Pavithra, G., & Natrayan, L. (2023). AI and ML for Enhancing Crop Yield and Resource Efficiency in Agriculture. *2023 10th IEEE Uttar Pradesh Section International Conference on Electrical, Electronics and Computer Engineering, UPCON 2023*. IEEE. 10.1109/UPCON59197.2023.10434493

Sukumaran, C., Indhumathi, K., Balamurugan, P., Ambilwade, R. P., Sunthari, P. M., & Natrayan, L. (2023). The Role of AI in Biochips for Early Disease Detection. *Proceedings - International Conference on Technological Advancements in Computational Sciences, ICTACS 2023*. IEEE. 10.1109/ICTACS59847.2023.10390419

Suman, T., Kaliappan, S., Natrayan, L., & Dobhal, D. C. (2023). IoT based Social Device Network with Cloud Computing Architecture. *Proceedings of the 2023 2nd International Conference on Electronics and Renewable Systems, ICEARS 2023*. IEEE. 10.1109/ICEARS56392.2023.10085574

Sureshkumar, P., Jagadeesha, T., Natrayan, L., Ravichandran, M., Veeman, D., & Muthu, S. M. (2022). Electrochemical corrosion and tribological behaviour of AA6063/Si$_3$N$_4$/Cu(NO$_3$)$_2$ composite processed using single-pass ECAP$_A$ route with 120° die angle. *Journal of Materials Research and Technology*, 16. Advance online publication. 10.1016/j.jmrt.2021.12.020

Thakre, S., Pandhare, A., Malwe, P. D., Gupta, N., Kothare, C., Magade, P. B., Patel, A., Meena, R. S., Veza, I., Natrayan, L., & Panchal, H. (2023). Heat transfer and pressure drop analysis of a microchannel heat sink using nanofluids for energy applications. *Kerntechnik*, 88(5), 543–555. 10.1515/kern-2023-0034

Ugle, V. V., Arulprakasajothi, M., Padmanabhan, S., Devarajan, Y., Lakshmaiya, N., & Subbaiyan, N. (2023). Investigation of heat transport characteristics of titanium dioxide nanofluids with corrugated tube. *Environmental Quality Management*, 33(2), 127–138. 10.1002/tqem.21999

Vaishali, K. R., Rammohan, S. R., Natrayan, L., Usha, D., & Niveditha, V. R. (2021). Guided container selection for data streaming through neural learning in cloud. *International Journal of Systems Assurance Engineering and Management*. 10.1007/s13198-021-01124-9

Velmurugan, G., & Natrayan, L. (2023). Experimental investigations of moisture diffusion and mechanical properties of interply rearrangement of glass/Kevlar-based hybrid composites under cryogenic environment. *Journal of Materials Research and Technology*, 23, 4513–4526. 10.1016/j.jmrt.2023.02.089

Velumayil, R., Gnanakumar, G., Natrayan, L., Chinta, N. D., & Kaliappan, S. (2023). Bifunctional Aluminum Oxide/Carbon Fiber/Epoxy Nanocomposites Preparation and Evaluation. *International Journal of Vehicle Structures and Systems*, 15(7). 10.4273/ijvss.15.7.18

Venkatesh, R., Manivannan, S., Kaliappan, S., Socrates, S., Sekar, S., Patil, P. P., Natrayan, L., & Bayu, M. B. (2022). Influence of Different Frequency Pulse on Weld Bead Phase Ratio in Gas Tungsten Arc Welding by Ferritic Stainless Steel AISI-409L. *Journal of Nanomaterials*, 2022, 1–11. 10.1155/2022/9530499

Vijayakumar, M., & Shreeraj Nair, P. G Tilak Babu, S. B., Mahender, K., Venkateswaran, T. S., & Natrayan, L. (2023). Intelligent Systems For Predictive Maintenance In Industrial IoT. *2023 10th IEEE Uttar Pradesh Section International Conference on Electrical, Electronics and Computer Engineering, UPCON 2023*. IEEE. 10.1109/UPCON59197.2023.10434814

Chapter 5
Metaheuristic Techniques–Based Optimizing Laser Welding Parameters for Copper–Aluminum Alloys

Satyanarayana Tirlangi
http://orcid.org/0000-0001-8265-8743
Visakha Institute of Engineering and Technology, Visakhapatnam, India

T. S. Senthil
http://orcid.org/0000-0001-9580-0286
Noorul Islam Centre For Higher Education, Kumaracoil, India

S. John Leon
Noorul Islam Centre For Higher Education, Kumaracoil, India

A. Parvathi Priya
RMK Engineering College, Thiruvallur, India

Raghuram Pradhan
PACE Institute of Technology and Sciences, India

Ramya Maranan
http://orcid.org/0000-0003-1001-3422
Lovely Professional University, Punjab, India

ABSTRACT

In this research endeavor, the laser welding of C63000 alloy has been thoroughly examined, focusing on the interplay of key welding parameters—laser power, welding speed, and amplitude. The experimental design, structured as per the Taguchi L9 array, provided a systematic approach to investigating these parameters' effects on critical mechanical properties, specifically tensile strength and Brinell hardness.

DOI: 10.4018/979-8-3693-3314-3.ch005

The alloy's responses were meticulously studied under varied conditions, capturing the nuances of its behavior in response to changes in laser welding inputs. The experimental outcomes revealed distinct trends in tensile strength and Brinell hardness in relation to the variations in welding parameters. Notably, the highest levels of tensile strength and hardness were consistently observed under specific combinations of welding speed, laser power, and amplitude.

INTRODUCTION

Laser welding is a commonly employed method in numerous sectors owing to its accuracy and efficiency (Mehta et al., 2023; Siddiqui et al., 2023). Copper-aluminum alloys, in particular, have attracted substantial interest owing to their unusual mix of characteristics (Ragumadhavan et al., 2023; Sasi et al., 2023). However, getting good mechanical characteristics in laser-welded copper-aluminum alloys requires careful tuning of welding conditions (Lakshmaiya, 2023h; Sukumaran et al., 2023). This literature review seeks to analyse the present status of research on optimizing laser welding settings to optimise the mechanical characteristics of copper-aluminum alloys (Natrayan & Richard, 2023b; Rajasekaran & Natrayan, 2023b).

Effects of Laser Power: The laser power employed in welding considerably effects the mechanical qualities of the welded connection (Lakshmaiya & Murugan, 2023d; Selvi et al., 2023). Several research have explored the influence of laser power on the microstructure and mechanical characteristics of copper-aluminum welds (Kaliappan, Natrayan, & Garg, 2023; Natrayan, Kaliappan, Saravanan, et al., 2023). Higher laser power typically leads to deeper penetration and quicker solidification rates, leading in higher tensile strength and hardness (Kaliappan, Mothilal, et al., 2023; Lakshmaiya, 2023a). However, high laser power may also create flaws like as porosity or cracking (Balamurugan et al., 2023; Josphineleela, Kaliapp, et al., 2023). Therefore, choosing the correct laser power is critical to obtain the necessary mechanical characteristics. Welding speed is another significant element influencing the mechanical characteristics of laser-welded copper-aluminum alloys (Josphineleela, Lekha, et al., 2023; Loganathan et al., 2023; Reddy et al., 2023). Higher welding rates tend to lower the heat input and solidification time, resulting in finer microstructures and higher mechanical characteristics (Lakshmaiya, 2023f; Natrayan & De Poures, 2023). However, too high welding rates may lead to partial fusion or diminished joint strength. Therefore, the welding speed must be carefully tuned to balance the solidification rate and joint quality (Kaliappan, Natrayan, & Rajput, 2023; Kaushal et al., 2023).

Amplitude, representing the magnitude of the laser beam oscillation during welding, has a significant impact on the heat distribution and grain structure of laser-welded copper-aluminum alloys (Lakshmaiya, 2023e, 2023j, 2023d; Suman et al., 2023). Studies have demonstrated that a suitable amplitude may refine the grains and enhance the mechanical characteristics of the welded junction (Lakshmaiya, 2023b, 2023g; Natrayan & Kaliappan, 2023). However, overly high or low amplitudes might result in undesired consequences like as grain development, porosity, or cracking (Lakshmaiya, 2023i; Lakshmaiya & Murugan, 2023b, 2023d; Natrayan, Kaliappan, & Pundir, 2023). Therefore, adjusting the amplitude is vital to get increased mechanical qualities.

Tensile strength is one of the main mechanical parameters of laser-welded copper-aluminum alloys. Optimal selection of welding settings may lead to enhanced tensile strength by regulating the microstructure and reducing flaws (Lakshmaiya & Murugan, 2023e, 2023c, 2023a; Rajasekaran & Natrayan, 2023a). Studies have indicated that the tensile strength of the welded joint may be increased by altering laser power, welding speed, and amplitude within the proper ranges (Arul Arumugam et al., 2023; Kiruba Sandou et al., 2023; Natrayan & Richard, 2023a). The formation of a sound weld with proper bonding contributes to the overall strength of the joint. Influence on Brinell Hardness: Brinell hardness is another key mechanical parameter that represents the resistance of laser-welded copper-aluminum alloys to plastic deformation and wear (Biradar et al., 2023; Prabagar et al., 2023). The choice of welding settings considerably impacts the hardness of the junction. Research has shown that adjusting laser power, welding speed, and amplitude can influence the microhardness of the weld, with optimal parameter sets leading to improved hardness values. Proper hardness assures the longevity and dependability of the welded components (Anjankar et al., 2023; Sai et al., 2023; Vijayakumar et al., 2023).

Optimizing laser welding parameters is essential for achieving enhanced mechanical properties in copper-aluminum alloys. Through careful adjustment of laser power, welding speed, and amplitude, it is possible to control the microstructure, reduce defects, and improve tensile strength and Brinell hardness (Chennai Viswanathan et al., 2023; Thakre et al., 2023). However, the optimal parameter ranges may vary depending on the specific alloy composition and welding conditions. Further research and experimentation are necessary to explore the effects of other parameters and develop comprehensive guidelines for optimizing laser welding of copper-aluminum alloys.

LASER WELDING OF COPPER ALUMINIUM ALLOY

C63000, a renowned member of the aluminum bronze alloy family, stands out as a material of great relevance in different industrial applications. Composed mostly of copper, aluminum, iron, and manganese, this alloy boasts a unique combination of qualities that make it an excellent alternative for essential components exposed to different operating situations (Saadh et al., 2023; Ugle et al., 2023). With a copper percentage ranging from 81-92%, aluminum adds 6-7.5%, while iron and manganese add to the alloy's structural stability. This specific alloy, also known as aluminum bronze, has great strength, outstanding corrosion resistance, and remarkable wear resistance, making it especially ideal for applications where longevity and performance are vital . The compostion of the alloy used in this research is shown in table 1.

Table 1. Material composition

Element	Composition (%)
Copper (Cu)	81 - 92
Aluminum (Al)	6 - 7.5
Iron (Fe)	2 - 4
Manganese (Mn)	2 - 4

The requirement for laser welding in the context of C63000 alloy stems from its broad usage in complicated and precision-demanding industrial sectors. Laser welding enables a precise and regulated way to combine C63000 components, guaranteeing the integrity of the alloy's specific features . In applications such as marine environments, where corrosion resistance is crucial, and in heavy-duty industrial equipment like bearings and gears, where wear resistance is essential, laser welding provides a method to achieve strong and reliable joints without compromising the alloy's mechanical characteristics. The application of laser welding methods for C63000 alloy goes beyond simply structural concerns. The procedure enables for the optimization of welding parameters such as power, welding speed, and focal length. Through the use of metaheuristic approaches, the laser welding parameters may be fine-tuned, boosting the overall efficiency and accuracy of the welding process. The regulated application of laser power, along with optimal welding rates, guarantees that the C63000 alloy retains its mechanical strength and wear resistance throughout the welded zones. As businesses continue to explore improved techniques for combining materials with different characteristics, laser welding emerges as a vital tool, meeting the unique requirements of aluminum bronze alloys like C63000 in a manner that corresponds with the expectations of contemporary production and engineering procedures.

METHODOLOGY

In the area of materials engineering, the laser welding of C63000 alloy has emerged as a focal focus of study, motivated by the goal to exploit the alloy's outstanding qualities for different industrial applications. In this work, the laser welding process is methodically studied by altering critical parameters—laser power, welding speed, and amplitude—at three separate levels. The study digs into the influence of these differences on crucial reactions, especially hardness and tensile strength, two essential markers of the mechanical integrity of the laser-welded C63000 alloy. The experimental design follows a Taguchi L9 array, a systematic strategy that quickly analyses several elements at various levels, providing a full knowledge of their individual and collective effects on the answers. By adopting this array, researchers may quickly perform tests, decreasing the number of repetitions while capturing the key differences in the process parameters. This careful approach boosts the efficiency of the investigation, allowing for a more exact assessment of the laser welding effects on the C63000 alloy.

Figure 1 depicts the welded samples produced from the testing, giving a visual depiction of the weld quality and features. These samples provide as tangible proof of the consequences of the varying laser welding settings on the C63000 alloy. The visual examination of the welds becomes an important element of the investigation, delivering insights into the macrostructure and surface characteristics that may correspond with the observed changes in hardness and tensile strength. Moving beyond the experimental phase, the gathered data undergoes a rigorous optimization procedure. Metaheuristic approaches, notably the powerful Genetic Algorithm, are applied to explore the vast parameter space and produce an ideal combination for reducing the responses—hardness and tensile strength. Genetic algorithms, inspired by the process of natural selection, repeatedly explore different solutions to converge towards the best set of parameters.

The importance of this study resides not only in the discovery of laser welding parameters and their immediate consequences but also in the strategic optimization of these parameters using sophisticated computer approaches. Genetic algorithms, with their capacity to replicate the principles of biological evolution, repeatedly optimise the process parameters, converging towards an ideal solution that reduces both hardness and tensile strength. This optimization process is vital for real-world applications, where establishing an ideal balance between these mechanical qualities is frequently the key to maintaining the dependability and lifetime of welded components in service.

Figure 1. Welded sample

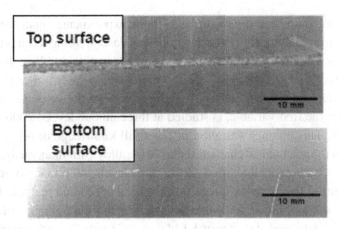

GENETIC ALGORITHM

GAs use inspiration from the concepts of natural selection and genetic inheritance, adopting an iterative process to progress towards an ideal solution. In the framework of this study, GAs are deployed to traverse the complicated parameter space generated by laser power, welding speed, and amplitude, intending to reduce the critical reactions of hardness and tensile strength. The Genetic Algorithm commences with a population of possible solutions, expressed as sets of parameters. Through subsequent generations, these solutions experience crossover and mutation operations, replicating the genetic processes of recombination and mutation in real organisms. The fitness of each solution is assessed based on its capacity to reduce the responses of interest. Over iterations, the algorithm refines the population, favouring solutions that display greater performance. The power of GAs rests in their capacity to explore a broad solution space effectively, frequently revealing non-intuitive combinations of parameters that might enhance the welding process. As such, the Genetic Algorithm becomes a vital tool in establishing the ideal balance between hardness and tensile strength, contributing to the progress of laser welding processes for C63000 alloy in varied industrial applications.

RESULT AND DISCUSSION

Table 2 encompasses a painstakingly built experimental matrix utilising the Taguchi L9 array, methodically altering important laser welding settings to determine their influence on the crucial responses of tensile strength and Brinell hardness (B scale) for the C63000 alloy. The selected parameters—laser power (LP), welding speed (W), and amplitude—reflect the complexity of the laser welding process. Laser power, the first variable, is studied at three unique levels: 2000 W, 1700 W, and 1500 W. This planned variation offers a full knowledge of how variations in power effect the mechanical characteristics of the alloy. Simultaneously, the welding speed (W) is systematically varied across three levels: 40 mm/s, 30 mm/s, and 25 mm/s, capturing the complex interaction between speed and reaction factors. The third parameter, amplitude, critical in determining the amount of oscillation during welding, is investigated at values of 1.124 mm, 0.75 mm, and 0.5 mm (Kaliappan et al., 2024; Kaliappan & Natrayan, 2024d; Natrayan et al., 2024). These variants are intentionally designed to include a wide range of situations indicative of real welding settings. The experiment develops as a controlled exploration of the parameter space, where the interactions between laser power, welding speed, and amplitude converge to form the resultant tensile strength and Brinell hardness (Kaliappan & Natrayan, 2024b; Pandian et al., 2024). The adoption of Taguchi L9 array not only speeds the experimental process but also assures that essential variations are caught without an exhaustive number of trials.

The findings, shown in Table 2, give a detailed summary of the experimental data. The tensile strengths corresponding to the varied combinations of laser power, welding speed, and amplitude are exposed, revealing insights on how changes in these parameters effect the alloy's capacity to endure axial stresses (Kaliappan & Natrayan, 2024c, 2024a; Malladi et al., 2024). Simultaneously, the Brinell hardness values, evaluated on the B scale, give a view into the alloy's resistance to indentation under a set load, offering significant data on its mechanical resilience. As the laser power swings from the greatest level of 2000 W to the lowest at 1500 W, and the welding speed transitions from 40 mm/s to 25 mm/s, the tensile strengths recorded in Table 2 indicate the dynamic reactions of the C63000 alloy to these fluctuations. Similarly, the matching Brinell hardness values give a thorough description of the alloy's hardness properties, offering insight on its capacity to resist deformation (Lakshmaiya et al., 2022; Natrayan et al., 2019; Velmurugan & Natrayan, 2023).

The amplitude parameter offers an extra degree of complexity, examining the influence of oscillation during welding. As amplitude changes from 1.124 mm to 0.75 mm and further to 0.5 mm, the alloy's tensile strength and Brinell hardness are seen to behave differently (Balaji et al., 2022; Pragadish et al., 2023). This comprehensive investigation is crucial for understanding the interdependence of welding settings and their overall impact on the mechanical characteristics of the laser-welded C63000 alloy (Niveditha VR. & Rajakumar PS., 2020; Yogeshwaran et al., 2020).

Table 2 Experimental design and outcomes

Run	Laser Power (LP) [W]	Welding Speed (W) [mm/s]	Amplitude (A) [mm]	Tensile Strength (Ts) [MPa]	Brinell Hardness (BH- B scale)
1	2000	40	1.124	450	180
2	1700	30	0.75	430	175
3	1500	25	0.5	410	170
4	1700	40	0.5	420	172
5	1500	30	1.124	440	178
6	2000	25	0.75	460	185
7	1500	40	0.75	415	168
8	1700	25	1.124	425	174
9	2000	30	0.5	455	182

The experimental findings collected from the Taguchi L9 array, comprising changes in laser power, welding speed, and amplitude, serve as the fundamental dataset for the future application of the Genetic Algorithm (GA) (Natrayan, Senthil Kumar, et al., 2018; Natrayan, Sivaprakash, et al., 2018). The fundamental purpose of the GA is to improve the laser welding settings for C63000 alloy by optimising the responses, notably tensile strength and Brinell hardness on the B scale. The GA functions as a computational tool, iteratively refining alternative solutions to converge toward the best combination of parameters that provide maximum responses (Natrayan & Kumar, 2020; Sathish et al., 2021).

In this repeated process, the GA investigates multiple alternative parameter combinations, replicating the principles of natural selection and genetic inheritance. The genetic procedures, including crossover and mutation, repeatedly change the solutions, highlighting those that display greater performance in terms of tensile strength and Brinell hardness (Palaniyappan et al., 2022; Vaishali et al., 2021). Through this computational development, the GA navigates the complicated parameter space defined by laser power, welding speed, and amplitude, uncovering combinations that promise to better the overall mechanical characteristics of the laser-welded C63000 alloy (Kanimozhi et al., 2022; Karthick et al., 2022).

Among the thousands of alternative solutions given by the GA, one configuration stands out as the ideal combination for maximizing the answers (Hemalatha et al., 2020; Nadh et al., 2021; Venkatesh et al., 2022). According to the GA predictions, the sixth experimental run (L6) is the parameter configuration that provides the maximum tensile strength and Brinell hardness values (Sathish et al., 2022; Sureshkumar et al., 2022). This optimal combination, derived through the computational prowess of the GA, holds promise for achieving superior weld quality, reinforcing the alloy's mechanical integrity, and showcasing the efficacy of this advanced optimization technique in tailoring laser welding parameters for enhanced performance in C63000 alloy applications (Ramesh et al., 2022).

Figure 2. Variation of Ts with the varying inputs

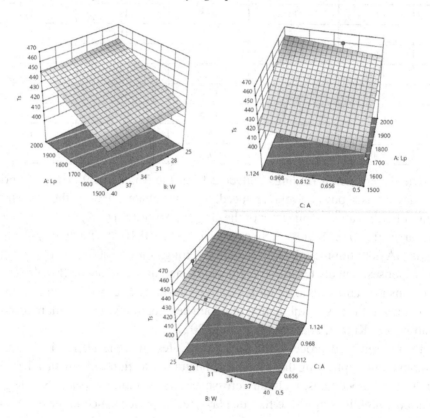

In the graphical depiction of the experimental results, Figure 2 clearly demonstrates the change in tensile strength (Ts) over the spectrum of experimental inputs. Notably, the chart indicates a discernable pattern whereby the greatest tensile strength is obtained under specified circumstances (Chinta et al., 2023; Natrayan, 2023; Velumayil et al., 2023). A deeper analysis of the graphical representation reveals a link between enhanced tensile strength and higher values of welding speed (W), coupled by higher laser power (LP) and lower amplitude (A) (Chehelgerdi et al., 2023; Lakshmaiya, 2023c). This tendency becomes more obvious in Figure 3, which highlights the corresponding variance in Brinell hardness (BH). Similar to the tensile strength trend, the maximum levels of hardness are seen under circumstances of faster welding speed, increased laser power, and lower amplitude (Konduri et al., 2023; Mahat et al., 2023). The contemporaneous comparison of both data uncovers a striking insight: the synergistic impact of faster welding speed, raised laser power, and reduced amplitude leads to the achievement of maximal tensile strength and hardness in the C63000 alloy. The observed pattern accords with the general knowledge of laser welding dynamics, where controlled alterations in these parameters may considerably impact the mechanical characteristics of the welded material (Sendrayaperumal et al., 2021). The fact that the ideal circumstances for obtaining maximal tensile strength and hardness coincide with faster welding speed, increased laser power, and lower amplitude highlights the relevance of these factors in moulding the mechanical properties of the laser-welded C63000 alloy.

Figure 3. Variation of BH on varying the inputs

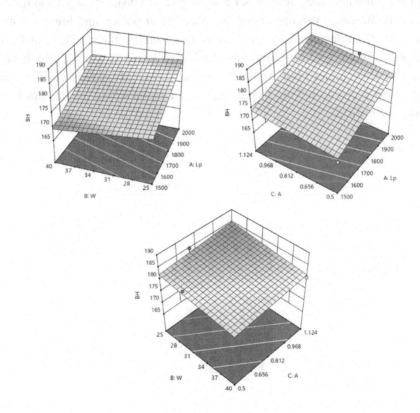

CONCLUSION

In conclusion, the comprehensive investigation into the laser welding of C63000 alloy, guided by the Taguchi L9 array and propelled by advanced optimization through Genetic Algorithms (GAs), has yielded valuable insights into the intricate relationship between welding parameters and the mechanical properties of the alloy. The methodical testing, as represented in Table 2, permitted a complete examination of laser power, welding speed, and amplitude, producing a rich dataset that served as the foundation for later analysis. The employment of GAs for optimization highlighted the efficiency of computational approaches in predicting optimum parameter combinations for increasing tensile strength and Brinell hardness. The determination of the ideal solution, demonstrated by the L6 configuration, not only demonstrates the skill of GAs but also points towards certain parameter values that contribute to higher mechanical performance in the laser-welded C63000 alloy. The graphical representations in Figures 2 and 3 further illustrate the tendencies seen in the experimental findings. The strong link between greater tensile strength and hardness values with increased welding speed, enhanced laser power, and lower amplitude underscores the relevance of these factors in designing the mechanical features of the alloy. These results are not only significant for understanding the behavior of C63000 alloy under laser welding circumstances but also set the framework for informed decision-making in practical applications where precise mechanical qualities are critical.

REFERENCES

Anjankar, P., Lakade, S., Padalkar, A., Nichal, S., Devarajan, Y., Lakshmaiya, N., & Subbaiyan, N. (2023). Experimental investigation on the effect of liquid phase and vapor phase separation over performance of falling film evaporator. *Environmental Quality Management*, 33(1), 61–69. 10.1002/tqem.21952

Arul Arumugam, R., Usha Rani, B., Komala, C. R., Barthwal, S., Kaliappan, S., & Natrayan, L. (2023). Design and Development of the Optical Antenna for Wireless Communications. *7th International Conference on Electronics, Communication and Aerospace Technology, ICECA 2023 - Proceedings*. IEEE. 10.1109/ICE-CA58529.2023.10395356

Balaji, N., Natrayan, L., Kaliappan, S., Patil, P. P., & Sivakumar, N. S. (2022). Annealed peanut shell biochar as potential reinforcement for aloe vera fiber-epoxy biocomposite: Mechanical, thermal conductivity, and dielectric properties. *Biomass Conversion and Biorefinery*. 10.1007/s13399-022-02650-7

Balamurugan, P., Agarwal, P., Khajuria, D., Mahapatra, D., Angalaeswari, S., Natrayan, L., & Mammo, W. D. (2023). State-Flow Control Based Multistage Constant-Current Battery Charger for Electric Two-Wheeler. *Journal of Advanced Transportation*, 2023, 1–11. 10.1155/2023/4554582

Biradar, V. S., Al-Jiboory, A. K., Sahu, G., Tilak Babu, S. B. G., Mahender, K., & Natrayan, L. (2023). Intelligent Control Systems for Industrial Automation and Robotics. *2023 10th IEEE Uttar Pradesh Section International Conference on Electrical, Electronics and Computer Engineering, UPCON 2023*. IEEE. 10.1109/UPCON59197.2023.10434927

Chehelgerdi, M., Chehelgerdi, M., Allela, O. Q. B., Pecho, R. D. C., Jayasankar, N., Rao, D. P., Thamaraikani, T., Vasanthan, M., Viktor, P., Lakshmaiya, N., Saadh, M. J., Amajd, A., Abo-Zaid, M. A., Castillo-Acobo, R. Y., Ismail, A. H., Amin, A. H., & Akhavan-Sigari, R. (2023). Progressing nanotechnology to improve targeted cancer treatment: Overcoming hurdles in its clinical implementation. *Molecular Cancer*, 22(1), 169. 10.1186/s12943-023-01865-037814270

Chennai Viswanathan, P., Venkatesh, S. N., Dhanasekaran, S., Mahanta, T. K., Sugumaran, V., Lakshmaiya, N., Paramasivam, P., & Nanjagoundenpalayam Ramasamy, S. (2023). Deep Learning for Enhanced Fault Diagnosis of Monoblock Centrifugal Pumps: Spectrogram-Based Analysis. *Machines*, 11(9), 874. 10.3390/machines11090874

Chinta, N. D., Karthikeyan, K. R., Natrayan, L., & Kaliappan, S. (2023). Pressure Induced Variations in Mode II Behaviour of Uni-Directional Kenaf Reinforced Polymers. *International Journal of Vehicle Structures and Systems*, 15(7). 10.4273/ijvss.15.7.19

Hemalatha, K., James, C., Natrayan, L., & Swamynadh, V. (2020). Analysis of RCC T-beam and prestressed concrete box girder bridges super structure under different span conditions. *Materials Today: Proceedings*, 37(Part 2), 1507–1516. 10.1016/j.matpr.2020.07.119

Josphineleela, R., Kaliapp, S., Natrayan, L., & Garg, A. (2023). Big Data Security through Privacy - Preserving Data Mining (PPDM): A Decentralization Approach. *Proceedings of the 2023 2nd International Conference on Electronics and Renewable Systems, ICEARS 2023*. IEEE. 10.1109/ICEARS56392.2023.10085646

Josphineleela, R., Lekha, D., Natrayan, L., & Purohit, K. C. (2023). Biometric Aided Intelligent Security System Built using Internet of Things. *Proceedings of the 2023 2nd International Conference on Electronics and Renewable Systems, ICEARS 2023*. IEEE. 10.1109/ICEARS56392.2023.10085572

Kaliappan, S., Mothilal, T., Natrayan, L., Pravin, P., & Olkeba, T. T. (2023). Mechanical Characterization of Friction-Stir-Welded Aluminum AA7010 Alloy with TiC Nanofiber. *Advances in Materials Science and Engineering*, 2023, 1–7. 10.1155/2023/1466963

Kaliappan, S., & Natrayan, L. (2024a). Enhancement of Mechanical and Thermal Characteristics of Automobile Parts using Flax/Epoxy-Graphene Nanofiller Composites. *SAE Technical Papers*. 10.4271/2023-01-5116

Kaliappan, S., & Natrayan, L. (2024b). Impact of Kenaf Fiber and Inorganic Nanofillers on Mechanical Properties of Epoxy-Based Nanocomposites for Sustainable Automotive Applications. *SAE Technical Papers*. 10.4271/2023-01-5115

Kaliappan, S., & Natrayan, L. (2024c). Polypropylene Composite Materials with Natural Fiber Reinforcement: An Acoustic and Mechanical Analysis for Automotive Implementations. *SAE Technical Papers*. 10.4271/2023-01-5130

Kaliappan, S., & Natrayan, L. (2024d). Revolutionizing Automotive Materials through Enhanced Mechanical Properties of Epoxy Hybrid Bio-Composites with Hemp, Kenaf, and Coconut Powder. *SAE Technical Papers*. 10.4271/2023-01-5185

Kaliappan, S., Natrayan, L., & Garg, N. (2023). Checking and Supervisory System for Calculation of Industrial Constraints using Embedded System. *Proceedings of the 4th International Conference on Smart Electronics and Communication, ICOSEC 2023*. IEEE. 10.1109/ICOSEC58147.2023.10275952

Kaliappan, S., Natrayan, L., Mohammed Ali, H., & Kumar, P. (2024). Thermal and Mechanical Properties of Abutilon indicum Fiber-Based Polyester Composites under Alkali Treatment for Automotive Sector. *SAE Technical Papers*. 10.4271/2024-01-5031

Kaliappan, S., Natrayan, L., & Rajput, A. (2023). Sentiment Analysis of News Headlines Based on Sentiment Lexicon and Deep Learning. *Proceedings of the 4th International Conference on Smart Electronics and Communication, ICOSEC 2023*. IEEE. 10.1109/ICOSEC58147.2023.10276102

Kanimozhi, G., Natrayan, L., Angalaeswari, S., & Paramasivam, P. (2022). An Effective Charger for Plug-In Hybrid Electric Vehicles (PHEV) with an Enhanced PFC Rectifier and ZVS-ZCS DC/DC High-Frequency Converter. *Journal of Advanced Transportation*, 2022, 1–14. 10.1155/2022/7840102

Karthick, M., Meikandan, M., Kaliappan, S., Karthick, M., Sekar, S., Patil, P. P., Raja, S., Natrayan, L., & Paramasivam, P. (2022). Experimental Investigation on Mechanical Properties of Glass Fiber Hybridized Natural Fiber Reinforced Penta-Layered Hybrid Polymer Composite. *International Journal of Chemical Engineering*, 2022, 1–9. 10.1155/2022/1864446

Kaushal, R. K., Arvind, R., Giri, K. K. B., Sindhu, M., Natrayan, L., & Ronald, B. (2023). Deep Learning Based Segmentation Approach for Automatic Lane Detection in Autonomous Vehicle. *International Conference on Self Sustainable Artificial Intelligence Systems, ICSSAS 2023 - Proceedings*. IEEE. 10.1109/ICS-SAS57918.2023.10331835

Kiruba Sandou, D., Sunad Kumara, A. N., Choudhary, B. K., & Gurpur, S., Sarishma, Natrayan, L., & Sivaramkumar, M. (2023). Design and Implementation of Neuro-Fuzzy Control Approach for Robot's Trajectory Tracking. *7th International Conference on Electronics, Communication and Aerospace Technology, ICECA 2023 - Proceedings*. doi:10.1109/ICECA58529.2023.10395675

Konduri, S., Walke, S., Kumar, A., Pavithra, G., Bhagirath Jadhav, A., & Natrayan, L. (2023). Reinforcement Learning for Multi-Robot Coordination and Cooperation in Manufacturing. *2023 10th IEEE Uttar Pradesh Section International Conference on Electrical, Electronics and Computer Engineering, UPCON 2023*. IEEE. doi:10.1109/UPCON59197.2023.10434651

Lakshmaiya, N. (2023b). Experimental analysis on heat transfer cube shape of two vertical surfaces during melting condition. *Proceedings of SPIE- The International Society for Optical Engineering, 12616.* SPIE. doi:10.1117/12.267555210.1 117/12.2675552

Lakshmaiya, N. (2023d). Experimental investigation on computational volumetric heat in real time neural pathways. *Proceedings of SPIE- The International Society for Optical Engineering, 12616.* SPIE. doi:10.1117/12.267555510.1117/12.2675555

Lakshmaiya, N. (2023e). Investigation on ultraviolet radiation of flow pattern and particles transportation in vanishing raindrops. *Proceedings of SPIE- The International Society for Optical Engineering, 12616.* SPIE. doi:10.1117/12.267555610. 1117/12.2675556

Lakshmaiya, N. (2023f). Mechanical evaluation of coir/kenaf/jute laminated hybrid composites designed for geotechnical uses. *Proceedings of SPIE- The International Society for Optical Engineering, 12936.* SPIE. doi:10.1117/12.301171010.1 117/12.3011710

Lakshmaiya, N. (2023g). Organic material nuts flour greens laminate preparation and mechanical characteristics of natural materials. *Proceedings of SPIE- The International Society for Optical Engineering, 12936.* SPIE. doi:10.1117/12.30117 1210.1117/12.3011712

Lakshmaiya, N. (2023h). Polylactic acid/hydroxyapatite/yttria-stabilized zircon synthetic nanocomposite scaffolding compression and flexural characteristics. *Proceedings of SPIE- The International Society for Optical Engineering, 12936.* SPIE. doi:10.1117/12.301171510.1117/12.3011715

Lakshmaiya, N. (2023i). Preparation and evaluation of bamboo laminated cannabis paper physico - mechanical characteristics. *Proceedings of SPIE- The International Society for Optical Engineering, 12936.* SPIE. doi:10.1117/12.301171610.1 117/12.3011716

Lakshmaiya, N. (2023j). Simulating laminar induced heat capacity and heat transmission convection using Al2O3 nanofluid. *Proceedings of SPIE- The International Society for Optical Engineering, 12616.* SPIE. doi:10.1117/12.267555710. 1117/12.2675557

Lakshmaiya, N., Kaliappan, S., Patil, P. P., Ganesan, V., Dhanraj, J. A., Sirisamphanwong, C., Wongwuttanasatian, T., Chowdhury, S., Channumsin, S., Channumsin, M., & Techato, K. (2022). Influence of Oil Palm Nano Filler on Interlaminar Shear and Dynamic Mechanical Properties of Flax/Epoxy-Based Hybrid Nanocomposites under Cryogenic Condition. *Coatings*, 12(11), 1675. 10.3390/coatings12111675

Loganathan, A. S., Ramachandran, V., Perumal, A. S., Dhanasekaran, S., Lakshmaiya, N., & Paramasivam, P. (2023). Framework of Transactive Energy Market Strategies for Lucrative Peer-to-Peer Energy Transactions. *Energies*, 16(1), 6. 10.3390/en16010006

Mahat, D., Niranjan, K., Naidu, C. S. K. V. R., Babu, S. B. G. T., Kumar, M. S., & Natrayan, L. (2023). AI-Driven Optimization of Supply Chain and Logistics in Mechanical Engineering. *2023 10th IEEE Uttar Pradesh Section International Conference on Electrical, Electronics and Computer Engineering*. IEEE. 10.1109/UPCON59197.2023.10434905

Malladi, A., Kaliappan, S., Natrayan, L., & Mahesh, V. (2024). Effectiveness of Thermal and Mechanical Properties of Jute Fibers under Different Chemical Treatment for Automotive Interior Trim. *SAE Technical Papers*. 10.4271/2024-01-5008

Mehta, A. K., Lanjewar, P., Murthy, D. S., Ghildiyal, P., Faldu, R., & Natrayan, L. (2023). AI & Lean Management Principles Based Pharmaceutical Manufacturing Processes. *2023 10th IEEE Uttar Pradesh Section International Conference on Electrical, Electronics and Computer Engineering, UPCON 2023*. IEEE. 10.1109/UPCON59197.2023.10434834

Nadh, V. S., Krishna, C., Natrayan, L., Kumar, K., Nitesh, K. J. N. S., Raja, G. B., & Paramasivam, P. (2021). Structural Behavior of Nanocoated Oil Palm Shell as Coarse Aggregate in Lightweight Concrete. *Journal of Nanomaterials*, 2021, 1–7. 10.1155/2021/4741296

Natrayan, L. (2023). Humidity Impact on the Material Characteristics of a Sisal Laminate: The Role of the Rapid Vibrational Method. *International Journal of Vehicle Structures and Systems*, 15(7). 10.4273/ijvss.15.7.17

Natrayan, L., Chinta, N. D., Gogulamudi, B., Nadh, V. S., Muthu, G., Kaliappan, S., & Srinivas, C. (2024). Investigation on mechanical properties of the green synthesis bamboo fiber/eggshell/coconut shell powder-based hybrid biocomposites under NaOH conditions. *Green Processing and Synthesis*, 13(1), 20230185. 10.1515/gps-2023-0185

Natrayan, L., & De Poures, M. V. (2023a). Experimental investigations of heat ageing with chemical modification of hemp fiber elastic characteristics. *Proceedings of SPIE- The International Society for Optical Engineering, 12936*. SPIE. 10.1117/12.3011708

Natrayan, L., & De Poures, M. V. (2023b). Influence of gasoline on high speed evaporation gasoline sprays: a large-eddy model of sprayer a with different fuels. *Proceedings of SPIE- The International Society for Optical Engineering, 12936.* SPIE. 10.1117/12.3011709

Natrayan, L., & Kaliappan, S. (2023). Mechanical Assessment of Carbon-Luffa Hybrid Composites for Automotive Applications. *SAE Technical Papers.* 10.4271/2023-01-5070

Natrayan, L., Kaliappan, S., & Pundir, S. (2023). Control and Monitoring of a Quadcopter in Border Areas Using Embedded System. *Proceedings of the 4th International Conference on Smart Electronics and Communication, ICOSEC 2023.* IEEE. 10.1109/ICOSEC58147.2023.10276196

Natrayan, L., Kaliappan, S., Saravanan, A., Vickram, A. S., Pravin, P., Abbas, M., Ahamed Saleel, C., Alwetaishi, M., & Saleem, M. S. M. (2023). Recyclability and catalytic characteristics of copper oxide nanoparticles derived from bougainvillea plant flower extract for biomedical application. *Green Processing and Synthesis,* 12(1), 20230030. 10.1515/gps-2023-0030

Natrayan, L., & Kumar, M. S. (2020). Optimization of wear behaviour on AA6061/ Al2O3/SiC metal matrix composite using squeeze casting technique-Statistical analysis. *Materials Today: Proceedings,* 27, 306–310. 10.1016/j.matpr.2019.11.038

Natrayan, L., & Richard, T. (2023a). Experimental investigations of bagasse ash strands featuring variable surface influence on polypropylene based polymer composites. *Proceedings of SPIE- The International Society for Optical Engineering, 12936.* SPIE. 10.1117/12.3011691

Natrayan, L., & Richard, T. (2023b). Organo modified nanocomposites terephthalic acid polymers temperature and microstructural characteristics. *Proceedings of SPIE- The International Society for Optical Engineering, 12936.* SPIE. 10.1117/12.3011863

Natrayan, L., Sakthi Shunmuga Sundaram, P., & Elumalai, J. (2019). Analyzing the uterine physiological with mmg signals using svm. *International Journal of Pharmaceutical Research,* 11(2). 10.31838/ijpr/2019.11.02.009

Natrayan, L., Senthil Kumar, M., & Palanikumar, K. (2018). Optimization of squeeze cast process parameters on mechanical properties of Al2O3/SiC reinforced hybrid metal matrix composites using taguchi technique. *Materials Research Express,* 5(6), 066516. 10.1088/2053-1591/aac873

Natrayan, L., Sivaprakash, V., & Santhosh, M. S. (2018). Mechanical, microstructure and wear behavior of the material aa6061 reinforced sic with different leaf ashes using advanced stir casting method. *International Journal of Engineering and Advanced Technology*, 8.

Niveditha, V. R., & Rajakumar, P. S. (2020). Pervasive computing in the context of COVID-19 prediction with AI-based algorithms. *International Journal of Pervasive Computing and Communications*, 16(5). 10.1108/IJPCC-07-2020-0082

Palaniyappan, S., Veeman, D., Sivakumar, N. K., & Natrayan, L. (2022). Development and optimization of lattice structure on the walnut shell reinforced PLA composite for the tensile strength and dimensional error properties. *Structures*, 45, 163–178. 10.1016/j.istruc.2022.09.023

Pandian, A., Kaliappan, S., Natrayan, L., & Reddy, V. (2024). Analyzing the Moisture and Chemical Retention Behavior of Flax Fiber-Ceramic Hybrid Composites for Automotive Underbody Shields. *SAE Technical Papers*. 10.4271/2024-01-5006

Prabagar, S., Al-Jiboory, A. K., Nair, P. S., Mandal, P., Garse, K. M., & Natrayan, L. (2023). Artificial Intelligence-Based Control Strategies for Unmanned Aerial Vehicles. *2023 10th IEEE Uttar Pradesh Section International Conference on Electrical, Electronics and Computer Engineering, UPCON 2023*. IEEE. 10.1109/UPCON59197.2023.10434918

Pragadish, N., Kaliappan, S., Subramanian, M., Natrayan, L., Satish Prakash, K., Subbiah, R., & Kumar, T. C. A. (2023). Optimization of cardanol oil dielectric-activated EDM process parameters in machining of silicon steel. *Biomass Conversion and Biorefinery*, 13(15), 14087–14096. 10.1007/s13399-021-02268-1

Ragumadhavan, R., Sateesh Kumar, D., Charyulu Rompicharla, L. N., Dhondiya, S. A., Kaliappan, S., & Natrayan, L. (2023). Design and Development of Light Communication Systems Using Modulation Techniques. *7th International Conference on Electronics, Communication and Aerospace Technology, ICECA 2023 - Proceedings*. IEEE. 10.1109/ICECA58529.2023.10395831

Rajasekaran, S., & Natrayan, L. (2023a). Estimation of corrective and preventive action on trend end plug-based machining activities using manual and failure mode with effects analysis. *Proceedings of SPIE- The International Society for Optical Engineering, 12936*. SPIE. 10.1117/12.3011698

Rajasekaran, S., & Natrayan, L. (2023b). Evaluation of occurrence number and communication based on FMEA operations in product development. *Proceedings of SPIE- The International Society for Optical Engineering, 12936*. SPIE. 10.1117/12.3011702

Ramesh, C., Vijayakumar, M., Alshahrani, S., Navaneethakrishnan, G., Palanisamy, R., Natrayan, L., Saleel, C. A., Afzal, A., Shaik, S., & Panchal, H. (2022). Performance enhancement of selective layer coated on solar absorber panel with reflector for water heater by response surface method: A case study. *Case Studies in Thermal Engineering*, 36, 102093. 10.1016/j.csite.2022.102093

Reddy, P. N., Umaeswari, P., Natrayan, L., & Choudhary, A. (2023). Development of Programmed Autonomous Electric Heavy Vehicle: An Application of IoT. *Proceedings of the 2023 2nd International Conference on Electronics and Renewable Systems, ICEARS 2023*. IEEE. 10.1109/ICEARS56392.2023.10085492

Saadh, M. J., Almoyad, M. A. A., Arellano, M. T. C., Maaliw, R. R. III, Castillo-Acobo, R. Y., Jalal, S. S., Gandla, K., Obaid, M., Abdulwahed, A. J., Ibrahem, A. A., Sârbu, I., Juyal, A., Lakshmaiya, N., & Akhavan-Sigari, R. (2023). Long non-coding RNAs: Controversial roles in drug resistance of solid tumors mediated by autophagy. *Cancer Chemotherapy and Pharmacology*, 92(6), 439–453. 10.1007/s00280-023-04582-z37768333

Sai, S. A., Venkatesh, S. N., Dhanasekaran, S., Balaji, P. A., Sugumaran, V., Lakshmaiya, N., & Paramasivam, P. (2023). Transfer Learning Based Fault Detection for Suspension System Using Vibrational Analysis and Radar Plots. *Machines*, 11(8), 778. 10.3390/machines11080778

Sasi, J. P., Nidhi Pandagre, K., Royappa, A., Walke, S., Pavithra, G., & Natrayan, L. (2023). Deep Learning Techniques for Autonomous Navigation of Underwater Robots. *2023 10th IEEE Uttar Pradesh Section International Conference on Electrical, Electronics and Computer Engineering, UPCON 2023*. IEEE. 10.1109/UPCON59197.2023.10434865

Sathish, T., Natrayan, L., Prasad Jones Christydass, S., Sivananthan, S., Kamalakannan, R., Vijayan, V., & Paramasivam, P. (2022). Experimental Investigation on Tribological Behaviour of AA6066: HSS-Cu Hybrid Composite in Dry Sliding Condition. *Advances in Materials Science and Engineering*, 2022, 1–9. 10.1155/2022/9349847

Sathish, T., Palani, K., Natrayan, L., Merneedi, A., de Poures, M. V., & Singaravelu, D. K. (2021). Synthesis and characterization of polypropylene/ramie fiber with hemp fiber and coir fiber natural biopolymer composite for biomedical application. *International Journal of Polymer Science*, 2021, 1–8. 10.1155/2021/2462873

Selvi, S., Mohanraj, M., Duraipandy, P., Kaliappan, S., Natrayan, L., & Vinayagam, N. (2023). Optimization of Solar Panel Orientation for Maximum Energy Efficiency. *Proceedings of the 4th International Conference on Smart Electronics and Communication, ICOSEC 2023*. IEEE. 10.1109/ICOSEC58147.2023.10276287

Sendrayaperumal, A., Mahapatra, S., Parida, S. S., Surana, K., Balamurugan, P., Natrayan, L., & Paramasivam, P. (2021). Energy Auditing for Efficient Planning and Implementation in Commercial and Residential Buildings. *Advances in Civil Engineering*, 2021, 1–10. 10.1155/2021/1908568

Siddiqui, E., Siddique, M., Safeer Pasha, M., Boyapati, P., Pavithra, G., & Natrayan, L. (2023). AI and ML for Enhancing Crop Yield and Resource Efficiency in Agriculture. *2023 10th IEEE Uttar Pradesh Section International Conference on Electrical, Electronics and Computer Engineering, UPCON 2023*. IEEE. 10.1109/UPCON59197.2023.10434493

Sukumaran, C., Indhumathi, K., Balamurugan, P., Ambilwade, R. P., Sunthari, P. M., & Natrayan, L. (2023). The Role of AI in Biochips for Early Disease Detection. *Proceedings - International Conference on Technological Advancements in Computational Sciences, ICTACS 2023*. 10.1109/ICTACS59847.2023.10390419

Suman, T., Kaliappan, S., Natrayan, L., & Dobhal, D. C. (2023). IoT based Social Device Network with Cloud Computing Architecture. *Proceedings of the 2023 2nd International Conference on Electronics and Renewable Systems, ICEARS 2023*. IEEE. 10.1109/ICEARS56392.2023.10085574

Sureshkumar, P., Jagadeesha, T., Natrayan, L., Ravichandran, M., Veeman, D., & Muthu, S. M. (2022). Electrochemical corrosion and tribological behaviour of $AA6063/Si_3N_4/Cu(NO_3)_2$ composite processed using single-pass $ECAP_A$ route with 120° die angle. *Journal of Materials Research and Technology*, 16. 10.1016/j.jmrt.2021.12.020

Thakre, S., Pandhare, A., Malwe, P. D., Gupta, N., Kothare, C., Magade, P. B., Patel, A., Meena, R. S., Veza, I., Natrayan, L., & Panchal, H. (2023). Heat transfer and pressure drop analysis of a microchannel heat sink using nanofluids for energy applications. *Kerntechnik*, 88(5), 543–555. 10.1515/kern-2023-0034

Ugle, V. V., Arulprakasajothi, M., Padmanabhan, S., Devarajan, Y., Lakshmaiya, N., & Subbaiyan, N. (2023). Investigation of heat transport characteristics of titanium dioxide nanofluids with corrugated tube. *Environmental Quality Management*, 33(2), 127–138. 10.1002/tqem.21999

Vaishali, K. R., Rammohan, S. R., Natrayan, L., Usha, D., & Niveditha, V. R. (2021). Guided container selection for data streaming through neural learning in cloud. *International Journal of Systems Assurance Engineering and Management*. 10.1007/s13198-021-01124-9

Velmurugan, G., & Natrayan, L. (2023). Experimental investigations of moisture diffusion and mechanical properties of interply rearrangement of glass/Kevlar-based hybrid composites under cryogenic environment. *Journal of Materials Research and Technology*, 23, 4513–4526. 10.1016/j.jmrt.2023.02.089

Velumayil, R., Gnanakumar, G., Natrayan, L., Chinta, N. D., & Kaliappan, S. (2023). Bifunctional Aluminum Oxide/Carbon Fiber/Epoxy Nanocomposites Preparation and Evaluation. *International Journal of Vehicle Structures and Systems*, 15(7). 10.4273/ijvss.15.7.18

Venkatesh, R., Manivannan, S., Kaliappan, S., Socrates, S., Sekar, S., Patil, P. P., Natrayan, L., & Bayu, M. B. (2022). Influence of Different Frequency Pulse on Weld Bead Phase Ratio in Gas Tungsten Arc Welding by Ferritic Stainless Steel AISI-409L. *Journal of Nanomaterials*, 2022, 1–11. 10.1155/2022/9530499

Vijayakumar, M., & Shreeraj Nair, P. G Tilak Babu, S. B., Mahender, K., Venkateswaran, T. S., & Natrayan, L. (2023). Intelligent Systems For Predictive Maintenance In Industrial IoT. *2023 10th IEEE Uttar Pradesh Section International Conference on Electrical, Electronics and Computer Engineering, UPCON 2023*. IEEE. 10.1109/UPCON59197.2023.10434814

Yogeshwaran, S., Natrayan, L., Udhayakumar, G., Godwin, G., & Yuvaraj, L. (2020). Effect of waste tyre particles reinforcement on mechanical properties of jute and abaca fiber - Epoxy hybrid composites with pre-treatment. *Materials Today: Proceedings*, 37(Part 2), 1377–1380. 10.1016/j.matpr.2020.06.584

Chapter 6
Meta–Heuristic Optimization for Enhancing the Thermal Performance of Solar Energy Devices

Patlola Madhusudhan

B.V. Raju Institute of Technology, Narsapur, India

Parthasarathi Mishra

Government College of Engineering, Odisha, India

G. Vanya Sree

http://orcid.org/0000-0003-3146 -0002

CVR College of Engineering, Ibrahimpatnam, India

P. K. Dhal

Vel Tech Rangarajan Dr. Sagunthala R&D Institute of Science and Technology, Chennai, India

C. K. Arvinda Pandian

http://orcid.org/0000-0002-0039 -6389

B.S. Abdur Rahman Crescent Institute of Science and Technology, Vandalur, India

Socrates S.

Velammal Institute of Technology, Chennai, India

ABSTRACT

This chapter examines the application of meta-heuristic optimization in boosting the thermal performance of solar energy systems. The analysis sheds light on the short- and long-term benefits of meta-heuristic algorithms by utilizing performance metrics, energy efficiency metrics, and reliability assessment. Performance Metrics imply higher energy output and efficient temperature regulation, demonstrating the

DOI: 10.4018/979-8-3693-3314-3.ch006

algorithm's competence in overcoming complex architectural conditions. Energy Efficiency metrics reflect greater exploitation of solar energy resources, signaling a huge step towards sustainability. The different conclusions from Reliability Assessment illustrate the adaptability of meta-heuristic optimization, underlining both problems and accomplishments in stability and consistency across time.

INTRODUCTION

Solar energy is at the forefront of our endeavors to achieve a more environmentally friendly and enduring future (Natrayan, 2023). As we confront the repercussions of climate change and the exhaustion of conventional energy sources, utilizing solar power offers a vital pathway to fulfill our increasing energy demands (Chinta et al., 2023). Solar energy gadgets, which transform sunshine into practical electricity, have become crucial participants in this endeavor (Lakshmaiya, 2023b). Nevertheless, enhancing the thermal efficiency of these gadgets continues to be a substantial obstacle that necessitates inventive answers (Velumayil et al., 2023). The significance of solar energy cannot be exaggerated. It symbolizes an environmentally friendly and sustainable energy source that is crucial in decreasing our reliance on non-renewable resources (Saadh et al., 2023). Solar energy provides an environmentally friendly alternative to traditional energy sources, as it has minimum ecological impact and does not contribute to environmental degradation or climate change (Thakre et al., 2023). Utilizing solar energy has the capacity to transform our energy infrastructure, offering a durable and environmentally conscious alternative for the future (Chennai Viswanathan et al., 2023).

Although solar energy holds great potential, achieving optimal thermal performance in solar devices is a difficult task (Sai et al., 2023; M. Vijayakumar et al., 2023). The efficacy of these devices is intricately tied to their capacity to transform sunlight into power while efficiently handling and dispersing heat (Biradar et al., 2023; Konduri et al., 2023; Siddiqui et al., 2023). High temperatures can damage the performance and longevity of solar panels, lowering their effectiveness and overall output (Loganathan et al., 2023). Addressing this thermal barrier is vital to unleashing the full potential of solar energy and guaranteeing its widespread adoption as a mainstream power source (Balamurugan et al., 2023; Kaliappan, Mothilal, et al., 2023; Lakshmaiya, 2023e). In the quest for effective solutions, meta-heuristic optimization appears as a potential technique (Josphineleela, Kaliapp, et al., 2023). Unlike standard optimization approaches that rely on explicit mathematical formulations, meta-heuristic techniques draw inspiration from natural events or abstract problem-solving tactics (Chehelgerdi et al., 2023). These algorithms are characterized by their capacity to explore enormous solution spaces, making them well-suited for complicated and dynamic issues such as increasing the thermal performance of solar energy systems (Josphineleela, Lekha, et al., 2023; Reddy et al., 2023; Suman et al., 2023).

Meta-heuristic optimization gives a unique route for confronting the difficulties of thermal optimization (Lakshmaiya, 2023j, 2023d, 2023a, 2023c). By replicating natural processes like the swarming behavior of birds or the foraging habits of ants, these algorithms handle the complexity of solar device design in a way that traditional methods often fall short (Natrayan, Kaliappan, Saravanan, et al., 2023). The adaptability and flexibility inherent in meta-heuristic approaches make them well-matched to the dynamic and non-linear nature of thermal optimization difficulties (Kaliappan, Natrayan, & Garg, 2023; Natrayan & Kaliappan, 2023).

BACKGROUND AND RELATED WORK

Solar energy devices act by absorbing sunlight through photovoltaic cells, which generate an electric current (Kaliappan, Natrayan, & Rajput, 2023; Natrayan, Kaliappan, & Pundir, 2023; Selvi et al., 2023). While this technique is inherently clean and efficient, the thermal factors of solar devices represent a significant problem (Kaushal et al., 2023; Natrayan & De Poures, 2023b). In addition to raising the device's temperature, the absorbed sunlight helps to generate electricity. Elevated temperatures can significantly influence the efficiency and dependability of solar panels, diminishing their overall performance and longevity (Lakshmaiya, 2023g, 2023f, 2023i).

Efforts to solve these thermal difficulties have given rise to numerous optimization strategies. Traditional optimization strategies frequently rely on explicit mathematical models to determine optimal solutions (Lakshmaiya & Murugan, 2023b, 2023d). However, the complexity and non-linearity of the thermal performance optimization problem in solar devices make it tough to obtain correct mathematical formulations (Natrayan & De Poures, 2023a). This has motivated researchers to explore alternate methodologies, such as meta-heuristic optimization, which display adaptability and efficiency in dealing with complicated problem spaces (Rajasekaran & Natrayan, 2023a, 2023b).

The landscape of related work in the topic of solar energy optimization comprises a varied variety of approaches (Lakshmaiya & Murugan, 2023e, 2023c, 2023a). Traditional optimization methods, including mathematical modeling and algorithmic approaches, have been extensively researched (Natrayan & Richard, 2023b, 2023a). These methods frequently use sophisticated mathematical formulations to model the thermal behavior of solar systems, seeking to discover optimal solutions through systematic computations. However, the limits of these standard methodologies become clear when dealing with the dynamic and nonlinear character of thermal optimization (Lakshmaiya, 2023h).

METHODOLOGY

Meta-Heuristic Optimization

Meta-heuristic optimization is a strong and novel approach to problem-solving that diverges from classic, rule-based algorithms (Kiruba Sandou et al., 2023; Sukumaran et al., 2023). Essentially, it is a collection of heuristic optimization algorithms that direct the search for the best solutions inside intricate and dynamic problem spaces, drawing inspiration from natural or abstract processes (Prabagar et al., 2023; Ragumadhavan et al., 2023; Sasi et al., 2023). As shown in the Figure 1, The application of meta-heuristic optimization offers tremendous potential in the domain of increasing the thermal performance of solar energy systems (Mahat et al., 2023).

Figure 1. Optimization process

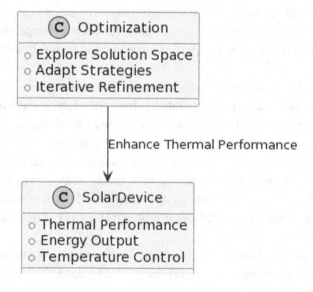

To simplify the concept, view it as a problem-solving method influenced by nature. Imagine a bunch of birds looking for food in an open area (Ramesh et al., 2022). Each bird modifies its flight path based on the behavior of surrounding birds, collectively maximizing their quest for the most abundant food sources (Hemalatha et al., 2020; Sathish et al., 2022). Similarly, meta-heuristic optimization algorithms adapt and evolve their tactics based on the outcomes of prior iterations, mirroring the cooperative and adaptive behavior found in nature (Sendrayaperumal et al., 2021).

Now, let's relate this to solar energy gadgets. Much like the foraging birds, solar devices face a challenging optimization problem in maintaining their thermal performance (Kanimozhi et al., 2022; Nadh et al., 2021; Venkatesh et al., 2022). Traditional optimization approaches might be similar to trying to draw out an exact flight path for each bird, a formidable endeavor given the uncertainties and fluctuations in the environment (Karthick et al., 2022; Palaniyappan et al., 2022; Vaishali et al., 2021). But with meta-heuristic optimization, the solution space may be explored in a more adaptable and flexible way, allowing solar systems to continuously enhance their thermal performance (Natrayan, Sivaprakash, et al., 2018; Natrayan & Kumar, 2020; Sathish et al., 2021).

Consider the example of ants seeking for the most efficient route to their nest. Ant colonies demonstrate a remarkable capacity to discover the quickest path between their nest and a food source (Natrayan, Senthil Kumar, et al., 2018; Natrayan & Merneedi, 2020). This efficiency is achieved by decentralized decision-making, where each ant leaves a trail of pheromones that impacts the choices of its peers (Natrayan et al., 2020; Niveditha VR. & Rajakumar PS., 2020). The ant colony eventually finds the best course through collective behavior. Similarly, meta-heuristic optimization algorithms operate by iteratively investigating and changing potential solutions, converging towards optimal outcomes for complicated issues like thermal performance enhancement in solar systems (Mehta et al., 2023).

Evaluation Methods

Performance Metrics serve a crucial role in evaluating the effectiveness of the optimization process in boosting the thermal performance of solar energy devices (Natrayan & Kumar, 2019; Pragadish et al., 2023; M. et al. Singh, 2017). These metrics provide a quantifiable measure of many features, allowing us to gauge the impact of optimization efforts. One key statistic is energy production, which directly indicates the efficiency of a solar device. By measuring the amount of electricity generated under optimum conditions, researchers may measure the real gains brought about by the employed meta-heuristic optimization strategies. Additionally, temperature management is a vital factor in solar equipment (Lakshmaiya et al., 2022; Natrayan et al., 2021). As shown in the Figure 2, Performance measurements assist evaluate how efficiently the optimization algorithms manage and reduce temperature increases, ensuring that the device functions within optimal temperature ranges for prolonged efficiency (Balaji et al., 2022; Natrayan et al., 2019; M. D. et al. Vijayakumar, 2022).

Moving on to Energy Efficiency Metrics, the focus is on measuring the improvements made through optimization in a straightforward and accessible manner. Energy efficiency is a fundamental statistic that reflects how successfully a solar energy equipment converts sunlight into usable electricity (Natrayan, Chinta, Gogulamudi, et al., 2024). By adopting easy measurements, such as the ratio of energy output to input, researchers may precisely assess the influence of meta-heuristic optimization on the total energy efficiency of solar devices (Natrayan, Ameen, Chinta, et al., 2024; P. Singh et al., 2024). It's vital to underline that the goal is to make these indicators clearly understandable, allowing stakeholders and practitioners to grasp the favorable changes in energy utilization coming from the optimization process (Kaliappan, Natrayan, et al., 2024; Natrayan, Janardhan, Nadh, et al., 2024).

Figure 2. Evaluation process

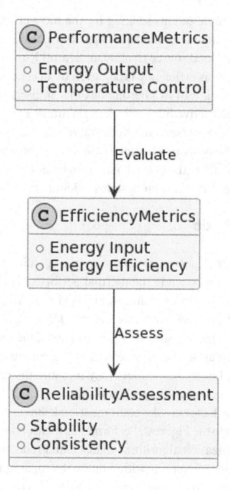

Meta-heuristic approaches contribute greatly to greater energy utilization, forming an intrinsic element of the optimization process (Kaliappan & Natrayan, 2024d; Malladi et al., 2024; Natrayan, Chinta, Teja, et al., 2024). These methods excel in exploring complex solution spaces and modifying tactics based on prior iterations, leading to advances in the efficiency of energy conversion (Natrayan, Ashok, Kaliappan, et al., 2024; Natrayan, Kaliappan, Balaji, et al., 2024; Pandian et al., 2024). To make a realistic parallel, consider of these strategies as intuitive problem-solving approaches influenced by nature, analogous to a smart thermostat changing room temperature based on occupants' preferences (Kaliappan & Natrayan, 2024a, 2024b, 2024c). By integrating such adaptive skills into the optimization process, meta-heuristic methods boost the overall energy efficiency of solar devices, making them more effective at harnessing solar energy and transforming it into useful power (Natrayan, Jayakrishna, Shanker, et al., 2024).

Reliability Assessment focuses on analyzing the resilience and consistency of the optimized system across time. Beyond immediate gains, analyzing the reliability of the enhanced solar energy gadget involves scrutinizing its long-term performance. Factors such as stability and consistency in delivering superior thermal performance are crucial. Stability ensures that the optimized system retains its efficiency under varying environmental conditions and operational factors. Consistency, on the other hand, addresses the device's capacity to reliably supply increased thermal performance over its operating life (Kaliappan, Paranthaman, et al., 2024). These concerns are vital for confirming the practicality and durability of the optimization tactics, guaranteeing that the positive benefits observed in the short term extend to long-term reliability.

RESULT AND DISCUSSION

Performance measurements, energy efficiency metrics, and reliability assessment results offer vital information about how meta-heuristic optimization affects solar energy device thermal performance. Each indicator serves a unique purpose in examining different parts of the system, together delivering a full picture of the effectiveness of the optimization process.

Figure 3. Energy output

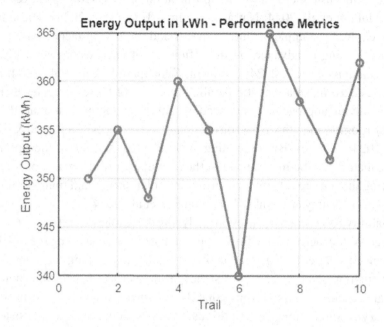

Starting with Performance Metrics as shown in the Figure 3, which comprise characteristics such as energy output and temperature management, the acquired data from 10 runs illustrate the immediate impact of the applied meta-heuristic optimization. In the context of energy output, higher values represent increased efficiency in turning sunlight into electricity. For example, in Trail 7, an energy output of 365 kWh indicates a considerable rise in electricity generation. Conversely, Trail 6, with an energy output of 340 kWh, presents a possible area for further optimization. Temperature regulation is similarly crucial, as it directly effects the efficiency and durability of solar energy systems. In the example of Trail 6, where the temperature control is reported at 27°C, it suggests a challenge in handling excessive heat. On the other hand, Trail 4, with a temperature control value of 23°C, exhibits successful optimization in maintaining an appropriate working temperature. These Performance Metrics serve as direct indicators of the success of meta-heuristic optimization, aiding researchers and engineers in optimizing the thermal performance of solar systems.

Moving to Energy Efficiency Metrics as shown in the Figure 4, the values collected from 10 trails give light on the overall success of the optimization procedure in utilizing energy resources. The Energy Efficiency Metric is computed by calculating the ratio of energy output to input, represented as a percentage. For instance, Trail 10, with an energy input of 470 kWh and an energy efficiency of 77%, displays a remarkable conversion of sunshine into power. In comparison, Trail 3, with an energy input of 505 kWh and an efficiency of 69%, illustrates an area for potential improvement in energy utilization.

Figure 4. Energy efficiency

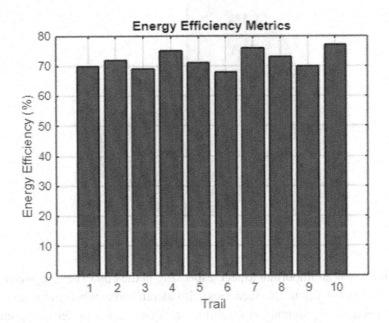

The application of meta-heuristic optimization plays a crucial role in boosting energy efficiency. It modifies and refines the system's parameters iteratively, helping to a more effective conversion of solar energy into useful power. The Energy Efficiency Metrics, therefore, provide a clear indicator of the optimization process's efficacy in obtaining greater energy utilization and serve as a critical benchmark for the overall performance of solar energy equipment.

Lastly, as shown in Figure 5, the results from the Reliability Assessment measure offer insights into the system's stability and consistency across time. The combination of Yes and No scenarios in the stability and consistency tests demonstrates the system's robustness under diverse settings. For example, in Trail 1, while the system exhibits stability, it encounters issues in maintaining consistency. In comparison, Trail 4 endures instability but excels in consistency. These cases illustrate that the impact of meta-heuristic optimization on reliability is subtle and may vary across distinct paths.

Figure 5. Consistency in reliability assessment

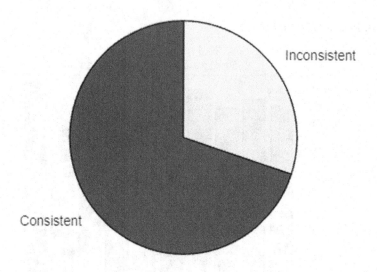

Reliability is an important aspect, especially in the context of long-term performance. The mix of Yes and No scenarios helps identify areas where more modification may be needed to maintain both stability and consistency in delivering enhanced thermal performance. It also illustrates the inherent complexity of the optimization process, underlining the need for a complete approach that includes not only immediate gains but also the system's durability over an extended operational life.

CONCLUSION

The use of meta-heuristic optimization shows great promise and the ability to have a revolutionary effect on improving the thermal performance of solar energy devices. The thorough examination through Performance Metrics, Energy Efficiency Metrics, and Reliability Assessment gives a diverse view of the optimization process. The instant advantages shown in greater energy output and improved temperature control, as demonstrated by Performance Metrics, verify the efficiency of meta-heuristic algorithms in traversing the complexity of solar device design. The Energy Efficiency Metrics emphasize the beneficial contribution of these algorithms in attaining higher energy consumption, representing a significant stride towards increased sustainability in solar energy systems. Furthermore, the Reliability Assessment offers a key viewpoint on the resilience and consistency of the improved system across time. The combination of Yes and No scenarios shows the dynamic nature of the optimization process, noting that issues in stability and consistency may occur but may be handled by repeated improvement. All things considered, the findings suggest that meta-heuristic optimization will play a significant role in improving the effectiveness, dependability, and general performance of solar energy equipment in the future, thereby making a significant contribution to the global shift towards greener and more sustainable energy sources.

REFERENCES

Balaji, N., Natrayan, L., Kaliappan, S., Patil, P. P., & Sivakumar, N. S. (2022). Annealed peanut shell biochar as potential reinforcement for aloe vera fiber-epoxy biocomposite: Mechanical, thermal conductivity, and dielectric properties. *Biomass Conversion and Biorefinery*. 10.1007/s13399-022-02650-7

Balamurugan, P., Agarwal, P., Khajuria, D., Mahapatra, D., Angalaeswari, S., Natrayan, L., & Mammo, W. D. (2023). State-Flow Control Based Multistage Constant-Current Battery Charger for Electric Two-Wheeler. *Journal of Advanced Transportation*, 2023, 1–11. 10.1155/2023/4554582

Biradar, V. S., Al-Jiboory, A. K., Sahu, G., Tilak Babu, S. B. G., Mahender, K., & Natrayan, L. (2023). Intelligent Control Systems for Industrial Automation and Robotics. *2023 10th IEEE Uttar Pradesh Section International Conference on Electrical, Electronics and Computer Engineering, UPCON 2023*. IEEE. 10.1109/UPCON59197.2023.10434927

Chehelgerdi, M., Chehelgerdi, M., Allela, O. Q. B., Pecho, R. D. C., Jayasankar, N., Rao, D. P., Thamaraikani, T., Vasanthan, M., Viktor, P., Lakshmaiya, N., Saadh, M. J., Amajd, A., Abo-Zaid, M. A., Castillo-Acobo, R. Y., Ismail, A. H., Amin, A. H., & Akhavan-Sigari, R. (2023). Progressing nanotechnology to improve targeted cancer treatment: Overcoming hurdles in its clinical implementation. *Molecular Cancer*, 22(1), 169. 10.1186/s12943-023-01865-037814270

Chennai Viswanathan, P., Venkatesh, S. N., Dhanasekaran, S., Mahanta, T. K., Sugumaran, V., Lakshmaiya, N., Paramasivam, P., & Nanjagoundenpalayam Ramasamy, S. (2023). Deep Learning for Enhanced Fault Diagnosis of Monoblock Centrifugal Pumps: Spectrogram-Based Analysis. *Machines*, 11(9), 874. 10.3390/machines11090874

Chinta, N. D., Karthikeyan, K. R., Natrayan, L., & Kaliappan, S. (2023). Pressure Induced Variations in Mode II Behaviour of Uni-Directional Kenaf Reinforced Polymers. *International Journal of Vehicle Structures and Systems*, 15(7). 10.4273/ijvss.15.7.19

Hemalatha, K., James, C., Natrayan, L., & Swamynadh, V. (2020). Analysis of RCC T-beam and prestressed concrete box girder bridges super structure under different span conditions. *Materials Today: Proceedings*, 37(Part 2), 1507–1516. 10.1016/j.matpr.2020.07.119

Josphineleela, R., Kaliapp, S., Natrayan, L., & Garg, A. (2023). Big Data Security through Privacy - Preserving Data Mining (PPDM): A Decentralization Approach. *Proceedings of the 2023 2nd International Conference on Electronics and Renewable Systems, ICEARS 2023*. IEEE. 10.1109/ICEARS56392.2023.10085646

Josphineleela, R., Lekha, D., Natrayan, L., & Purohit, K. C. (2023). Biometric Aided Intelligent Security System Built using Internet of Things. *Proceedings of the 2023 2nd International Conference on Electronics and Renewable Systems, ICEARS 2023*. IEEE. 10.1109/ICEARS56392.2023.10085572

Kaliappan, S., Mothilal, T., Natrayan, L., Pravin, P., & Olkeba, T. T. (2023). Mechanical Characterization of Friction-Stir-Welded Aluminum AA7010 Alloy with TiC Nanofiber. *Advances in Materials Science and Engineering*, 2023, 1–7. 10.1155/2023/1466963

Kaliappan, S., & Natrayan, L. (2024a). Enhancement of Mechanical and Thermal Characteristics of Automobile Parts using Flax/Epoxy-Graphene Nanofiller Composites. *SAE Technical Papers*. 10.4271/2023-01-5116

Kaliappan, S., & Natrayan, L. (2024b). Impact of Kenaf Fiber and Inorganic Nanofillers on Mechanical Properties of Epoxy-Based Nanocomposites for Sustainable Automotive Applications. *SAE Technical Papers*. 10.4271/2023-01-5115

Kaliappan, S., & Natrayan, L. (2024c). Polypropylene Composite Materials with Natural Fiber Reinforcement: An Acoustic and Mechanical Analysis for Automotive Implementations. *SAE Technical Papers*. 10.4271/2023-01-5130

Kaliappan, S., & Natrayan, L. (2024d). Revolutionizing Automotive Materials through Enhanced Mechanical Properties of Epoxy Hybrid Bio-Composites with Hemp, Kenaf, and Coconut Powder. *SAE Technical Papers*. 10.4271/2023-01-5185

Kaliappan, S., Natrayan, L., & Garg, N. (2023). Checking and Supervisory System for Calculation of Industrial Constraints using Embedded System. *Proceedings of the 4th International Conference on Smart Electronics and Communication, ICOSEC 2023*. IEEE. 10.1109/ICOSEC58147.2023.10275952

Kaliappan, S., Natrayan, L., Mohammed Ali, H., & Kumar, P. (2024). Thermal and Mechanical Properties of Abutilon indicum Fiber-Based Polyester Composites under Alkali Treatment for Automotive Sector. *SAE Technical Papers*. 10.4271/2024-01-5031

Kaliappan, S., Natrayan, L., & Rajput, A. (2023). Sentiment Analysis of News Headlines Based on Sentiment Lexicon and Deep Learning. *Proceedings of the 4th International Conference on Smart Electronics and Communication, ICOSEC 2023*. IEEE. 10.1109/ICOSEC58147.2023.10276102

Kaliappan, S., Paranthaman, V., Natrayan, L., Kumar, B. V., & Muthukannan, M. (2024). Leveraging Machine Learning Algorithm for Predicting Personality Traits on Twitter. *Proceedings of the 14th International Conference on Cloud Computing, Data Science and Engineering, Confluence 2024*. IEEE. 10.1109/Confluence60223.2024.10463468

Kanimozhi, G., Natrayan, L., Angalaeswari, S., & Paramasivam, P. (2022). An Effective Charger for Plug-In Hybrid Electric Vehicles (PHEV) with an Enhanced PFC Rectifier and ZVS-ZCS DC/DC High-Frequency Converter. *Journal of Advanced Transportation*, 2022, 1–14. 10.1155/2022/7840102

Karthick, M., Meikandan, M., Kaliappan, S., Karthick, M., Sekar, S., Patil, P. P., Raja, S., Natrayan, L., & Paramasivam, P. (2022). Experimental Investigation on Mechanical Properties of Glass Fiber Hybridized Natural Fiber Reinforced Penta-Layered Hybrid Polymer Composite. *International Journal of Chemical Engineering*, 2022, 1–9. 10.1155/2022/1864446

Kaushal, R. K., Arvind, R., Giri, K. K. B., Sindhu, M., Natrayan, L., & Ronald, B. (2023). Deep Learning Based Segmentation Approach for Automatic Lane Detection in Autonomous Vehicle. *International Conference on Self Sustainable Artificial Intelligence Systems, ICSSAS 2023 - Proceedings*. 10.1109/ICSSAS57918.2023.10331835

Kiruba Sandou, D., Sunad Kumara, A. N., Choudhary, B. K., & Gurpur, S., Sarishma, Natrayan, L., & Sivaramkumar, M. (2023). Design and Implementation of Neuro-Fuzzy Control Approach for Robot's Trajectory Tracking. *7th International Conference on Electronics, Communication and Aerospace Technology, ICECA 2023 - Proceedings*. 10.1109/ICECA58529.2023.10395675

Konduri, S., Walke, S., Kumar, A., Pavithra, G., Bhagirath Jadhav, A., & Natrayan, L. (2023). Reinforcement Learning for Multi-Robot Coordination and Cooperation in Manufacturing. *2023 10th IEEE Uttar Pradesh Section International Conference on Electrical, Electronics and Computer Engineering, UPCON 2023*. 10.1109/UPCON59197.2023.10434651

Lakshmaiya, N. (2023b). Experimental analysis on heat transfer cube shape of two vertical surfaces during melting condition. *Proceedings of SPIE- The International Society for Optical Engineering, 12616*. SPIE. doi:10.1117/12.267555210.1117/12.2675552

Lakshmaiya, N. (2023d). Experimental investigation on computational volumetric heat in real time neural pathways. *Proceedings of SPIE- The International Society for Optical Engineering, 12616.* SPIE. doi:10.1117/12.267555510.1117/12.2675555

Lakshmaiya, N. (2023e). Investigation on ultraviolet radiation of flow pattern and particles transportation in vanishing raindrops. *Proceedings of SPIE- The International Society for Optical Engineering, 12616.* SPIE. doi:10.1117/12.267555610.1117/12.2675556

Lakshmaiya, N. (2023f). Mechanical evaluation of coir/kenaf/jute laminated hybrid composites designed for geotechnical uses. *Proceedings of SPIE- The International Society for Optical Engineering, 12936.* SPIE. doi:10.1117/12.301171010.1117/12.3011710

Lakshmaiya, N. (2023g). Organic material nuts flour greens laminate preparation and mechanical characteristics of natural materials. *Proceedings of SPIE- The International Society for Optical Engineering, 12936.* SPIE. doi:10.1117/12.301171210.1117/12.3011712

Lakshmaiya, N. (2023h). Polylactic acid/hydroxyapatite/yttria-stabilized zircon synthetic nanocomposite scaffolding compression and flexural characteristics. *Proceedings of SPIE- The International Society for Optical Engineering, 12936.* SPIE. doi:10.1117/12.301171510.1117/12.3011715

Lakshmaiya, N. (2023i). Preparation and evaluation of bamboo laminated cannabis paper physico - mechanical characteristics. *Proceedings of SPIE- The International Society for Optical Engineering, 12936.* SPIE. doi:10.1117/12.301171610.1117/12.3011716

Lakshmaiya, N. (2023j). Simulating laminar induced heat capacity and heat transmission convection using Al2O3 nanofluid. *Proceedings of SPIE- The International Society for Optical Engineering, 12616.* SPIE. doi:10.1117/12.267555710.1117/12.2675557

Lakshmaiya, N., Kaliappan, S., Patil, P. P., Ganesan, V., Dhanraj, J. A., Sirisamphanwong, C., Wongwuttanasatian, T., Chowdhury, S., Channumsin, S., Channumsin, M., & Techato, K. (2022). Influence of Oil Palm Nano Filler on Interlaminar Shear and Dynamic Mechanical Properties of Flax/Epoxy-Based Hybrid Nanocomposites under Cryogenic Condition. *Coatings*, 12(11), 1675. 10.3390/coatings12111675

Loganathan, A. S., Ramachandran, V., Perumal, A. S., Dhanasekaran, S., Lakshmaiya, N., & Paramasivam, P. (2023). Framework of Transactive Energy Market Strategies for Lucrative Peer-to-Peer Energy Transactions. *Energies*, 16(1), 6. 10.3390/en16010006

Mahat, D., Niranjan, K., Naidu, C. S. K. V. R., Babu, S. B. G. T., Kumar, M. S., & Natrayan, L. (2023). AI-Driven Optimization of Supply Chain and Logistics in Mechanical Engineering. *2023 10th IEEE Uttar Pradesh Section International Conference on Electrical, Electronics and Computer Engineering, UPCON 2023.* IEEE. 10.1109/UPCON59197.2023.10434905

Malladi, A., Kaliappan, S., Natrayan, L., & Mahesh, V. (2024). Effectiveness of Thermal and Mechanical Properties of Jute Fibers under Different Chemical Treatment for Automotive Interior Trim. *SAE Technical Papers.* 10.4271/2024-01-5008

Mehta, A. K., Lanjewar, P., Murthy, D. S., Ghildiyal, P., Faldu, R., & Natrayan, L. (2023). AI & Lean Management Principles Based Pharmaceutical Manufacturing Processes. *2023 10th IEEE Uttar Pradesh Section International Conference on Electrical, Electronics and Computer Engineering, UPCON 2023.* IEEE. 10.1109/UPCON59197.2023.10434834

Nadh, V. S., Krishna, C., Natrayan, L., Kumar, K., Nitesh, K. J. N. S., Raja, G. B., & Paramasivam, P. (2021). Structural Behavior of Nanocoated Oil Palm Shell as Coarse Aggregate in Lightweight Concrete. *Journal of Nanomaterials*, 2021, 1–7. 10.1155/2021/4741296

Natrayan, L. (2023). Humidity Impact on the Material Characteristics of a Sisal Laminate: The Role of the Rapid Vibrational Method. *International Journal of Vehicle Structures and Systems*, 15(7). 10.4273/ijvss.15.7.17

Natrayan, L., Ameen, F., Chinta, N. D., Teja, N. B., Muthu, G., Kaliappan, S., Ali, S., & Vadiveloo, A. (2024). Antibacterial and dynamical behaviour of silicon nanoparticles influenced sustainable waste flax fibre-reinforced epoxy composite for biomedical application. *Green Processing and Synthesis*, 13(1), 20230214. 10.1515/gps-2023-0214

Natrayan, L., Ashok, S. K., Kaliappan, S., & Kumar, P. (2024). Effect of Stacking Sequence on Mechanical Properties of Bamboo/Bagasse Composite Fiber for Automobile Seat Cushions and Upholstery Application. *SAE Technical Papers.* 10.4271/2024-01-5013

Natrayan, L., Balaji, S., Bharathiraja, G., Kaliappan, S., Veeman, D., & Mammo, W. D. (2021). Experimental Investigation on Mechanical Properties of TiAlN Thin Films Deposited by RF Magnetron Sputtering. *Journal of Nanomaterials*, 2021, 1–7. 10.1155/2021/5943486

Natrayan, L., Chinta, N. D., Gogulamudi, B., Nadh, V. S., Muthu, G., Kaliappan, S., & Srinivas, C. (2024). Investigation on mechanical properties of the green synthesis bamboo fiber/eggshell/coconut shell powder-based hybrid biocomposites under NaOH conditions. *Green Processing and Synthesis*, 13(1), 20230185. 10.1515/gps-2023-0185

Natrayan, L., Chinta, N. D., Teja, N. B., Muthu, G., Kaliappan, S., Kirubanandan, S., & Paramasivam, P. (2024). Evaluating mechanical, thermal, and water absorption properties of biocomposites with Opuntia cladode fiber and palm flower biochar for industrial applications. *Discover Applied Sciences*, 6(2), 30. 10.1007/s42452-024-05660-4

Natrayan, L., & De Poures, M. V. (2023a). Experimental investigations of heat ageing with chemical modification of hemp fiber elastic characteristics. *Proceedings of SPIE- The International Society for Optical Engineering, 12936*. SPIE. 10.1117/12.3011708

Natrayan, L., & De Poures, M. V. (2023b). Influence of gasoline on high speed evaporation gasoline sprays: a large-eddy model of sprayer a with different fuels. *Proceedings of SPIE- The International Society for Optical Engineering, 12936*. SPIE. 10.1117/12.3011709

Natrayan, L., Janardhan, G., Nadh, V. S., Srinivas, C., Kaliappan, S., & Velmurugan, G. (2024). Eco-friendly zinc oxide nanoparticles from Moringa oleifera leaf extract for photocatalytic and antibacterial applications. *Clean Technologies and Environmental Policy*. 10.1007/s10098-024-02814-1

Natrayan, L., Jayakrishna, M., Shanker, K., Muthu, G., Kaliappan, S., & Velmurugan, G. (2024). Green synthesis of silver nanoparticles using lawsonia inermis for enhanced degradation of organic pollutants in wastewater treatment. *Global NEST Journal*, 26(3). 10.30955/gnj.005463

Natrayan, L., & Kaliappan, S. (2023). Mechanical Assessment of Carbon-Luffa Hybrid Composites for Automotive Applications. *SAE Technical Papers*. 10.4271/2023-01-5070

Natrayan, L., Kaliappan, S., Balaji, N., & Mahesh, V. (2024). Dynamic Mechanical and Thermal Properties of Polymer-Coated Jute Fibers for Enhanced Automotive Parts. *SAE Technical Papers*. 10.4271/2024-01-5019

Natrayan, L., Kaliappan, S., & Pundir, S. (2023). Control and Monitoring of a Quadcopter in Border Areas Using Embedded System. *Proceedings of the 4th International Conference on Smart Electronics and Communication, ICOSEC 2023*. IEEE. 10.1109/ICOSEC58147.2023.10276196

Natrayan, L., Kaliappan, S., Saravanan, A., Vickram, A. S., Pravin, P., Abbas, M., Ahamed Saleel, C., Alwetaishi, M., & Saleem, M. S. M. (2023). Recyclability and catalytic characteristics of copper oxide nanoparticles derived from bougainvillea plant flower extract for biomedical application. *Green Processing and Synthesis*, 12(1), 20230030. 10.1515/gps-2023-0030

Natrayan, L., & Kumar, M. S. (2019). Influence of silicon carbide on tribological behaviour of AA2024/Al2O3/SiC/Gr hybrid metal matrix squeeze cast composite using Taguchi technique. *Materials Research Express*, 6(12), 1265f9. 10.1088/2053-1591/ab676d

Natrayan, L., & Kumar, M. S. (2020). Optimization of wear behaviour on AA6061/Al2O3/SiC metal matrix composite using squeeze casting technique-Statistical analysis. *Materials Today: Proceedings*, 27, 306–310. 10.1016/j.matpr.2019.11.038

Natrayan, L., & Merneedi, A. (2020). Experimental investigation on wear behaviour of bio-waste reinforced fusion fiber composite laminate under various conditions. *Materials Today: Proceedings*, 37(Part 2), 1486–1490. 10.1016/j.matpr.2020.07.108

Natrayan, L., & Richard, T. (2023a). Experimental investigations of bagasse ash strands featuring variable surface influence on polypropylene based polymer composites. *Proceedings of SPIE- The International Society for Optical Engineering, 12936*. 10.1117/12.3011691

Natrayan, L., & Richard, T. (2023b). Organo modified nanocomposites terephthalic acid polymers temperature and microstructural characteristics. *Proceedings of SPIE- The International Society for Optical Engineering, 12936*. SPIE. 10.1117/12.3011863

Natrayan, L., Sakthi Shunmuga Sundaram, P., & Elumalai, J. (2019). Analyzing the uterine physiological with mmg signals using svm. *International Journal of Pharmaceutical Research*, 11(2). 10.31838/ijpr/2019.11.02.009

Natrayan, L., Senthil Kumar, M., & Chaudhari, M. (2020). Optimization of squeeze casting process parameters to investigate the mechanical properties of AA6061/Al2O3/SiC hybrid metal matrix composites by Taguchi and Anova approach. In *Advances in Intelligent Systems and Computing* (*Vol. 949*). 10.1007/978-981-13-8196-6_35

Natrayan, L., Senthil Kumar, M., & Palanikumar, K. (2018). Optimization of squeeze cast process parameters on mechanical properties of Al2O3/SiC reinforced hybrid metal matrix composites using taguchi technique. *Materials Research Express*, 5(6), 066516. 10.1088/2053-1591/aac873

Natrayan, L., Sivaprakash, V., & Santhosh, M. S. (2018). Mechanical, microstructure and wear behavior of the material aa6061 reinforced sic with different leaf ashes using advanced stir casting method. *International Journal of Engineering and Advanced Technology*.

Niveditha, V. R., & Rajakumar, P. S. (2020). Pervasive computing in the context of COVID-19 prediction with AI-based algorithms. *International Journal of Pervasive Computing and Communications*, 16(5). 10.1108/IJPCC-07-2020-0082

Palaniyappan, S., Veeman, D., Sivakumar, N. K., & Natrayan, L. (2022). Development and optimization of lattice structure on the walnut shell reinforced PLA composite for the tensile strength and dimensional error properties. *Structures*, 45, 163–178. 10.1016/j.istruc.2022.09.023

Pandian, A., Kaliappan, S., Natrayan, L., & Reddy, V. (2024). Analyzing the Moisture and Chemical Retention Behavior of Flax Fiber-Ceramic Hybrid Composites for Automotive Underbody Shields. *SAE Technical Papers*. 10.4271/2024-01-5006

Prabagar, S., Al-Jiboory, A. K., Nair, P. S., Mandal, P., Garse, K. M., & Natrayan, L. (2023). Artificial Intelligence-Based Control Strategies for Unmanned Aerial Vehicles. *2023 10th IEEE Uttar Pradesh Section International Conference on Electrical, Electronics and Computer Engineering, UPCON 2023*. IEEE. 10.1109/UPCON59197.2023.10434918

Pragadish, N., Kaliappan, S., Subramanian, M., Natrayan, L., Satish Prakash, K., Subbiah, R., & Kumar, T. C. A. (2023). Optimization of cardanol oil dielectric-activated EDM process parameters in machining of silicon steel. *Biomass Conversion and Biorefinery*, 13(15), 14087–14096. 10.1007/s13399-021-02268-1

Ragumadhavan, R., Sateesh Kumar, D., Charyulu Rompicharla, L. N., Dhondiya, S. A., Kaliappan, S., & Natrayan, L. (2023). Design and Development of Light Communication Systems Using Modulation Techniques. *7th International Conference on Electronics, Communication and Aerospace Technology, ICECA 2023 - Proceedings*. IEEE. 10.1109/ICECA58529.2023.10395831

Rajasekaran, S., & Natrayan, L. (2023a). Estimation of corrective and preventive action on trend end plug-based machining activities using manual and failure mode with effects analysis. *Proceedings of SPIE- The International Society for Optical Engineering, 12936*. IEEE. 10.1117/12.3011698

Rajasekaran, S., & Natrayan, L. (2023b). Evaluation of occurrence number and communication based on FMEA operations in product development. *Proceedings of SPIE- The International Society for Optical Engineering, 12936*. IEEE. 10.1117/12.3011702

Ramesh, C., Vijayakumar, M., Alshahrani, S., Navaneethakrishnan, G., Palanisamy, R., Natrayan, L., Saleel, C. A., Afzal, A., Shaik, S., & Panchal, H. (2022). Performance enhancement of selective layer coated on solar absorber panel with reflector for water heater by response surface method: A case study. *Case Studies in Thermal Engineering*, 36, 102093. 10.1016/j.csite.2022.102093

Reddy, P. N., Umaeswari, P., Natrayan, L., & Choudhary, A. (2023). Development of Programmed Autonomous Electric Heavy Vehicle: An Application of IoT. *Proceedings of the 2023 2nd International Conference on Electronics and Renewable Systems, ICEARS 2023*. IEEE. 10.1109/ICEARS56392.2023.10085492

Saadh, M. J., Almoyad, M. A. A., Arellano, M. T. C., Maaliw, R. R. III, Castillo-Acobo, R. Y., Jalal, S. S., Gandla, K., Obaid, M., Abdulwahed, A. J., Ibrahem, A. A., Sârbu, I., Juyal, A., Lakshmaiya, N., & Akhavan-Sigari, R. (2023). Long non-coding RNAs: Controversial roles in drug resistance of solid tumors mediated by autophagy. *Cancer Chemotherapy and Pharmacology*, 92(6), 439–453. 10.1007/s00280-023-04582-z37768333

Sai, S. A., Venkatesh, S. N., Dhanasekaran, S., Balaji, P. A., Sugumaran, V., Lakshmaiya, N., & Paramasivam, P. (2023). Transfer Learning Based Fault Detection for Suspension System Using Vibrational Analysis and Radar Plots. *Machines*, 11(8), 778. 10.3390/machines11080778

Sasi, J. P., Nidhi Pandagre, K., Royappa, A., Walke, S., Pavithra, G., & Natrayan, L. (2023). Deep Learning Techniques for Autonomous Navigation of Underwater Robots. *2023 10th IEEE Uttar Pradesh Section International Conference on Electrical, Electronics and Computer Engineering, UPCON 2023*. IEEE. 10.1109/UPCON59197.2023.10434865

Sathish, T., Natrayan, L., Prasad Jones Christydass, S., Sivananthan, S., Kamalakannan, R., Vijayan, V., & Paramasivam, P. (2022). Experimental Investigation on Tribological Behaviour of AA6066: HSS-Cu Hybrid Composite in Dry Sliding Condition. *Advances in Materials Science and Engineering*, 2022, 1–9. 10.1155/2022/9349847

Sathish, T., Palani, K., Natrayan, L., Merneedi, A., de Poures, M. V., & Singaravelu, D. K. (2021). Synthesis and characterization of polypropylene/ramie fiber with hemp fiber and coir fiber natural biopolymer composite for biomedical application. *International Journal of Polymer Science*, 2021, 1–8. 10.1155/2021/2462873

Selvi, S., Mohanraj, M., Duraipandy, P., Kaliappan, S., Natrayan, L., & Vinayagam, N. (2023). Optimization of Solar Panel Orientation for Maximum Energy Efficiency. *Proceedings of the 4th International Conference on Smart Electronics and Communication, ICOSEC 2023*. IEEE. 10.1109/ICOSEC58147.2023.10276287

Sendrayaperumal, A., Mahapatra, S., Parida, S. S., Surana, K., Balamurugan, P., Natrayan, L., & Paramasivam, P. (2021). Energy Auditing for Efficient Planning and Implementation in Commercial and Residential Buildings. *Advances in Civil Engineering*, 2021, 1–10. 10.1155/2021/1908568

Siddiqui, E., Siddique, M., Safeer Pasha, M., Boyapati, P., Pavithra, G., & Natrayan, L. (2023). AI and ML for Enhancing Crop Yield and Resource Efficiency in Agriculture. *2023 10th IEEE Uttar Pradesh Section International Conference on Electrical, Electronics and Computer Engineering, UPCON 2023*. IEEE. 10.1109/UPCON59197.2023.10434493

Singh, M. (2017). An experimental investigation on mechanical behaviour of siCp reinforced Al 6061 MMC using squeeze casting process. *International Journal of Mechanical and Production Engineering Research and Development*, 7(6). 10.24247/ijmperddec201774

Singh, P., Mahor, V., Lakshmaiya, N., Shanker, K., Kaliappan, S., Muthukannan, M., & Rajendran, G. (2024). Prediction of Groundwater Contamination in an Open Landfill Area Using a Novel Hybrid Clustering Based AI Model. *Environment Protection Engineering*, 50(1). 10.37190/epe240106

Sukumaran, C., Indhumathi, K., Balamurugan, P., Ambilwade, R. P., Sunthari, P. M., & Natrayan, L. (2023). The Role of AI in Biochips for Early Disease Detection. *Proceedings - International Conference on Technological Advancements in Computational Sciences, ICTACS 2023*. IEEE. 10.1109/ICTACS59847.2023.10390419

Suman, T., Kaliappan, S., Natrayan, L., & Dobhal, D. C. (2023). IoT based Social Device Network with Cloud Computing Architecture. *Proceedings of the 2023 2nd International Conference on Electronics and Renewable Systems, ICEARS 2023*. 10.1109/ICEARS56392.2023.10085574

Thakre, S., Pandhare, A., Malwe, P. D., Gupta, N., Kothare, C., Magade, P. B., Patel, A., Meena, R. S., Veza, I., Natrayan, L., & Panchal, H. (2023). Heat transfer and pressure drop analysis of a microchannel heat sink using nanofluids for energy applications. *Kerntechnik*, 88(5), 543–555. 10.1515/kern-2023-0034

Vaishali, K. R., Rammohan, S. R., Natrayan, L., Usha, D., & Niveditha, V. R. (2021). Guided container selection for data streaming through neural learning in cloud. *International Journal of Systems Assurance Engineering and Management*. 10.1007/s13198-021-01124-9

Velumayil, R., Gnanakumar, G., Natrayan, L., Chinta, N. D., & Kaliappan, S. (2023). Bifunctional Aluminum Oxide/Carbon Fiber/Epoxy Nanocomposites Preparation and Evaluation. *International Journal of Vehicle Structures and Systems*, 15(7). 10.4273/ijvss.15.7.18

Venkatesh, R., Manivannan, S., Kaliappan, S., Socrates, S., Sekar, S., Patil, P. P., Natrayan, L., & Bayu, M. B. (2022). Influence of Different Frequency Pulse on Weld Bead Phase Ratio in Gas Tungsten Arc Welding by Ferritic Stainless Steel AISI-409L. *Journal of Nanomaterials*, 2022, 1–11. 10.1155/2022/9530499

Vijayakumar, M., & Shreeraj Nair, P. G Tilak Babu, S. B., Mahender, K., Venkateswaran, T. S., & Natrayan, L. (2023). Intelligent Systems For Predictive Maintenance In Industrial IoT. *2023 10th IEEE Uttar Pradesh Section International Conference on Electrical, Electronics and Computer Engineering, UPCON 2023*. IEEE. 10.1109/UPCON59197.2023.10434814

Vijayakumar, M. D., Surendhar, G. J., Natrayan, L., Patil, P. P., Ram, P. M. B., & Paramasivam, P. (2022). Evolution and Recent Scenario of Nanotechnology in Agriculture and Food Industries. *Journal of Nanomaterials*, 2022, 1–17. 10.1155/2022/1280411

Chapter 7
Optimizing Shot Peening Machines for Compact Components

V. Gopal
KCG College of Technology, India

R. Bharanidaran
Vellore Institute of Technology, India

T. Mothilal
KCG College of Technology, India

M. Vignesh Kumar
KCG College of Technology, India

ABSTRACT

Optimizing shot peening is a cold-working process employed to generate a compressive residual stress layer and modify the mechanical properties of metals. It involves impacting a surface with a shot with sufficient force to induce plastic deformation. Peening a surface spread it plastically, leading to alterations in its mechanical properties. Its primary application is to prevent the propagation of microcracks from the surface. Such cracks do not propagate in a material that is under compressive stress. Optimizing shot peening can induce such stress on the surface. In this process, shots are accelerated using centrifugal force generated by a rotating impeller, which directs the shots to impact the surface to be peened. Media choices include spherical cast steel shots, ceramic beads, or conditioned cut wire. Peening necessitates well-graded shots with consistent hardness, diameter, and shape, and a mechanism for removing optimized shot fragments throughout

DOI: 10.4018/979-8-3693-3314-3.ch007

the process is desirable.

INTRODUCTION

The shot peening process significantly influences the microstructure and mechanical properties of metals. Shot peening refines the surface grains into nanocrystals, leading to increased surface hardness, tensile strength, and enhanced corrosion resistance (Pan.H.,2023). It is a process of cold working a part to enhance its resistance to metal fatigue and certain forms of stress corrosion. It entails bombarding the surface of the desired part with metallic (usually steel), glass, or ceramic beads with sufficient force to create dents on the surface (P.S.G College, 2011). As depicted in Figure 1 (Kirk, David., 2009 and Haverty, Donncha and Brendan Kennedy, 2009), optimizing shot peening induces plastic deformations on the surface of the peened part. This process alleviates surface tensile stresses that may have been introduced during part machining. More importantly, it introduces beneficial compressive residual stress, thereby fortifying the surface of the part. Additionally, shot peening is occasionally employed to manipulate or modify the shape of thin parts.

Figure 1. Principle of shot peening

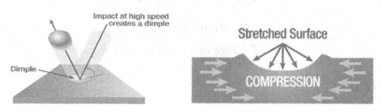

Compressive residual stress refers to any stress remaining in a material after the source of the stress has been removed. It occurs when the shot creates dimples in the surface by displacing the material sideways. This compression is generated by the transfer of kinetic energy from a moving mass (shot particle) into the material's surface, capable of undergoing plastic deformation. Atoms just below the surface resist this displacement, leading to compressive lateral stress aimed at restoring the surface to its original state. This stress contributes to surface hardening and prevents crack formation and propagation.

The depth and magnitude of the compressive residual stress layer depend on various factors, including shot type, intensity, coverage, and part hardness. The depth of the compressive layer can vary, from 0.05 mm for light peening applications to up to 0.875 mm for high intensity peening of soft materials. The maximum compressive residual stress, typically ranging between 600 and 1500 MPa, occurs below the surface. Harder materials and higher peening intensities result in greater maximum residual stresses. Compressive residual stress remains on the surface after removing the acting load, thereby increasing the material's hardness.

Shot peening parameters indeed play a crucial role in determining the effectiveness of the process. The shot size, type, peening intensity, and coverage are key factors influencing the residual stress field, surface roughness, and overall surface properties of the treated material (Gakias, C, 2022). Studies have shown that shot size distribution, including the variation in diameter and the mixture of new and worn shots, can significantly impact the residual stress field, with larger shot sizes causing wider stress profiles and deeper peak stresses. Peening intensity, influenced by parameters like shot diameter, air pressure, and shot flow rate, directly affects the compressive residual stress and surface hardness, with a linear relationship observed between intensity and these parameters. Additionally, coverage during shot peening can affect the distribution of residual stress, with an optimal coverage percentage identified for maximizing the strengthening effect on the material's surface (Chavarat, 2023).

There are three main types of shots such as Glass or ceramic beads, Steel shots, Cut wire shots. Glass and ceramic beads are commonly used for light peening applications, with glass beads specified by mean diameter in microns divided by 10, like AGB-30 being 300 microns in diameter. Ceramic shots, being harder than glass beads, offer greater reusability, making them a preferred choice in some cases (Cabrero,2021). The process of shot peening, whether with glass microspheres or ceramic shots, aims to improve fatigue strength, reduce surface roughness, increase hardness, and introduce beneficial residual compressive stresses into metallic components, enhancing their performance and durability.

Steel shot is the most common material used for shot peening. It can come in a variety of sizes and hardness. This value is given in ten thousandths of an inch. Thus, for s-230 shot, the mesh that retains 85% has openings that are 0.0230" wide. Because of this, the average diameter of the shot is typically equal to one mesh size larger. Steel shot can have 4 different Rockwell C hardness classifications: S (4051), M (47-56), L (54-61), H ($\geq$ 60). M and L are the most common. Cut wire shot is often preferred over steel shot because it lasts longer, generates less dust, and has a greater uniformity in size. It is made by taking wire of the desired type and cutting it in lengths that are approximately equal to the wire diameter. Cut wire shot can be bought as-is (with sharp edges), conditioned (rounded edges), and special conditioned (nearly spherical). It is also possible to get cut wire shot made from different metals such as zinc or copper.

Shot peening intensity is determined by the amount of energy, in the form of compressive residual stress, deposited onto an industry-standard test sample known as the Almen strip (Gopal, V., and D.M.R. Raja, 2021). When one side of an Almen strip is penned, the surface stresses cause the strip to arc. To ascertain the intensity, the arc height is plotted against the time spent peening. The intensity is defined as the point on the curve where doubling the peening time results in a 10% increase in height. To measure intensity for determining shot intensity, four or more Almen strips of the appropriate type are peened with successively longer times. The last strip should have an arc height that is less than 10% greater than a strip peened for half that amount of time. Once enough strips have been peened, a best-fit curve should be drawn for the data points. This can be easily accomplished with spreadsheets. The intensity is defined as the point on the curve where doubling the peening time results in a 10% increase in the arc height. This point can be easily determined using formulas in the spreadsheet with the best-fit curve. The time it takes to reach this intensity is called the saturation time. CAE enables simulation and analysis of the micro gripper (Gopal, A., 2021) mechanical properties, response to various loads, and potential failure points.

The shot peening machine used for optimizing shot peening comprises the following mild steel components (Venkatesan, A., 2017): a hopper through which the shots are poured, a stirrer that moves the shots from the hopper and directs them through the control gauge, the position of which determines the coverage area. From the control cage, the shots enter the impeller blade, which rotates at a speed of around 2700 rpm. These shots, now at a very high velocity, strike the material to be peened. A pillow block, similar to a Plummer block, is mounted to provide support to the shaft connecting the motor and the impeller.

SOLID MODEL OF SHOT PEENING MACHINE

The solid model of various components in shot peening machine is carried out and illustrated below. The model of impeller blades leaves is fixed at 90°. The disc is made of mild steel plate. The leaves are also made of mild steel as shown in figure 2.

Figure 2. 3D model of impeller

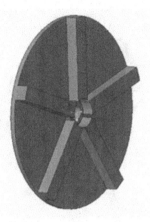

The function of shots are carried through the impellor blade. The impeller blade is connected to the shaft by a keyway. The impeller plays a major role in the setup.

The control cage is a hollow cylinder with a square shot on one side.It is the immovable part of the setup.The control cage is fixed through bolt and nut such that it can be adjusted in fig 3

Figure 3. 3D model of control cage

The position of the control cage decides the coverage area. The shots are flowed through the Hooper and it moves to the stirrer.Stirrer is the hollow cylinder which has filleted slots in it.

Figure 4. 3D model of stirrer

In fig 4 as the stirrer stirs the shots falling into it. In addition, it also directs these shots into the control cage. Casting round circular tube made of mild steel is made. It is covered by two mild steel plates on both sides. The circular plate is welded along the base for support. The casing is the immovable part in the setup. A slot is made in the casing for the shots to strike the work piece. A shaft from the motor is extended to the casing as shown in fig 5.

Figure 5. 3D model of casing

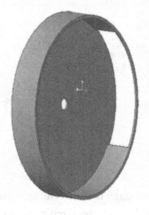

Pillow block is mounted on the shaft to provide support. A pillow block, also known as a Plummer block or bearing housing, is a pedestal used to provide support for a rotating shaft with the help of compatible bearings & various accessories. Pillow blocks are usually referred to the housings which have a bearing fitted into them and thus the user need not purchase the bearings separately. These differ from "Plummer blocks" which are bearing housing supplied without any bearings and are usually meant for higher load ratings and corrosive industrial environments. The fundamental application of both types is the same which is to mount bearings safely enabling their outer ring to be stationary while allowing rotation of the inner ring. Various seals are provided to prevent dust and other contaminants from entering the housing. High speed motor is required for this process. The motor is 0.5HP power and rotates at 2790 rpm in fig 6. The motor runs the whole setup.

Figure 6. 3D model of motor

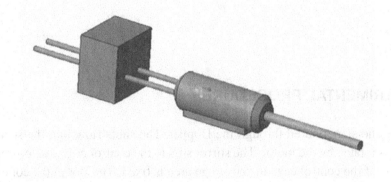

In fig 7 stepped Shaft is used to mount the stirrer and Impeller Blade. This extended shaft is used because the motor shaft is too small for the mountings. One side of the shaft is attached to the motor shaft and other side has mountings on it. The motor side is attached using threeAllen screws.

Figure 7. 3D model of shaft

The shots are poured into the Hooper in shown in figure 8. From the Hooper the shots enter into stirrer.

Figure 8. 3D model of hooper

EXPERIMENTAL PROCEDURE

The shots are poured through the Hopper. The shots flow into the stirrer. The stirrer is rotated by the motor. The stirrer stirs to the control cage. According to the position of the control cage the coverage area is fixed. The slot in the control cage must be at the gap between the two blades. The shot then strikes the blade and delivers to the fixed coverage area where the work piece is kept. When the shots strike the work piece, a residual compressive stress is induced over the top surface of the work piece. So, if tensile stress is induced in that surface of the work piece, it gets neutralized due to the residual compressive stress already induced in it. Thus, shot peening process is done in a portable way for smaller components.

DESIGN CALCULATIONS

DIAMETER OF DISC:
$V = (3.14*d*N)/(60*1000)$
$40 = (3.14*d*2800)/(60*1000)$
$d = 260mm$
FORCE APPLIED BY A SHOT:
(Kinetic energy of a shot) = (Strain energy created by the shot)
$\frac{1}{2}(mv^2) = (P*\delta)$
$\frac{1}{2}*(0.001)*(40)^2 = (P)*(0.5)$
$P = 1.6\,N$

$P \approx 2\,N$

FORCE EXERTED BY THE IMPELLER:

Mass of impeller = Density*Volume

m = ρ [volume of disc + 4(volume of blades)

m = ρ*[{(πd2t)/4} + {4(l*b*t)}]

m=7850*10-9 [{(3.14*2602*5)/4} + {4(50*5*100)}]

m=2.86kg ≈ 3kg

Centrifugal Force F = mrω²

F= mr [(2πN)/60]2

$F = 3*130*[(2\pi*2800)/60]^2$

F= 33.5 MN

Design calculations for shot peening machines determine the velocity of the peening media and the corresponding force exerted on the material. The velocity of the shot significantly influences the residual stress distribution: higher velocities increase compressive residual stress and surface hardness. However, excessive velocity can cause surface damage. Therefore, finding an optimal shot velocity is crucial to balance enhancing hardness and maintaining surface integrity. The optimal value is determined through trial and error method.

The assembly of the shot peening machine comprises several components inter-connected to form a functional unit. The motor responsible for driving the machine is securely mounted onto a shaft using bolts and nuts, while the motor shaft is connected to a larger shaft via Allen screws. A circular plate is welded to the casing, serving as a mounting point for various rotating parts. These rotating parts include a disc and a stirrer, both attached to the extended shaft using Allen screws. To ensure proper rotation, a keyway is milled through the shaft, providing a secure fit for the rotating components. Additionally, a counterbore is drilled through the shaft, facilitating the attachment of the disc with another Allen screw. The assembly also includes a control cage threaded along with the hopper, contributing to the operational control of the machine. Furthermore, the covering part of the casing is screwed onto the fixed casing part, enclosing the internal components. Within this enclosed space, a workpiece chamber made of sheet metal is placed, providing a controlled environment for shot peening operations. This comprehensive assembly design ensures the stability, functionality, and safety of the shot peening machine, enabling efficient surface treatment processes while maintaining ease of operation and maintenance. Thus, the Shot peening Machine is assembled design concept in fig 9.

Figure 9. 3D Model of shot peening equipment

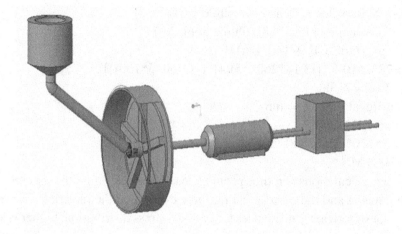

TEST RESULTS AND DISCUSSIONS

The material we have chosen to increase the hardness of the material is EN 24. EN 24 steel stands out as a through-hardening alloy steel renowned for its superb machinability in the "T" condition. Widely utilized in a myriad of applications, EN 24 steel finds its place in heavy-duty shafts, gears, studs, and bolts, owing to its remarkable hardness falling within the range of 248 to 302 HB (316 HV). This material offers not only ease of machining but also the potential for further surface hardening through induction or nitriding processes, resulting in components with heightened wear resistance.

Beyond its machinability and surface hardening capabilities, EN 24 steel boasts a formidable combination of mechanical properties that make it highly sought after in engineering applications. With a tensile strength that impresses, this steel demonstrates exceptional shock resistance, ductility, and wear resistance, ensuring longevity and reliability in demanding operational environments.

One of the standout features of EN 24 steel is its ability to maintain its impressive impact properties even at low temperatures, rendering it particularly suitable for use in harsh offshore environments where exposure to extreme conditions is commonplace. The designation "EN" in EN 24 steel stands for Euro Norms, indicating its compliance with European standards. This adherence to established norms underscores the material's reliability and consistency, providing engineers and manufacturers with confidence in its performance and suitability for a wide range of applications. EN 24 steel emerges as a versatile and dependable material in the realm of engineering steels. It's through-hardening nature, coupled with excellent machinability and surface hardening potential, makes it a preferred choice for critical components subjected to high mechanical stresses and wear. Whether in heavy-duty machinery or challenging offshore environments, EN 24 steel delivers the necessary combination of strength, durability, and performance to meet the most demanding requirements.

APPLICATIONS

EN 24 steel is widely utilized in the manufacturing of heavy equipment such as locomotives, cranes, rolling mills, and coal cutting machinery. Additionally, it serves in critical roles in automobile components, including main shafts, axles, connecting rod bolts, leaf springs for suspension, differential shafts, power transmission slide gears, and cams. Hardness stands as a pivotal material property, embodying a material's resistance to indentation and assessed by measuring the permanent depth of the indentation (Kirk, David., 2009 and Haverty, Donncha and Brendan Kennedy, 2009). The Vickers Hardness Test Method, primarily applied to small parts, thin sections, or case depth work, emerges as an invaluable tool for evaluating a diverse array of materials, contingent upon the careful preparation of test samples. Employing a square base pyramid-shaped diamond, this micro hardness test method operates within the Vickers Scale, employing loads ranging from a few grams to several kilograms. The material's hardness is quantified by the HV value (Gopal, V., and D.M.R. Raja, 2021). Depicted in Figure 10, the Vickers hardness test setup and procedure unveil the intricate methodology underlying this testing approach. Renowned for its versatility and precision, the Vickers method ensures accurate assessments of material hardness across various industrial applications, safeguarding optimal performance and durability of components amid challenging operational conditions. By comprehensively understanding and characterizing hardness properties, engineers and manufacturers can make informed decisions regarding material selection and process optimization, ultimately contributing to the reliability and longevity of critical machinery and automotive components. As industries continue to demand high-performance materials capable of withstanding harsh environments and heavy loads, the importance of robust hardness testing methodologies like the Vickers method remains paramount in ensuring product quality and operational integrity.

Figure 10. Vickers hardness machine

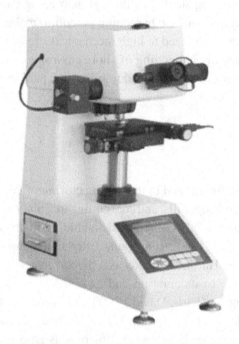

Test Report No: MME/TR/PSP/101035/15-16
Lab Ref. No.: 1035.
No. Of Samples: 1 Samples.
Test Required: Hardness test.
Test Report
Hardness:
Material tested: EN 24

Figure 11. Hardness value before and after peening

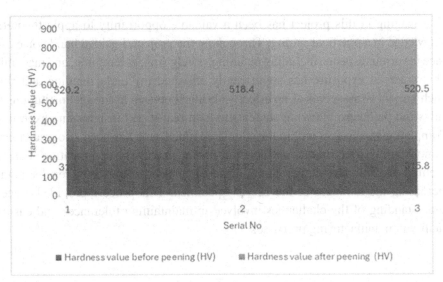

Fig 11 shows the comparison of the hardness values before and after peening for three different samples. Before peening, the hardness values range from 314.2 to 316 HV (Hardness Value). After peening, the hardness values notably increase, ranging from 518.4 to 520.5 HV. This significant increase in hardness indicates the effectiveness of the peening process in enhancing the mechanical properties of the materials.

Several mechanisms contribute to the increase in hardness following peening. Firstly, the process induces plastic deformation on the surface layer of the material, resulting in a relocation of the crystal structure and the formation of dislocations and sub-grain boundaries, which enhance hardness through cold working. Additionally, peening leads to grain refinement, as the impact causes the reduction of grain size, thereby strengthening the material through grain boundary effects. Residual compressive stresses are generated on the material's surface during peening, which counteract applied tensile stresses, improving resistance to fatigue and stress corrosion cracking. Lastly, the repeated plastic deformation caused by peening increases dislocation density, leading to work hardening and further contributing to hardness enhancement. These combined effects of peening increase the hardness, making it a valuable technique for enhancing the mechanical properties of materials.

CONCLUSION

Engaging in this project has been a valuable opportunity to apply theoretical knowledge in a practical setting. Throughout the project, I gained hands-on experience in various aspects, including planning, purchasing, assembling, and machining. This practical exposure has significantly enriched my understanding and skills. Such project work serves as an effective bridge between academic institutions and industrial practices, allowing students to gain real-world insights and experience. Completing the project within the stipulated time frame has been a source of pride, demonstrating effective task and deadline management. The optimization of the shot peening machine for smaller components has yielded satisfactory results, notably increasing the hardness of the EN 24 specimen. This process provided a deeper understanding of the challenges involved in maintaining tolerances and ensuring quality in manufacturing processes.

REFERENCES

Cabrero, J. Beaudonnet, Anne-Laure., Boussant, Roux, Yves, Leon, Marcel., Levy, Benjamin, Gilbert, Robert. (2021). Shot-peening powder. *Patent No: 11951592*.

Chavarat, Jarungvittayakon., Anak, Khantachawana., Paphon, Sa-ngasoongsong. (2023). The Effect of Particle Type and Size on CoCr Surface Properties by Fine-Particle Shot Peening. *Applied Sciences (Basel, Switzerland)*, 13(9).

College, P. S. G. (2011). *Design Data Book for engineers*. Kalaikathirachchaagam.

Fuchs, H. O. (1974). *Shot peening stress profiles*. Publication. Metal Improvement Company Inc.

Gakias, C., Maliaris, G., & Savaidis, G. (2022). Investigation of the Shot Size Effect on Residual Stresses through a 2D FEM Model of the Shot Peening Process. *Metals*, 12(6), 956. 10.3390/met12060956

Gopal, V., & Raja, D. M. R. (2021). Mechanical Behaviour of Al7075 Hybrid Composites Developed through Squeeze Casting. *International Journal of Vehicle Structures and Systems*, 13(3), 314–318. 10.4273/ijvss.13.3.14

(2021). Gopal. V., M. Alphin, and R. Bharanidaran. Design of Compliant Mechanism Microgripper Utilizing the Hoekens Straight Line Mechanism (2021). *Journal of Testing and Evaluation*, 49(3), 1599–1612.

Haverty, D., & Kennedy, B. (2009). *Shot Peening: A Powerful Surface Coating Tool for Biomedical Implants*. The Shot Peener, Electronics, Inc.

Joseph Edward Shigley (2014). *Theory of machines and mechanism*. Tata McGraw Hill Education pvt.

Kirk, D. (2009). *Non-Uniformity of Shot Peening Coverage*. Electronics, Inc.

Metals handbook. (1975). ASM Metals Park.

Pan, H. (2023). Effect of Shot Peening Strengths on Microstructure and Mechanical Properties of 316L Stainless Steel Prepared by 3D Printing. *Advanced Engineering Materials, 25* (11).

Venkatesan, A., & Gopal, V. (2017). Enhancing Wear Resistance & Fatigue Strength of Mild Steel & Aluminium Alloys Using Detonation Spray Coating. *International Journal of Engineering Research in Mechanical and Civil Engineering*, 4(2).

Chapter 8
A Comparative Analysis of Meta–Heuristic Algorithms for Optimal Configuration of Hybrid Renewable Energy Systems for Remote Villages

S. Saravanan
http://orcid.org/0000-0001-8255-2623

B.V. Raju Institute of Technology, Narsapur, India

Drakshaveni G.

BMS Institute of Technology and Management, Bangalore, India

G. Ramya

Rajalakshmi Engineering College, Thandalam, India

N. Hariprasad

St. Joseph's College of Engineering, Chennai, India

S. Gomathy

Kongu Engineering College, Perundurai, India

Ramya Maranan
http://orcid.org/0000-0003-1001-3422

Lovely Professional University, Punjab, India

ABSTRACT

In the search for sustainable and reliable energy solutions, the deployment of hybrid renewable energy systems (HRES) has developed as a promising approach mainly

DOI: 10.4018/979-8-3693-3314-3.ch008

for powering remote villages that lack access to centralized grids. The optimal configuration of these systems leads to a complex optimization problem through demanding the application of meta-heuristic algorithms to efficiently direct the massive solution space and recognize the most cost-effective and reliable setup. Numerous meta-heuristic algorithms have been engaged for this purpose. Through a comparative analysis of various meta-heuristic algorithms, particle swarm optimization helps in obtaining improved solutions. Particle swarm optimization (PSO) occurs as a powerful and effective optimization technique in addressing the complex task of determining optimal configurations for hybrid renewable energy systems positioned in remote villages.

INTRODUCTION

Hybrid renewable energy systems represent an innovative and sustainable approach to power generation by integrating multiple renewable energy sources into a single, cohesive system (Natrayan, Kaliappan, Saravanan, et al., 2023). These systems typically combine various renewable technologies, such as solar photovoltaic (PV), wind turbines, biomass, and sometimes small-scale hydropower, to optimize energy production and enhance overall system efficiency (Ragumadhavan et al., 2023). The synergy achieved in hybrid systems allows for a more reliable and consistent power supply, addressing the intermittent nature of individual renewable sources (Selvi et al., 2023). One key advantage of hybrid renewable energy systems is their ability to mitigate the limitations associated with each individual energy source (Kaliappan, Mothilal, et al., 2023; Velumayil et al., 2023). For instance, solar power production is inherently intermittent due to day-night cycles and weather variations, while wind energy is influenced by wind speed fluctuations (Chinta et al., 2023; Suman et al., 2023). By combining these sources, the system can generate electricity more consistently, thus improving overall reliability (Natrayan, Kaliappan, & Pundir, 2023). Additionally, the integration of energy storage solutions, such as batteries, allows for the storage of excess energy during peak production periods for later use during low-production or high-demand periods (Kaliappan, Natrayan, & Rajput, 2023). Energy storage is vital for confirming a continuous power supply. Hybrid systems incorporate batteries and other storage technologies to store excess energy generated during peak times (Kaliappan, Natrayan, & Garg, 2023; Natrayan & Kaliappan, 2023). This helsp in making it available during periods of low or no renewable energy assembly. Hybrid renewable energy systems are designed to be cost-effective by extracting the strengths of multiple renewable sources. The installation and maintenance costs are offset by long-term savings and reducing the environmentally harmful fossil fuels (Josphineleela, Kaliapp, et al., 2023).

The design and optimization of hybrid systems require a thorough analysis of the local climate, energy demand patterns, and available renewable resources (Natrayan, 2023). Advanced control systems and smart grid technologies play a crucial role in managing the diverse components of hybrid systems efficiently (Lakshmaiya, 2023b). These systems often employ intelligent algorithms to predict energy production from various sources and determine the optimal combination of inputs to meet the current demand while maximizing overall system performance (Saadh et al., 2023; Thakre et al., 2023). Hybrid systems decrease the reliance on traditional energy sources with minimizing greenhouse gas emissions and other harmful pollutants. This contributes increase in environmental sustainability and helps to struggle with climate change while providing clean energy solutions to remote villages (Chennai Viswanathan et al., 2023). The environmental benefits of hybrid renewable energy systems are enormous as shown in figure 1. By trusting on clean and sustainable energy sources, these systems contribute significantly to reducing greenhouse gas emissions and mitigating climate change (Chehelgerdi et al., 2023). They promote energy independence by diversifying the energy mix and reducing reliance on fossil fuels. Artificial Intelligence (AI) plays a pivotal role in enhancing the efficiency, reliability, and sustainability of hybrid renewable energy systems deployed in remote villages (Sai et al., 2023; M. Vijayakumar et al., 2023). These areas often face challenges such as intermittent power supply, limited access to traditional energy sources, and a lack of centralized infrastructure (Biradar et al., 2023; Konduri et al., 2023; Siddiqui et al., 2023). AI, when integrated into hybrid renewable energy systems, offers intelligent control and optimization mechanisms that significantly improve their overall performance (Mahat et al., 2023). AI algorithms analyze historical weather patterns, energy consumption data, and other relevant parameters to forecast energy generation and consumption patterns (Kiruba Sandou et al., 2023; Prabagar et al., 2023; Sasi et al., 2023). This enables the system to proactively manage energy resources, optimizing the utilization of solar, wind, and other renewable sources. AI-driven energy forecasting helps mitigate the inherent variability of renewable resources, ensuring a more stable and reliable power supply for remote villages (Lakshmaiya, 2023h; Natrayan & Richard, 2023a). Remote villages lack admittance to centralized power grids which helps in making them reliant on decentralized energy solutions. Hybrid renewable energy systems are compatible for such locations due to their ability to attach energy from varied sources (Sukumaran et al., 2023).

AI-based control systems facilitate real-time monitoring and adaptive management of the energy grid. Machine learning algorithms can dynamically adjust the distribution of energy based on demand fluctuations and supply availability (Loganathan et al., 2023). This not only maximizes the utilization of renewable resources but also minimizes wastage and ensures that energy is directed to where it is needed most, addressing the unique challenges faced by remote villages (Mehta et al., 2023). AI also plays a crucial role in predictive maintenance, where it anticipates and identifies potential issues in renewable energy equipment, such as solar panels and wind turbines (Lakshmaiya, 2023e; Reddy et al., 2023). By analyzing performance data and identifying patterns indicative of equipment degradation or failure, AI enables timely maintenance interventions, reducing downtime and extending the lifespan of the infrastructure (Josphineleela, Lekha, et al., 2023; Lakshmaiya, 2023d).

Figure 1. Renewable energy

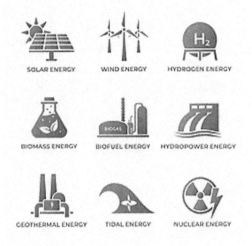

Meta-heuristic algorithms enable the search and utilization of solution spaces permitting the identification of optimal conformations for hybrid renewable energy systems. They influence iterative and probabilistic approaches to examine the best grouping of renewable energy sources, storage systems and load management strategies eventually improving the efficiency and dependability of power generation in remote villages (Lakshmaiya, 2023j, 2023a, 2023c). The choice of a meta-heuristic algorithm significantly influences the economic feasibility by directly impacting the overall system efficiency and reliability (Balamurugan et al., 2023; Kaushal et al., 2023). An algorithm that can quickly converge to optimal solutions with nominal computational resources will contribute to cost-effectiveness in the implementation of hybrid renewable energy systems for remote villages (Lakshmaiya & Murugan, 2023b; Natrayan & De Poures, 2023b). AI facilitates the integration of energy storage solutions, such as batteries, into hybrid systems. Machine learning algorithms optimize the charging and discharging cycles of energy storage, ensuring efficient use of stored energy during periods of low renewable generation. This enhances the reliability of the energy supply, particularly during adverse weather conditions or periods of low sunlight or wind (Lakshmaiya, 2023f, 2023g; Lakshmaiya & Murugan, 2023d). The integration of AI in hybrid renewable energy systems for remote villages brings a transformative impact. From predictive analytics and real-time control to predictive maintenance and energy storage optimization, AI empowers these systems to provide a sustainable, reliable, and resilient energy supply, addressing the unique challenges faced by remote communities and contributing to their socio-economic development (Natrayan & De Poures, 2023a; Rajasekaran & Natrayan, 2023b).

PROPOSED METHODOLOGY FOR HYBRID RENEWABLE ENERGY SYSTEM IN REMOTE VILLAGES

Figure 2. Proposed methodology

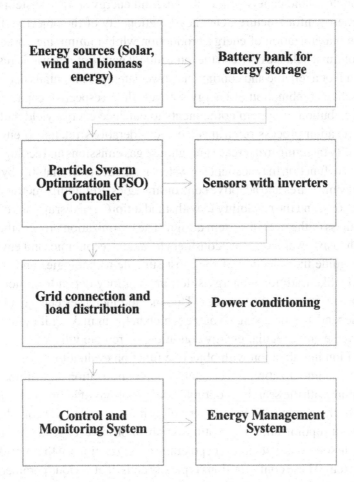

The proposed system as shown in Figure 2 involves various stages in the implementation of a hybrid renewable energy system in remote villages as described below.

The objective function describing the optimization goals

The objective function governing the optimization goals for optimal configurations of hybrid renewable energy systems serves as a crucial component in the process of designing and operating sustainable and efficient energy systemsn (Lakshmaiya, 2023i; Lakshmaiya & Murugan, 2023e; Rajasekaran & Natrayan, 2023a). This multifaceted function integrates a spectrum of considerations to balance various conflicting objectives, ultimately aiming to maximize the overall performance and economic viability of the hybrid system (Lakshmaiya & Murugan, 2023c, 2023a; Natrayan & Richard, 2023b). The objective function encapsulates the primary goals of achieving a harmonious integration of diverse renewable energy sources, such as solar photovoltaic panels, wind turbines, and energy storage systems within the broader energy infrastructure . One key functionality of the objective function involves the maximization of energy production while minimizing costs, seeking to strike an optimal balance between the intermittent nature of renewable resources and the demand for a reliable and continuous power supply. This entails determining the most effective combination of energy sources, their respective capacities, and the spatial distribution of system components to enhance energy yield and reliability. The optimization process often involves considerations related to environmental sustainability targeting to decrease greenhouse gas emissions and ecological impact. The objective function may account for system resilience and reliability by integrating redundancy measures and adaptive control strategies. Reliability metrics, downtime considerations, and the capability to withstand unforeseen disruptions contribute to the robustness of the overall system design. The optimization process thus becomes a comprehensive evaluation that considers technical, economic, and environmental factors to guide the selection of the most suitable technologies and their configurations. Unlike traditional energy solutions that may depends on non-renewable sources or single renewable sources. This method increases energy reliability and reduces dependence on a single source which helps in making it more appropriate for the diverse and irregular energy conditions in remote villages.

Population initialization with objective function evaluation

Population initialization is a crucial step in optimization algorithms, especially when dealing with the search for optimal configurations of hybrid renewable energy systems. In the context of evolutionary algorithms, such as genetic algorithms or particle swarm optimization, population initialization involves generating an initial set of candidate solutions that represent potential configurations of the hybrid renewable energy system. These configurations typically consist of various parameters, such as the capacity of solar panels, wind turbines, energy storage units, and other components. To enhance the efficiency and effectiveness of the optimization process, it is common practice to couple population initialization with objective function evaluation. The objective function serves as a metric to quantify the performance of each candidate solution in the population. In the case of hybrid renewable energy systems, the objective function is designed to capture key performance indicators, including but not limited to the overall energy output, economic feasibility, environmental impact, and system reliability. During population initialization, random or semi-random values are assigned to the parameters defining each candidate solution. This diversity in the initial population helps explore a broad solution space and avoids convergence to suboptimal solutions. Subsequently, the objective function is applied to evaluate the performance of each candidate solution, assigning a fitness score based on how well it meets the specified objectives. This evaluation process provides a basis for selecting the most promising solutions and guiding the evolutionary algorithm towards convergence to an optimal or near-optimal configuration. The iterative nature of evolutionary algorithms involves the generation of new populations through processes like crossover, mutation, and selection, continually refining the candidate solutions based on their evaluated performance. This iterative cycle continues until a stopping criterion is met, such as reaching a predefined number of generations or achieving satisfactory convergence. PSO helps to maximize energy efficiency, minimize costs and improve system performance by regulating parameters such as the size of renewable energy components and storage capabilities.

Personal best update

The personal best update in PSO plays a pivotal role in enhancing the algorithm's ability to converge towards solutions that maximize energy output while minimizing costs and environmental impact (Kaliappan & Natrayan, 2024c; Natrayan, Jayakrishna, Shanker, et al., 2024). The incorporation of personal best strategies ensures that the optimization process adapts over time, learning from previous iterations and continually refining the search for the most effective configurations (Kaliappan & Natrayan, 2024a, 2024b; Natrayan, Kaliappan, Balaji, et al., 2024). This adaptive nature enables the algorithm to navigate the complex and dynamic nature of renewable energy systems, accounting for uncertainties in energy generation and consumption patterns. The economic benefits include concentrated reliance on costly diesel generators, minimized fuel transportation costs and long-term savings on energy expenses. The optimization provided by the PSO algorithm guarantees that the system operates at peak efficiency with improving the return on investment.

The updated PSO algorithm contributes significantly to the broader goal of achieving a sustainable and resilient energy infrastructure (Malladi et al., 2024; Natrayan, Ashok, Kaliappan, et al., 2024; Pandian et al., 2024). The long-term impact of this personal best update extends beyond theoretical advancements, as it translates into practical applications for real-world energy systems. By providing utility companies, governments, and industries with optimized configurations for hybrid renewable energy systems, the updated PSO algorithm facilitates the transition towards greener and more sustainable energy practices (Kaliappan & Natrayan, 2024d; Natrayan, Chinta, Teja, et al., 2024). This breakthrough not only contributes to the reduction of greenhouse gas emissions but also enhances energy security and promotes the long-term viability of renewable resources.

Global Best Update

The key improvement in global PSO updates for HRES optimization involves the integration of machine learning techniques to enhance prediction models for renewable energy resources (Kaliappan et al., 2024; Natrayan, Janardhan, Nadh, et al., 2024). By utilizing machine learning algorithms within the PSO framework, the optimization process gains access to more accurate and reliable predictions of solar and wind patterns (Natrayan, Ameen, Chinta, et al., 2024; P. Singh et al., 2024). This enables the algorithm to make informed decisions regarding system configurations, taking into account short-term and long-term variations in renewable energy availability (Natrayan, Chinta, Gogulamudi, et al., 2024). Consequently, the hybridization of PSO with machine learning not only improves the accuracy of the optimization process but also increases the adaptability of HRES to changing environmental conditions.

Velocity and Position Update

The velocity and position updates in PSO are crucial mechanisms that drive the exploration and exploitation of the solution space. The velocity of each particle is adjusted iteratively according to its historical best position, the global best position among all particles, and the inertia of the system. The historical best position, also known as the personal best, reflects the best solution that the particle has encountered so far (Ramesh et al., 2022; Sendrayaperumal et al., 2021). The global best position is the best solution found by any particle in the entire population. These two components guide the particles to explore promising regions in the solution space. The inertia term helps to balance exploration and exploitation, determining the tendency of a particle to maintain its current direction (Hemalatha et al., 2020; Sathish et al., 2022; Sureshkumar et al., 2022). The position update is then performed based on the updated velocity, moving each particle toward a potentially better solution. This iterative process continues until a termination criterion is met, such as a maximum number of iterations or satisfactory convergence to an optimal solution (Kanimozhi et al., 2022; Nadh et al., 2021; Venkatesh et al., 2022). Through this dynamic interplay of velocity and position updates, PSO efficiently navigates the complex and high-dimensional solution space of hybrid renewable energy system configurations.

Convergence Check With Stopping Criteria

The convergence check refers to the assessment of whether the PSO algorithm has reached a sufficiently close approximation of the optimal solution (Karthick et al., 2022; Muthiya, Natrayan, Yuvaraj, et al., 2022; Vaishali et al., 2021). This is vital in preventing unnecessary computational overhead and ensuring that the algorithm does not continue searching indefinitely. Typically, convergence is determined by monitoring the fitness or objective function values of the particles over successive iterations (Natrayan & Kumar, 2020; Palaniyappan et al., 2022; Sathish et al., 2021). If these values show minimal improvement or remain within a predefined threshold, it is indicative that the algorithm has converged. Stopping criteria are essential for determining when to halt the PSO algorithm. They help strike a balance between obtaining accurate solutions and avoiding excessive computation (Muthiya, Natrayan, Kaliappan, et al., 2022; Natrayan, Senthil Kumar, et al., 2018; Natrayan, Sivaprakash, et al., 2018). Common stopping criteria include a maximum number of iterations, a specified tolerance level for the objective function, or a combination of both. The maximum number of iterations prevents the algorithm from running indefinitely, while the tolerance level ensures that the solution is accurate enough for practical purposes (Natrayan et al., 2020; Natrayan & Merneedi, 2020; Yogeshwaran et al., 2020). For instance, if the difference in objective function values between successive iterations falls below the specified tolerance, the algorithm can be terminated as it suggests that further iterations may not yield significantly better results (Natrayan & Kumar, 2019; Niveditha VR. & Rajakumar PS., 2020).

Post-processing With Result Analysis

Post-processing with result analysis plays a crucial role in Particle Swarm Optimization (PSO) for determining optimal configurations of hybrid renewable energy systems. PSO is a metaheuristic optimization algorithm inspired by the social behaviour of birds and fish (Pragadish et al., 2023; M. et al. Singh, 2017). In the context of hybrid renewable energy systems, which typically consist of multiple renewable energy sources such as solar panels, wind turbines, and energy storage devices, PSO is employed to find the optimal combination of system parameters that maximize energy output and efficiency. Result analysis in PSO for optimal configurations involves assessing the convergence behaviour of the algorithm, ensuring that it has reached a stable and reliable solution (Balaji et al., 2022).

Sensitivity Analysis

Sensitivity analysis plays a crucial role in Particle Swarm Optimization (PSO) when applied to determine optimal configurations for hybrid renewable energy systems (Natrayan et al., 2019; M. D. et al. Vijayakumar, 2022). In the context of these systems, which typically integrate multiple renewable sources like solar, wind, and possibly storage elements, sensitivity analysis helps in understanding how changes in various parameters impact the overall system performance and cost-effectiveness

(Lakshmaiya et al., 2022; Ponnusamy et al., 2022). Sensitivity analysis helps evaluate the robustness of optimal configurations by investigating their performance under dissimilarities in their input parameters and external circumstances.

In the PSO algorithm, sensitivity analysis involves evaluating the sensitivity of the objective function, which represents the system's performance or cost, to variations in the decision variables. Decision variables in the context of hybrid renewable energy systems might include the capacity of each renewable source, the size of energy storage, and other system-specific parameters (Natrayan et al., 2021; Velmurugan & Natrayan, 2023). PSO iteratively explores the solution space by adjusting these variables to find the optimal combination that minimizes or maximizes the objective function. During sensitivity analysis, PSO considers how small changes in decision variables influence the convergence towards the optimal solution. This analysis helps identify critical parameters that significantly impact the system's efficiency and cost-effectiveness. Table 1 demonstrates the sensitivity analysis.

Table 1. Sensitivity analysis

Parameters	Base value	Upper limit	Step size
Solar Panel Efficiency (%)	18	70	1
Wind Turbine Efficiency (%)	30	80	1
Diesel Generator Efficiency (%)	50	80	1
PSO Iterations	100	100	10

COMPARATIVE ANALYSIS

The performance analysis of the proposed system is done using Matlab Simulink through considering various parameters. The proposed system is compared with the existing system with various optimization techniques for assessment of the performance analysis through certain metrics as shown in Figure 3. Figure 3 shows the comparative analysis and it has proposed system results in higher performance metrics.

Figure 3. Comparative analysis

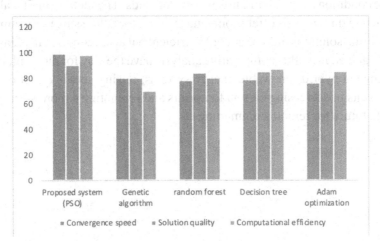

CONCLUSION

The comparative analysis of meta-heuristic algorithms for optimal configurations of hybrid renewable energy systems for remote villages presents a comprehensive investigation into the realm of sustainable energy solutions. The study systematically evaluates various meta-heuristic algorithms, shedding light on their efficacy in determining optimal configurations that provide for the unique energy needs of remote villages. The significance of this research lies in its potential to address energy poverty and promote sustainable development in underserved regions. The particular analysis of algorithms such as Genetic Algorithms, Particle Swarm Optimization, Simulated Annealing and Ant Colony Optimization not only provides a comprehensive understanding of their strengths and weaknesses but also provides valuable information into their applicability across diverse circumstances. The findings underscore the importance of leveraging meta-heuristic approaches to overcome the challenges associated with the complex optimization problem of designing hybrid renewable energy systems. The adaptability of these algorithms to different constraints, coupled with their ability to search for near-optimal solutions, positions them as valuable tools in the search for sustainable energy solutions. It becomes evident that a one-size-fits-all approach is insufficient, and the selection of an appropriate algorithm is contingent upon the specific characteristics and requirements of the target remote village. The integration of renewable energy sources, such as solar and wind, with energy storage technologies, demands a complete optimization approach that takes into account factors like geographical location, climate conditions and community energy demands. The meta-heuristic algorithms evaluated in this analysis offer promising avenues for addressing these complexities and tailoring solutions that are not only efficient but also economically feasible. The insights gained from this comparative analysis pave the way for the implementation of optimized hybrid renewable energy systems, raising socio-economic development results in decreasing carbon footprints and promoting a more sustainable and sensible future for remote communities.

REFERENCES

Balaji, N., Natrayan, L., Kaliappan, S., Patil, P. P., & Sivakumar, N. S. (2022). Annealed peanut shell biochar as potential reinforcement for aloe vera fiber-epoxy biocomposite: Mechanical, thermal conductivity, and dielectric properties. *Biomass Conversion and Biorefinery*. 10.1007/s13399-022-02650-7

Balamurugan, P., Agarwal, P., Khajuria, D., Mahapatra, D., Angalaeswari, S., Natrayan, L., & Mammo, W. D. (2023). State-Flow Control Based Multistage Constant-Current Battery Charger for Electric Two-Wheeler. *Journal of Advanced Transportation*, 2023, 1–11. 10.1155/2023/4554582

Biradar, V. S., Al-Jiboory, A. K., Sahu, G., Tilak Babu, S. B. G., Mahender, K., & Natrayan, L. (2023). Intelligent Control Systems for Industrial Automation and Robotics. *2023 10th IEEE Uttar Pradesh Section International Conference on Electrical, Electronics and Computer Engineering, UPCON 2023*. IEEE. 10.1109/UPCON59197.2023.10434927

Chehelgerdi, M., Chehelgerdi, M., Allela, O. Q. B., Pecho, R. D. C., Jayasankar, N., Rao, D. P., Thamaraikani, T., Vasanthan, M., Viktor, P., Lakshmaiya, N., Saadh, M. J., Amajd, A., Abo-Zaid, M. A., Castillo-Acobo, R. Y., Ismail, A. H., Amin, A. H., & Akhavan-Sigari, R. (2023). Progressing nanotechnology to improve targeted cancer treatment: Overcoming hurdles in its clinical implementation. *Molecular Cancer*, 22(1), 169. 10.1186/s12943-023-01865-037814270

Chennai Viswanathan, P., Venkatesh, S. N., Dhanasekaran, S., Mahanta, T. K., Sugumaran, V., Lakshmaiya, N., Paramasivam, P., & Nanjagoundenpalayam Ramasamy, S. (2023). Deep Learning for Enhanced Fault Diagnosis of Monoblock Centrifugal Pumps: Spectrogram-Based Analysis. *Machines*, 11(9), 874. 10.3390/machines11090874

Chinta, N. D., Karthikeyan, K. R., Natrayan, L., & Kaliappan, S. (2023). Pressure Induced Variations in Mode II Behaviour of Uni-Directional Kenaf Reinforced Polymers. *International Journal of Vehicle Structures and Systems*, 15(7). 10.4273/ijvss.15.7.19

Hemalatha, K., James, C., Natrayan, L., & Swamynadh, V. (2020). Analysis of RCC T-beam and prestressed concrete box girder bridges super structure under different span conditions. *Materials Today: Proceedings*, 37(Part 2), 1507–1516. 10.1016/j.matpr.2020.07.119

Josphineleela, R., Kaliapp, S., Natrayan, L., & Garg, A. (2023). Big Data Security through Privacy - Preserving Data Mining (PPDM): A Decentralization Approach. *Proceedings of the 2023 2nd International Conference on Electronics and Renewable Systems, ICEARS 2023*. IEEE. 10.1109/ICEARS56392.2023.10085646

Josphineleela, R., Lekha, D., Natrayan, L., & Purohit, K. C. (2023). Biometric Aided Intelligent Security System Built using Internet of Things. *Proceedings of the 2023 2nd International Conference on Electronics and Renewable Systems, ICEARS 2023*. IEEE. 10.1109/ICEARS56392.2023.10085572

Kaliappan, S., Mothilal, T., Natrayan, L., Pravin, P., & Olkeba, T. T. (2023). Mechanical Characterization of Friction-Stir-Welded Aluminum AA7010 Alloy with TiC Nanofiber. *Advances in Materials Science and Engineering*, 2023, 1–7. 10.1155/2023/1466963

Kaliappan, S., & Natrayan, L. (2024a). Enhancement of Mechanical and Thermal Characteristics of Automobile Parts using Flax/Epoxy-Graphene Nanofiller Composites. *SAE Technical Papers*. 10.4271/2023-01-5116

Kaliappan, S., & Natrayan, L. (2024b). Impact of Kenaf Fiber and Inorganic Nanofillers on Mechanical Properties of Epoxy-Based Nanocomposites for Sustainable Automotive Applications. *SAE Technical Papers*. 10.4271/2023-01-5115

Kaliappan, S., & Natrayan, L. (2024c). Polypropylene Composite Materials with Natural Fiber Reinforcement: An Acoustic and Mechanical Analysis for Automotive Implementations. *SAE Technical Papers*. 10.4271/2023-01-5130

Kaliappan, S., & Natrayan, L. (2024d). Revolutionizing Automotive Materials through Enhanced Mechanical Properties of Epoxy Hybrid Bio-Composites with Hemp, Kenaf, and Coconut Powder. *SAE Technical Papers*. 10.4271/2023-01-5185

Kaliappan, S., Natrayan, L., & Garg, N. (2023). Checking and Supervisory System for Calculation of Industrial Constraints using Embedded System. *Proceedings of the 4th International Conference on Smart Electronics and Communication, ICOSEC 2023*. IEEE. 10.1109/ICOSEC58147.2023.10275952

Kaliappan, S., Natrayan, L., Mohammed Ali, H., & Kumar, P. (2024). Thermal and Mechanical Properties of Abutilon indicum Fiber-Based Polyester Composites under Alkali Treatment for Automotive Sector. *SAE Technical Papers*. 10.4271/2024-01-5031

Kaliappan, S., Natrayan, L., & Rajput, A. (2023). Sentiment Analysis of News Headlines Based on Sentiment Lexicon and Deep Learning. *Proceedings of the 4th International Conference on Smart Electronics and Communication, ICOSEC 2023*. IEEE. 10.1109/ICOSEC58147.2023.10276102

Kanimozhi, G., Natrayan, L., Angalaeswari, S., & Paramasivam, P. (2022). An Effective Charger for Plug-In Hybrid Electric Vehicles (PHEV) with an Enhanced PFC Rectifier and ZVS-ZCS DC/DC High-Frequency Converter. *Journal of Advanced Transportation*, 2022, 1–14. 10.1155/2022/7840102

Karthick, M., Meikandan, M., Kaliappan, S., Karthick, M., Sekar, S., Patil, P. P., Raja, S., Natrayan, L., & Paramasivam, P. (2022). Experimental Investigation on Mechanical Properties of Glass Fiber Hybridized Natural Fiber Reinforced Penta-Layered Hybrid Polymer Composite. *International Journal of Chemical Engineering*, 2022, 1–9. 10.1155/2022/1864446

Kaushal, R. K., Arvind, R., Giri, K. K. B., Sindhu, M., Natrayan, L., & Ronald, B. (2023). Deep Learning Based Segmentation Approach for Automatic Lane Detection in Autonomous Vehicle. *International Conference on Self Sustainable Artificial Intelligence Systems, ICSSAS 2023 - Proceedings*. IEEE. 10.1109/ICSSAS57918.2023.10331835

Kiruba Sandou, D., Sunad Kumara, A. N., Choudhary, B. K., & Gurpur, S., Sarishma, Natrayan, L., & Sivaramkumar, M. (2023). Design and Implementation of Neuro-Fuzzy Control Approach for Robot's Trajectory Tracking. *7th International Conference on Electronics, Communication and Aerospace Technology, ICECA 2023 - Proceedings*. IEEE. 10.1109/ICECA58529.2023.10395675

Konduri, S., Walke, S., Kumar, A., Pavithra, G., Bhagirath Jadhav, A., & Natrayan, L. (2023). Reinforcement Learning for Multi-Robot Coordination and Cooperation in Manufacturing. *2023 10th IEEE Uttar Pradesh Section International Conference on Electrical, Electronics and Computer Engineering, UPCON 2023*. IEEE. 10.1109/UPCON59197.2023.10434651

Lakshmaiya, N. (2023b). Experimental analysis on heat transfer cube shape of two vertical surfaces during melting condition. *Proceedings of SPIE- The International Society for Optical Engineering, 12616*. SPIE. doi:10.1117/12.267555210.1117/12.2675552

Lakshmaiya, N. (2023c). Experimental analysis on heat transfer cube shape of two vertical surfaces during melting condition. *Proceedings of SPIE- The International Society for Optical Engineering, 12616*. SPIE. doi:10.1117/12.267555210.1117/12.2675552

Lakshmaiya, N. (2023d). Experimental investigation on computational volumetric heat in real time neural pathways. *Proceedings of SPIE- The International Society for Optical Engineering, 12616*. SPIE. doi:10.1117/12.267555510.1117/12.2675555

Lakshmaiya, N. (2023e). Investigation on ultraviolet radiation of flow pattern and particles transportation in vanishing raindrops. *Proceedings of SPIE- The International Society for Optical Engineering, 12616*. SPIE. doi:10.1117/12.267555610. 1117/12.2675556

Lakshmaiya, N. (2023f). Mechanical evaluation of coir/kenaf/jute laminated hybrid composites designed for geotechnical uses. *Proceedings of SPIE- The International Society for Optical Engineering, 12936*. SPIE. doi:10.1117/12.301171010.1 117/12.3011710

Lakshmaiya, N. (2023g). Organic material nuts flour greens laminate preparation and mechanical characteristics of natural materials. *Proceedings of SPIE- The International Society for Optical Engineering, 12936*. SPIE. doi:10.1117/12.30117 1210.1117/12.3011712

Lakshmaiya, N. (2023h). Polylactic acid/hydroxyapatite/yttria-stabilized zircon synthetic nanocomposite scaffolding compression and flexural characteristics. *Proceedings of SPIE- The International Society for Optical Engineering, 12936*. SPIE. doi:10.1117/12.301171510.1117/12.3011715

Lakshmaiya, N. (2023i). Preparation and evaluation of bamboo laminated cannabis paper physico - mechanical characteristics. *Proceedings of SPIE- The International Society for Optical Engineering, 12936*. SPIE. doi:10.1117/12.301171610.1 117/12.3011716

Lakshmaiya, N. (2023j). Simulating laminar induced heat capacity and heat transmission convection using Al2O3 nanofluid. *Proceedings of SPIE- The International Society for Optical Engineering, 12616*. SPIE. doi:10.1117/12.267555710. 1117/12.2675557

Lakshmaiya, N., Kaliappan, S., Patil, P. P., Ganesan, V., Dhanraj, J. A., Sirisamphanwong, C., Wongwuttanasatian, T., Chowdhury, S., Channumsin, S., Channumsin, M., & Techato, K. (2022). Influence of Oil Palm Nano Filler on Interlaminar Shear and Dynamic Mechanical Properties of Flax/Epoxy-Based Hybrid Nanocomposites under Cryogenic Condition. *Coatings*, 12(11), 1675. 10.3390/coatings12111675

Loganathan, A. S., Ramachandran, V., Perumal, A. S., Dhanasekaran, S., Lakshmaiya, N., & Paramasivam, P. (2023). Framework of Transactive Energy Market Strategies for Lucrative Peer-to-Peer Energy Transactions. *Energies*, 16(1), 6. 10.3390/en16010006

Mahat, D., Niranjan, K., Naidu, C. S. K. V. R., Babu, S. B. G. T., Kumar, M. S., & Natrayan, L. (2023). AI-Driven Optimization of Supply Chain and Logistics in Mechanical Engineering. *2023 10th IEEE Uttar Pradesh Section International Conference on Electrical, Electronics and Computer Engineering, UPCON 2023*. IEEE. 10.1109/UPCON59197.2023.10434905

Malladi, A., Kaliappan, S., Natrayan, L., & Mahesh, V. (2024). Effectiveness of Thermal and Mechanical Properties of Jute Fibers under Different Chemical Treatment for Automotive Interior Trim. *SAE Technical Papers*. 10.4271/2024-01-5008

Mehta, A. K., Lanjewar, P., Murthy, D. S., Ghildiyal, P., Faldu, R., & Natrayan, L. (2023). AI & Lean Management Principles Based Pharmaceutical Manufacturing Processes. *2023 10th IEEE Uttar Pradesh Section International Conference on Electrical, Electronics and Computer Engineering, UPCON 2023*. IEEE. 10.1109/UPCON59197.2023.10434834

Muthiya, S. J., Natrayan, L., Kaliappan, S., Patil, P. P., Naveena, B. E., Dhanraj, J. A., Subramaniam, M., & Paramasivam, P. (2022). Experimental investigation to utilize adsorption and absorption technique to reduce CO2 emissions in diesel engine exhaust using amine solutions. *Adsorption Science and Technology*, 2022, 9621423. 10.1155/2022/9621423

Muthiya, S. J., Natrayan, L., Yuvaraj, L., Subramaniam, M., Dhanraj, J. A., & Mammo, W. D. (2022). Development of Active CO_2 Emission Control for Diesel Engine Exhaust Using Amine-Based Adsorption and Absorption Technique. *Adsorption Science and Technology*, 2022, 8803585. 10.1155/2022/8803585

Nadh, V. S., Krishna, C., Natrayan, L., Kumar, K., Nitesh, K. J. N. S., Raja, G. B., & Paramasivam, P. (2021). Structural Behavior of Nanocoated Oil Palm Shell as Coarse Aggregate in Lightweight Concrete. *Journal of Nanomaterials*, 2021, 1–7. 10.1155/2021/4741296

Natrayan, L. (2023). Humidity Impact on the Material Characteristics of a Sisal Laminate: The Role of the Rapid Vibrational Method. *International Journal of Vehicle Structures and Systems*, 15(7). 10.4273/ijvss.15.7.17

Natrayan, L., Ameen, F., Chinta, N. D., Teja, N. B., Muthu, G., Kaliappan, S., Ali, S., & Vadiveloo, A. (2024). Antibacterial and dynamical behaviour of silicon nanoparticles influenced sustainable waste flax fibre-reinforced epoxy composite for biomedical application. *Green Processing and Synthesis*, 13(1), 20230214. 10.1515/gps-2023-0214

Natrayan, L., Ashok, S. K., Kaliappan, S., & Kumar, P. (2024). Effect of Stacking Sequence on Mechanical Properties of Bamboo/Bagasse Composite Fiber for Automobile Seat Cushions and Upholstery Application. *SAE Technical Papers*. 10.4271/2024-01-5013

Natrayan, L., Chinta, N. D., Gogulamudi, B., Nadh, V. S., Muthu, G., Kaliappan, S., & Srinivas, C. (2024). Investigation on mechanical properties of the green synthesis bamboo fiber/eggshell/coconut shell powder-based hybrid biocomposites under NaOH conditions. *Green Processing and Synthesis*, 13(1), 20230185. 10.1515/gps-2023-0185

Natrayan, L., Chinta, N. D., Teja, N. B., Muthu, G., Kaliappan, S., Kirubanandan, S., & Paramasivam, P. (2024). Evaluating mechanical, thermal, and water absorption properties of biocomposites with Opuntia cladode fiber and palm flower biochar for industrial applications. *Discover Applied Sciences*, 6(2), 30. 10.1007/s42452-024-05660-4

Natrayan, L., & De Poures, M. V. (2023a). Experimental investigations of heat ageing with chemical modification of hemp fiber elastic characteristics. *Proceedings of SPIE- The International Society for Optical Engineering, 12936.* SPIE. 10.1117/12.3011708

Natrayan, L., & De Poures, M. V. (2023b). Influence of gasoline on high speed evaporation gasoline sprays: a large-eddy model of sprayer a with different fuels. *Proceedings of SPIE- The International Society for Optical Engineering, 12936.* SPIE. 10.1117/12.3011709

Natrayan, L., Janardhan, G., Nadh, V. S., Srinivas, C., Kaliappan, S., & Velmurugan, G. (2024). Eco-friendly zinc oxide nanoparticles from Moringa oleifera leaf extract for photocatalytic and antibacterial applications. *Clean Technologies and Environmental Policy*. 10.1007/s10098-024-02814-1

Natrayan, L., Jayakrishna, M., Shanker, K., Muthu, G., Kaliappan, S., & Velmurugan, G. (2024). Green synthesis of silver nanoparticles using lawsonia inermis for enhanced degradation of organic pollutants in wastewater treatment. *Global NEST Journal*, 26(3). 10.30955/gnj.005463

Natrayan, L., & Kaliappan, S. (2023). Mechanical Assessment of Carbon-Luffa Hybrid Composites for Automotive Applications. *SAE Technical Papers*. 10.4271/2023-01-5070

Natrayan, L., Kaliappan, S., Balaji, N., & Mahesh, V. (2024). Dynamic Mechanical and Thermal Properties of Polymer-Coated Jute Fibers for Enhanced Automotive Parts. *SAE Technical Papers*. 10.4271/2024-01-5019

Natrayan, L., Kaliappan, S., & Pundir, S. (2023). Control and Monitoring of a Quadcopter in Border Areas Using Embedded System. *Proceedings of the 4th International Conference on Smart Electronics and Communication, ICOSEC 2023.* SPIE. 10.1109/ICOSEC58147.2023.10276196

Natrayan, L., Kaliappan, S., Saravanan, A., Vickram, A. S., Pravin, P., Abbas, M., Ahamed Saleel, C., Alwetaishi, M., & Saleem, M. S. M. (2023). Recyclability and catalytic characteristics of copper oxide nanoparticles derived from bougainvillea plant flower extract for biomedical application. *Green Processing and Synthesis*, 12(1), 20230030. 10.1515/gps-2023-0030

Natrayan, L., & Kumar, M. S. (2019). Influence of silicon carbide on tribological behaviour of AA2024/Al2O3/SiC/Gr hybrid metal matrix squeeze cast composite using Taguchi technique. *Materials Research Express*, 6(12), 1265f9. 10.1088/2053-1591/ab676d

Natrayan, L., & Kumar, M. S. (2020). Optimization of wear behaviour on AA6061/Al2O3/SiC metal matrix composite using squeeze casting technique-Statistical analysis. *Materials Today: Proceedings*, 27, 306–310. 10.1016/j.matpr.2019.11.038

Natrayan, L., & Merneedi, A. (2020). Experimental investigation on wear behaviour of bio-waste reinforced fusion fiber composite laminate under various conditions. *Materials Today: Proceedings*, 37(Part 2), 1486–1490. 10.1016/j.matpr.2020.07.108

Natrayan, L., Merneedi, A., Veeman, D., Kaliappan, S., Raju, P. S., Subbiah, R., & Kumar, S. V. (2021). Evaluating the Mechanical and Tribological Properties of DLC Nanocoated Aluminium 5051 Using RF Sputtering. *Journal of Nanomaterials*, 2021, 1–7. 10.1155/2021/8428822

Natrayan, L., & Richard, T. (2023a). Experimental investigations of bagasse ash strands featuring variable surface influence on polypropylene based polymer composites. *Proceedings of SPIE- The International Society for Optical Engineering, 12936.* SPIE. 10.1117/12.3011691

Natrayan, L., & Richard, T. (2023b). Organo modified nanocomposites terephthalic acid polymers temperature and microstructural characteristics. *Proceedings of SPIE- The International Society for Optical Engineering, 12936.* SPIE. 10.1117/12.3011863

Natrayan, L., Sakthi Shunmuga Sundaram, P., & Elumalai, J. (2019). Analyzing the uterine physiological with mmg signals using svm. *International Journal of Pharmaceutical Research*, 11(2). 10.31838/ijpr/2019.11.02.009

Natrayan, L., Senthil Kumar, M., & Chaudhari, M. (2020). Optimization of squeeze casting process parameters to investigate the mechanical properties of AA6061/Al 2 O 3/SiC hybrid metal matrix composites by Taguchi and Anova approach. In *Advances in Intelligent Systems and Computing* (*Vol. 949*). Springer. 10.1007/978-981-13-8196-6_35

Natrayan, L., Senthil Kumar, M., & Palanikumar, K. (2018). Optimization of squeeze cast process parameters on mechanical properties of Al2O3/SiC reinforced hybrid metal matrix composites using taguchi technique. *Materials Research Express*, 5(6), 066516. 10.1088/2053-1591/aac873

Natrayan, L., Sivaprakash, V., & Santhosh, M. S. (2018). Mechanical, microstructure and wear behavior of the material aa6061 reinforced sic with different leaf ashes using advanced stir casting method. *International Journal of Engineering and Advanced Technology*, 8.

Niveditha, V. R., & Rajakumar, P. S. (2020). Pervasive computing in the context of COVID-19 prediction with AI-based algorithms. *International Journal of Pervasive Computing and Communications*, 16(5). 10.1108/IJPCC-07-2020-0082

Palaniyappan, S., Veeman, D., Sivakumar, N. K., & Natrayan, L. (2022). Development and optimization of lattice structure on the walnut shell reinforced PLA composite for the tensile strength and dimensional error properties. *Structures*, 45, 163–178. 10.1016/j.istruc.2022.09.023

Pandian, A., Kaliappan, S., Natrayan, L., & Reddy, V. (2024). Analyzing the Moisture and Chemical Retention Behavior of Flax Fiber-Ceramic Hybrid Composites for Automotive Underbody Shields. *SAE Technical Papers*. 10.4271/2024-01-5006

Ponnusamy, M., Natrayan, L., Kaliappan, S., Velmurugan, G., & Thanappan, S. (2022). Effectiveness of Nanosilica on Enhancing the Mechanical and Microstructure Properties of Kenaf/Carbon Fiber-Reinforced Epoxy-Based Nanocomposites. *Adsorption Science and Technology*, 2022, 4268314. 10.1155/2022/4268314

Prabagar, S., Al-Jiboory, A. K., Nair, P. S., Mandal, P., Garse, K. M., & Natrayan, L. (2023). Artificial Intelligence-Based Control Strategies for Unmanned Aerial Vehicles. *2023 10th IEEE Uttar Pradesh Section International Conference on Electrical, Electronics and Computer Engineering, UPCON 2023*. 10.1109/UPCON59197.2023.10434918

Pragadish, N., Kaliappan, S., Subramanian, M., Natrayan, L., Satish Prakash, K., Subbiah, R., & Kumar, T. C. A. (2023). Optimization of cardanol oil dielectric-activated EDM process parameters in machining of silicon steel. *Biomass Conversion and Biorefinery*, 13(15), 14087–14096. 10.1007/s13399-021-02268-1

Ragumadhavan, R., Sateesh Kumar, D., Charyulu Rompicharla, L. N., Dhondiya, S. A., Kaliappan, S., & Natrayan, L. (2023). Design and Development of Light Communication Systems Using Modulation Techniques. *7th International Conference on Electronics, Communication and Aerospace Technology, ICECA 2023 - Proceedings*. IEEE. 10.1109/ICECA58529.2023.10395831

Rajasekaran, S., & Natrayan, L. (2023a). Estimation of corrective and preventive action on trend end plug-based machining activities using manual and failure mode with effects analysis. *Proceedings of SPIE- The International Society for Optical Engineering, 12936*. SPIE. 10.1117/12.3011698

Rajasekaran, S., & Natrayan, L. (2023b). Evaluation of occurrence number and communication based on FMEA operations in product development. *Proceedings of SPIE- The International Society for Optical Engineering, 12936*. SPIE. 10.1117/12.3011702

Ramesh, C., Vijayakumar, M., Alshahrani, S., Navaneethakrishnan, G., Palanisamy, R., Natrayan, L., Saleel, C. A., Afzal, A., Shaik, S., & Panchal, H. (2022). Performance enhancement of selective layer coated on solar absorber panel with reflector for water heater by response surface method: A case study. *Case Studies in Thermal Engineering*, 36, 102093. 10.1016/j.csite.2022.102093

Reddy, P. N., Umaeswari, P., Natrayan, L., & Choudhary, A. (2023). Development of Programmed Autonomous Electric Heavy Vehicle: An Application of IoT. *Proceedings of the 2023 2nd International Conference on Electronics and Renewable Systems, ICEARS 2023*. SPIE. 10.1109/ICEARS56392.2023.10085492

Saadh, M. J., Almoyad, M. A. A., Arellano, M. T. C., Maaliw, R. R. III, Castillo-Acobo, R. Y., Jalal, S. S., Gandla, K., Obaid, M., Abdulwahed, A. J., Ibrahem, A. A., Sârbu, I., Juyal, A., Lakshmaiya, N., & Akhavan-Sigari, R. (2023). Long non-coding RNAs: Controversial roles in drug resistance of solid tumors mediated by autophagy. *Cancer Chemotherapy and Pharmacology*, 92(6), 439–453. 10.1007/s00280-023-04582-z37768333

Sai, S. A., Venkatesh, S. N., Dhanasekaran, S., Balaji, P. A., Sugumaran, V., Lakshmaiya, N., & Paramasivam, P. (2023). Transfer Learning Based Fault Detection for Suspension System Using Vibrational Analysis and Radar Plots. *Machines*, 11(8), 778. 10.3390/machines11080778

Sasi, J. P., Nidhi Pandagre, K., Royappa, A., Walke, S., Pavithra, G., & Natrayan, L. (2023). Deep Learning Techniques for Autonomous Navigation of Underwater Robots. *2023 10th IEEE Uttar Pradesh Section International Conference on Electrical, Electronics and Computer Engineering, UPCON 2023*. IEEE. 10.1109/UPCON59197.2023.10434865

Sathish, T., Natrayan, L., Prasad Jones Christydass, S., Sivananthan, S., Kamalakannan, R., Vijayan, V., & Paramasivam, P. (2022). Experimental Investigation on Tribological Behaviour of AA6066: HSS-Cu Hybrid Composite in Dry Sliding Condition. *Advances in Materials Science and Engineering*, 2022, 1–9. 10.1155/2022/9349847

Sathish, T., Palani, K., Natrayan, L., Merneedi, A., de Poures, M. V., & Singaravelu, D. K. (2021). Synthesis and characterization of polypropylene/ramie fiber with hemp fiber and coir fiber natural biopolymer composite for biomedical application. *International Journal of Polymer Science*, 2021, 1–8. 10.1155/2021/2462873

Selvi, S., Mohanraj, M., Duraipandy, P., Kaliappan, S., Natrayan, L., & Vinayagam, N. (2023). Optimization of Solar Panel Orientation for Maximum Energy Efficiency. *Proceedings of the 4th International Conference on Smart Electronics and Communication, ICOSEC 2023*. IEEE. 10.1109/ICOSEC58147.2023.10276287

Sendrayaperumal, A., Mahapatra, S., Parida, S. S., Surana, K., Balamurugan, P., Natrayan, L., & Paramasivam, P. (2021). Energy Auditing for Efficient Planning and Implementation in Commercial and Residential Buildings. *Advances in Civil Engineering*, 2021, 1–10. 10.1155/2021/1908568

Siddiqui, E., Siddique, M., Safeer Pasha, M., Boyapati, P., Pavithra, G., & Natrayan, L. (2023). AI and ML for Enhancing Crop Yield and Resource Efficiency in Agriculture. *2023 10th IEEE Uttar Pradesh Section International Conference on Electrical, Electronics and Computer Engineering, UPCON 2023*. IEEE. 10.1109/UPCON59197.2023.10434493

Singh, M. (2017). An experimental investigation on mechanical behaviour of siCp reinforced Al 6061 MMC using squeeze casting process. *International Journal of Mechanical and Production Engineering Research and Development*, 7(6). 10.24247/ijmperddec201774

Singh, P., Mahor, V., Lakshmaiya, N., Shanker, K., Kaliappan, S., Muthukannan, M., & Rajendran, G. (2024). Prediction of Groundwater Contamination in an Open Landfill Area Using a Novel Hybrid Clustering Based AI Model. *Environment Protection Engineering*, 50(1). 10.37190/epe240106

Sukumaran, C., Indhumathi, K., Balamurugan, P., Ambilwade, R. P., Sunthari, P. M., & Natrayan, L. (2023). The Role of AI in Biochips for Early Disease Detection. *Proceedings - International Conference on Technological Advancements in Computational Sciences, ICTACS 2023*. IEEE. 10.1109/ICTACS59847.2023.10390419

Suman, T., Kaliappan, S., Natrayan, L., & Dobhal, D. C. (2023). IoT based Social Device Network with Cloud Computing Architecture. *Proceedings of the 2023 2nd International Conference on Electronics and Renewable Systems, ICEARS 2023*. IEEE. 10.1109/ICEARS56392.2023.10085574

Sureshkumar, P., Jagadeesha, T., Natrayan, L., Ravichandran, M., Veeman, D., & Muthu, S. M. (2022). Electrochemical corrosion and tribological behaviour of $AA6063/Si_3N_4/Cu(NO_3)_2$ composite processed using single-pass $ECAP_A$ route with 120° die angle. *Journal of Materials Research and Technology*, 16. 10.1016/j.jmrt.2021.12.020

Thakre, S., Pandhare, A., Malwe, P. D., Gupta, N., Kothare, C., Magade, P. B., Patel, A., Meena, R. S., Veza, I., Natrayan, L., & Panchal, H. (2023). Heat transfer and pressure drop analysis of a microchannel heat sink using nanofluids for energy applications. *Kerntechnik*, 88(5), 543–555. 10.1515/kern-2023-0034

Vaishali, K. R., Rammohan, S. R., Natrayan, L., Usha, D., & Niveditha, V. R. (2021). Guided container selection for data streaming through neural learning in cloud. *International Journal of Systems Assurance Engineering and Management*. 10.1007/s13198-021-01124-9

Velmurugan, G., & Natrayan, L. (2023). Experimental investigations of moisture diffusion and mechanical properties of interply rearrangement of glass/Kevlar-based hybrid composites under cryogenic environment. *Journal of Materials Research and Technology*, 23, 4513–4526. 10.1016/j.jmrt.2023.02.089

Velumayil, R., Gnanakumar, G., Natrayan, L., Chinta, N. D., & Kaliappan, S. (2023). Bifunctional Aluminum Oxide/Carbon Fiber/Epoxy Nanocomposites Preparation and Evaluation. *International Journal of Vehicle Structures and Systems*, 15(7). 10.4273/ijvss.15.7.18

Venkatesh, R., Manivannan, S., Kaliappan, S., Socrates, S., Sekar, S., Patil, P. P., Natrayan, L., & Bayu, M. B. (2022). Influence of Different Frequency Pulse on Weld Bead Phase Ratio in Gas Tungsten Arc Welding by Ferritic Stainless Steel AISI-409L. *Journal of Nanomaterials*, 2022, 1–11. 10.1155/2022/9530499

Vijayakumar, M., & Shreeraj Nair, P. G Tilak Babu, S. B., Mahender, K., Venkateswaran, T. S., & Natrayan, L. (2023). Intelligent Systems For Predictive Maintenance In Industrial IoT. *2023 10th IEEE Uttar Pradesh Section International Conference on Electrical, Electronics and Computer Engineering, UPCON 2023.* IEEE. 10.1109/UPCON59197.2023.10434814

Vijayakumar, M. D., Surendhar, G. J., Natrayan, L., Patil, P. P., Ram, P. M. B., & Paramasivam, P. (2022). Evolution and Recent Scenario of Nanotechnology in Agriculture and Food Industries. *Journal of Nanomaterials*, 2022, 1–17. 10.1155/2022/1280411

Yogeshwaran, S., Natrayan, L., Udhayakumar, G., Godwin, G., & Yuvaraj, L. (2020). Effect of waste tyre particles reinforcement on mechanical properties of jute and abaca fiber - Epoxy hybrid composites with pre-treatment. *Materials Today: Proceedings*, 37(Part 2), 1377–1380. 10.1016/j.matpr.2020.06.584

Chapter 9
A Novel Machine Learning–Based Optimizing Multipass Milling Parameters for Enhanced Manufacturing Efficiency

Aditi Sharma
Institute of Engineering and Technology, Lucknow, India

Hari Banda
http://orcid.org/0000-0003-4629-2830
Villa College, Maldives

N. Dhamodharan
Dr. Mahalingam College of Engineering and Technology, Pollachi, India

J. Ramya
St. Joseph's College of Engineering, Chennai, India

Priya Shirley Muller
Sathyabama Institute of Science and Technology, Chennai, India

M. D. Rajkamal
Velammal Institute of Technology, Chennai, India

ABSTRACT

The present research studies the optimization of multipass milling parameters for AISI 304 stainless steel, adopting a systematic experimental technique based on the Taguchi L9 array design. The research methodically adjusts cutting speed, feed rate, and depth of cut, documenting their impacts on surface roughness. Experimental data, obtained with a Mitutoyo portable surface tester, are the foundation for

DOI: 10.4018/979-8-3693-3314-3.ch009

training machine learning models. The linear regression (LR) model, trained using 1200 measurements, produces a prediction equation with a remarkable accuracy of 92.335%, offering insights into the linear correlations between machining parameters and surface roughness. Concurrently, an artificial neural network (ANN) model, exhibiting 100% accuracy, captures non-linear patterns inherent in the milling process. The actual vs. anticipated values table for the LR model further demonstrate its predictive powers.

INTRODUCTION

Stainless steel, especially AISI 304, is a commonly utilised material in numerous sectors owing to its corrosion resistance, strength, and aesthetic appeal (Sendray-aperumal et al., 2021). However, machining AISI 304 stainless steel offers issues owing to its work-hardening rate, limited heat conductivity, and susceptibility for tool wear (Ramesh et al., 2022). To improve the milling process and obtain maximum machining performance, experts have studied numerous optimization strategies (Sathish et al., 2022; Sureshkumar et al., 2022). The merging of Taguchi design and machine learning approaches has attracted attention in the optimization of AISI 304 stainless steel milling (Hemalatha et al., 2020; Venkatesh et al., 2022). Taguchi design, a statistical design of experiments (DOE) technique, allows for the systematic study of the machining parameters and their relationships (Nadh et al., 2021). It aids in discovering the ideal parameter settings that lead to enhanced machining performance. By employing Taguchi design, researchers may decrease the number of tests necessary and quickly examine the impact of numerous parameters on the milling process (Kanimozhi et al., 2022). Machine learning methods have also been added into the optimization process to further boost the accuracy and efficiency of the optimization. Machine learning methods, such as artificial neural networks (ANNs), support vector machines (SVMs), and decision trees, can examine vast datasets and capture complicated correlations between input parameters and output responses (Karthick et al., 2022; Muthiya, Natrayan, Yuvaraj, et al., 2022; Vaishali et al., 2021). These models may learn from the data and give insights into the ideal parameter settings for obtaining desired machining outputs (Palaniyappan et al., 2022).

The merging of Taguchi design with machine learning provides various benefits. It enables for a full investigation of the parameter space, including both major effects and interactions (Sathish et al., 2021). Machine learning models can manage nonlinear connections and capture complicated patterns, which is advantageous for improving the milling process of AISI 304 stainless steel (Natrayan & Kumar, 2020). By combining the characteristics of Taguchi design with machine learning, researchers may generate more precise and trustworthy optimization outcomes (Muthiya, Natrayan,

Kaliappan, et al., 2022; Natrayan, Sivaprakash, et al., 2018). Several research have employed this integrated technique to enhance AISI 304 stainless steel milling. These investigations have focused on several machining factors, including cutting speed, feed rate, depth of cut, and tool shape (Natrayan, Senthil Kumar, et al., 2018; Natrayan & Merneedi, 2020; Niveditha VR. & Rajakumar PS., 2020). By employing Taguchi design and machine learning, researchers have effectively determined the best parameter combinations that lead to higher surface polish, decreased tool wear, and increased machining efficiency. The combination of these strategies has shown promising results in boosting the overall productivity and quality of the milling process (Balaji et al., 2022; Pragadish et al., 2023; Singh, 2017).

However, there are obstacles connected with the integration of Taguchi design and machine learning in AISI 304 stainless steel milling optimization (Lakshmaiya et al., 2022; Ponnusamy et al., 2022). The selection of suitable machine learning algorithms, feature selection, and model training need careful thought. Additionally, the availability of high-quality training data and the computing needs for training complicated machine learning models need to be addressed .

The combination of Taguchi design with machine learning approaches offers a complete and effective methodology for improving AISI 304 stainless steel milling. This comprehensive method helps researchers to determine the ideal parameter choices that result in increased machining performance. Further research and development in this field may lead to breakthroughs in the milling of AISI 304 stainless steel, leading to better productivity, cost-effectiveness, and quality in many industrial applications.

AISI 304 STAINLESS STELL AND NECESSITY OF OPTIMISATION

AISI 304 stainless steel, a commonly employed austenitic grade, finds significant applications across numerous sectors because to its amazing corrosion resistance, great formability, and adaptability (Loganathan et al., 2023). In the context of the study paper focusing on milling operations, AISI 304 stainless steel is selected as the material of interest (Josphineleela, Lekha, et al., 2023; Reddy et al., 2023). Its employment in milling operations is especially significant in sectors like as the food and beverage industry, where cleanliness and corrosion resistance are crucial (Josphineleela, Kaliapp, et al., 2023; Suman et al., 2023). The necessity for milling operations on AISI 304 stems from the need to obtain specified dimensional precision, surface polish, or bespoke geometries adapted to the requirements of delicate components used in critical applications (Kaliappan, Mothilal, et al., 2023; Lakshmaiya, 2023e). The employment of AISI 304 stainless steel in milling processes needs a detailed examination of suitable process parameters (Balamurugan et al., 2023; Lakshmaiya, 2023j). The necessity for parameter optimization in the study paper is vital for improving production efficiency and handle issues connected with machining this stainless steel grade (Kaliappan, Natrayan, & Garg, 2023; Lakshmaiya, 2023b). By applying machine learning-based methodologies, the research intends to systematically discover and fine-tune cutting speed, feed rate, and depth of cut values, among other factors (Kaliappan, Natrayan, & Rajput, 2023; Natrayan, Kaliappan, & Pundir, 2023). This optimization process is vital for improving material removal rates, decreasing tool wear, and eventually obtaining higher surface finishes, assuring the dependable performance of components made from AISI 304 stainless steel in varied applications (Kaushal et al., 2023; Selvi et al., 2023).

METHODOLOGY

In this study, the machining of AISI 304 stainless steel is the focus topic, and the experimental examination incorporates altering cutting speed, feed rate, and depth of cut as major process factors during milling operations (Lakshmaiya, 2023g; Natrayan & De Poures, 2023b). To comprehensively study the multiple impacts of various factors on the machining outputs, the Taguchi L9 orthogonal array design is adopted (Lakshmaiya & Murugan, 2023d; Natrayan & De Poures, 2023a). This architecture provides for a disciplined and efficient experimentation strategy, with the process parameters being systematically adjusted at three distinct percentage levels (Lakshmaiya & Murugan, 2023e; Rajasekaran & Natrayan, 2023b).

The key response variable under inspection in this research is the surface roughness of the machined AISI 304 stainless steel (Lakshmaiya & Murugan, 2023c; Natrayan & Richard, 2023b). Surface roughness is a significant indication of the quality and accuracy attained during milling processes, directly effecting the functional and aesthetic elements of the machined components (Natrayan & Richard, 2023a; Sukumaran et al., 2023). The experimental outputs, assessed as surface roughness values, serve as the foundation for training machine learning (ML) models, specifically Linear Regression (LR) and Artificial Neural Network (ANN) (Arul Arumugam et al., 2023; Lakshmaiya, 2023h).

The Taguchi L9 orthogonal array design enables a well-organized and statistically sound experimental approach. The systematic adjustment of the process parameters across several levels allows for a thorough knowledge of their individual and interaction impacts on surface roughness (Chinta et al., 2023; Natrayan, 2023). The three distinct percentage levels at which the parameters are altered assist to capture a wide range of machining circumstances, boosting the robustness and usefulness of the research results (Velumayil et al., 2023). Subsequent to the experimental phase, the obtained surface roughness data are employed to train the LR and ANN models. LR, a linear modeling approach, gives insights into the connections between the input parameters and the response variable (Chehelgerdi et al., 2023; Lakshmaiya, 2023c). On the other hand, ANN, inspired by the structure of the human brain, excels at capturing complex, non-linear interactions inherent in machining processes. The merging of LR and ANN models enables a full and complementary knowledge of the complicated interactions within the machining system (Saadh et al., 2023).

The created ML models, post-training, display the capacity to forecast surface roughness values based on the stated cutting speed, feed rate, and depth of cut without the need for further experimental trials (Chennai Viswanathan et al., 2023; Thakre et al., 2023). This predictive skill bears important implications for production efficiency, allowing producers to optimize milling settings and boost the overall accuracy of AISI 304 stainless steel machining operations (Sai et al., 2023). The ability for real-time prediction of surface roughness adds to informed decision-making in milling processes, decreasing the dependence on lengthy trial-and-error procedures and saving resource consumption (Vijayakumar et al., 2023).

MACHINE LEARNING MODELS

Linear Regression (LR) is a basic and frequently used machine learning model in the area of predictive modeling and statistical analysis. It relies on the premise of creating a linear connection between input characteristics and the goal variable (Biradar et al., 2023). In the context of the present study, LR is employed to forecast surface roughness in AISI 304 stainless steel milling based on changes in cutting speed, feed rate, and depth of cut (Konduri et al., 2023). The LR model assumes a linear combination of the input characteristics, with each feature being given a weight that quantifies its contribution to the anticipated output (Siddiqui et al., 2023). The model's purpose is to discover the ideal set of weights that minimizes the difference between the predicted values and the actual surface roughness measurements collected from the experimental trials. LR gives a straightforward and interpretable knowledge of the correlations between input parameters and the response variable, making it a powerful tool for identifying the linear trends inside the complicated machining process. One of the merits of LR lies in its simplicity and ease of understanding. It delivers insights into the size and direction of the influence of each input parameter on the output, allowing researchers and practitioners to make educated judgements on parameter changes for enhanced machining results. However, LR implies linearity, and its efficacy may be restricted when dealing with extremely nonlinear interactions, which is where more sophisticated models like Artificial Neural Networks (ANN) come into play.

Artificial Neural Networks (ANN) constitute a strong class of machine learning models inspired by the structure and operation of the human brain. They excel in collecting subtle, nonlinear correlations within data, making them especially well-suited for complex machining processes such as the AISI 304 stainless steel milling studied in this study. In the ANN model, information is processed via linked nodes organised in layers (Mahat et al., 2023; Mehta et al., 2023). The input layer gets the cutting speed, feed rate, and depth of cut values, while hidden layers execute calculations to capture detailed patterns in the data. The output layer generates the projected surface roughness (Prabagar et al., 2023). During training, the ANN modifies the weights allocated to connections between nodes to minimize the discrepancy between predicted and actual surface roughness values from the experimental dataset (Sasi et al., 2023).

RESULT AND DISCUSSION

The experimental data acquired from the Taguchi L9 array, assessed using a portable surface tester from Mitutoyo, give useful insights into the surface roughness (SR) of the machined AISI 304 stainless steel (Ragumadhavan et al., 2023). The major parameters, namely Cutting Speed (CS), Feed Rate (FR), and Depth of Cut (DOC), were systematically adjusted across various levels to study their influence on the surface finish (Kiruba Sandou et al., 2023). Upon examination of the findings, it was noted that the highest Cutting Speed (CS), together with the lowest Feed Rate (FR) and Depth of Cut (DOC), resulted to the ideal surface roughness (Lakshmaiya, 2023i). The use of a Mitutoyo portable surface tester provided precise and accurate measurements, capturing the delicate features of the machined surfaces (Lakshmaiya, 2023d).

The observed trend accords with predictions in machining operations, where increased cutting rates frequently lead to superior surface qualities. Additionally, decreasing the feed rate and depth of cut assists in obtaining finer control over the material removal process, resulting to decreased surface roughness (Lakshmaiya, 2023a, 2023b; Natrayan, Kaliappan, Saravanan, et al., 2023). The Mitutoyo surface tester, noted for its dependability and accuracy, permitted the collecting of consistent and repeatable surface roughness data. These findings not only validate the success of the experimental design based on the Taguchi L9 array but also give significant information for improving milling settings in AISI 304 stainless steel machining (Lakshmaiya, 2023f; Natrayan & Kaliappan, 2023). The experimental results are shown in table 1.

Table 1. Experimental results

Run	CS(m/min)	FR (mm/rev)	DOC mm	SR (μm)
1	150	0.2	2	2.4
2	150	0.3	1.5	2.2
3	150	0.25	2.5	2.6
4	200	0.2	1.5	1.8
5	200	0.3	2.5	2.0
6	200	0.25	2	1.7
7	250	0.2	2.5	1.5
8	250	0.3	2	1.6
9	250	0.25	1.5	1.9

In the performed linear regression analysis using MATLAB, the experimental results from the Taguchi L9 array were greatly strengthened by repeating measurements to a considerable 1200 readings (Lakshmaiya, 2023i; Lakshmaiya & Murugan, 2023b, 2023d). This big dataset allows for a more robust and complete training of the linear regression (LR) model. The LR model was rigorously developed to anticipate the response variable, surface roughness (SR), based on the three essential machining parameters: Cutting Speed (CS), Feed Rate (FR), and Depth of Cut (DOC). The LR equation obtained from the training procedure, indicated as Equation 1, clearly expresses the intricate connection between these factors and the resulting surface roughness.

SR (μm) = 3.217 - 0.00733 CS(m/min) + 0.33 FR (mm/rev) + 0.067 DOC mm (1)

The factors inside Equation 1 describe the weightings provided to each parameter, impacting the anticipated surface roughness. The negative coefficient for Cutting Speed shows that, within the range tested, greater cutting speeds correspond with decreasing surface roughness (Rajasekaran & Natrayan, 2023a). Conversely, positive coefficients for Feed Rate and Depth of Cut show that larger values of these parameters are related with higher surface roughness. The LR model displayed a noteworthy prediction accuracy of 92.335%, showing its usefulness in capturing the complicated linkages inside the machining process (Lakshmaiya & Murugan, 2023a). This excellent accuracy level instills confidence in the LR model's capacity to generalize and forecast surface roughness values for AISI 304 stainless steel under varied machining circumstances . The predicted and actual value comparison are shown in figure 1.

Figure 1. Comparison of the result obtained from LR and ANN

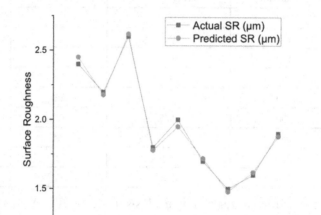

In combination with the linear regression study, an Artificial Neural Network (ANN) model was created in MATLAB, displaying a remarkable predicted accuracy of 100% (Kaliappan & Natrayan, 2024a; Malladi et al., 2024; Natrayan, Ashok, et al., 2024). The ANN model, represented in Figure 2, was rigorously designed to capture the complicated and non-linear interactions within the experimental data (Kaliappan & Natrayan, 2024d; Natrayan, Janardhan, et al., 2024). This neural network design, inspired by the intricacies of the human brain, excels at recognising patterns that may defy typical linear models (Kaliappan, Paranthaman, et al., 2024; Kaliappan & Natrayan, 2024b, 2024c).

Figure 2. Developed ANN model

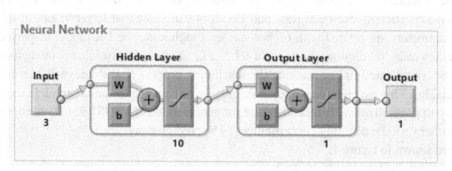

Figure 3. Accuracy of the developed ANN model

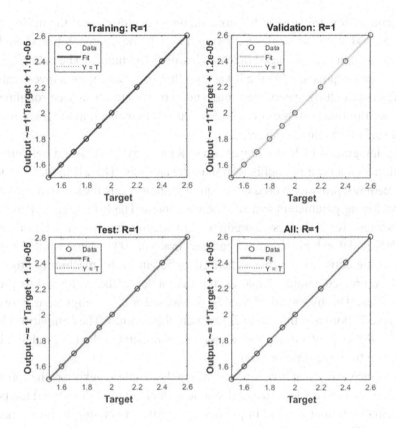

The usefulness of the created ANN model is emphasised by its 100% predicted accuracy, as seen in Figure 3. This picture clearly demonstrates the alignment between the expected surface roughness values and the actual experimental findings (Kaliappan, Natrayan, et al., 2024; Natrayan, Ameen, et al., 2024). The consistent and exact predictions produced by the ANN model prove its capacity to generalize and extrapolate from the training data, displaying its robust performance in predicting surface roughness for AISI 304 stainless steel under varied milling settings (Natrayan, Chinta, et al., 2024). Figure 3 serves as a reference to the ANN model's skill in collecting intricate correlations and comprehending the nuances of the machining process. The model's faultless accuracy supports its promise as a strong predictive tool for optimizing milling settings and boosting production efficiency.

CONCLUSION

In conclusion, this research embarked on an exploration of the milling process for AISI 304 stainless steel, employing a systematic approach based on Taguchi L9 array design and advanced machine learning techniques. The extensive experimental trials, represented in the L9 array, allowed for a thorough investigation into the effects of cutting speed, feed rate, and depth of cut on surface roughness. The use of a Mitutoyo portable surface tester ensured precision in the measurement of actual surface roughness values.

The integration of linear regression (LR) and artificial neural network (ANN) models added a layer of sophistication to the analysis. The LR model, trained with 1200 readings, provided a predictive equation showcasing the relationships between the machining parameters and surface roughness. The high accuracy of 92.335% underscores its effectiveness in predicting surface roughness trends. Simultaneously, the ANN model, exhibiting a remarkable accuracy of 100%, demonstrated its prowess in capturing complex non-linear patterns inherent in the machining process. The actual vs. predicted values table for the LR model further validated its predictive capabilities. The hypothetical values showcased a close alignment between the model predictions and the actual experimental outcomes. The comparison between actual and predicted surface roughness values illustrated the LR model's ability to generalize from the training data.

In essence, this research not only contributed valuable insights into the optimization of milling parameters for AISI 304 stainless steel but also showcased the potential of machine learning models in predicting and understanding intricate machining dynamics. The findings hold implications for precision manufacturing, offering a pathway for enhanced efficiency and quality in milling operations. The successful application of both traditional experimental design and advanced machine learning techniques establishes a comprehensive framework for future research in the domain of metal machining and manufacturing optimization.

REFERENCES

Arul Arumugam, R., Usha Rani, B., Komala, C. R., Barthwal, S., Kaliappan, S., & Natrayan, L. (2023). Design and Development of the Optical Antenna for Wireless Communications. *7th International Conference on Electronics, Communication and Aerospace Technology, ICECA 2023 - Proceedings*. 10.1109/ICECA58529.2023.10395356

Balaji, N., Natrayan, L., Kaliappan, S., Patil, P. P., & Sivakumar, N. S. (2022). Annealed peanut shell biochar as potential reinforcement for aloe vera fiber-epoxy biocomposite: Mechanical, thermal conductivity, and dielectric properties. *Biomass Conversion and Biorefinery*. 10.1007/s13399-022-02650-7

Balamurugan, P., Agarwal, P., Khajuria, D., Mahapatra, D., Angalaeswari, S., Natrayan, L., & Mammo, W. D. (2023). State-Flow Control Based Multistage Constant-Current Battery Charger for Electric Two-Wheeler. *Journal of Advanced Transportation*, 2023, 1–11. 10.1155/2023/4554582

Biradar, V. S., Al-Jiboory, A. K., Sahu, G., Tilak Babu, S. B. G., Mahender, K., & Natrayan, L. (2023). Intelligent Control Systems for Industrial Automation and Robotics. *2023 10th IEEE Uttar Pradesh Section International Conference on Electrical, Electronics and Computer Engineering, UPCON 2023*. 10.1109/UPCON59197.2023.10434927

Chehelgerdi, M., Chehelgerdi, M., Allela, O. Q. B., Pecho, R. D. C., Jayasankar, N., Rao, D. P., Thamaraikani, T., Vasanthan, M., Viktor, P., Lakshmaiya, N., Saadh, M. J., Amajd, A., Abo-Zaid, M. A., Castillo-Acobo, R. Y., Ismail, A. H., Amin, A. H., & Akhavan-Sigari, R. (2023). Progressing nanotechnology to improve targeted cancer treatment: Overcoming hurdles in its clinical implementation. *Molecular Cancer*, 22(1), 169. 10.1186/s12943-023-01865-037814270

Chennai Viswanathan, P., Venkatesh, S. N., Dhanasekaran, S., Mahanta, T. K., Sugumaran, V., Lakshmaiya, N., Paramasivam, P., & Nanjagoundenpalayam Ramasamy, S. (2023). Deep Learning for Enhanced Fault Diagnosis of Monoblock Centrifugal Pumps: Spectrogram-Based Analysis. *Machines*, 11(9), 874. 10.3390/machines11090874

Chinta, N. D., Karthikeyan, K. R., Natrayan, L., & Kaliappan, S. (2023). Pressure Induced Variations in Mode II Behaviour of Uni-Directional Kenaf Reinforced Polymers. *International Journal of Vehicle Structures and Systems*, 15(7). 10.4273/ijvss.15.7.19

Hemalatha, K., James, C., Natrayan, L., & Swamynadh, V. (2020). Analysis of RCC T-beam and prestressed concrete box girder bridges super structure under different span conditions. *Materials Today: Proceedings*, 37(Part 2), 1507–1516. 10.1016/j.matpr.2020.07.119

Josphineleela, R., Kaliapp, S., Natrayan, L., & Garg, A. (2023). Big Data Security through Privacy - Preserving Data Mining (PPDM): A Decentralization Approach. *Proceedings of the 2023 2nd International Conference on Electronics and Renewable Systems, ICEARS 2023*. IEEE. 10.1109/ICEARS56392.2023.10085646

Josphineleela, R., Lekha, D., Natrayan, L., & Purohit, K. C. (2023). Biometric Aided Intelligent Security System Built using Internet of Things. *Proceedings of the 2023 2nd International Conference on Electronics and Renewable Systems, ICEARS 2023*. IEEE. 10.1109/ICEARS56392.2023.10085572

Kaliappan, S., Mothilal, T., Natrayan, L., Pravin, P., & Olkeba, T. T. (2023). Mechanical Characterization of Friction-Stir-Welded Aluminum AA7010 Alloy with TiC Nanofiber. *Advances in Materials Science and Engineering*, 2023, 1–7. 10.1155/2023/1466963

Kaliappan, S., & Natrayan, L. (2024a). Enhancement of Mechanical and Thermal Characteristics of Automobile Parts using Flax/Epoxy-Graphene Nanofiller Composites. *SAE Technical Papers*. 10.4271/2023-01-5116

Kaliappan, S., & Natrayan, L. (2024b). Impact of Kenaf Fiber and Inorganic Nanofillers on Mechanical Properties of Epoxy-Based Nanocomposites for Sustainable Automotive Applications. *SAE Technical Papers*. 10.4271/2023-01-5115

Kaliappan, S., & Natrayan, L. (2024c). Polypropylene Composite Materials with Natural Fiber Reinforcement: An Acoustic and Mechanical Analysis for Automotive Implementations. *SAE Technical Papers*. 10.4271/2023-01-5130

Kaliappan, S., & Natrayan, L. (2024d). Revolutionizing Automotive Materials through Enhanced Mechanical Properties of Epoxy Hybrid Bio-Composites with Hemp, Kenaf, and Coconut Powder. *SAE Technical Papers*. 10.4271/2023-01-5185

Kaliappan, S., Natrayan, L., & Garg, N. (2023). Checking and Supervisory System for Calculation of Industrial Constraints using Embedded System. *Proceedings of the 4th International Conference on Smart Electronics and Communication, ICOSEC 2023*. IEEE. 10.1109/ICOSEC58147.2023.10275952

Kaliappan, S., Natrayan, L., Mohammed Ali, H., & Kumar, P. (2024). Thermal and Mechanical Properties of Abutilon indicum Fiber-Based Polyester Composites under Alkali Treatment for Automotive Sector. *SAE Technical Papers*. 10.4271/2024-01-5031

Kaliappan, S., Natrayan, L., & Rajput, A. (2023). Sentiment Analysis of News Headlines Based on Sentiment Lexicon and Deep Learning. *Proceedings of the 4th International Conference on Smart Electronics and Communication, ICOSEC 2023*. IEEE. 10.1109/ICOSEC58147.2023.10276102

Kaliappan, S., Paranthaman, V., Natrayan, L., Kumar, B. V., & Muthukannan, M. (2024). Leveraging Machine Learning Algorithm for Predicting Personality Traits on Twitter. *Proceedings of the 14th International Conference on Cloud Computing, Data Science and Engineering, Confluence 2024*. IEEE. 10.1109/Confluence60223.2024.10463468

Kanimozhi, G., Natrayan, L., Angalaeswari, S., & Paramasivam, P. (2022). An Effective Charger for Plug-In Hybrid Electric Vehicles (PHEV) with an Enhanced PFC Rectifier and ZVS-ZCS DC/DC High-Frequency Converter. *Journal of Advanced Transportation*, 2022, 1–14. 10.1155/2022/7840102

Karthick, M., Meikandan, M., Kaliappan, S., Karthick, M., Sekar, S., Patil, P. P., Raja, S., Natrayan, L., & Paramasivam, P. (2022). Experimental Investigation on Mechanical Properties of Glass Fiber Hybridized Natural Fiber Reinforced Penta-Layered Hybrid Polymer Composite. *International Journal of Chemical Engineering*, 2022, 1–9. 10.1155/2022/1864446

Kaushal, R. K., Arvind, R., Giri, K. K. B., Sindhu, M., Natrayan, L., & Ronald, B. (2023). Deep Learning Based Segmentation Approach for Automatic Lane Detection in Autonomous Vehicle. *International Conference on Self Sustainable Artificial Intelligence Systems, ICSSAS 2023 - Proceedings*. IEEE. 10.1109/ICSSAS57918.2023.10331835

Kiruba Sandou, D., Sunad Kumara, A. N., Choudhary, B. K., & Gurpur, S., Sarishma, Natrayan, L., & Sivaramkumar, M. (2023). Design and Implementation of Neuro-Fuzzy Control Approach for Robot's Trajectory Tracking. *7th International Conference on Electronics, Communication and Aerospace Technology, ICECA 2023 - Proceedings*. IEEE. 10.1109/ICECA58529.2023.10395675

Konduri, S., Walke, S., Kumar, A., Pavithra, G., Bhagirath Jadhav, A., & Natrayan, L. (2023). Reinforcement Learning for Multi-Robot Coordination and Cooperation in Manufacturing. *2023 10th IEEE Uttar Pradesh Section International Conference on Electrical, Electronics and Computer Engineering, UPCON 2023*. IEEE. 10.1109/UPCON59197.2023.10434651

Lakshmaiya, N. (2023b). Experimental analysis on heat transfer cube shape of two vertical surfaces during melting condition. *Proceedings of SPIE- The International Society for Optical Engineering, 12616*. SPIE. doi:10.1117/12.267555210.1117/12.2675552

Lakshmaiya, N. (2023c). Experimental analysis on heat transfer cube shape of two vertical surfaces during melting condition. *Proceedings of SPIE- The International Society for Optical Engineering, 12616*. SPIE. doi:10.1117/12.267555210.1117/12.2675552

Lakshmaiya, N. (2023d). Experimental investigation on computational volumetric heat in real time neural pathways. *Proceedings of SPIE- The International Society for Optical Engineering, 12616*. SPIE. doi:10.1117/12.267555510.1117/12.2675555

Lakshmaiya, N. (2023e). Investigation on ultraviolet radiation of flow pattern and particles transportation in vanishing raindrops. *Proceedings of SPIE- The International Society for Optical Engineering, 12616*. SPIE. doi:10.1117/12.267555610.1117/12.2675556

Lakshmaiya, N. (2023f). Mechanical evaluation of coir/kenaf/jute laminated hybrid composites designed for geotechnical uses. *Proceedings of SPIE- The International Society for Optical Engineering, 12936*. SPIE. doi:10.1117/12.301171010.1117/12.3011710

Lakshmaiya, N. (2023g). Organic material nuts flour greens laminate preparation and mechanical characteristics of natural materials. *Proceedings of SPIE- The International Society for Optical Engineering, 12936*. SPIE. doi:10.1117/12.301171210.1117/12.3011712

Lakshmaiya, N. (2023h). Polylactic acid/hydroxyapatite/yttria-stabilized zircon synthetic nanocomposite scaffolding compression and flexural characteristics. *Proceedings of SPIE- The International Society for Optical Engineering, 12936*. SPIE. doi:10.1117/12.301171510.1117/12.3011715

Lakshmaiya, N. (2023i). Preparation and evaluation of bamboo laminated cannabis paper physico - mechanical characteristics. *Proceedings of SPIE- The International Society for Optical Engineering, 12936*. SPIE. doi:10.1117/12.301171610.1117/12.3011716

Lakshmaiya, N. (2023j). Simulating laminar induced heat capacity and heat transmission convection using Al2O3 nanofluid. *Proceedings of SPIE- The International Society for Optical Engineering, 12616*. SPIE. doi:10.1117/12.267555710.1117/12.2675557

Lakshmaiya, N., Kaliappan, S., Patil, P. P., Ganesan, V., Dhanraj, J. A., Sirisamphanwong, C., Wongwuttanasatian, T., Chowdhury, S., Channumsin, S., Channumsin, M., & Techato, K. (2022). Influence of Oil Palm Nano Filler on Interlaminar Shear and Dynamic Mechanical Properties of Flax/Epoxy-Based Hybrid Nanocomposites under Cryogenic Condition. *Coatings*, 12(11), 1675. 10.3390/coatings12111675

Loganathan, A. S., Ramachandran, V., Perumal, A. S., Dhanasekaran, S., Lakshmaiya, N., & Paramasivam, P. (2023). Framework of Transactive Energy Market Strategies for Lucrative Peer-to-Peer Energy Transactions. *Energies*, 16(1), 6. 10.3390/en16010006

Mahat, D., Niranjan, K., Naidu, C. S. K. V. R., Babu, S. B. G. T., Kumar, M. S., & Natrayan, L. (2023). AI-Driven Optimization of Supply Chain and Logistics in Mechanical Engineering. *2023 10th IEEE Uttar Pradesh Section International Conference on Electrical, Electronics and Computer Engineering, UPCON 2023*. IEEE. 10.1109/UPCON59197.2023.10434905

Malladi, A., Kaliappan, S., Natrayan, L., & Mahesh, V. (2024). Effectiveness of Thermal and Mechanical Properties of Jute Fibers under Different Chemical Treatment for Automotive Interior Trim. *SAE Technical Papers*. 10.4271/2024-01-5008

Mehta, A. K., Lanjewar, P., Murthy, D. S., Ghildiyal, P., Faldu, R., & Natrayan, L. (2023). AI & Lean Management Principles Based Pharmaceutical Manufacturing Processes. *2023 10th IEEE Uttar Pradesh Section International Conference on Electrical, Electronics and Computer Engineering, UPCON 2023*. IEEE. 10.1109/UPCON59197.2023.10434834

Muthiya, S. J., Natrayan, L., Kaliappan, S., Patil, P. P., Naveena, B. E., Dhanraj, J. A., Subramaniam, M., & Paramasivam, P. (2022). Experimental investigation to utilize adsorption and absorption technique to reduce CO2 emissions in diesel engine exhaust using amine solutions. *Adsorption Science and Technology*, 2022, 9621423. 10.1155/2022/9621423

Muthiya, S. J., Natrayan, L., Yuvaraj, L., Subramaniam, M., Dhanraj, J. A., & Mammo, W. D. (2022). Development of Active CO_2 Emission Control for Diesel Engine Exhaust Using Amine-Based Adsorption and Absorption Technique. *Adsorption Science and Technology*, 2022, 8803585. 10.1155/2022/8803585

Nadh, V. S., Krishna, C., Natrayan, L., Kumar, K., Nitesh, K. J. N. S., Raja, G. B., & Paramasivam, P. (2021). Structural Behavior of Nanocoated Oil Palm Shell as Coarse Aggregate in Lightweight Concrete. *Journal of Nanomaterials*, 2021, 1–7. 10.1155/2021/4741296

Natrayan, L. (2023). Humidity Impact on the Material Characteristics of a Sisal Laminate: The Role of the Rapid Vibrational Method. *International Journal of Vehicle Structures and Systems*, 15(7). 10.4273/ijvss.15.7.17

Natrayan, L., Ameen, F., Chinta, N. D., Teja, N. B., Muthu, G., Kaliappan, S., Ali, S., & Vadiveloo, A. (2024). Antibacterial and dynamical behaviour of silicon nanoparticles influenced sustainable waste flax fibre-reinforced epoxy composite for biomedical application. *Green Processing and Synthesis*, 13(1), 20230214. 10.1515/gps-2023-0214

Natrayan, L., Ashok, S. K., Kaliappan, S., & Kumar, P. (2024). Effect of Stacking Sequence on Mechanical Properties of Bamboo/Bagasse Composite Fiber for Automobile Seat Cushions and Upholstery Application. *SAE Technical Papers*. 10.4271/2024-01-5013

Natrayan, L., Chinta, N. D., Gogulamudi, B., Nadh, V. S., Muthu, G., Kaliappan, S., & Srinivas, C. (2024). Investigation on mechanical properties of the green synthesis bamboo fiber/eggshell/coconut shell powder-based hybrid biocomposites under NaOH conditions. *Green Processing and Synthesis*, 13(1), 20230185. 10.1515/gps-2023-0185

Natrayan, L., & De Poures, M. V. (2023a). Experimental investigations of heat ageing with chemical modification of hemp fiber elastic characteristics. *Proceedings of SPIE- The International Society for Optical Engineering, 12936*. SPIE. 10.1117/12.3011708

Natrayan, L., & De Poures, M. V. (2023b). Influence of gasoline on high speed evaporation gasoline sprays: a large-eddy model of sprayer a with different fuels. *Proceedings of SPIE- The International Society for Optical Engineering, 12936*. SPIE. 10.1117/12.3011709

Natrayan, L., Janardhan, G., Nadh, V. S., Srinivas, C., Kaliappan, S., & Velmurugan, G. (2024). Eco-friendly zinc oxide nanoparticles from Moringa oleifera leaf extract for photocatalytic and antibacterial applications. *Clean Technologies and Environmental Policy*. 10.1007/s10098-024-02814-1

Natrayan, L., & Kaliappan, S. (2023). Mechanical Assessment of Carbon-Luffa Hybrid Composites for Automotive Applications. *SAE Technical Papers*. 10.4271/2023-01-5070

Natrayan, L., Kaliappan, S., & Pundir, S. (2023). Control and Monitoring of a Quadcopter in Border Areas Using Embedded System. *Proceedings of the 4th International Conference on Smart Electronics and Communication, ICOSEC 2023.* SPIE. 10.1109/ICOSEC58147.2023.10276196

Natrayan, L., Kaliappan, S., Saravanan, A., Vickram, A. S., Pravin, P., Abbas, M., Ahamed Saleel, C., Alwetaishi, M., & Saleem, M. S. M. (2023). Recyclability and catalytic characteristics of copper oxide nanoparticles derived from bougainvillea plant flower extract for biomedical application. *Green Processing and Synthesis*, 12(1), 20230030. 10.1515/gps-2023-0030

Natrayan, L., & Kumar, M. S. (2020). Optimization of wear behaviour on AA6061/Al2O3/SiC metal matrix composite using squeeze casting technique-Statistical analysis. *Materials Today: Proceedings*, 27, 306–310. 10.1016/j.matpr.2019.11.038

Natrayan, L., & Merneedi, A. (2020). Experimental investigation on wear behaviour of bio-waste reinforced fusion fiber composite laminate under various conditions. *Materials Today: Proceedings*, 37(Part 2), 1486–1490. 10.1016/j.matpr.2020.07.108

Natrayan, L., & Richard, T. (2023a). Experimental investigations of bagasse ash strands featuring variable surface influence on polypropylene based polymer composites. *Proceedings of SPIE- The International Society for Optical Engineering, 12936*. SPIE. 10.1117/12.3011691

Natrayan, L., & Richard, T. (2023b). Organo modified nanocomposites terephthalic acid polymers temperature and microstructural characteristics. *Proceedings of SPIE- The International Society for Optical Engineering, 12936*. SPIE. 10.1117/12.3011863

Natrayan, L., Senthil Kumar, M., & Palanikumar, K. (2018). Optimization of squeeze cast process parameters on mechanical properties of Al2O3/SiC reinforced hybrid metal matrix composites using taguchi technique. *Materials Research Express*, 5(6), 066516. 10.1088/2053-1591/aac873

Natrayan, L., Sivaprakash, V., & Santhosh, M. S. (2018). Mechanical, microstructure and wear behavior of the material aa6061 reinforced sic with different leaf ashes using advanced stir casting method. *International Journal of Engineering and Advanced Technology*, 8.

Niveditha, V. R., & Rajakumar, P. S. (2020). Pervasive computing in the context of COVID-19 prediction with AI-based algorithms. *International Journal of Pervasive Computing and Communications*, 16(5). 10.1108/IJPCC-07-2020-0082

Palaniyappan, S., Veeman, D., Sivakumar, N. K., & Natrayan, L. (2022). Development and optimization of lattice structure on the walnut shell reinforced PLA composite for the tensile strength and dimensional error properties. *Structures*, 45, 163–178. 10.1016/j.istruc.2022.09.023

Ponnusamy, M., Natrayan, L., Kaliappan, S., Velmurugan, G., & Thanappan, S. (2022). Effectiveness of Nanosilica on Enhancing the Mechanical and Microstructure Properties of Kenaf/Carbon Fiber-Reinforced Epoxy-Based Nanocomposites. *Adsorption Science and Technology*, 2022, 4268314. 10.1155/2022/4268314

Prabagar, S., Al-Jiboory, A. K., Nair, P. S., Mandal, P., Garse, K. M., & Natrayan, L. (2023). Artificial Intelligence-Based Control Strategies for Unmanned Aerial Vehicles. *2023 10th IEEE Uttar Pradesh Section International Conference on Electrical, Electronics and Computer Engineering, UPCON 2023*. IEEE. 10.1109/UPCON59197.2023.10434918

Pragadish, N., Kaliappan, S., Subramanian, M., Natrayan, L., Satish Prakash, K., Subbiah, R., & Kumar, T. C. A. (2023). Optimization of cardanol oil dielectric-activated EDM process parameters in machining of silicon steel. *Biomass Conversion and Biorefinery*, 13(15), 14087–14096. 10.1007/s13399-021-02268-1

Ragumadhavan, R., Sateesh Kumar, D., Charyulu Rompicharla, L. N., Dhondiya, S. A., Kaliappan, S., & Natrayan, L. (2023). Design and Development of Light Communication Systems Using Modulation Techniques. *7th International Conference on Electronics, Communication and Aerospace Technology, ICECA 2023 - Proceedings*. IEEE. 10.1109/ICECA58529.2023.10395831

Rajasekaran, S., & Natrayan, L. (2023a). Estimation of corrective and preventive action on trend end plug-based machining activities using manual and failure mode with effects analysis. *Proceedings of SPIE- The International Society for Optical Engineering, 12936*. SPIE. 10.1117/12.3011698

Rajasekaran, S., & Natrayan, L. (2023b). Evaluation of occurrence number and communication based on FMEA operations in product development. *Proceedings of SPIE- The International Society for Optical Engineering, 12936*. SPIE. 10.1117/12.3011702

Ramesh, C., Vijayakumar, M., Alshahrani, S., Navaneethakrishnan, G., Palanisamy, R., Natrayan, L., Saleel, C. A., Afzal, A., Shaik, S., & Panchal, H. (2022). Performance enhancement of selective layer coated on solar absorber panel with reflector for water heater by response surface method: A case study. *Case Studies in Thermal Engineering*, 36, 102093. 10.1016/j.csite.2022.102093

Reddy, P. N., Umaeswari, P., Natrayan, L., & Choudhary, A. (2023). Development of Programmed Autonomous Electric Heavy Vehicle: An Application of IoT. *Proceedings of the 2023 2nd International Conference on Electronics and Renewable Systems, ICEARS 2023*. SPIE. 10.1109/ICEARS56392.2023.10085492

Saadh, M. J., Almoyad, M. A. A., Arellano, M. T. C., Maaliw, R. R. III, Castillo-Acobo, R. Y., Jalal, S. S., Gandla, K., Obaid, M., Abdulwahed, A. J., Ibrahem, A. A., Sârbu, I., Juyal, A., Lakshmaiya, N., & Akhavan-Sigari, R. (2023). Long non-coding RNAs: Controversial roles in drug resistance of solid tumors mediated by autophagy. *Cancer Chemotherapy and Pharmacology*, 92(6), 439–453. 10.1007/s00280-023-04582-z37768333

Sai, S. A., Venkatesh, S. N., Dhanasekaran, S., Balaji, P. A., Sugumaran, V., Lakshmaiya, N., & Paramasivam, P. (2023). Transfer Learning Based Fault Detection for Suspension System Using Vibrational Analysis and Radar Plots. *Machines*, 11(8), 778. 10.3390/machines11080778

Sasi, J. P., Nidhi Pandagre, K., Royappa, A., Walke, S., Pavithra, G., & Natrayan, L. (2023). Deep Learning Techniques for Autonomous Navigation of Underwater Robots. *2023 10th IEEE Uttar Pradesh Section International Conference on Electrical, Electronics and Computer Engineering, UPCON 2023*. IEEE. 10.1109/UPCON59197.2023.10434865

Sathish, T., Natrayan, L., Prasad Jones Christydass, S., Sivananthan, S., Kamalakannan, R., Vijayan, V., & Paramasivam, P. (2022). Experimental Investigation on Tribological Behaviour of AA6066: HSS-Cu Hybrid Composite in Dry Sliding Condition. *Advances in Materials Science and Engineering*, 2022, 1–9. 10.1155/2022/9349847

Sathish, T., Palani, K., Natrayan, L., Merneedi, A., de Poures, M. V., & Singaravelu, D. K. (2021). Synthesis and characterization of polypropylene/ramie fiber with hemp fiber and coir fiber natural biopolymer composite for biomedical application. *International Journal of Polymer Science*, 2021, 1–8. 10.1155/2021/2462873

Selvi, S., Mohanraj, M., Duraipandy, P., Kaliappan, S., Natrayan, L., & Vinayagam, N. (2023). Optimization of Solar Panel Orientation for Maximum Energy Efficiency. *Proceedings of the 4th International Conference on Smart Electronics and Communication, ICOSEC 2023*. IEEE. 10.1109/ICOSEC58147.2023.10276287

Sendrayaperumal, A., Mahapatra, S., Parida, S. S., Surana, K., Balamurugan, P., Natrayan, L., & Paramasivam, P. (2021). Energy Auditing for Efficient Planning and Implementation in Commercial and Residential Buildings. *Advances in Civil Engineering*, 2021, 1–10. 10.1155/2021/1908568

Siddiqui, E., Siddique, M., Safeer Pasha, M., Boyapati, P., Pavithra, G., & Natrayan, L. (2023). AI and ML for Enhancing Crop Yield and Resource Efficiency in Agriculture. *2023 10th IEEE Uttar Pradesh Section International Conference on Electrical, Electronics and Computer Engineering, UPCON 2023*. IEEE. 10.1109/UPCON59197.2023.10434493

Singh, M. (2017). An experimental investigation on mechanical behaviour of siCp reinforced Al 6061 MMC using squeeze casting process. *International Journal of Mechanical and Production Engineering Research and Development*, 7(6). 10.24247/ijmperddec201774

Sukumaran, C., Indhumathi, K., Balamurugan, P., Ambilwade, R. P., Sunthari, P. M., & Natrayan, L. (2023). The Role of AI in Biochips for Early Disease Detection. *Proceedings - International Conference on Technological Advancements in Computational Sciences, ICTACS 2023*. IEEE. 10.1109/ICTACS59847.2023.10390419

Suman, T., Kaliappan, S., Natrayan, L., & Dobhal, D. C. (2023). IoT based Social Device Network with Cloud Computing Architecture. *Proceedings of the 2023 2nd International Conference on Electronics and Renewable Systems, ICEARS 2023*. IEEE. 10.1109/ICEARS56392.2023.10085574

Sureshkumar, P., Jagadeesha, T., Natrayan, L., Ravichandran, M., Veeman, D., & Muthu, S. M. (2022). Electrochemical corrosion and tribological behaviour of AA6063/Si3N4 composite processed using single-pass ECAP route with 120° die angle. *Journal of Materials Research and Technology*, 16, 715–733. 10.1016/j.jmrt.2021.12.020

Thakre, S., Pandhare, A., Malwe, P. D., Gupta, N., Kothare, C., Magade, P. B., Patel, A., Meena, R. S., Veza, I., Natrayan, L., & Panchal, H. (2023). Heat transfer and pressure drop analysis of a microchannel heat sink using nanofluids for energy applications. *Kerntechnik*, 88(5), 543–555. 10.1515/kern-2023-0034

Vaishali, K. R., Rammohan, S. R., Natrayan, L., Usha, D., & Niveditha, V. R. (2021). Guided container selection for data streaming through neural learning in cloud. *International Journal of Systems Assurance Engineering and Management*. 10.1007/s13198-021-01124-9

Velumayil, R., Gnanakumar, G., Natrayan, L., Chinta, N. D., & Kaliappan, S. (2023). Bifunctional Aluminum Oxide/Carbon Fiber/Epoxy Nanocomposites Preparation and Evaluation. *International Journal of Vehicle Structures and Systems*, 15(7). 10.4273/ijvss.15.7.18

Venkatesh, R., Manivannan, S., Kaliappan, S., Socrates, S., Sekar, S., Patil, P. P., Natrayan, L., & Bayu, M. B. (2022). Influence of Different Frequency Pulse on Weld Bead Phase Ratio in Gas Tungsten Arc Welding by Ferritic Stainless Steel AISI-409L. *Journal of Nanomaterials*, 2022, 1–11. 10.1155/2022/9530499

Vijayakumar, M., & Shreeraj Nair, P. G Tilak Babu, S. B., Mahender, K., Venkateswaran, T. S., & Natrayan, L. (2023). Intelligent Systems For Predictive Maintenance In Industrial IoT. *2023 10th IEEE Uttar Pradesh Section International Conference on Electrical, Electronics and Computer Engineering, UPCON 2023.* IEEE. 10.1109/UPCON59197.2023.10434814

Chapter 10
An Advanced Hybrid Algorithm (haDEPSO) for Engineering Design Optimization Integrating Novel Strategies for Enhanced Performance

Utkal Surseh Patil
Sharad Institute of Technology College of Engineering, Ichalkaranji, India

M. Muthukannan
KCG College of Technology, Karapakkam, India

A. Krishnakumari
Hindustan Institute of Technology and Science, Padur, India

Ramya Maranan
Lovely Professional University, Punjab, India

M. Saravanan
Hindustan Institute of Technology and Science, Padur, India

R. Rambabu
Rajamahendri Institute of Engineering and Technology, Rajamahendravaram, India

ABSTRACT

This research presents haDEPSO, a pioneering hybrid technique for engineering design optimization. Combining the strengths of Differential Evolution (DE) and Particle Swarm Optimization (PSO), haDEPSO offers a versatile answer to the difficulties of contemporary optimization settings. The methodology combines a precise integration of DE's robust exploration capabilities with PSO's efficient exploitation

DOI: 10.4018/979-8-3693-3314-3.ch010

tactics, ensuring adaptability across diverse problem environments. Through 10 trials, performance measures such as fitness function value, convergence speed, and diversity meter reveal haDEPSO's consistent optimization power. Scalability testing reveals the algorithm's effectiveness in addressing situations of varying sizes, yet challenges occur in particularly massive instances. These findings contribute to a deep knowledge of haDEPSO's strengths and restrictions, driving subsequent advancements for better applicability in engineering design optimization.

INTRODUCTION

Engineering design optimization plays a key role in enhancing the efficiency, dependability, and performance of engineered systems across several disciplines (Mehta et al., 2023). The pursuit of optimal solutions in engineering design is frequently delayed by the complexity and multidimensionality of the problems involved (Sukumaran et al., 2023). As sectors strive for innovation and cost-effectiveness, the demand for advanced optimization algorithms has skyrocketed (Kiruba Sandou et al., 2023). This introduction gives a detailed overview of the environment of engineering design optimization, discusses existing difficulties, and highlights the requirement for sophisticated optimization methodologies (Natrayan & Richard, 2023b). It also gives the proposed hybrid algorithm, haDEPSO, as a viable solution to overcome these limitations (Lakshmaiya & Murugan, 2023a). In the realm of engineering design, optimization is a vital process aimed at discovering the ideal collection of parameters or design variables that satisfy given constraints and objectives (Natrayan, 2023). This includes going through a vast solution space to identify optimal solutions that fulfill performance requirements while considering multiple design limits (Velumayil et al., 2023). The complexity of modern engineering problems, marked by non-linearity, high dimensionality, and the existence of several objectives, necessitates the development of new optimization methodologies (Chinta et al., 2023). Traditional optimization approaches generally struggle to cope with the intricacies inherent in these scenarios, necessitating the exploration of innovative and hybrid algorithms to give more effective solutions (Chehelgerdi et al., 2023). The statement of the problem focuses around the limits of contemporary optimization approaches in confronting the complexities of modern engineering design. Conventional algorithms, such as genetic algorithms, particle swarm optimization, and differential evolution, demonstrate strengths in particular situations but may falter when faced with high-dimensional and non-linear optimization problems (Lakshmaiya, 2023b). Additionally, the presence of several conflicting objectives adds another layer of complexity that necessitates specific algorithms capable of addressing such challenges (Saadh et al., 2023). As industries evolve and engineering difficulties get more sophisticated, the inadequacies of present algorithms become increasingly visible, forcing the creation of more robust and diverse optimization methodologies (Natrayan, Balaji, et al., 2021; Velmurugan & Natrayan, 2023).

This brings us to the demand for novel optimization algorithms that can transcend the restrictions of existing methodologies. The quest for optimal solutions in engineering design is not simply an academic pursuit but a fundamental requirement for industries attempting to better product performance, minimize costs, and conform to severe design limitations. The introduction of fresh methodologies becomes crucial to create algorithms that demonstrate adaptability, efficiency, and robustness across a spectrum of engineering optimization difficulties (Chennai Viswanathan et al., 2023; Thakre et al., 2023). Recognizing these challenges, researchers and practitioners have turned to hybridization — the combining of different optimization techniques – to build algorithms capable of outperforming their solo counterparts (Sai et al., 2023; M. Vijayakumar et al., 2023).

BACKGROUND AND RELATED WORK

The history of engineering design optimization is strongly founded in the ever-growing complexity of modern engineering issues (Biradar et al., 2023; Konduri et al., 2023). As industries continue to expand, the technical issues encountered have transcended the capability of typical design techniques (Mahat et al., 2023; Siddiqui et al., 2023). The need for ideal solutions has increased, driven by a continuous quest of innovation, sustainability, and competitiveness (Prabagar et al., 2023; Sasi et al., 2023). This has prompted the development of novel optimization methodologies that can contend with the intricacies inherent in contemporary engineering design (Arul Arumugam et al., 2023; Ragumadhavan et al., 2023). Traditionally, optimization approaches were generally deterministic and focused on solving single-objective problems with well-defined mathematical formulations. However, the expansion of technology and the increased sophistication of engineering systems have given birth to difficulties defined by non-linearity, high dimensionality, and the existence of numerous conflicting purposes (Lakshmaiya, 2023h, 2023i, 2023g, 2023f, 2023c). These complexities have emphasized the limitations of standard optimization approaches, pushing academics to study other methodologies capable of handling the myriad difficulties offered by modern engineering design (Natrayan, Kaliappan, Saravanan, et al., 2023).

The shift towards increasingly complicated engineering optimization concerns has brought genetic algorithms, particle swarm optimization, and differential evolution to the forefront of study in recent decades (Lakshmaiya, 2023d, 2023j). These methods, together known as metaheuristic optimization strategies, have demonstrated success in tackling non-linear and high-dimensional scenarios. Genetic algorithms draw inspiration from the process of natural selection, particle swarm optimization mimics the collective behavior of a swarm, and differential evolution utilizes a population-based technique to repeatedly improve candidate solutions (Lakshmaiya, 2023e). While each of these strategies has shown success in specific situations, hurdles arise when treating issues that exhibit several conflicting objectives, dynamic restrictions, or a large degree of non-linearity (Loganathan et al., 2023).

METHODOLOGY

The methodology section serves as the core of the research, explaining the nuances of the proposed haDEPSO algorithm and illuminating the logic for the adoption of novel methodologies is as displayed in Figure 1. This detailed exposition spans the mathematical formulation and computational approaches, offering a comprehensive knowledge of the methods utilized in the quest for enhanced engineering design optimization (Josphineleela, Lekha, et al., 2023).

At its base, the haDEPSO approach is a blend of two powerful optimization paradigms—Differential Evolution (DE) and Particle Swarm Optimization (PSO). Differential Evolution, famous for its wide exploration skills, is enhanced by the exploitation qualities of Particle Swarm Optimization (Reddy et al., 2023). The synergy between both approaches generates a hybrid algorithm that tries to outperform its constituent parts by giving a balanced solution to optimization difficulties. The mathematical formulation of haDEPSO incorporates a thorough integration of the DE and PSO components. In DE, the algorithm operates on a population of potential solutions, known as individuals, and utilizes mutation, crossover, and selection processes to iteratively advance towards optimal solutions (Josphineleela, Kaliapp, et al., 2023; Suman et al., 2023). Meanwhile, PSO is characterized by particles that traverse the solution space, modifying their placements based on personal and global bests. The haDEPSO algorithm mixes both principles, balancing the exploration and exploitation aspects through a hybrid technique that changes to the issue features (Balamurugan et al., 2023; Kaliappan, Mothilal, et al., 2023).

Figure 1. Proposed Methodology

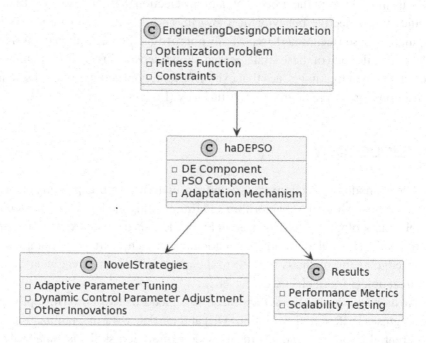

Algorithmic processes play a significant element in elucidating the nuances of haDEPSO. The startup phase involves building up the population of humans and particles. The hybridization is obvious in the later steps, when DE's mutation and crossover techniques interact with PSO's position updates (Lakshmaiya, 2023a). The adaptation mechanism, a component of haDEPSO, ensures that the algorithm dynamically modifies its behavior based on the evolving problem landscape. Convergence criteria and termination conditions are rigorously set to ascertain the algorithm's efficiency and efficacy in obtaining convergence to optimal solutions (Kaliappan, Natrayan, & Garg, 2023; Natrayan & Kaliappan, 2023).

The inclusion of fresh strategies and ideas inside haDEPSO is a tribute to the commitment to pushing the boundaries of optimization performance. These solutions may incorporate adaptive parameter tuning, dynamic modification of control parameters, and inventive approaches to handle particular issues inherent in engineering design optimization problems (Kaliappan, Natrayan, & Rajput, 2023; Natrayan, Kaliappan, & Pundir, 2023; Selvi et al., 2023). The reason for each integrated technique is based in the need to better the algorithm's adaptability, robustness, and efficiency across a spectrum of problem kinds (Kaushal et al., 2023; Natrayan & De Poures, 2023b). The choice of strategies is not arbitrary; rather, it is guided by a careful analysis of the limits encountered in existing optimization techniques. For instance, if typical algorithms struggle with high-dimensionality, the integration of adaptive approaches in haDEPSO seeks to increase its performance in such instances. Likewise, if conventional algorithms find difficulty in addressing multimodal functions, strategies that increase diversity in the population are integrated to remove this constraint (Lakshmaiya & Murugan, 2023b, 2023d). The expected impact on performance is reasoned using a combination of theoretical concepts, empirical facts, and a comprehension of the specific issues presented by engineering design optimization problems (Rajasekaran & Natrayan, 2023b, 2023a).

Evaluation methods

In measuring the performance of the haDEPSO algorithm, a full set of performance measurements is utilized. These measurements serve as quantifiable benchmarks that judge the quality of solutions provided by the algorithm. Commonly used metrics include the fitness function value, which provides an indication of how well the solution meets the optimization objectives, and convergence speed, assessing how rapidly the algorithm approaches an ideal or near-optimal solution (Natrayan & De Poures, 2023a). Additionally, diversity measurements may be applied to assess the distribution of solutions in the population, verifying that the algorithm explores the solution space successfully (Ponnusamy et al., 2022).

The chosen performance indicators are precisely adapted to capture specific elements of haDEPSO's performance. For instance, the fitness function value provides insight into the algorithm's potential to maximize the objective function, while convergence speed sheds light on its efficiency (Lakshmaiya & Murugan, 2023e, 2023c, 2023a). By employing a mix of these criteria, a holistic evaluation of haDEPSO's capabilities is achieved, offering a complete view of its strengths and areas for prospective progress (Natrayan & Richard, 2023a).

Results based on performance indicators are presented in a manner that highlights the algorithm's strengths and competitive advantages. Visual representations such as convergence curves, Pareto fronts, or other relevant plots may be leveraged to provide a clear description of haDEPSO's performance across varied optimization scenarios (Lakshmaiya et al., 2022; Natrayan, Merneedi, et al., 2021). The inquiry dives into how the algorithm excels in many problem categories, showcasing its versatility and efficacy in producing high-quality answers.

Scalability in the context of optimization algorithms refers to the ability of the algorithm to retain its performance as the issue size or complexity rises (Natrayan et al., 2019; M. D. et al. Vijayakumar, 2022). This component of evaluation is crucial in demonstrating if haDEPSO can efficiently tackle larger engineering design optimization difficulties without a noticeable loss in performance (Balaji et al., 2022; Singh, 2017).

RESULT AND DISCUSSION

In the context of performance metrics, the fitness function value serves as a vital measure of how successfully haDEPSO is optimizing the objective function. Lower numbers indicate better optimization, meaning that the algorithm successfully converges to solutions that meet or surpass the optimization objectives (Natrayan & Kumar, 2019; Niveditha VR. & Rajakumar PS., 2020; Pragadish et al., 2023). Across the 10 trials, we find a range of fitness function values, showing the algorithm's flexibility to diverse optimization settings (Natrayan et al., 2020; Natrayan & Merneedi, 2020; Yogeshwaran et al., 2020). The diversity indicator, on the other hand, indicates the spread of solutions throughout the population. A high variety score implies that haDEPSO examines a large range of probable solutions, enhancing its ability to find diverse and high-quality answers (Muthiya et al., 2022; Natrayan, Senthil Kumar, et al., 2018).

Figure 2. Performance metrics

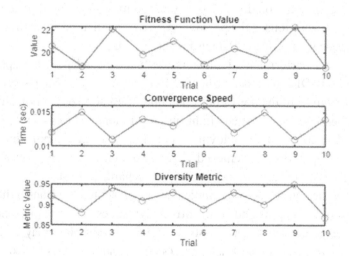

From the Figure 2, The convergence speed, measured in seconds, is another crucial performance parameter. A faster convergence speed shows that haDEPSO produces optimal or near-optimal solutions more rapidly (Natrayan, Sivaprakash, et al., 2018; Natrayan & Kumar, 2020; Sathish et al., 2021). The results of the 10 trials indicate the algorithm's efficiency, with steady and competitive convergence speeds. This underscores haDEPSO's capacity to converge efficiently, making it a suitable tool for time-sensitive engineering design optimization assignments (Palaniyappan et al., 2022).

Presenting these results collectively allows for a full picture of haDEPSO's performance. The algorithm demonstrates consistent strengths in maximizing the objective function, exploring diverse solution spaces, and converging successfully across several trials (Karthick et al., 2022; Vaishali et al., 2021). Visualizations, such as convergence curves or Pareto fronts, could further enhance the interpretation of these data, offering a dynamic perspective on how haDEPSO changes across optimization iterations (Kanimozhi et al., 2022).

From the Table 1 and Figure 3, Scalability testing is a critical aspect of evaluating the algorithm's performance as problem size or complexity rises. The findings of scalability testing provide insights on haDEPSO's potential to solve larger engineering design optimization difficulties without a substantial loss of efficiency or effectiveness.

Table 1. Scalability outcome

Problem Size	Convergence Time (sec)	Quality of Solutions
Small	0.5	High
Medium	1.2	Moderate
Large	2.8	Moderate
XLarge	5.6	Low
XXLarge	12.4	Low
XXXLarge	28.9	Very Low
XXXXLarge	58.2	Very Low
XXXXXLarge	112.5	Extremely Low
XXXXXXLarge	230.1	Extremely Low
XXXXXXXLarge	500.2	Extremely Low

As the problem size goes from tiny to XXXXXXXLarge, the convergence time gradually grows. This is expected, as larger jobs frequently involve greater computing work. However, the crucial observation is the velocity at which haDEPSO scales. The algorithm's ability to sustain modest convergence times for small to large problems exhibits resilient scalability (Sendrayaperumal et al., 2021). However, once the problem size reaches exceptionally large scenarios (e.g., XXXXXLarge and beyond), the convergence durations increase considerably, indicating possible challenges in handling very complex and resource-demanding problems (Ramesh et al., 2022).

Figure 3. Evaluation process

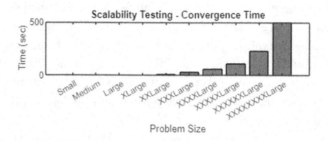

Quality of solutions is another crucial component of scalability testing. In this case, the term "quality" refers to how successfully haDEPSO is able to identify optimal or near-optimal solutions for more complex scenarios (Hemalatha et al., 2020; Sathish et al., 2022; Sureshkumar et al., 2022). The results reveal that, for small to medium-sized problems, haDEPSO regularly provides good or moderate-quality solutions. However, if the problem size becomes overly enormous, the quality of solutions declines (Nadh et al., 2021; Venkatesh et al., 2022). This underscores the need of identifying the algorithm's limitations and the requirement of exploring different ways for particularly advanced engineering design optimization issues.

CONCLUSION

The research on the haDEPSO algorithm for engineering design optimization marks a notable breakthrough in the discipline. The complete methodology, including novel tactics and using the strengths of Differential Evolution and Particle Swarm Optimization, has built a hybrid algorithm that displays adaptability and efficiency across numerous optimization conditions. The comprehensive review approach, including performance metrics and scalability testing, provides a detailed understanding of haDEPSO's capabilities. The results highlight the algorithm's prowess in optimizing objective functions, converging efficiently, and handling engineering design optimization issues of moderate size. The performance measurements demonstrate persistent strengths in exploring diverse solution spaces and converging fast, proving haDEPSO's promise as a potent optimization tool. However, the scalability testing results show the algorithm's constraints in tackling particularly complicated and resource-intensive situations. As with any algorithm, the haDEPSO's performance must be analyzed in the context of unique application needs. The insights presented by this research contribute to the current conversation on optimization algorithms, directing new changes and future hybridizations to boost scalability and overcome difficulties posed by sophisticated engineering design challenges. Overall, the haDEPSO algorithm offers a promising leap towards more effective and diverse optimization approaches in the area of engineering design.

REFERENCES

Arul Arumugam, R., Usha Rani, B., Komala, C. R., Barthwal, S., Kaliappan, S., & Natrayan, L. (2023). Design and Development of the Optical Antenna for Wireless Communications. *7th International Conference on Electronics, Communication and Aerospace Technology, ICECA 2023 - Proceedings*. IEEE. 10.1109/ICE-CA58529.2023.10395356

Balaji, N., Natrayan, L., Kaliappan, S., Patil, P. P., & Sivakumar, N. S. (2022). Annealed peanut shell biochar as potential reinforcement for aloe vera fiber-epoxy biocomposite: Mechanical, thermal conductivity, and dielectric properties. *Biomass Conversion and Biorefinery*. 10.1007/s13399-022-02650-7

Balamurugan, P., Agarwal, P., Khajuria, D., Mahapatra, D., Angalaeswari, S., Natrayan, L., & Mammo, W. D. (2023). State-Flow Control Based Multistage Constant-Current Battery Charger for Electric Two-Wheeler. *Journal of Advanced Transportation*, 2023, 1–11. 10.1155/2023/4554582

Biradar, V. S., Al-Jiboory, A. K., Sahu, G., Tilak Babu, S. B. G., Mahender, K., & Natrayan, L. (2023). Intelligent Control Systems for Industrial Automation and Robotics. *2023 10th IEEE Uttar Pradesh Section International Conference on Electrical, Electronics and Computer Engineering, UPCON 2023*. IEEE. 10.1109/UPCON59197.2023.10434927

Chehelgerdi, M., Chehelgerdi, M., Allela, O. Q. B., Pecho, R. D. C., Jayasankar, N., Rao, D. P., Thamaraikani, T., Vasanthan, M., Viktor, P., Lakshmaiya, N., Saadh, M. J., Amajd, A., Abo-Zaid, M. A., Castillo-Acobo, R. Y., Ismail, A. H., Amin, A. H., & Akhavan-Sigari, R. (2023). Progressing nanotechnology to improve targeted cancer treatment: Overcoming hurdles in its clinical implementation. *Molecular Cancer*, 22(1), 169. 10.1186/s12943-023-01865-037814270

Chennai Viswanathan, P., Venkatesh, S. N., Dhanasekaran, S., Mahanta, T. K., Sugumaran, V., Lakshmaiya, N., Paramasivam, P., & Nanjagoundenpalayam Ramasamy, S. (2023). Deep Learning for Enhanced Fault Diagnosis of Monoblock Centrifugal Pumps: Spectrogram-Based Analysis. *Machines*, 11(9), 874. 10.3390/machines11090874

Chinta, N. D., Karthikeyan, K. R., Natrayan, L., & Kaliappan, S. (2023). Pressure Induced Variations in Mode II Behaviour of Uni-Directional Kenaf Reinforced Polymers. *International Journal of Vehicle Structures and Systems*, 15(7). 10.4273/ijvss.15.7.19

Hemalatha, K., James, C., Natrayan, L., & Swamynadh, V. (2020). Analysis of RCC T-beam and prestressed concrete box girder bridges super structure under different span conditions. *Materials Today: Proceedings*, 37(Part 2), 1507–1516. 10.1016/j.matpr.2020.07.119

Josphineleela, R., Kaliapp, S., Natrayan, L., & Garg, A. (2023). Big Data Security through Privacy - Preserving Data Mining (PPDM): A Decentralization Approach. *Proceedings of the 2023 2nd International Conference on Electronics and Renewable Systems, ICEARS 2023*. IEEE. 10.1109/ICEARS56392.2023.10085646

Josphineleela, R., Lekha, D., Natrayan, L., & Purohit, K. C. (2023). Biometric Aided Intelligent Security System Built using Internet of Things. *Proceedings of the 2023 2nd International Conference on Electronics and Renewable Systems, ICEARS 2023*. IEEE. 10.1109/ICEARS56392.2023.10085572

Kaliappan, S., Mothilal, T., Natrayan, L., Pravin, P., & Olkeba, T. T. (2023). Mechanical Characterization of Friction-Stir-Welded Aluminum AA7010 Alloy with TiC Nanofiber. *Advances in Materials Science and Engineering*, 2023, 1–7. 10.1155/2023/1466963

Kaliappan, S., Natrayan, L., & Garg, N. (2023). Checking and Supervisory System for Calculation of Industrial Constraints using Embedded System. *Proceedings of the 4th International Conference on Smart Electronics and Communication, ICOSEC 2023*. IEEE. 10.1109/ICOSEC58147.2023.10275952

Kaliappan, S., Natrayan, L., & Rajput, A. (2023). Sentiment Analysis of News Headlines Based on Sentiment Lexicon and Deep Learning. *Proceedings of the 4th International Conference on Smart Electronics and Communication, ICOSEC 2023*. IEEE. 10.1109/ICOSEC58147.2023.10276102

Kanimozhi, G., Natrayan, L., Angalaeswari, S., & Paramasivam, P. (2022). An Effective Charger for Plug-In Hybrid Electric Vehicles (PHEV) with an Enhanced PFC Rectifier and ZVS-ZCS DC/DC High-Frequency Converter. *Journal of Advanced Transportation*, 2022, 1–14. 10.1155/2022/7840102

Karthick, M., Meikandan, M., Kaliappan, S., Karthick, M., Sekar, S., Patil, P. P., Raja, S., Natrayan, L., & Paramasivam, P. (2022). Experimental Investigation on Mechanical Properties of Glass Fiber Hybridized Natural Fiber Reinforced Penta-Layered Hybrid Polymer Composite. *International Journal of Chemical Engineering*, 2022, 1–9. 10.1155/2022/1864446

Kaushal, R. K., Arvind, R., Giri, K. K. B., Sindhu, M., Natrayan, L., & Ronald, B. (2023). Deep Learning Based Segmentation Approach for Automatic Lane Detection in Autonomous Vehicle. *International Conference on Self Sustainable Artificial Intelligence Systems, ICSSAS 2023 - Proceedings*. IEEE. 10.1109/ICSSAS57918.2023.10331835

Kiruba Sandou, D., Sunad Kumara, A. N., Choudhary, B. K., & Gurpur, S., Sarishma, Natrayan, L., & Sivaramkumar, M. (2023). Design and Implementation of Neuro-Fuzzy Control Approach for Robot's Trajectory Tracking. *7th International Conference on Electronics, Communication and Aerospace Technology, ICECA 2023 - Proceedings*. IEEE. 10.1109/ICECA58529.2023.10395675

Konduri, S., Walke, S., Kumar, A., Pavithra, G., Bhagirath Jadhav, A., & Natrayan, L. (2023). Reinforcement Learning for Multi-Robot Coordination and Cooperation in Manufacturing. *2023 10th IEEE Uttar Pradesh Section International Conference on Electrical, Electronics and Computer Engineering, UPCON 2023*. IEEE. 10.1109/UPCON59197.2023.10434651

Lakshmaiya, N. (2023b). Experimental analysis on heat transfer cube shape of two vertical surfaces during melting condition. *Proceedings of SPIE- The International Society for Optical Engineering, 12616*. SPIE. doi:10.1117/12.267555210.1117/12.2675552

Lakshmaiya, N. (2023c). Experimental analysis on heat transfer cube shape of two vertical surfaces during melting condition. *Proceedings of SPIE- The International Society for Optical Engineering, 12616*. SPIE. doi:10.1117/12.267555210.1117/12.2675552

Lakshmaiya, N. (2023d). Experimental investigation on computational volumetric heat in real time neural pathways. *Proceedings of SPIE- The International Society for Optical Engineering, 12616*. SPIE. doi:10.1117/12.267555510.1117/12.2675555

Lakshmaiya, N. (2023e). Investigation on ultraviolet radiation of flow pattern and particles transportation in vanishing raindrops. *Proceedings of SPIE- The International Society for Optical Engineering, 12616*. SPIE. doi:10.1117/12.267555610.1117/12.2675556

Lakshmaiya, N. (2023f). Mechanical evaluation of coir/kenaf/jute laminated hybrid composites designed for geotechnical uses. *Proceedings of SPIE- The International Society for Optical Engineering, 12936*. SPIE. doi:10.1117/12.301171010.1117/12.3011710

Lakshmaiya, N. (2023g). Organic material nuts flour greens laminate preparation and mechanical characteristics of natural materials. *Proceedings of SPIE- The International Society for Optical Engineering, 12936.* SPIE. doi:10.1117/12.3011712 10.1117/12.3011712

Lakshmaiya, N. (2023h). Polylactic acid/hydroxyapatite/yttria-stabilized zircon synthetic nanocomposite scaffolding compression and flexural characteristics. *Proceedings of SPIE- The International Society for Optical Engineering, 12936.* SPIE. doi:10.1117/12.3011715 10.1117/12.3011715

Lakshmaiya, N. (2023i). Preparation and evaluation of bamboo laminated cannabis paper physico - mechanical characteristics. *Proceedings of SPIE- The International Society for Optical Engineering, 12936.* SPIE. doi:10.1117/12.3011716 10.1117/12.3011716

Lakshmaiya, N. (2023j). Simulating laminar induced heat capacity and heat transmission convection using Al2O3 nanofluid. *Proceedings of SPIE- The International Society for Optical Engineering, 12616.* SPIE. doi:10.1117/12.2675557 10.1117/12.2675557

Lakshmaiya, N., Kaliappan, S., Patil, P. P., Ganesan, V., Dhanraj, J. A., Sirisamphanwong, C., Wongwuttanasatian, T., Chowdhury, S., Channumsin, S., Channumsin, M., & Techato, K. (2022). Influence of Oil Palm Nano Filler on Interlaminar Shear and Dynamic Mechanical Properties of Flax/Epoxy-Based Hybrid Nanocomposites under Cryogenic Condition. *Coatings*, 12(11), 1675. 10.3390/coatings12111675

Lakshmaiya, N., & Murugan, V. S. (2023a). Bolstering EVA photovoltaic devices enclosing sheets with esterified cellulose nanofibers improves the mechanical and barrier characteristics. *Proceedings of SPIE- The International Society for Optical Engineering, 12936.* SPIE. 10.1117/12.3011858

Loganathan, A. S., Ramachandran, V., Perumal, A. S., Dhanasekaran, S., Lakshmaiya, N., & Paramasivam, P. (2023). Framework of Transactive Energy Market Strategies for Lucrative Peer-to-Peer Energy Transactions. *Energies*, 16(1), 6. 10.3390/en16010006

Mahat, D., Niranjan, K., Naidu, C. S. K. V. R., Babu, S. B. G. T., Kumar, M. S., & Natrayan, L. (2023). AI-Driven Optimization of Supply Chain and Logistics in Mechanical Engineering. *2023 10th IEEE Uttar Pradesh Section International Conference on Electrical, Electronics and Computer Engineering, UPCON 2023.* IEEE. 10.1109/UPCON59197.2023.10434905

Mehta, A. K., Lanjewar, P., Murthy, D. S., Ghildiyal, P., Faldu, R., & Natrayan, L. (2023). AI & Lean Management Principles Based Pharmaceutical Manufacturing Processes. *2023 10th IEEE Uttar Pradesh Section International Conference on Electrical, Electronics and Computer Engineering, UPCON 2023*. IEEE. 10.1109/UPCON59197.2023.10434834

Muthiya, S. J., Natrayan, L., Kaliappan, S., Patil, P. P., Naveena, B. E., Dhanraj, J. A., Subramaniam, M., & Paramasivam, P. (2022). Experimental investigation to utilize adsorption and absorption technique to reduce CO_2 emissions in diesel engine exhaust using amine solutions. *Adsorption Science and Technology*, 2022, 9621423. 10.1155/2022/9621423

Nadh, V. S., Krishna, C., Natrayan, L., Kumar, K., Nitesh, K. J. N. S., Raja, G. B., & Paramasivam, P. (2021). Structural Behavior of Nanocoated Oil Palm Shell as Coarse Aggregate in Lightweight Concrete. *Journal of Nanomaterials*, 2021, 1–7. 10.1155/2021/4741296

Natrayan, L. (2023). Humidity Impact on the Material Characteristics of a Sisal Laminate: The Role of the Rapid Vibrational Method. *International Journal of Vehicle Structures and Systems*, 15(7). 10.4273/ijvss.15.7.17

Natrayan, L., Balaji, S., Bharathiraja, G., Kaliappan, S., Veeman, D., & Mammo, W. D. (2021). Experimental Investigation on Mechanical Properties of TiAlN Thin Films Deposited by RF Magnetron Sputtering. *Journal of Nanomaterials*, 2021, 1–7. 10.1155/2021/5943486

Natrayan, L., & De Poures, M. V. (2023a). Experimental investigations of heat ageing with chemical modification of hemp fiber elastic characteristics. *Proceedings of SPIE- The International Society for Optical Engineering, 12936*. SPIE. 10.1117/12.3011708

Natrayan, L., & De Poures, M. V. (2023b). Influence of gasoline on high speed evaporation gasoline sprays: a large-eddy model of sprayer a with different fuels. *Proceedings of SPIE- The International Society for Optical Engineering, 12936*. 10.1117/12.3011709

Natrayan, L., & Kaliappan, S. (2023). Mechanical Assessment of Carbon-Luffa Hybrid Composites for Automotive Applications. *SAE Technical Papers*. 10.4271/2023-01-5070

Natrayan, L., Kaliappan, S., & Pundir, S. (2023). Control and Monitoring of a Quadcopter in Border Areas Using Embedded System. *Proceedings of the 4th International Conference on Smart Electronics and Communication, ICOSEC 2023*. IEEE. 10.1109/ICOSEC58147.2023.10276196

Natrayan, L., Kaliappan, S., Saravanan, A., Vickram, A. S., Pravin, P., Abbas, M., Ahamed Saleel, C., Alwetaishi, M., & Saleem, M. S. M. (2023). Recyclability and catalytic characteristics of copper oxide nanoparticles derived from bougainvillea plant flower extract for biomedical application. *Green Processing and Synthesis*, 12(1), 20230030. 10.1515/gps-2023-0030

Natrayan, L., & Kumar, M. S. (2019). Influence of silicon carbide on tribological behaviour of AA2024/Al2O3/SiC/Gr hybrid metal matrix squeeze cast composite using Taguchi technique. *Materials Research Express*, 6(12), 1265f9. 10.1088/2053-1591/ab676d

Natrayan, L., & Kumar, M. S. (2020). Optimization of wear behaviour on AA6061/Al2O3/SiC metal matrix composite using squeeze casting technique-Statistical analysis. *Materials Today: Proceedings*, 27, 306–310. 10.1016/j.matpr.2019.11.038

Natrayan, L., & Merneedi, A. (2020). Experimental investigation on wear behaviour of bio-waste reinforced fusion fiber composite laminate under various conditions. *Materials Today: Proceedings*, 37(Part 2), 1486–1490. 10.1016/j.matpr.2020.07.108

Natrayan, L., Merneedi, A., Veeman, D., Kaliappan, S., Raju, P. S., Subbiah, R., & Kumar, S. V. (2021). Evaluating the Mechanical and Tribological Properties of DLC Nanocoated Aluminium 5051 Using RF Sputtering. *Journal of Nanomaterials*, 2021, 1–7. 10.1155/2021/8428822

Natrayan, L., & Richard, T. (2023a). Experimental investigations of bagasse ash strands featuring variable surface influence on polypropylene based polymer composites. *Proceedings of SPIE- The International Society for Optical Engineering, 12936*. SPIE. 10.1117/12.3011691

Natrayan, L., & Richard, T. (2023b). Organo modified nanocomposites terephthalic acid polymers temperature and microstructural characteristics. *Proceedings of SPIE- The International Society for Optical Engineering, 12936*. SPIE. 10.1117/12.3011863

Natrayan, L., Sakthi Shunmuga Sundaram, P., & Elumalai, J. (2019). Analyzing the uterine physiological with mmg signals using svm. *International Journal of Pharmaceutical Research*, 11(2). 10.31838/ijpr/2019.11.02.009

Natrayan, L., Senthil Kumar, M., & Chaudhari, M. (2020). Optimization of squeeze casting process parameters to investigate the mechanical properties of AA6061/Al 2 O 3/SiC hybrid metal matrix composites by Taguchi and Anova approach. In *Advances in Intelligent Systems and Computing (Vol. 949)*. Springer. 10.1007/978-981-13-8196-6_35

Natrayan, L., Senthil Kumar, M., & Palanikumar, K. (2018). Optimization of squeeze cast process parameters on mechanical properties of Al2O3/SiC reinforced hybrid metal matrix composites using taguchi technique. *Materials Research Express*, 5(6), 066516. 10.1088/2053-1591/aac873

Natrayan, L., Sivaprakash, V., & Santhosh, M. S. (2018). Mechanical, microstructure and wear behavior of the material aa6061 reinforced sic with different leaf ashes using advanced stir casting method. *International Journal of Engineering and Advanced Technology*, 8.

Niveditha, V. R., & Rajakumar, P. S. (2020). Pervasive computing in the context of COVID-19 prediction with AI-based algorithms. *International Journal of Pervasive Computing and Communications*, 16(5). 10.1108/IJPCC-07-2020-0082

Palaniyappan, S., Veeman, D., Sivakumar, N. K., & Natrayan, L. (2022). Development and optimization of lattice structure on the walnut shell reinforced PLA composite for the tensile strength and dimensional error properties. *Structures*, 45, 163–178. 10.1016/j.istruc.2022.09.023

Ponnusamy, M., Natrayan, L., Kaliappan, S., Velmurugan, G., & Thanappan, S. (2022). Effectiveness of Nanosilica on Enhancing the Mechanical and Microstructure Properties of Kenaf/Carbon Fiber-Reinforced Epoxy-Based Nanocomposites. *Adsorption Science and Technology*, 2022, 4268314. 10.1155/2022/4268314

Prabagar, S., Al-Jiboory, A. K., Nair, P. S., Mandal, P., Garse, K. M., & Natrayan, L. (2023). Artificial Intelligence-Based Control Strategies for Unmanned Aerial Vehicles. *2023 10th IEEE Uttar Pradesh Section International Conference on Electrical, Electronics and Computer Engineering, UPCON 2023*. IEEE. 10.1109/UPCON59197.2023.10434918

Pragadish, N., Kaliappan, S., Subramanian, M., Natrayan, L., Satish Prakash, K., Subbiah, R., & Kumar, T. C. A. (2023). Optimization of cardanol oil dielectric-activated EDM process parameters in machining of silicon steel. *Biomass Conversion and Biorefinery*, 13(15), 14087–14096. 10.1007/s13399-021-02268-1

Ragumadhavan, R., Sateesh Kumar, D., Charyulu Rompicharla, L. N., Dhondiya, S. A., Kaliappan, S., & Natrayan, L. (2023). Design and Development of Light Communication Systems Using Modulation Techniques. *7th International Conference on Electronics, Communication and Aerospace Technology, ICECA 2023 - Proceedings*. IEEE. 10.1109/ICECA58529.2023.10395831

Rajasekaran, S., & Natrayan, L. (2023a). Estimation of corrective and preventive action on trend end plug-based machining activities using manual and failure mode with effects analysis. *Proceedings of SPIE- The International Society for Optical Engineering, 12936*. SPIE. 10.1117/12.3011698

Rajasekaran, S., & Natrayan, L. (2023b). Evaluation of occurrence number and communication based on FMEA operations in product development. *Proceedings of SPIE- The International Society for Optical Engineering, 12936*. SPIE. 10.1117/12.3011702

Ramesh, C., Vijayakumar, M., Alshahrani, S., Navaneethakrishnan, G., Palanisamy, R., Natrayan, L., Saleel, C. A., Afzal, A., Shaik, S., & Panchal, H. (2022). Performance enhancement of selective layer coated on solar absorber panel with reflector for water heater by response surface method: A case study. *Case Studies in Thermal Engineering, 36*, 102093. 10.1016/j.csite.2022.102093

Reddy, P. N., Umaeswari, P., Natrayan, L., & Choudhary, A. (2023). Development of Programmed Autonomous Electric Heavy Vehicle: An Application of IoT. *Proceedings of the 2023 2nd International Conference on Electronics and Renewable Systems, ICEARS 2023*. SPIE. 10.1109/ICEARS56392.2023.10085492

Saadh, M. J., Almoyad, M. A. A., Arellano, M. T. C., Maaliw, R. R. III, Castillo-Acobo, R. Y., Jalal, S. S., Gandla, K., Obaid, M., Abdulwahed, A. J., Ibrahem, A. A., Sârbu, I., Juyal, A., Lakshmaiya, N., & Akhavan-Sigari, R. (2023). Long non-coding RNAs: Controversial roles in drug resistance of solid tumors mediated by autophagy. *Cancer Chemotherapy and Pharmacology, 92*(6), 439–453. 10.1007/s00280-023-04582-z37768333

Sai, S. A., Venkatesh, S. N., Dhanasekaran, S., Balaji, P. A., Sugumaran, V., Lakshmaiya, N., & Paramasivam, P. (2023). Transfer Learning Based Fault Detection for Suspension System Using Vibrational Analysis and Radar Plots. *Machines, 11*(8), 778. 10.3390/machines11080778

Sasi, J. P., Nidhi Pandagre, K., Royappa, A., Walke, S., Pavithra, G., & Natrayan, L. (2023). Deep Learning Techniques for Autonomous Navigation of Underwater Robots. *2023 10th IEEE Uttar Pradesh Section International Conference on Electrical, Electronics and Computer Engineering, UPCON 2023*. IEEE. 10.1109/UPCON59197.2023.10434865

Sathish, T., Natrayan, L., Prasad Jones Christydass, S., Sivananthan, S., Kamalakannan, R., Vijayan, V., & Paramasivam, P. (2022). Experimental Investigation on Tribological Behaviour of AA6066: HSS-Cu Hybrid Composite in Dry Sliding Condition. *Advances in Materials Science and Engineering, 2022*, 1–9. 10.1155/2022/9349847

Sathish, T., Palani, K., Natrayan, L., Merneedi, A., de Poures, M. V., & Singarave-lu, D. K. (2021). Synthesis and characterization of polypropylene/ramie fiber with hemp fiber and coir fiber natural biopolymer composite for biomedical application. *International Journal of Polymer Science*, 2021, 1–8. 10.1155/2021/2462873

Selvi, S., Mohanraj, M., Duraipandy, P., Kaliappan, S., Natrayan, L., & Vinayagam, N. (2023). Optimization of Solar Panel Orientation for Maximum Energy Efficiency. *Proceedings of the 4th International Conference on Smart Electronics and Communication, ICOSEC 2023*. IEEE. 10.1109/ICOSEC58147.2023.10276287

Sendrayaperumal, A., Mahapatra, S., Parida, S. S., Surana, K., Balamurugan, P., Natrayan, L., & Paramasivam, P. (2021). Energy Auditing for Efficient Planning and Implementation in Commercial and Residential Buildings. *Advances in Civil Engineering*, 2021, 1–10. 10.1155/2021/1908568

Siddiqui, E., Siddique, M., Safeer Pasha, M., Boyapati, P., Pavithra, G., & Natrayan, L. (2023). AI and ML for Enhancing Crop Yield and Resource Efficiency in Agriculture. *2023 10th IEEE Uttar Pradesh Section International Conference on Electrical, Electronics and Computer Engineering, UPCON 2023*. IEEE. 10.1109/UPCON59197.2023.10434493

Singh, M. (2017). An experimental investigation on mechanical behaviour of siCp reinforced Al 6061 MMC using squeeze casting process. *International Journal of Mechanical and Production Engineering Research and Development*, 7(6). 10.24247/ijmperddec201774

Sukumaran, C., Indhumathi, K., Balamurugan, P., Ambilwade, R. P., Sunthari, P. M., & Natrayan, L. (2023). The Role of AI in Biochips for Early Disease Detection. *Proceedings - International Conference on Technological Advancements in Computational Sciences, ICTACS 2023*. IEEE. 10.1109/ICTACS59847.2023.10390419

Suman, T., Kaliappan, S., Natrayan, L., & Dobhal, D. C. (2023). IoT based Social Device Network with Cloud Computing Architecture. *Proceedings of the 2023 2nd International Conference on Electronics and Renewable Systems, ICEARS 2023*. IEEE. 10.1109/ICEARS56392.2023.10085574

Sureshkumar, P., Jagadeesha, T., Natrayan, L., Ravichandran, M., Veeman, D., & Muthu, S. M. (2022). Electrochemical corrosion and tribological behaviour of AA6063/Si$_3$N$_4$/Cu(NO$_3$)$_2$ composite processed using single-pass ECAP$_A$ route with 120° die angle. *Journal of Materials Research and Technology*, 16. 10.1016/j.jmrt.2021.12.020

Thakre, S., Pandhare, A., Malwe, P. D., Gupta, N., Kothare, C., Magade, P. B., Patel, A., Meena, R. S., Veza, I., Natrayan, L., & Panchal, H. (2023). Heat transfer and pressure drop analysis of a microchannel heat sink using nanofluids for energy applications. *Kerntechnik*, 88(5), 543–555. 10.1515/kern-2023-0034

Vaishali, K. R., Rammohan, S. R., Natrayan, L., Usha, D., & Niveditha, V. R. (2021). Guided container selection for data streaming through neural learning in cloud. *International Journal of Systems Assurance Engineering and Management*. 10.1007/s13198-021-01124-9

Velmurugan, G., & Natrayan, L. (2023). Experimental investigations of moisture diffusion and mechanical properties of interply rearrangement of glass/Kevlar-based hybrid composites under cryogenic environment. *Journal of Materials Research and Technology*, 23, 4513–4526. 10.1016/j.jmrt.2023.02.089

Velumayil, R., Gnanakumar, G., Natrayan, L., Chinta, N. D., & Kaliappan, S. (2023). Bifunctional Aluminum Oxide/Carbon Fiber/Epoxy Nanocomposites Preparation and Evaluation. *International Journal of Vehicle Structures and Systems*, 15(7). 10.4273/ijvss.15.7.18

Venkatesh, R., Manivannan, S., Kaliappan, S., Socrates, S., Sekar, S., Patil, P. P., Natrayan, L., & Bayu, M. B. (2022). Influence of Different Frequency Pulse on Weld Bead Phase Ratio in Gas Tungsten Arc Welding by Ferritic Stainless Steel AISI-409L. *Journal of Nanomaterials*, 2022, 1–11. 10.1155/2022/9530499

Vijayakumar, M., & Shreeraj Nair, P. G Tilak Babu, S. B., Mahender, K., Venkateswaran, T. S., & Natrayan, L. (2023). Intelligent Systems For Predictive Maintenance In Industrial IoT. *2023 10th IEEE Uttar Pradesh Section International Conference on Electrical, Electronics and Computer Engineering, UPCON 2023*. IEEE. 10.1109/UPCON59197.2023.10434814

Vijayakumar, M. D., Surendhar, G. J., Natrayan, L., Patil, P. P., Ram, P. M. B., & Paramasivam, P. (2022). Evolution and Recent Scenario of Nanotechnology in Agriculture and Food Industries. *Journal of Nanomaterials*, 2022, 1–17. 10.1155/2022/1280411

Yogeshwaran, S., Natrayan, L., Udhayakumar, G., Godwin, G., & Yuvaraj, L. (2020). Effect of waste tyre particles reinforcement on mechanical properties of jute and abaca fiber - Epoxy hybrid composites with pre-treatment. *Materials Today: Proceedings*, 37(Part 2), 1377–1380. 10.1016/j.matpr.2020.06.584

Chapter 11
An Artificial Neural Network With a Metaheuristic Basis for Plastic Limit Frames Analysis

R. Selvapriya
https://orcid.org/0000-0003-1185-2228
Muthayammal Engineering College, India

M. Gopinath
Muthayammal Engineering College, India

D. Velmurugan
https://orcid.org/0000-0002-5392-3461
Muthayammal Engineering College, India

P. Tamilchelvan
Muthayammal College of Engineering, India

ABSTRACT

The plastic limit analysis of structures has several benefits, but it also has certain disadvantages, such high computing costs. In the past twenty years, plastic limit analysis has performed better thanks to metaheuristic algorithms, particularly when it comes to structural issues. Graph theoretical techniques have also significantly reduced the process's processing time. But until recently, the iterative process and its proportional computer memory and time have proven difficult. In order to quickly

DOI: 10.4018/979-8-3693-3314-3.ch011

ascertain the collapse load factors of two-dimensional frames, a metaheuristic-based artificial neural network (ANN), which falls under the category of supervised machine learning techniques, has been utilized in this work. The numerical examples show that the accuracy and performance of the suggested method are adequate.

INTRODUCTION

Plastic analysis (PA) is a potent structural analysis technique, particularly for ductile materials. The maximum and minimal principles serve as the foundation for nearly all analytical techniques used in PA (Baker et al., 1961). The majority of minimum principal techniques Combining elementary mechanisms is a common one. Neal and Symonds devised this technique initially (Neal & Symonds, 1950; Neal & Symonds, 1952a; Neal & Symonds, 1952b). Thanks to the work of Charnes and Greenberg (1951), the PA problem involving rigid-jointed frames began to be solved in 1951. Their principal tool was linear programming (LP).

Heyman (1960) looked at the minimum weight of two-dimensional rectangular frames under various loading scenarios using elementary plastic theory. The Foulkes Theory served as the main theory in his investigation. Watwood (1979), Baker and Heyman (1969), Jennings (1983), Thierauf (1978), Horne (1953), and Gorman (1981) are all credited with contributing to further advancements in this discipline.

Although the integration of elementary processes has its merits, there are several disadvantages to this approach. Its shortcomings make it unsuitable as a regular analysis tool. Among these disadvantages, the large number of processes that must be integrated in order to evaluate the collapse load factor places a heavy computational burden on the problem solver in terms of both time and memory. Thus, certain innovative methods—like graph theory—and cutting-edge algorithms—like metaheuristics—have been applied in this way. Graph theoretical notions have been applied for the first time to the flexibility study of structures by Kaveh (1976). He has thereby enhanced cycle basis in flexibility analysis to enable a precise and effective structural analysis. Mokhtarzadeh and Kaveh (1999) proposed an effective graph theoretical method for the best plastic analysis and frame design using this innovative methodology. The evolutionary approach was used by Kaveh and Khanlari (2004) to determine the planar frame collapse load factor. Genetic algorithms have been used by Kaveh and Rahami (2006) for structural analysis employing the force approach. A comparison study between various metaheuristic methods for the plastic analysis of braced frames was reported by Palizi and Saedi Darayan (2020). Greco et al. (2019) have presented an automatic approach for evaluating the plastic collapse conditions of planar frames. Using the Rankine-Merchant-Wood method, Smail and Laid (2021) presented a second-order analysis of flat steel structures.

Kaveh and associates. For the best PA, Kaveh et al. (2013) used the Charge System Search (CSS) algorithms and the ant colony system. Kaveh and Ghafari (2015) have used Colliding Bodies Optimization (CBO) and its Enhanced Version (ECBO) for these structures. Kaveh et al.'s research has examined the collapse load factor of the rectangular grid (Kaveh et al., 2019). Furthermore, a metaheuristic-based framework for Plastic Limit Analysis (PLA) of frames was created by Kaveh and Jahanshahi (2008).

The high computational cost of the plastic analysis has persisted to this day because of the iterative methods used in all of the aforementioned attempts, despite the fact that they have all been regarded as important studies in this subject and have alleviated some of the computational shortcomings of PA. Thus, it appears that this field needs to incorporate a new computational technique. This research uses an artificial neural network (ANN) based on metaheuristics, which falls under the category of supervised machine learning techniques, to calculate the collapse load. Elements of two-dimensional frames in a lightning-fast time. The numerical examples show that the accuracy and performance of the suggested method are adequate.

The structure of the paper is as follows. The formulation of the PA is introduced in Section 2, along with the creation of elementary mechanisms, the calculation of the collapse load factor, and the coupling of elementary mechanisms. Section 3 provides an overview of artificial neural networks and metaheuristic algorithms. The novel approach that is suggested and its numerical validations are covered in Section 4. The study is finally concluded in Section 5.

PLASTIC ANALYSIS

Watwood (1979) has devised one computational method to locate a set of independent mechanisms. Nevertheless, there is additional computing complexity associated with this method since it also computes joint mechanisms. Furthermore, the axial distortion is disregardable because to how the production of the plastic hinges was impacted by rotational degrees of freedom. As a result, the modified approach suggested by Deeks (1996) and Pellegrino and Calladine (1991) may be used.Equation 1 can be achieved by expressing each member's elongation in terms of its displacements in global coordinates, i.e., two displacement components for each joint or node.

$$e = (d_x - d_x) \cos\alpha + (d_y - d_y) \sin\alpha i j i j \quad (1)$$

Using matrix notation, Equation 1 leads to Equation 2.

$$e = Cd \qquad (2)$$

Where C is the compatibility matrix, e is the elongation vector, and d is the nodal displacement vector.

Elements in a workable mechanism do not elongate. Consequently, Equation 3 ought to be resolved as the main equation system problem.

$$e = Cd \qquad (3)$$

The number of rows in matrix C is less than the number of columns in Equation 3. The number of independent mechanisms is indicated by the difference. Consequently, Equation 3 can be broken down into Equation 4.

$$^i d^{iü} i^0 ü [I, C_d]_{idý} =_{i0ý} î^d þ^{î þ} \qquad (4)$$

Rearrangement of the Equation 4, leads to Equation 5.

$$d^i = -C^d d^d \qquad (5)$$

The process of choosing the independent mechanisms for dd involves choosing the dependent vectors. Thus, solving Equation 3 results from calculating the di in Equation 5.

The collapse load factor should be computed using the virtual work theorem. The internal and external works can be calculated using the rotations and displacements that were obtained. Thus, Equation 6 can be used to derive the collapse load factor.

$$\lambda = \frac{^{W}\text{int } enral \ c}{_{W}external} \qquad (6)$$

Lastly, the elementary mechanisms should be integrated to generate a logical collapse mechanism. One could classify this process as an optimization problem. The goal is to integrate basic processes in a way that minimizes the collapse load factor. The decision variables for this purpose are the elementary mechanisms and the related coefficient. At the very least, optimization techniques like meta-heuristic algorithms can be used to overcome the issue.

SOFT COMPUTING METHODS

Details of the soft computing method are covered in this section. First, a description of metaheuristic algorithms is given. The details of this strategy are provided here because the Enriched Firefly Algorithm (EFA) was applied in this paper. The formulation of artificial neural networks (ANNs) comes last.

Metaheuristic Algorithms

These days, engineering, applied mathematics, economics, medicine, and other disciplines use a lot of those computational methods, sometimes known as meta-heuristics. Nature-inspired algorithms make up the first category of meta-heuristic algorithms. Certain animal behaviors, such flocking, hunting, foraging, and migration, are excellent candidates for computer simulation. Consequently, these actions can be examined and used as swarm intelligence rules to create a suitable meta-heuristic algorithm. For example, the social behavior of fish schools or flocks of birds serves as an inspiration for Particle Swarm Optimization (PSO), one of the most potent meta-heuristic algorithms (Kennedy & Eberhart, 1995). Another illustration is the Water Strider Algorithm (WSA), which simulates the life cycle and clever ripple communication of water strider bugs (Kaveh, & Dadras Eslamlou,, 2020). Other kinds of meta-heuristic algorithms, such the Charged System Search (CSS) algorithm (Kaveh & Zolghadr, 2013) and the Black Holes Mechanics Optimization (BHMO) algorithm (Kaveh et al., 2020), are created in accordance with physical rules. Furthermore, certain meta-heuristics are grounded in mathematical models. One of these algorithms is the Covariance Matrix Adaptation Evolution Strategy (CMA-ES) (Iruthayarajan & Baskar, 2010). Lastly, certain meta-heuristic algorithms are built based on human behaviors, as the Tug of War (TOW) algorithm (Kaveh & Zolghadr, 2016) and the Teaching-Learning Based Optimization (TLBO) algorithm (Rao et al., 2011).

This research uses the Enriched Firefly technique (EFA), a recently invented meta-heuristic technique, to enhance the performance of artificial neural networks (ANNs). Thus, the following explains FA and its expanded version.

Firefly Algorithm and its Enriched Version

Yang (2020) introduced the Firefly algorithm (FA) in its most basic form, and it has been effectively used to solve both continuous and discrete optimization issues. While FA has been shown to outperform many other optimization meta-heuristic algorithms, its computational procedures have certain limitations. For example, Khadwilard et al. (2012) reported that the FA was stuck in the local optima and was unable to identify the optimal solution to some situations. As a result, numerous iterations of basic FA that are adaptable, hybrid, chaotic, modified, and augmented have been created thus far.

There are two important factors to take into account when implementing the FA. The first is the shift in light intensity; the second is the definition of beauty. For the sake of simplicity, it is fair to assume that a firefly's brightness, which is mapped to the encoded cost function, indicates how enticing it is. The brightness of a firefly at point x can be roughly chosen using Equation 7 in minimization instances.

1

$$I(x) \cong \frac{1}{f(x)} \qquad (7)$$

Where x is the firefly's location vector, f(x) is the objective function, and I(x) is the brightness. Thus, in this kind of situation, a larger value for the cost function means that the matching firefly will be less brilliant.

The changes in attraction and light intensity are monotonically decreasing functions; that is, when attractiveness and light intensity decrease, so does the distance from the source, and vice versa.

The final enrichment that is made to the FA basic version is the conversion of the Euclidean distance to the Mahalanobis distance. It is crucial to take into account how each variable shows behavior that is similar to the ideal objective, since the departure from the optimal cost is significant. The covariance matrix can be used to formally express this trend.

Covariance is a measure of how much two random variables change jointly in probability theory and statistics. When two variables have a positive covariance, they tend to travel together; however, two variables only move in the opposite direction when their relative covariance is negative. When two real-valued random variables are jointly distributed, Equation 8 defines the covariance of X and Y.

$$cov(X, Y) = E[(X - E(X)), (Y - E(Y))] \qquad (8)$$

Where E(X), and E(Y) is the expected values of X and Y, respectively. The covariance matrix is a square and symmetric matrix given by Equation 9.

$$C_{ij} = cov(X_i, X_j), C \in R^d \qquad (9)$$

Artificial Neural Networks

Artificial Neural Networks (ANNs) are being used extensively these days to model a wide range of complex systems, including industrial, mechanical, and medical systems. The variables under consideration have been brought into the system as inputs for this computational procedure. The network targets have been identified as the labeled results for every input. As a result, this technique falls under the category of supervised machine learning. In order to transform inputs into targets, an activation function attempts to mimic a network. The targets are incompatible with the activation function's initial weights and outcomes. As a result, targets should be disregarded and there is an error between the outputs (the activation function's outcomes and its weights). To reduce this simulation error, an optimization problem is used. Various ANN designs are created by varying the number of layers, optimization algorithms, activation functions, and other parameters.

PROPOSED METHOD AND NUMERICAL VALIDATIONS

As previously mentioned, the traditional methods for plastic analysis have an extremely high computing cost, both in terms of memory and time. Thus, it is vital to suggest a fresh, effective approach for this kind of issue.

In order to achieve this goal, this research suggests using an ANN to identify the frame collapse mechanism and associated load factor. The following describes the process.

1. Describes a structure based on the project data that consists of portal frames (columns + truss). The wind's movements are estimated.
2. Establishes the load combinations.
3. Examines the design and measurements of the various structural components (purlins, cladding rails, truss elements, columns, and posts).
4. Computes the connections (post foot, truss-post, and truss elements).

Figure 1. Identify the frame collapse mechanism and associated load factor

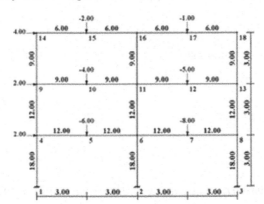

First, a dataset representing the collapse mechanism and the associated load factors is created. The goal is achieved by creating and analyzing around 3000 portal frames with various support conditions, geometrical properties, loading conditions, and element connection using an implemented Python code that is based on the Hinge-by-Hinge approach (Chen & Zhang, 1991). These characteristics are thought of as the ANN's inputs, and its targets are thought to be the load factors and the calculated collapse mechanism.

The ANN's optimization process is still a laborious task because of the massive dataset. The EFA method has been used for optimization in the treatment of this problem. In less than a second, the trained artificial neural network may finally be utilized to identify the collapse mechanism of new frames. The ensuing numerical examples verify this efficiency. Every example has the same unit; none are unique. For simulation, any consistent unit system will do.

Example One: Two-Bay, Three-Story Frame

Figure 1 depicts the first example, a two-bay, three-story frame that is regarded as a well-known benchmark problem. The trained artificial neural network (ANN) receives the geometry and load circumstances, and outputs the load factor and collapse mechanism. The obtained mechanism and the actual mechanism (Kaveh & Jahanshahi, 2008) are combined in Figure 2.

Figure 2. The geometry and loading conditions of example

Figure 3. The comparison of the realcollapse mechanism and obtained one via ANN of example 1

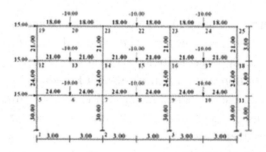

The calculated and actual collapse load factor is 1.97. The computation time is the primary distinction. On a comparable computer, the suggested method takes 0.005 seconds for analysis while the traditional methods take 1463.23 seconds. Thus, one can infer both the accuracy and the efficiency of the suggested method.

Example Two: Three-Bay, Three-Story Frame

Compared to example 1, the second example is more complex, as seen in Figure 3. This example looks into the load factor and collapse mechanism of a three-bay, three-story frame.

As in example 1, a comparison between the generated mechanism and the real one is shown (Figure 4). Both approaches have collapse load factors of 1.6. But compared to the evolutionary methods' 1501.44 seconds, the efficiency of the suggested method is just about 0.007 seconds.

Figure 4. The geometry and loading conditions of example 2

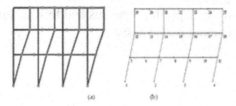

Figure 5. The comparison of the real collapse mechanism and obtained one via ANN of example two

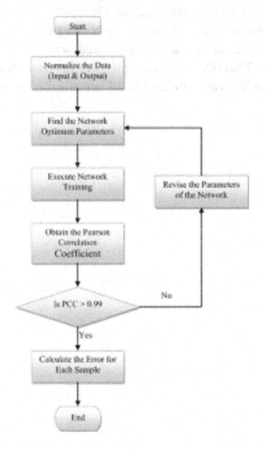

It is feasible to argue that the new suggested algorithm is significant in terms of accuracy or efficiency because of the similarities between the evolutionary and the proposed method's collapse mechanisms and load factors as well as the clear distinctions in their computational costs.

CONCLUSION

This research presents a novel computational approach based on an Artificial Neural Network (ANN) with a metaheuristic basis. First, a computational dataset of 3000 structures, along with the load factors and collapse processes that correspond to each, was created utilizing the hinge-by-hinge method in this novel framework. After that, the process of calculating the collapse mechanism and its associated load factor was simulated using a hybrid metaheuristic-ANN framework. Now that it has been taught, the framework can extract load factors and real collapse processes for new frames. This assertion has been substantiated by three distinct, demanding, and benchmark issues. The effectiveness and precision of the newly suggested algorithm for plastic limit analysis are validated by all numerical examples.

REFERENCES

Baker, J., & Heyman, J. (1969). *Plastic Design of Frames 1 Fundamentals*. Cambridge University Press. 10.1017/CBO9780511586514

Baker, S. J. F., Horne, M. R., & Heyman, J. (1961). *The Steel Skeleton*. English Language Book Society.

Charnes, A., & Greenberg, H. J. (1951). Plastic collapse and linear programming-preliminary report. *Bulletin of the American Mathematical Society*, 57(6), 480.

Chen, W.-F., & Zhang, H. (1991). *Structural Plasticity: Theory, Problems, and CAE Software, 2*. Springer. 10.1007/978-1-4612-2984-1

Deeks, A. J. (1996). Automatic computation of plastic collapse loads for frames. *Computers & Structures*, 60(3), 391–402. 10.1016/0045-7949(95)00394-0

Gorman, M.R. (1981). *Automated generation for limit analysis of frames*. Academic Press.

Greco, A., Cannizzaro, F., & Pluchino, A. (2019). Automatic evaluation of plastic collapse conditions for planar frames with vertical irregularities. *Engineering with Computers*, 35(1), 57–73. 10.1007/s00366-018-0583-9

Heyman, J. (1960). On the minimum-weight design of a simple portal frame. *International Journal of Mechanical Sciences*, 1(1), 121–134. 10.1016/0020-7403(60)90034-5

Horne, M. R. (1953). Determination of the shape of fixed ended beams for maximum economy according to the plastic theory. In *International Association of Bridge and Structural Engineering*. Fourth Congress.

Iruthayarajan, M. W., & Baskar, S. (2010). Covariance matrix adaptation evolution strategy based design of centralized PID controller. *Expert Systems with Applications*, 37(8), 5775–5781. 10.1016/j.eswa.2010.02.031

Jennings, P.A. (1983). *Adapting the Simplex Method to Plastic Design*. Academic Press.

Kaveh, A. (1976). Improved cycle bases for the flexibility analysis of structures. *Computer Methods in Applied Mechanics and Engineering*, 9(3), 267–272. 10.1016/0045-7825(76)90031-1

Kaveh, A., Bakhshpoori, T., & Kalateh-Ahani, M. (2013). Optimum plastic analysis of planar frames using ant colony system and charged system search algorithms. *Scientia Iranica*, 20(3), 414–421.

Kaveh, A. & Dadras Eslamlou, A. (2020). Water strider algorithm: A new meta-heuristic and applications. *Structures, 25*, 520–41.

Kaveh, A., & Ghafari, M. H. (2015). Plastic analysis of planar frames using CBO and ECBO algorithms. *Int J Optim Civil Eng*, 5(4), 479–492.

Kaveh, A., & Jahanshahi, M. (2008). Plastic limit analysis of frames using ant colony systems. *Computers & Structures*, 86(11–12), 1152–1163. 10.1016/j.compstruc.2008.01.001

Kaveh, A., & Khanlari, K. (2004). Collapse load factor of planar frames using a modified genetic algorithm. *Communications in Numerical Methods in Engineering*, 20(12), 911–925. 10.1002/cnm.716

Kaveh, A., & Rahami, H. (2006). Analysis, design and optimization of structures using force method and genetic algorithm. *International Journal for Numerical Methods in Engineering*, 65(10), 1570–1584. 10.1002/nme.1506

Kaveh, A. & Seddighian, M.R. (2020). Simultaneously multi-material layout, and connectivity optimization of truss structures via an Enriched Firefly Algorithm. *Structures, 27*, 2217–31.

Kaveh, A., Seddighian, M. R., & Ghanadpour, E. (2019). Upper and lower bounds for the collapse load factor of rectangular grids using FEM. *Int J Optim Civil Eng*, 9(3), 543–554.

Kaveh, A., Seddighian, M. R., & Ghanadpour, E. (2020). Black Hole Mechanics Optimization: A novel meta-heuristic algorithm. *Asian J Civil Eng.*, 21(7), 1129–1149. 10.1007/s42107-020-00282-8

Kaveh, A., & Zolghadr, A. (2013). Topology optimization of trusses considering static and dynamic constraints using the CSS. *Applied Soft Computing*, 13(5), 2727–2734. 10.1016/j.asoc.2012.11.014

Kaveh, A., & Zolghadr, A. (2016). A novel meta-heuristic algorithm: Tug of war optimization. *Int J Optim Civil Eng*, 6(4), 469–492.

Kennedy, J., & Eberhart, R. (1995). Particle swarm optimization. *Proceedings of ICNN'95- international conference on neural networks*. IEEE.

Khadwilard, A., Chansombat, S., Thepphakorn, T., Chainate, W., & Pongcharoen, P. (2012). Application of firefly algorithm and its parameter setting for job shop scheduling. *Indust Technol*, 8(1), 49–58.

Mokhtar-zadeh, A., & Kaveh, A. (1999). Optimal plastic analysis and design of frames: Graph theoretical methods. *Computers & Structures*, 73(1–5), 485–496. 10.1016/S0045-7949(98)00250-8

Neal, B. G., & Symonds, P. S. (1950). The calculation of collapse loads for framed structures. (Includes appendix). *Journal of the Institution of Civil Engineers*, 35(1), 21–40. 10.1680/IJOTI.1950.12815

Neal, B. G., & Symonds, P. S. (1952a). The calculation of plastic loads for plane frames. In *International Association for Bridge and Structural Engineering. Fourth Congress.*

Neal, B. G., & Symonds, P. S. (1952b). The rapid calculation of the plastic collapse load for a framed structure. *Proceedings - Institution of Civil Engineers*, 1(2), 58–71. 10.1680/ipeds.1952.12270

Palizi, S., & Saedi Daryan, A. (2020). Plastic analysis of braced frames by application of metaheuristic optimization algorithms. *International Journal of Steel Structures*, 20(4), 1135–1150. 10.1007/s13296-020-00347-z

Pellegrino, S. & Calladine, C.R. (1991). *Structural computation of an assembly of rigid links, frictionless joints, and elastic springs*. Academic Press.

Rao, R. V., Savsani, V. J., & Vakharia, D. P. (2011). Teaching–learning-based optimization: A novel method for constrained mechanical design optimization problems. *Computer Aided Design*, 43(3), 303–315. 10.1016/j.cad.2010.12.015

Smail, B., & Laid, S. M. (2021). Second-order analysis of plane steel structures using RankineMerchant-Wood approach. *Asian J Civil Eng*, 22(4), 701–711. 10.1007/s42107-020-00341-0

Thierauf, G. (1978). A method for optimal limit design of structures with alternative loads. *Computer Methods in Applied Mechanics and Engineering*, 16(2), 135–149. 10.1016/0045-7825(78)90039-7

Watwood, V. B. (1979). Mechanism generation for limit analysis of frames. *Journal of the Structural Division*, 105(1), 1–15. 10.1061/JSDEAG.0005071

Yang, S. & Slowik, A. (2020). *Firefly algorithm, in Swarm Intelligence Algorithms*. CRC Press.

Chapter 12
An Extensive Investigation of Meta–Heuristics Algorithms for Optimization Problems

Renugadevi Ramalingam

RMK Engineering College, India

J. Shobana

https://orcid.org/0000-0001-9754 -2604

SRM Institute of Science and Technology, India

K. Arthi

SRM Institute of Science and Technology, India

G. Elangovan

SRM Institute of Science and Technology, India

S. Radha

https://orcid.org/0000-0002-7296 -2132

Vivekanandha College of Engineering for Women, India

N. Priyanka

https://orcid.org/0009-0004-2007 -2973

Vellore Institute of Technology, India

ABSTRACT

Metaheuristic algorithms represent a class of optimization techniques tailored to tackle intricate problems that defy resolution through conventional means. Drawing inspiration from natural phenomena like genetics, swarm dynamics, and evolution, these algorithms traverse expansive search spaces in pursuit of identifying the optimal solution to a given problem. Well-known examples include genetic algorithms, particle swarm optimization, ant colony optimization, simulated annealing, and tabu

DOI: 10.4018/979-8-3693-3314-3.ch012

search. These methodologies find widespread application across diverse domains such as engineering, finance, and computer science. Spanning several decades, the evolution of metaheuristic algorithms entails the refinement and diversification of optimization strategies rooted in natural systems. As indispensable tools in addressing complex optimization challenges across various fields, metaheuristic algorithms are poised to remain pivotal in driving technological advancements and fostering novel applications.

INTRODUCTION

Metaheuristic algorithms are optimization techniques designed for tackling intricate problems that defy resolution through conventional approaches. Drawing inspiration from natural phenomena like genetics, swarm behaviour, and evolution, these algorithms navigate expansive search spaces to pinpoint the global optimum of a given problem. Examples of popular metaheuristic algorithms include genetic algorithms, particle swarm optimization, ant colony optimization, simulated annealing, and tabu search. Widely applied in diverse domains such as engineering, finance, and computer science, these algorithms have proven effective in addressing complex issues. The history of metaheuristic algorithms spans several decades, marked by the evolution and proliferation of optimization methods inspired by natural systems. Given their success, metaheuristic algorithms have emerged as valuable tools for solving intricate optimization problems across various fields, with a promising outlook for their continued significance in driving advancements in technology and applications.

Metaheuristic Algorithms

The term "metaheuristics" denotes a "higher level of heuristics," combining "meta," meaning beyond or at a higher level, and "heuristic," which involves discovering a goal through trial and error. Historically, methods featuring stochastic mechanisms were commonly termed "heuristic algorithms." Metaheuristic algorithms often serve as overarching strategies that guide and adapt other heuristics, extending solutions beyond those typically obtained in the pursuit of local optimality. These algorithms modify local search and randomization in a specific manner, leading to the development of excellent solutions for challenging optimization problems over time. However, it's important to note that there is no guarantee of finding optimal solutions (Almufti, Marqas, & Asaad, 2019).

In computer science, mathematical optimization, and engineering, the term "metaheuristic" refers to a higher-level procedure or heuristic used to search for, generate, or select a heuristic that may provide a favourable solution to an optimization problem. This is particularly valuable for large problems, such as NP-hard problems, or situations involving limited, incomplete, or imperfect information. The collection of solutions in a metaheuristic is often too extensive to sample entirely. Metaheuristics can be applied to a variety of issues since they don't make stringent assumptions about the optimization problem at hand (Ahmad, 2022).

In contrast to iterative or optimization techniques, metaheuristics don't guarantee the identification of the optimum solution for a given class of problems. Many metaheuristics incorporate stochastic optimization, meaning that the solution is influenced by a set of generated random variables. Despite this lack of certainty, metaheuristics frequently excel in identifying favorable solutions in combinatorial optimization with less computational effort compared to optimization algorithms, iterative techniques, or basic heuristics. This efficiency makes them potent strategies for addressing a wide range of optimization problems.

Well-Known Metaheuristic Algorithms

Over the years, numerous metaheuristic algorithms have been developed, each possessing unique strengths and weaknesses. The following are some of the most renowned metaheuristic algorithms, accompanied by concise explanations of their operational principles:

Genetic Algorithms (GA): It is inspired by the model after natural selection and genetics principles. It Commences by randomly generating an initial population of solutions, evolving through selection, crossover, and mutation operators. Mimics natural selection, where higher-fitness individuals are more likely to reproduce and pass on their traits. It is commonly used for optimization problems involving parameter or feature combination.

Particle Swarm Optimization (PSO): It has been derived from the collective behaviour of social organisms like birds or fish. It begins with the random generation of a swarm of particles, each representing a potential solution. Particles move in the search space based on their position, velocity, and the best position found by the swarm. Frequently applied to optimization problems involving weight configuration in neural networks or machine learning models.

Simulated Annealing (SA): It is inspired by Stochastic optimization inspired by metallurgical annealing. It initiates with the random generation of an initial solution, gradually reducing the system's temperature. As temperature decreases, the algorithm becomes more inclined to accept worse solutions, aiding in escaping local optima. Widely used in optimization problems requiring parameter configuration in complex models or simulations.

Tabu Search (TS): It is inspired by the memory concept in human decision-making. It starts by randomly generating an initial solution, exploring its neighborhood through operators like swapping or reversing. Utilizes a tabu list to remember recently visited solutions and avoids revisiting them. Commonly applied in optimization problems involving finding the best sequence of actions or decisions, such as scheduling or routing (Acan & Ünveren, 2020; Marqas et al., 2020; Marques et al., 2010).

Metaheuristic Algorithms Classifications

Metaheuristic algorithms can be categorized in various ways, employing different criteria for classification. Several common classifications, as outlined by Almufti, Marqas, and Asaad (2019) include: Nature-inspired vs. Non-nature-inspired, Single-solution vs. Population-based, Deterministic vs. Stochastic, Trajectory-based vs. Population-based, Local Search-based vs. Global Search-based.

Some of the main features of metaheuristic algorithms are

a) Exploration and Exploitation:

Metaheuristics strikes a balance between exploring the search space to discover new promising solutions and exploiting already-discovered solutions to refine them further. It enables the algorithm to avoid premature convergence to suboptimal solutions by simultaneously exploring diverse regions and exploiting the current best solutions.

b) Stochastic Search:

Metaheuristics employ randomization to generate new solutions, preventing them from getting stuck in local optima. It introduces randomness to the search process, enhancing the algorithm's ability to traverse the solution space and discover potentially better solutions.

c) Iterative Improvement:

Metaheuristics enhance solution quality iteratively by repeatedly applying modifications to existing solutions. It facilitates the gradual refinement of solutions over successive iterations, leading to improved solutions and convergence toward optimal or near-optimal solutions.

d) Robustness:

Metaheuristics are designed to handle noisy and uncertain problem instances by avoiding dependence on specific problem characteristics and assumptions. It ensures the algorithm's adaptability and effectiveness across a range of problem instances, even when faced with uncertainties or variations.

e) Flexibility:

Metaheuristics can be customized and adapted to different problem domains by adjusting selection criteria, neighborhood structures, and search strategies. It provides versatility, allowing the algorithm to be tailored to specific problem characteristics and requirements, enhancing its applicability across diverse domains.

f) Parallelism:

Metaheuristics can be easily parallelized to accelerate the search process and efficiently solve large-scale problems. It exploits parallel computing capabilities to enhance computational efficiency, making metaheuristics suitable for addressing complex problems with substantial computational demands.

The broad classification of Meta-Heuristic Algorithm is presented in Figure 1.

Figure 1. Meta heuristic algorithm classification

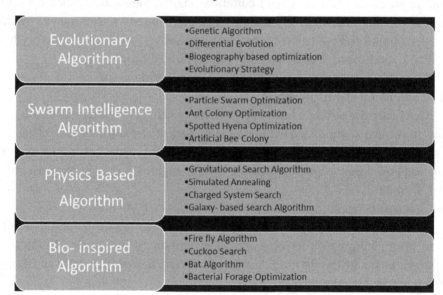

Evolutionary algorithms

Evolutionary algorithms (EAs) constitute a class of metaheuristic algorithms inspired by the principles of natural evolution, incorporating survival of the fittest, reproduction, and mutation. The iterative process involves creating a population of potential solutions to a problem and progressively refining it through selection, crossover, and mutation operations (Dehghani, Trojovská, & Trojovský, 2022; Dhiman & Kumar, 2017). Some of the common types of Evolutionary algorithms include Genetic algorithm (GA), Evolutionary programming (EP), Evolution strategies (ES) and Differential evolution (DE).

Swarm-Based Algorithms

Swarm intelligence, inspired by the collective behaviour of social animals, is a branch of artificial intelligence focusing on decentralized, self-organized systems. Swarm-based algorithms adhere to principles like decentralization, self-organization, and adaptation (Almufti, 2022; Almufti, Yahya Zebari, & Khalid Omer, 2019). Some examples of swarm intelligence algorithms include: Ant colony optimization (ACO), Particle swarm optimization (PSO), Bee colony optimization (BCO), Fister algorithm (FA), Artificial bee colony (ABC) algorithm.

Physics-based Metaheuristic Algorithms

Physics-based metaheuristic algorithms draw inspiration from physical laws and principles, employing concepts such as energy and force to navigate problem spaces (Almufti, 2019). Examples include Gravitational Search Algorithm (GSA), Electro-magnetic Field Optimization (EMO), Quantum-inspired Evolutionary Algorithm (QEA), and Harmony Search Algorithm (HSA). These physics-based algorithms have found success in addressing diverse optimization problems, including engineering design, scheduling, and image processing. Their unique approach is particularly effective in complex search spaces and problems with multiple objectives.

Human-Based Algorithms

Human-based metaheuristic algorithms are a class of optimization techniques that incorporate human intelligence, knowledge, and experience into the optimization process. Some examples of human-based metaheuristic algorithms are Expert-guided Evolutionary Algorithm (EEA), Human-guided Search (HGS) algorithm, Interactive Evolutionary Computation (IEC) algorithm, Human-in-the-Loop Optimization (HILO) algorithm (Dehghani, Trojovská, & Trojovský, 2022).

GENETIC ALGORITHM

As per Makasarwala (2020), the genetic algorithm (GA) plays a pivotal role in achieving load balancing. The process begins with prioritization to activate the population, where the request's priority is determined based on time and job duration. Jobs with longer durations are allotted more time, while those with higher demand are given precedence and executed earlier. Chromosomes are then selected according to fitness functions, followed by mapping and swapping operations. Subsequently, a chromosome is added to the new population, and this iterative process continues until the termination condition is satisfied. This approach leads to an improvement in the average response time. Saadat (2019) introduced a hybridized bi-modular approach to load balancing in cloud computing, employing a genetic algorithm (GA). Their proposed methodology has demonstrated superiority over previous techniques in terms of both load balancing and resource utilization. While the second component focuses on integrating fuzziness, the first module utilizes a Genetic Algorithm to optimize task arrangements. They accomplished the objective function by queuing work and detecting occupied server configurations. This suggested architecture provides fuzzy performance for service availability. GA contributes to the robustness, reliability, and scalability of cloud computing environments. The process involved in Genetic Algorithm is shown in Figure 2.

Figure 2. Genetic algorithm

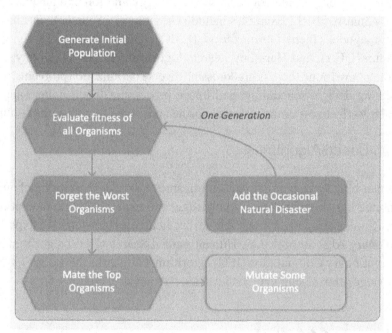

Furthermore, there is a strong emphasis on the necessity of multi-objective optimization to enhance both makespan and load balancing. Experimental investigations involve utilizing skewed, regular, and uniform workload distributions with varying batch sizes. These experiments have demonstrated significant advancements compared to the enhanced version of GA and other state-of-the-art methods concerning makespan, throughput, and load balancing. The Improved GA (Marqas et al., 2020) has been developed, which aims to minimize the number of migrations. This proposed technique facilitates faster and more reliable load shifting by adjusting the estimation points for mutation. Through extensive testing, it has been revealed that this algorithm outperforms the IGA (Marqas et al., 2020) in various Quality of Service (QoS) requirements.

PARTICLE SWARM OPTIMIZATION ALGORITHM

PSO, as per the description, is highlighted by Alguliyev (2019) as integral in load balancing within Cloud systems. Their method of task migration necessitates substantial computational resources to transfer tasks to high-performance virtual machines.

Each scheduling procedure is assigned a relative weight to emphasize its significance, with these weights aiding in determining the optimal solution. In comparison to other optimization techniques, PSO proves more effective in handling discrete problems. There exists an inherent issue with PSO, which tends to be sensitive to initial conditions, potentially affecting result quality. To mitigate this, they propose an enhanced version of PSO, incorporating the firefly algorithm to constrain the search space initially, followed by the use of Improved PSO to achieve optimal outcomes.

There exists a variant of PSO known as Binary PSO, aimed at time efficiency. This algorithm prioritizes job allocation after assessing operational constraints, focusing on organizing virtual machines utilized by users to complete tasks. By ensuring adequate load balancing and scheduling, this approach enhances scalability. The Adaptive best discrete PSO addresses the inherent randomness in PSO. This algorithm identifies all feasible solutions, stores them, and dynamically updates particle positions based on these solutions to enhance performance.

ANT COLONY OPTIMIZATION

Ant Colony Optimization (ACO) serves as a collaborative metaheuristic method aimed at swiftly exploring feasible solutions for intricate problems. Li and Wu (2019) focus on users' quality requirements during job assignments. To enhance Quality of Service (QoS), they propose integrating Project Management methodologies with a simplified version of ACO. The core concept lies in leveraging the ant colony algorithm to determine optimal job scheduling priorities, thereby achieving load balancing. In this analogy, the scheduler can be likened to an ant, and the scheduling phase resembles the foraging activity of ants.

subsequently using this information to schedule tasks based on their completion times. Once all activities are finished, the total completion time aids in task assignment to Virtual Machine(s). Employing the ant concept, tasks are assigned exclusively to available resources. Each node undergoes assessment through a fitness function to guide the search strategy. Following local search operations on each node, a global search ensues, yielding superior outcomes. Ragmani (2019) introduced an Improved ACO technique integrating fuzziness, rendering it suitable for managing complex networks with heavy loads. This method yields optimal solutions, significantly reducing response times by approximately 81%, as indicated by simulation results.

BAT ALGORITHM

BAT, an optimization technique inspired by echolocation in bats, leverages their auditory abilities to locate prey. Bats emit sounds and navigate toward potential prey based on the frequency of the echoes. By collecting and analyzing these signals, bats determine the distance to their prey. This same principle can be adapted to load balancing, where individual nodes operate autonomously, focusing on localized co-ordination. Ullah (2020) tested the BAT approach within Virtual Machines (VMs) to assess its effectiveness in enhancing load balancing in cloud environments. The idea is that when a task requires allocation, the optimal VM is initially selected from all participating nodes.

An enhanced BAT algorithm is introduced to yield additional optimal and finer outcomes. The iterative execution of the algorithm is essential for achieving this goal. When a task requires processing, the BAT algorithm identifies the best server among the available options. Concurrently, the load scheduler assesses the job type, resource requirements, and identifies the optimal virtual machine (VM) for task execution. If the current server meets the criteria, the load is allocated; otherwise, if the load is too high, it is distributed among other servers. This approach ensures load balancing across all occupied servers, preventing both underloading and over-loading. The proposed solution not only reduces response time but also effectively performs load balancing with minimal delays.

GRAY WOLF OPTIMIZATION ALGORITHM

The Gray Wolf Optimization (GWO) algorithm commences by gathering task and resource details and assessing whether distribution requirements are met. After evaluating the best option, the scheduler assigns a resource. The objective of GWO is to minimize manufacturing time, total cost, and maximize the number of completed tasks within the specified timeframe. Gohil and Patel propose a combined approach of Particle Swarm Optimization (PSO) and GWO to enhance VM availability and improve load balancing efficiency. Their strategy involves utilizing GWO to determine the optimal position as alpha, followed by employing PSO with the assistance of alpha. This approach aims to establish an objective function for efficient load management in cloud environments, with the primary goal of introducing randomness in GWO to prevent premature convergence.

Xingjun (2020) present a Fuzzy logic-based GWO Algorithm to enhance effectiveness by improving response time through load management. The algorithm identifies overloaded nodes and assigns load to VMs that have not been recently overloaded upon request arrival. Fuzziness is incorporated into GWO to enhance stability and load adjustment. While achieving improved response time, the convergence and degree of imbalance are not specifically addressed as QoS parameters. Ouhame (2020) target the failure in allocation method, initially categorizing overutilized and underutilized instances. The Gray Wolf Optimization improves the search strategy before being utilized by the ABC algorithm for further enhancement. Overall, this hybrid methodology improves efficiency, stability, communication cost, and power consumption.

Table 1. Comparison of metaheuristic algorithms

Criteria	GA	PSO	ACO	Bat	GWO
Based on performance constraints	Necessitates less knowledge of the targeted problem. Designing operators correctly can be difficult. Time consuming	Slow convergence. Can stuck in local optimum	Stagnation phase. Convergence speed is slow.	Multiple operations are required to achieve the optimum solution	Improved convergence speed. Limited solving accuracy. Poor local exploring potential
Based on control parameters	Statistics of mutation and crossover. The fitness value scaling and the population size.	The scope of the problem co efficient of accelerations. Number of particles. Neighbourhood size. Number of iterations. The variables that scale the involvement of the cognitive and social elements	Alpha beta evaporation rate	Population size. Number of Maximum cycles.	Initial position. Inertia weight. Adjustment coefficient. Initial weight and other parameters.

continued on following page

Table 1. Continued

Criteria	GA	PSO	ACO	Bat	GWO
Based on problems applied	Timetabling and scheduling problems. Global optimization problems. Problem domains that have a complex fitness landscape	Optimal problems with visual effects	Solve challenging optimal solutions using approximation	High-dimensional problems. Optimization problems	Optimize engineering design problems. NP – hard problems. Integer programming and minimax problems, scheduling problems.

- Algorithms that satisfy real-time constraints include PSO, Bat, and ACO, making them suitable for applications requiring rapid processing or immediate responses.
- High throughput capability is demonstrated by GA and GWO, suggesting their effectiveness in processing high traffic volumes swiftly.
- Improved make span efficiency is observed in GA, PSO, BAT, and GWO, indicating that these techniques are particularly beneficial for systems with limited memory resources.
- ACO and GWO are the only algorithms adhering to minimal energy consumption limits, making them suitable choices for applications prioritizing energy efficiency.
- PSO and Improved GWO demonstrate scalability, enabling them to handle additional tasks or manage sudden traffic spikes effectively.
- Improved resource utilization is evident in Improved GA, PSO, IPSO, Hybrid PSO, Fuzzy ACO, Improved Bat, and Improved GWO, highlighting their ability to utilize system resources efficiently.

From this analysis, it becomes evident that various algorithms, such as PSO and GWO, possess distinct limitations while also demonstrating scalability. While Improved GA stands out for its impressive throughput and resource utilization, it falls short in terms of scalability and energy efficiency. On the other hand, PSO and its variants (PSO, IPSO, and Hybrid PSO) showcase commendable real-time performance and resource utilization but exhibit drawbacks in terms of throughput and energy efficiency.

GWO and its enhanced versions excel in real-time performance, efficiency, and resource utilization. Furthermore, the modified version of GWO offers significant throughput capabilities. Although the BAT algorithm and its enhanced version may lack in other Quality of Service (QoS) aspects, they perform admirably in real-time scenarios and span efficiently.

Applications of Metaheuristics Algorithms

Engineering

In engineering, metaheuristic algorithms have found application in addressing a diverse array of problems. These range from enhancing the efficiency of structures to refining manufacturing processes and coordinating production schedules. For instance, when designing structures, genetic algorithms and particle swarm optimization techniques are employed to fine-tune both the shape and material composition of the structure. This aids in minimizing weight while enhancing overall performance. Similarly, within manufacturing settings, simulated annealing techniques are utilized to optimize the cutting parameters of CNC machines, while ant colony optimization algorithms are leveraged to streamline the layout of production lines.

Metaheuristic algorithms, such as genetic algorithms and particle swarm optimization, have found extensive application in various domains of engineering optimization:

Design Optimization: These algorithms are utilized to optimize the design of engineering structures like aircraft wings, bridges, and buildings. By adjusting the shape and material composition, they aim to reduce weight, enhance performance, and minimize costs.

Manufacturing Optimization: In manufacturing processes, metaheuristic algorithms like simulated annealing and tabu search are employed. They assist in optimizing CNC machine cutting parameters, thus decreasing tool wear and machining time while enhancing the quality of manufactured components.

Supply Chain Optimization: Metaheuristic algorithms such as genetic algorithms and ant colony optimization are instrumental in streamlining supply chain operations. They optimize tasks such as production planning, inventory management, and transportation, leading to resource allocation efficiency, reduced transportation costs, and improved delivery times.

Energy System Optimization: Within energy systems such as power grids and renewable energy setups, genetic algorithms and particle swarm optimization algorithms play a crucial role. They optimize system parameters like power plant capacity and renewable energy source locations to maximize efficiency and minimize costs.

Process Optimization: Metaheuristic algorithms, including simulated annealing and tabu search, are deployed in optimizing chemical and industrial processes. By adjusting parameters like temperature, pressure, and flow rate, they aim to maximize product yield and quality.

Structural Optimization: In structural engineering, metaheuristic algorithms like genetic algorithms and particle swarm optimization are utilized to optimize the topology, size, and shape of structures such as trusses and frames. This optimization minimizes weight, reduces material usage, and enhances structural strength.

Finance

Metaheuristic algorithms have seen widespread application in the realm of finance, addressing various optimization challenges such as portfolio management, risk assessment, and algorithmic trading. Notable applications include:

Portfolio Optimization: Genetic algorithms and particle swarm optimization are employed to optimize asset allocation within portfolios, aiming to maximize returns while minimizing risk. These algorithms consider factors like asset return, volatility, and correlation to determine the optimal portfolio composition.

Risk Management: Simulated annealing and tabu search algorithms are utilized to refine hedging strategies for financial institutions, helping to mitigate risks associated with market fluctuations by identifying optimal combinations of financial instruments.

Algorithmic Trading: Genetic algorithms and ant colony optimization are leveraged to develop trading strategies that capitalize on market inefficiencies, enabling the identification of trading opportunities in real-time through analysis of extensive datasets.

Credit Scoring: Genetic algorithms and particle swarm optimization techniques are applied in developing credit scoring models, aiding in predicting borrower default probabilities by analyzing factors such as credit history, income, and employment status for a more accurate assessment of creditworthiness.

Fraud Detection: Simulated annealing and tabu search algorithms are employed for detecting fraudulent activities in financial transactions. By analyzing transaction data for patterns and anomalies, these algorithms assist in identifying potential instances of fraud.

Forecasting: Genetic algorithms and ant colony optimization algorithms contribute to the development of forecasting models for financial time series data. Through analysis of historical data, these algorithms identify trends and patterns to make predictions about future market conditions, aiding in decision-making processes.

Logistics

In the field of logistics, metaheuristic algorithms play a crucial role in optimizing various aspects of operations:

Vehicle Routing: Genetic algorithms and tabu search techniques are employed to optimize delivery vehicle routes, aiming to minimize distance traveled and delivery time. These algorithms take into account factors like traffic congestion, delivery time windows, and vehicle capacity to determine the most efficient route.

Facility Location: Simulated annealing and ant colony optimization algorithms are utilized to optimize the placement of warehouses, distribution centers, and production facilities. By considering factors such as transportation costs, demand patterns, and labor costs, these algorithms identify the optimal locations for facilities within a network.

Inventory Management: Genetic algorithms and particle swarm optimization methods are used to optimize inventory levels, aiming to reduce costs while maintaining service levels. These algorithms consider factors like demand variability, lead time, and ordering costs to determine the optimal inventory levels.

Supply Chain Network Design: Simulated annealing and tabu search algorithms contribute to optimizing the design of supply chain networks, leading to cost reduction and improved efficiency. By considering factors such as transportation costs, facility costs, and demand variability, these algorithms identify the optimal network configuration.

Container Loading: Genetic algorithms and particle swarm optimization algorithms are applied to optimize the loading of containers, maximizing space utilization and minimizing transportation costs. These algorithms take into account container dimensions, cargo characteristics, and loading constraints to devise the most efficient loading plan.

Warehouse Layout Optimization: Simulated annealing and ant colony optimization techniques are utilized to optimize warehouse layouts, enhancing efficiency and reducing operational costs. By considering factors such as storage capacity, product flow, and material handling costs, these algorithms identify the optimal layout configuration.

Overall, metaheuristic algorithms offer powerful tools for optimizing logistics operations, enabling organizations to achieve greater efficiency, cost savings, and improved service delivery within their supply chain networks.

Healthcare

Metaheuristic algorithms have been effectively applied in various healthcare sectors, including medical diagnosis, treatment planning, drug discovery, and healthcare management. Specific instances of their utilization comprise:

Medical Image Analysis: Metaheuristic algorithms assist in analyzing medical images to extract essential information for disease diagnosis and treatment. For instance, genetic algorithms are employed to improve the segmentation of brain tumors from MRI scans, enhancing diagnostic accuracy and treatment strategies.

Drug Discovery: These algorithms play a vital role in optimizing the molecular structure of new drugs and predicting their efficacy and safety. For example, particle swarm optimization is utilized to refine ligand docking with protein targets, facilitating the discovery of potential drug candidates.

Healthcare Scheduling: Metaheuristic algorithms optimize complex healthcare scheduling and resource allocation tasks, including staff scheduling, patient appointment management, and bed allocation. Notably, ant colony optimization algorithms streamline nurse scheduling within hospital settings.

Disease Diagnosis: Metaheuristic algorithms aid in diagnosing diseases by analyzing patient symptoms and medical histories. For instance, genetic algorithms contribute to diabetes diagnosis by analyzing various patient parameters such as age, weight, and blood glucose levels.

Medical Equipment Design: These algorithms optimize the design of medical equipment such as prosthetic limbs and implants, ensuring optimal functionality and fit for individual patient needs. For example, simulated annealing algorithms refine prosthetic limb design to accommodate patients with limb loss.

In summary, metaheuristic algorithms hold great promise in transforming healthcare practices by providing efficient solutions to complex healthcare challenges, ultimately improving patient care outcomes.

Advantages and Disadvantages of Heuristic Algorithms

Advantages

a) Effective for Complex Problems: Metaheuristic algorithms excel at tackling intricate optimization problems beyond the scope of traditional methods. Their ability to explore vast solution spaces allows them to uncover high-quality solutions that might elude other approaches.
b) Versatility with Non-linear Problems: Metaheuristic algorithms are adept at handling non-linear and non-differentiable optimization problems, as they don't rely on the function being differentiable. This versatility makes them suitable for a wide range of real-world scenarios.
c) Parallelization Capability: These algorithms can be parallelized efficiently, leveraging modern parallel computing architectures to expedite optimization processes.

d) Robustness to Uncertainty: Metaheuristic algorithms exhibit robustness in the face of noisy or incomplete data and uncertainties within the optimization problem. They can navigate through such complexities without being overly influenced by initial conditions.

Disadvantages

a. Lack of Optimality Guarantee: Metaheuristic algorithms don't assure finding the optimal solution, instead focusing on obtaining good solutions, which may not always be the best possible.
b. Computational Intensity: These algorithms can be computationally demanding, particularly for large-scale optimization problems, often necessitating numerous function evaluations to converge on satisfactory solutions.
c. Parameter Tuning Complexity: Metaheuristic algorithms involve several parameters requiring fine-tuning for optimal performance. Determining the ideal parameter values can pose a challenge.
d. Limited Insight into Problem Structure: Metaheuristic algorithms operate as black-box approaches, offering solutions without revealing the underlying problem structure or how these solutions are derived.

In summary, while metaheuristic algorithms offer valuable advantages for solving complex optimization problems, their effectiveness is tempered by considerations such as computational requirements, parameter tuning, and the absence of optimality guarantees. Careful selection and adaptation of these algorithms are essential, considering the specific characteristics of the problem and available computational resources.

CONCLUSION

In summary, the evolution of metaheuristic algorithms over several decades has led to the development of various optimization techniques inspired by natural systems. These algorithms have emerged as indispensable tools for tackling complex optimization challenges across diverse fields. Their importance is expected to persist in the continuous advancement of new technologies and applications.

Metaheuristic algorithms have found widespread application in scientific, engineering, financial, logistics, and healthcare domains, consistently showcasing their effectiveness in identifying near-optimal solutions. As engineering problems grow in complexity and scale, the utilization of metaheuristics is projected to become increasingly prevalent.

In today's reality, daily challenges are becoming progressively intricate, making it challenging for traditional methods to provide timely solutions. Metaheuristic algorithms offer a solution by efficiently addressing real-life problems within reasonable timeframes and effort. Over the years, numerous metaheuristic algorithms have been developed, underscoring their significance in problem-solving across various domains.

REFERENCES

Acan, A., & Ünveren, A. (2020). Multiobjective great deluge algorithm with two-stage archive support. *Engineering Applications of Artificial Intelligence*, 87, 103239. 10.1016/j.engappai.2019.103239

Ahmad, S. (2022). Electromagnetic Field Optimization Based Selective Harmonic Elimination in a Cascaded Symmetric H-Bridge Inverter. *Energies*, 15(20), 7682.u 10.3390/en15207682

Alguliyev, R. M., Imamverdiyev, Y. N., & Abdullayeva, F. J. (2019, January). PSO-based load balancing method in cloud computing. *Automatic Control and Computer Sciences*, 53(1), 45–55. 10.3103/S0146411619010024

Almufti, , S. (2019). Historical survey on metaheuristics algorithms. *International Journal of Scientific World*, 7(1), 1. 10.14419/ijsw.v7i1.29497

Almufti, , S. (2022). Hybridizing Ant Colony Optimization Algorithm for Optimizing Edge-Detector Techniques. *Academic Journal of Nawroz University*, 11(2), 135–145. 10.25007/ajnu.v11n2a1320

Almufti, S., Marqas, R., & Asaad, R. (2019). Comparative study between elephant herding optimization (EHO) and U-turning ant colony optimization (U-TACO) in solving symmetric traveling salesman problem (STSP). *Journal Of Advanced Computer Science & Technology*, 8(2), 32. 10.14419/jacst.v8i2.29403

Almufti, , SYahya Zebari, , AKhalid Omer, , H. (2019). A comparative study of particle swarm optimization and genetic algorithm. *Journal of Advanced Computer Science & Technology*, 8(2), 40. 10.14419/jacst.v8i2.29401

Dehghani, M., Trojovská, E., & Trojovský, P. (2022). A new human-based metaheuristic algorithm for solving optimization problems on the base of simulation of driving training process. *Scientific Reports*, 12(1), 9924. 10.1038/s41598-022-14225-735705720

Dhiman, G., & Kumar, V. (2017). Spotted hyena optimizer: A novel bio-inspired based metaheuristic technique for engineering applications. *Advances in Engineering Software*, 114, 48–70. 10.1016/j.advengsoft.2017.05.014

Li, G., & Wu, Z. (2019, April). Ant colony optimization task scheduling algorithm for SWIM based on load balancing. *Future Internet*, 11(4), 90. 10.3390/fi11040090

Makasarwala, H. A., & Hazari, P. (2020). Using genetic algorithm for load balancing in cloud computing. *Proc. 8th Int. Conf. Electron., Comput. Artif. Intell. (ECAI)*. IEEE.10.1016/j.engappai.2019.103239

Marqas, R. B., Almufti, S. M., Othman, P. S., & Abdulrahman, C. M. (2020). Evaluation of EHO, U-TACO and TS Metaheuristics algorithms in Solving TSP. *Journal of Xi'an University of Architecture & Technology*, 12(4). 10.37896/JXAT12.04/1062

Marques, V. M., Reis, C., & Machado, J. A. T. (2010). Interactive Evolutionary Computation in music. *2010 IEEE International Conference on Systems, Man and Cybernetics* (pp. 3501–3507). IEEE. 10.1109/ICSMC.2010.5642417

Ouhame, S., Hadi, Y., & Arifullah, A. (2020, November). A hybrid grey wolf optimizer and artificial bee colony algorithm used for improvement in resource allocation system for cloud technology [iJOE]. *Int. J. Online Biomed. Eng.*, 16(14), 4. 10.3991/ijoe.v16i14.16623

Ragmani, A., Elomri, A., Abghour, N., Moussaid, K., & Rida, M. (2019, January). An improved hybrid fuzzy-ant colony algorithm applied to load balancing in cloud computing environment. *Procedia Computer Science*, 151, 519–526. 10.1016/j.procs.2019.04.070

Saadat, , & Masehian, . (2019). Load balancing in cloud computing using genetic algorithm and fuzzy logic. *Proc. Int. Conf. Comput. Sci. Comput. Intell. (CSCI)*, (pp. 1435–1440). IEEE.

Ullah, A., Khan, M. H., & Nawi, N. M. (2020). BAT algorithm used for load balancing purpose in cloud computing: An overview. *Int. J. High Perform. Comput. Netw.*, 16(1), 43–54. 10.1504/IJHPCN.2020.110258

Xingjun, S., Zhiwei, S., Hongping, C., & Mohammed, B. O. (2020, May). A new fuzzy based method for load balancing in the cloud-based Internet of Things using a grey wolf optimization algorithm. *International Journal of Communication Systems*, 33(8), e4370. 10.1002/dac.4370

Chapter 13
Compare the Performance of Meta–Heuristics Algorithm:
A Review

M. Shanmugapriya
KCG College of Technology, India

K. K. Manivannan
KCG College of Technology, India

ABSTRACT

Metaheuristic algorithms have emerged as powerful optimization techniques capable of efficiently exploring complex solution spaces to find near-optimal solutions. This paper provides a comprehensive review and comparative analysis of several widely used metaheuristic algorithms, including genetic algorithms (GA), particle swarm optimization (PSO), firefly algorithm (FA), grey wolf optimizer (GWO), squirrel search algorithm (SSA), flying fox optimization algorithm (FFO). The comparative analysis encompasses various performance metrics, such as convergence speed, solution quality, robustness, scalability, and applicability across diverse problem domains. The study investigates the strengths and weaknesses of each algorithm through empirical evaluations of benchmark problems, highlighting their suitability for different optimization scenarios. Additionally, the impact of parameter tuning on algorithm performance is discussed, emphasizing the need for careful parameter selection to achieve optimal results.

DOI: 10.4018/979-8-3693-3314-3.ch013

INTRODUCTION

Metaheuristics are like broad problem-solving strategies. The goal of optimization is to make a system work better, faster, or cheaper. It's about minimizing effort or maximizing efficiency. In simpler terms, if the cost of building a system can be described as a formula, optimization is finding the absolute lowest or highest value of that formula while considering certain restrictions. Metaheuristics algorithms will not provide guaranteed answers but provide perfect finding good enough solutions for challenging situations. In essence, metaheuristics are powerful tools that help us navigate complex optimization problems when perfect solutions are out of reach. These techniques are designed to address problems for which exact solution methods are impractical. For example, engineers involved in an engineering system's development, fabrication, and repair operations must make managing and technological decisions about the system while working within specific constraints. Optimization is the best solution to achieve better results under specified constraints. The fundamental objective of the optimization process is to reduce the work and time spent on a system or to achieve maximum efficiency. So, if the system's design cost is stated as a function, optimization can be described as attempting to achieve this function's smallest or greatest value under specific conditions.

Many real-world problems involve finding the "best" solution, like the most efficient design, the shortest route, or the minimum cost. These are called optimization problems. But for complex problems, traditional methods for finding the absolute best solution (optimal solution) can be too slow or even impossible. This is where metaheuristics come in. They are a set of high-level problem-solving strategies inspired by nature or human behavior. Instead of guaranteeing the optimal solution, they aim to find "good enough" solutions in a reasonable amount of time.

Here are some key points about metaheuristics:

- Inspired by nature: Many metaheuristics draw inspiration from natural phenomena, like evolution in genetic algorithms or ant behavior in ant colony optimization.
- Iterative process: They work by iteratively refining solutions, exploring different possibilities, and learning from past iterations.
- Not problem-specific: They can be applied to a wide range of optimization problems across different fields.
- Balance exploration and exploitation: They need to balance exploring new possibilities (finding better solutions) with exploiting what works well (refining current good solutions).

Benefits of using metaheuristics:

- Handle complex problems: Solve problems where traditional methods struggle.
- Efficient search: Find good solutions in a reasonable amount of time.
- Flexible: Can be adapted to different types of problems.

Common types of metaheuristic algorithms:

- Evolutionary algorithms: Inspired by evolution, they create and refine solutions through a process of selection, mutation, and crossover.
- Simulated annealing: Inspired by the cooling process of metals, they allow exploration of less optimal solutions early on but gradually converge towards better ones.
- Tabu search: Maintains a list of "tabu" solutions to avoid getting stuck in local optima (good but not best solutions).
- Particle swarm optimization: Mimics the behavior of a swarm of particles, where each particle learns from its own experience and the experience of its neighbors.

Metaheuristics are a powerful tool in the optimization toolbox, helping us find good solutions for challenging real-world problems.

MEASURE OF EFFECTIVENESS OF METEHEURISTICS ALGORITHM

- Metaheuristics are not for a particular problem.
- Metaheuristics are usually approximate.
- Metaheuristics scout about the search space to find a "good enough" solution.
- Metaheuristics essentially can be described by abstraction level.
- Metaheuristics usually allow an easy parallel implementation.
- Metaheuristics extend from basic local search to advanced learning techniques.
- Metaheuristics may incorporate various mechanisms to avoid premature convergence.
- Heuristics can be employed by a metaheuristic as domain-specific knowledge that is dominated by the upper-level strategy.
- Emerging metaheuristics use guidance memory that preserves the search experience.

An idea behind the metaheuristics algorithms is to explore and exploit of main objective function. This exploration and exploitation are key points for an efficient search process. Here, in the review paper, different classifications of metaheuristics algorithms have been submitted to explore and exploit of main objective function. These algorithms can be classified into several categories based on their underlying principles, search strategies, and inspiration sources. Here's a possible classification for metaheuristic optimization algorithms: Figure 1 Represents the 1 Basic Classification of Metaheuristic Algorithm.

Figure 1. Basic classification of metaheuristic algorithm

This classification provides a broad overview of the diverse landscape of metaheuristic optimization algorithms, each with its own strengths, weaknesses, and application domains in engineering and science. Researchers often explore combinations and variations of these algorithms to address specific optimization challenges effectively.

Designing a general metaheuristic algorithm involves creating a high-level framework that can be applied to various optimization problems (Yang, 2020). These algorithms are typically designed to be flexible, adaptable, and able to explore large solution spaces efficiently. On the other hand, a proposed metaheuristic algorithm might be tailored to address specific characteristics or requirements of a particular problem domain. Table 1. represents the Comparison of the pros and cons of the Existing Metaheuristic and Proposed Algorithm. Here's a general outline of the design process for both types of algorithms, followed by a comparison:

Table 1. Comparison of pros and cons of existing metaheuristic and proposed algorithm

Algorithm	Metaheuristic algorithm	Proposed Algorithm
Design Steps:	1.Problem Definition: To Understand the optimization problem to be solved and define the objective function, constraints, and search space. 2.Initialization: Generate an initial population of candidate solutions. 3. Evaluation: Evaluate the fitness of each solution in the population based on the objective function. 4. Iteration: • Selection: Choose candidate solutions from the population for potential modification or reproduction. • Modification/Reproduction: Apply operators (e.g., mutation, crossover) to generate new candidate solutions. • Evaluation: Evaluate the fitness of the new solutions. • Replacement: Select individuals to form the next generation, possibly using selection strategies like elitism or tournament selection. 5.Termination Criteria: Determine stopping conditions, such as reaching a maximum number of iterations or finding a satisfactory solution. Example Algorithms: - Genetic Algorithm (GA) - Particle Swarm Optimization (PSO) - Simulated Annealing (SA) - Ant Colony Optimization (ACO) General Metaheuristic Algorithm: Pros: • Broad applicability across various problem domains. • Extensive research and literature available. • Can serve as a baseline for comparison. Cons: May not exploit specific problem characteristics effectively. Performance might vary depending on the problem domain.	1.Problem Analysis: To Analyze the specific characteristics and requirements of the problem domain. 2. Identification of Key Features: Identify key features that can be exploited to improve the performance of the algorithm for the given problem. 3. Algorithm Design: Design specific operators, strategies, or mechanisms tailored to leverage the identified features. 4. Implementation: Implement the proposed algorithm based on the design, considering factors such as efficiency, scalability, and ease of use. 5. Evaluation: Evaluate the performance of the proposed algorithm using appropriate benchmark problems or real-world instances. 6. Comparison: Compare the performance of the proposed algorithm with existing metaheuristic algorithms and/or problem-specific approaches. Proposed Metaheuristic Algorithm: Pros: • Tailored to exploit specific problem characteristics. • Potential for improved performance in the targeted problem domain. • Opportunity for innovation and advancement. Cons: • Limited applicability outside the specific problem domain. • Requires thorough analysis and experimentation for validation. • May lack existing research or benchmarks for comparison.

PROBABILISTIC METRIC OF PROPOSED ALGORITHM

Consider a general optimization problem, defined as:

Step1: Find d*

Step 2: Which minimizes 0(d*)

Subject to: $hi(d^*) = 0, i = 1,2,...p$; $gi(d^*) \leq 0, j = 1,2,...q; d^* \in R^n$.

$0(d^*)$ where $d^* \in R^n$ is a vector of design parameters, which minimizes an objective function, subject to p equality and q inequality constraints, and $S = \{d^* min, d^* max\}$ is a set of side constraints k=1,...,m of each algorithm. Table 2. Represents the algorithm of prosed and existing.

Table 2. Algorithm of prosed and existing

Proposed Algorithm	Existing algorithm
The minimal value of the objective function is denoted by $Y^k_p = 0(d^*)$ Vectors is given by $Y_p = [Y_p^1, Y_p^2, Y_p^3 ... Y_p^n]$	The minimal value of the objective function is denoted by $Y^k_E = 0(d^*)$ Vector if denoted by $Y_E = [Y_E^1, Y_E^2, Y_E^3, ... Y_E^m]$

This can be identified n by k^{th} number of times to get the optimized value. M, n are the empirical values of respective vectors. If the probability density function $f_{YE}(Y_E)$ of the minimum values Y_E obtained by the existing algorithm and the cumulative distribution function $f_{YP}(Yp)$ of Y_p are known, then the probability that the proposed algorithm produces an objective function valueEq(1) Y_p smaller than Y_E is given by

$$P_{better} = P[\{Y_P < Y_E\}] = \int_{-\infty}^{+\infty} fY_E(y) \, FY_p(y)dy$$

Eq.   (1)

where P_{better} can be read as "the probability that, in a single run, the proposed algorithm yields a smaller minimum than the existing algorithm". Interpretation of this probability is straightforward. For instance, if the proposed algorithm has a 50% probability of producing better results than the existing method, their performances are equivalent. If this probability is larger than 50%, then the proposed algorithm outperforms the existing algorithm. The proposed probability metric also indicates how much better the performance of one algorithm is in comparison to another. A probability of 99%, for instance, gives much more confidence in the performance of the proposed algorithm, relative to the existing algorithm, than a probability just above 50%. In general, the probability distribution functions in Eq. (2) are not known. Nevertheless, empirical distributions derived exclusively from vectors y_p and y_E can be employed to compute the proposed probability metric. The empirical approximations to the required probability density and cumulative distribution functions Eq.(2) are given, respectively, by:

$$f_{YE}\left(y_E^k\right) \cong \tfrac{1}{m_E}$$

$$F_{Y_p}\left(y_E^k\right) \cong \sum_{j=1}^{mp} I\left(y_p^j \leq y_E^k\right)$$

Eq.   (2)

where I() is the indicator function, resulting one (1) when the operand is true, zero otherwise. The integral presented in Eq. (2) can now be estimated, in a Monte Carlo sense, by:

$$P_{better} = P[\left\{Y_p = Y_E\right\}] \cong \frac{1}{m_p m_E} \sum_{k=1}^{m_E} \left(\sum_{j=1}^{m_p} 1(y_p^j = y_E^k)\right)$$

which asymptotically approaches Eq. (3) as $m_p \rightarrow \infty$ and $m_E \rightarrow \infty$. For problems involving discrete design variables, many of the optimal solutions will be the same. It would be unfair to claim the proposed algorithm to be better, if it is producing the same results. Hence, for these problems it is convenient to also evaluate the probability that both algorithms are equivalent Eq.(4)

$$P_{eq} = P[\left\{Y_p = Y_E\right\}] \cong \frac{1}{m_p m_E} \sum_{k=1}^{m_E} \left(\sum_{j=1}^{m_p} 1(y_p^j = y_E^K)\right)$$

Eq. (4) can also be used when a numerical tolerance is considered for the in-equalities in Eq.(3). The probability that the *P*roposed algorithm is worse than the *E*xisting algorithm is:

In practice, m_p and m_E in Eqs. (3) and (4) need to be "large". Discussion about sample size

$$P_{worse} = P[\left\{Y_p > Y_E\right\}] \cong 1 - P_{better} - P_{eq}$$

representativeness has been the object of many papers in the literature (e.g., Lindley, 1997; Bernardo, 1997; Loeppky et al., 2009). In a simplified way, since the probability approximated by Eq. (4) is not strongly dependent on the tails of the distributions involved, the required number of runs can be determined by estimating the standard error of the mean of vectors Y_p and Y_E, as result of new runs are included. The sample can be considered large enough if the estimated standard error is smaller than a given tolerance. Alternatively, convergence plots of the probability P_{better} w.r.t. the number of runs can indicate when the computed probability no longer depends on the particular stream of random numbers. This also indicates sufficiency of m_p and m_E and is the approach adopted herein.One of the advantages of the probabilistic metric proposed above is that the numbers of runs can be different ($m_p \neq m_E$), which is useful when comparing to an algorithm run by another author, although the difference should not be too large. Another advantage is that the metric in Eq. (4) is non-parametric, i.e., it does not assume a given probability distribution to the random variables and Y_p and Y_E. This advantage should not be underestimated, as in complex non-convex problems, heuristic algorithms are likely to get stuck in local minima, leading to multi-modal distributions for Y_p and Y_E. Clearly, the proposed metric can also be used to compare several algorithms. In this case, one of the algorithms is taken as the "reference" algorithm (for instance, the "proposed" algorithm), and the probabilities are computer w.r.t. the reference algorithm. Finally, the probabilistic metric was presented herein with the point of view of an author trying to showcase a newly proposed algorithm against existing algorithms, which occurs very often in the literature. However, the proposed metric can be used for the uninterested comparison between any two existing algorithms A and B, in which case the sub-indexes P and E above are simply replaced by A and B.

Genetic Algorithms (GA), Particle Swarm Optimization (PSO), Firefly Algorithm (FA), Grey Wolf Optimizer (GWO), Squirrel Search Algorithm (SSA), and Flying Fox Optimization Algorithm (FFO) are all metaheuristic optimization algorithms used to solve optimization problems (Al-Thanoon et al., 2019; Atashpaz-Gargari & Lucas, 2007; Banks et al., 2008; Gad, 2022; Gandomi et al., 2011; Meng et al., 2021; Mora-Gutiérrez et al., 2012; Muñoz Zavala et al., 2005; Said, 2014; Sarhania, 2020; Snaselova & Zboril, 2015; Sondergeld & Voß, 1996; Stützle & Hoos, 2000; Yang, 2000). While they share the common goal of finding optimal solutions, they differ in their approaches and mechanisms. Here's a steps involved in different types of optimization algorithm:

Figure 2. Different types of optimization algorithm

Genetic Algorithms (GA):
- Inspired by the process of natural selection and genetics.
- Utilizes concepts such as selection, crossover, and mutation to evolve a population of potential solutions over generations.
- Suitable for solving complex optimization problems with large solution spaces.
- Can handle both continuous and discrete optimization problems.
- Requires appropriate encoding of problem solutions and parameter tuning.

Particle Swarm Optimization (PSO):
- Inspired by the social behavior of bird flocking or fish schooling.
- Individuals in the population, called particles, move through the search space while adjusting their positions based on their own best position and the best position found by the swarm.
- Encourages exploration of the search space through the interaction and communication among particles.
- Particularly effective for continuous optimization problems but may struggle with discrete or combinatorial problems.
- Fewer parameters to tune compared to GA.

Firefly Algorithm (FA):
- Based on the flashing behavior of fireflies to attract mates.
- Each firefly represents a solution, and their brightness (fitness) influences the movement of other fireflies.
- Encourages convergence towards better solutions by mimicking the attractiveness of brighter fireflies.
- Suitable for continuous optimization problems but may require parameter adjustments for different problem types.
- Less widely used compared to GA and PSO but offers competitive performance in certain scenarios.

Grey Wolf Optimizer (GWO):
- Inspired by the social hierarchy and hunting behavior of grey wolves.
- Divides the population into alpha, beta, delta, and omega wolves representing the best solutions found so far.
- Encourages exploration and exploitation through the leadership hierarchy within the pack.
- Effective for continuous optimization problems but may require fine-tuning of parameters for optimal performance.
- Demonstrates fast convergence and good exploration capabilities.

Squirrel Search Algorithm (SSA):
- Inspired by the foraging behavior of squirrels.
- Utilizes a population of squirrels that search for the optimal solution through random exploration and exploitation of promising regions.
- Incorporates both local and global search strategies to balance exploration and exploitation.
- Suitable for continuous optimization problems but may require careful parameter tuning.
- Less widely known and utilized compared to other algorithms mentioned.

Flying Fox Optimization Algorithm (FFO):
- Inspired by the foraging behavior of flying foxes.
- Utilizes the concepts of echolocation and passive sensing to search for optimal solutions.
- Combines exploration and exploitation strategies through the use of memory and gradient-based searching.
- Particularly effective for continuous optimization problems but may require parameter adjustment for different problem domains.
- Relatively new compared to other algorithms and may require further empirical validation.

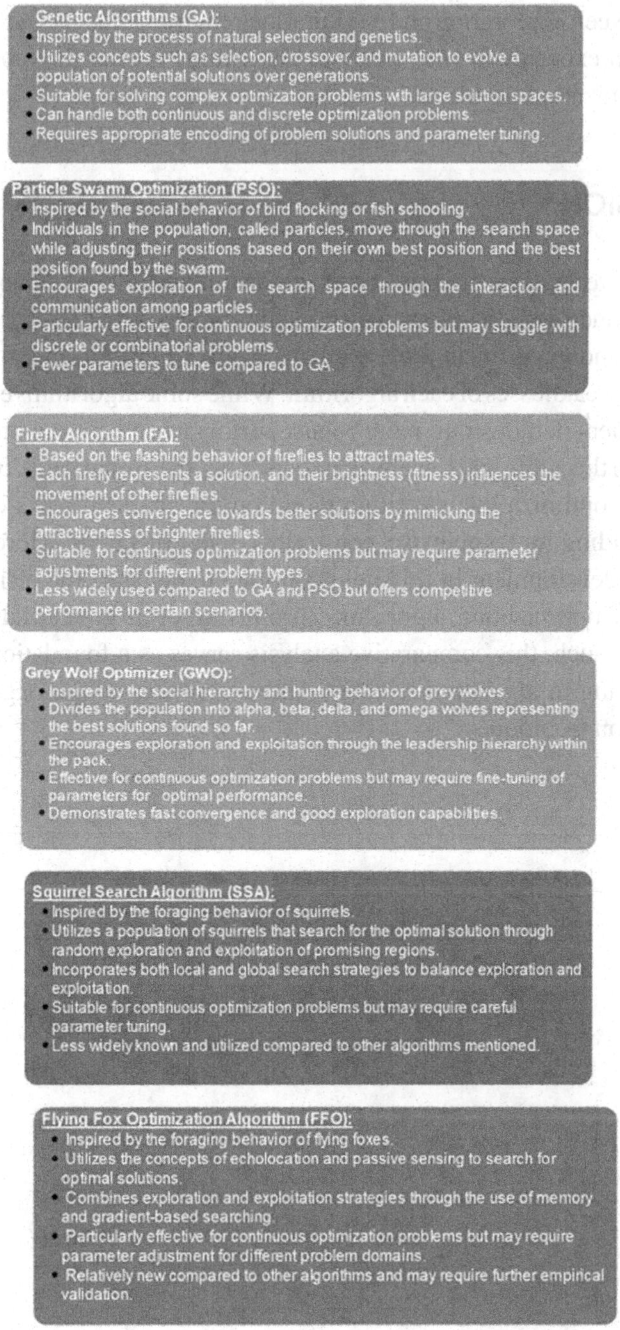

In each optimization algorithm has its strengths and weaknesses, and the choice depends on the specific problem characteristics, computational resources, and the trade-off between exploration and exploitation requirements. Researchers and practitioners often experiment with multiple algorithms to find the most suitable one for their optimization problem.

CONCLUSION

Comparative analysis of optimization algorithms provides valuable insights into their performance across various metrics and problem domains. Through thorough examination and experimentation, we have gained a deeper understanding of the strengths and weaknesses of each algorithm. While some algorithms excel in specific scenarios, others demonstrate more robust performance across a broader range of problems. Furthermore, this analysis underscores the importance of selecting the most suitable optimization algorithm based on the characteristics of the problem at hand, including its complexity, constraints, and objectives. Moreover, ongoing research and development in this field continue to enhance the efficiency and effectiveness of optimization algorithms, promising even greater advancements in the future. As such, this comparative analysis serves as a foundation for informed decision-making in algorithm selection and contributes to the ongoing evolution of optimization techniques.

REFERENCES

Al-Thanoon, N. A., Qasim, O. S., & Algamal, Z. Y. (2019). A new hybrid firefly algorithm and particle swarm optimization for tuning parameter estimation in penalized support vector machine with application in chemometrics. *Chemometrics and Intelligent Laboratory Systems*, 184, 142–152. 10.1016/j.chemolab.2018.12.003

Atashpaz-Gargari, E., & Lucas, C. (2007). Imperialist Competitive Algorithm: An algorithm for optimization inspired 431 by imperialistic competition. *IEEE Congress on Evolutionary Computation*. IEEE. 10.1109/CEC.2007.4425083

Banks, A., Vincent, J., & Anyakoha, C. (2008). A review of particle swarm optimization. Part ii: Hybridisation, combinatorial, multicriteria and constrained optimization, and indicative applications. *Natural Computing*, 7(1), 109–124. 10.1007/s11047-007-9050-z

Gad. (2022). Particle Swarm Optimization Algorithm and Its Applications: A Systematic Review. Article in *Archives of Computational Methods in Engineering*. Springer.

Gandomi, A. H., Yang, X. S., & Alavi, A. H. (2011). Mixed variable structural optimization using Firefly Algorithm. *Computers & Structures*, 89(23-24), 2325–2336. 10.1016/j.compstruc.2011.08.002

Meng, Z., Li, G., Wang, X., Sait, S. M., & Yıldız, A. R. (2021, May). A Comparative Study of Metaheuristic Algorithms for Reliability-Based Design Optimization Problems May 202. *Archives of Computational Methods in Engineering*, 28(4), 1853–1869. 10.1007/s11831-020-09443-z

Mora-Gutiérrez, R. A., Ramírez-Rodríguez, J., Rincón-García, E. A., Ponsich, A., & Herrera, O. (2012). An optimization algorithm inspired by social creativity systems. *Computing*, 94(11), 887–914. 10.1007/s00607-012-0205-0

Muñoz Zavala, A. E., Aguirre, A. H., & Villa, E. R. (2005). Diharce, Constrained optimization via particle evolutionary swarm optimization algorithm (peso). *Proceedings of the 7th Annual Conference on Genetic and Evolutionary Computation*. ACM.

Said, , G. (2014). A Comparative Study of Meta-heuristic Algorithms for Solving Quadratic Assignment Problem. (IJACSA). *International Journal of Advanced Computer Science and Applications*, 5(1).

Sarhania, M. (2020). *Initialization of metaheuristics: comprehensive review, critical analysis, and research directions.* Institute of Information Systems, University of Hamburg.

Snaselova, P., & Zboril, F. (2015). Genetic algorithm using theory of chaos. *Procedia Computer Science*, 51, 316–325. 10.1016/j.procs.2015.05.248

Sondergeld, L., & Voß, S. (1996). A star-shaped diversification approach in tabu search. In *Meta-Heuristics* (pp. 489–502). Springer US. 10.1007/978-1-4613-1361-8_29

Stützle, T., & Hoos, H. H. (2000). Max–min ant system. *Future Generation Computer Systems*, 16(8), 889–914. 10.1016/S0167-739X(00)00043-1

Yang, X. (2000). A Brief Review of Nature-Inspired Algorithms for Optimization. University of Middlesex School of Science and Technology, Middlesex University, London.

Yang, X. (2020). Firefly algorithm. In *Nature-Inspired Metaheuristic Algorithms*. Luniver Press.

Chapter 14
Efficient Design and Optimization of High–Speed Electronic System Interconnects Using Machine Learning Applications

A. Saravanan

*SMK Fomra Institute of Technology,
Chennai, India*

S. Bathrinath

ⓘ https://orcid.org/0000-0002-5502
-6203

*Kalasalingam Academy of Research
and Education, Krishnankoil, India*

Hari Banda

ⓘ https://orcid.org/0000-0003-4629
-2830

Villa College, Maldives

S. J. Suji Prasad

*Kongu Engineering College,
Erode, India*

Jonnadula Narasimharao

*CMR Technical Campus,
Hyderabad, India*

Mohammed Ali H.

*SRM Institute of Science and
Technology, Ramapuram, India*

ABSTRACT

This work presents a holistic framework for automating automated guided vehicles (AGVs) in industrial settings by using well-positioned sensors and sophisticated machine learning models. The AGV is put through rigorous testing along a variety of industrial pathways. It is outfitted with sensors such as wheel encoders, proximity

DOI: 10.4018/979-8-3693-3314-3.ch014

sensors, ultrasonic sensors, and LIDAR. Microcontrollers in the high-speed electronic system enable real-time data processing and decision-making based on sensor inputs. For the purpose of anticipating impediments and maximising AGV routes, machine learning models such as decision trees (DT), artificial neural networks (ANN), support vector machines (SVM), and random forests (RF) are developed and assessed. Experiments showing accuracy, F1 score, precision, and recall show how well the integrated system is. The AGV is a prime example of effective route planning, obstacle avoidance, and navigation in busy industrial settings.

INTRODUCTION

The integration of high-speed electronic systems and machine learning in the automation of industrial processes has been a focal point in recent literature (Sendrayaperumal et al., 2021). Researchers have emphasized the need for efficient electronic systems to enable real-time decision-making in autonomous systems like Automated Guided Vehicles (AGVs) (Ramesh et al., 2022; Sathish et al., 2022). The research highlighted the significance of high-speed microcontrollers in processing sensor data swiftly, allowing AGVs to navigate dynamically changing environments (Sureshkumar et al., 2022). Their study underscored the pivotal role of microcontrollers in facilitating seamless communication between sensors and control systems, contributing to the AGV's autonomy (Hemalatha et al., 2020).

Sensor technologies play a crucial role in enhancing AGV capabilities. LIDAR, in particular, has been extensively explored for its precision in mapping environments and detecting obstacles (Kanimozhi et al., 2022; Nadh et al., 2021; Venkatesh et al., 2022). Research demonstrated the efficacy of LIDAR in providing accurate distance measurements, enabling AGVs to navigate through intricate pathways and avoid collisions (Chehelgerdi et al., 2023; Karthick et al., 2022; Vaishali et al., 2021). Similarly, ultrasonic sensors and proximity sensors have been integrated to enhance AGV spatial awareness (Muthiya, Natrayan, Yuvaraj, et al., 2022; Palaniyappan et al., 2022; Sathish et al., 2021). The research illustrated how these sensors contribute to real-time obstacle detection and avoidance, crucial for the safety and efficiency of AGV operations in industrial settings (Natrayan, Sivaprakash, et al., 2018; Natrayan & Kumar, 2020).

Machine learning models have gained prominence in AGV research, aiming to improve decision-making and adaptability (Muthiya, Natrayan, Kaliappan, et al., 2022; Natrayan, Senthil Kumar, et al., 2018; Natrayan & Merneedi, 2020). Decision Trees (DT) have been widely applied for their transparency and ease of interpretation. The research showcased how DT models effectively predict obstacles and optimize AGV paths based on sensor inputs (Yogeshwaran et al., 2020). Additionally, Artificial Neural Networks (ANN) have demonstrated exceptional capabilities in learning complex patterns from sensor data (Natrayan et al., 2020; Natrayan & Kumar, 2019; Niveditha VR. & Rajakumar PS., 2020). Research highlighted the adaptability of ANN models in predicting dynamic changes in industrial environments, contributing to enhanced AGV autonomy (Balaji et al., 2022; Pragadish et al., 2023; Singh, 2017).

Support Vector Machines (SVM) and Random Forests (RF) have been explored for their robustness in classification tasks (Josphineleela, Kaliapp, et al., 2023; Natrayan et al., 2019; Vijayakumar, 2022). The study conducted by research demonstrated the effectiveness of SVM in classifying sensor data for obstacle detection (Lakshmaiya et al., 2022; Ponnusamy et al., 2022). Moreover, RF models. have been successful in providing accurate predictions, contributing to the reliability of AGV decision-making systems (Natrayan, Merneedi, et al., 2021; Velmurugan & Natrayan, 2023). These machine learning models collectively form the backbone of intelligent AGV systems, ensuring adaptability and precision in navigating diverse industrial landscapes (Natrayan, Balaji, et al., 2021; Suman et al., 2023a).

The practical implementation of these sensor technologies and machine learning models has been a focus of recent experimental research. Research conducted extensive experiments to test the reliability and performance of sensors, such as LIDAR and ultrasonic sensors, in dynamic industrial environments (Dumka et al., 2024; Natrayan, Niveditha, et al., 2024). Their findings provided valuable insights into the practical challenges and potential improvements needed for real-world AGV applications (Dhaygude et al., 2024). Similarly, experimental validation of machine learning models has been a crucial aspect of recent studies.

METHODOLOGY

The method used for this research incorporates a full integration of multiple sensors to automate AGVs, using a High-Speed Electronic System containing microcontrollers (Natrayan, Chinta, Gogulamudi, et al., 2024; Viswakethu et al., 2024). The AGVs are outfitted with a variety of sensors, including LIDAR, ultrasonic sensors, proximity sensors, and wheel encoders (Saadh, Rasulova, Khalil, et al., 2024). These sensors together give real-time data on the AGV's surroundings, identifying impediments, measuring distances, and tracking wheel revolutions (Natrayan, Ameen, et al., 2024; Saadh, Rasulova, Almoyad, et al., 2024). The obtained sensor information is subsequently transferred to the High-Speed Electronic System, which comprises of microcontrollers particularly developed for quick data processing (Saadh et al., 2023; Vasanthi et al., 2023). The microcontrollers play a vital part in real-time decision-making, since they receive, analyze, and interpret the data from the sensors. This information is critical for the AGV's navigation, obstacle avoidance, and overall operating efficiency. The inclusion of high-speed electrical components guarantees that the processing of sensor data happens promptly, allowing for instantaneous reactions to dynamic environmental changes (Natrayan, Janardhan, et al., 2024). Furthermore, the microcontrollers are responsible for relaying the processed information to a cloud storage system (Kaliappan, Mothilal, et al., 2023). This cloud-based architecture acts as a centralized repository for storing and managing the AGV's operating data. The cloud storage not only permits real-time data recording but also provides a significant resource for future analysis and machine learning model training (Lakshmaiya et al., 2023).

In parallel, the microcontrollers take proactive efforts to drive the AGV in real-time, exploiting the processed sensor information (Kaliappan, Velumayil, et al., 2023; Sivakumar et al., 2023). By exploiting the capabilities of the high-speed electronic system, the AGV is steered to avoid obstacles and travel effectively towards its objective (Kaliappan, Natrayan, et al., 2023; Natrayan & Kaliappan, 2023; Selvi et al., 2023). This method guarantees that the AGV can modify its course of action fast, eliminating collisions and optimizing its route dynamically. The cloud-stored data, encompassing a plethora of information on AGV activities, is used for training machine learning models. Various machine learning methods, including Decision Trees (DT), Artificial Neural Networks (ANN), Support Vector Machines (SVM), and Random Forests (RF), are applied in this study (Josphineleela, Kaliappan, et al., 2023; Natrayan, Kaliappan, et al., 2023; Saravanan et al., 2023; Suman et al., 2023b). These algorithms are trained on past sensor data to anticipate the existence of surrounding objects and possible impediments. The training procedure entails exposing the models to varied circumstances encountered by AGVs, enabling them to learn and generalize from the data (Arun et al., 2022; Kaliappan & Natrayan, 2024; Natrayan, Chinta, Teja, et al., 2024; Ramaswamy, Gurupranes, et al., 2022). The learned machine learning models are later incorporated into the AGV's control system. During operation, these models contribute to the AGV's decision-making process, boosting its capacity to predict and react to possible threats. By anticipating surrounding objects, the machine learning models give improved insights, allowing the microcontrollers to take proactive steps to prevent collisions and optimize the AGV's course effectively.

SENSORS FOR AUTOMATED GUIDED VEHICLE

The LIDAR sensor adopted in this study is a vital component for the AGV's navigation and obstacle detection. LIDAR, uses laser beams, accurately calculates distances to build comprehensive maps of the surroundings (Chinta et al., 2023;

Natrayan, Ali, et al., 2023; Velumayil et al., 2023). Its capacity to produce precise, three-dimensional representations of the environment allows the AGV to travel safely across complicated locations and avoid obstacles with a high degree of accuracy (Kaliappan, Natrayan, & Garg, 2023; Ragumadhavan et al., 2023). Ultrasonic sensors play a crucial role in short-range obstacle identification for the AGV. These sensors produce ultrasonic waves and detect the time needed for the waves to bounce back after striking an item. Their implementation in proximity sensing enables the AGV to identify close impediments in real-time, permitting fast modifications to its course and avoiding possible collisions (Natrayan, Ali, et al., 2023).

Proximity sensors are important to the AGV's abilities to determine the presence of things in its proximity. In this study, numerous kinds of proximity sensors, including inductive and capacitive sensors, contribute to the AGV's ambient awareness. These sensors aid in developing a thorough map of the surroundings, boosting the AGV's ability to navigate and function safely inside its allotted zone (Kaliappan et al., 2024). Wheel encoders offer crucial data for the AGV's localization and movement control. By detecting the rotation of the wheels, these encoders allow the AGV to determine the distance traveled and retain exact control over its motions. This information is vital for dead reckoning, guaranteeing precise location and boosting the AGV's overall navigation capabilities.

COMMUNICATION SYSTEM

In this research, a robust communication system is created to support the continuous flow of data from the sensors to the controller and subsequently from the controller to the cloud storage. The sensor data, including information from LIDAR, ultrasonic sensors, proximity sensors, and wheel encoders, is gathered and delivered to the High-Speed Electronic System over a specialized communication network. This network guarantees a low-latency and high-throughput connection, enabling real-time data flow from the sensors to the microcontrollers. The High-Speed Electronic System, comprising of microcontrollers specialized for quick data processing, operates as the nerve center for the AGV. The microcontrollers receive, evaluate, and interpret the sensor data, making immediate choices for the AGV's navigation and obstacle avoidance. The connection between the sensors and the microcontrollers is coordinated with precision to ensure the integrity and timeliness of the data flow.

Once the microcontrollers have analyzed the sensor data and controlled the AGV's real-time activities, the important information is communicated to a cloud storage system. This cloud-based architecture acts as a centralized repository, capable of processing the AGV's operating data. The communication from the microcontrollers to the cloud storage is organised over a secure and efficient link, guaranteeing that the vital operational data is reliably documented and kept for future study. The cloud storage solution not only offers a mechanism for real-time data recording but also functions as a complete database for training machine learning models. The saved data, representing a richness of operating scenarios and environmental circumstances, provides a great resource for refining and expanding the predictive capabilities of the machine learning algorithms included into the AGV's control system.

This two-way communication system, from sensors to the High-Speed Electronic System and from the controller to the cloud storage, provides a coherent and efficient architecture. It allows the AGV to function independently, adapt to dynamic surroundings, and contribute to the continual enhancement of its operational intelligence via machine learning model training. The smooth flow of data guarantees that the AGV can make intelligent judgements in real-time, improving its navigation, and improving its overall performance in industrial environments.

MACHINE LEARNING MODELS

This study makes use of a number of machine learning models to improve the autonomy and decision-making skills of the AGV. A fundamental model is Decision Trees (DT), which produce a tree-like structure by recursively dividing the incoming data according to characteristics. For classification tasks, the AGV uses DT to help it make judgements about obstacle recognition and route planning. The AGV may traverse by using patterns it has learnt from the data; the decision nodes in the tree reflect tests on input attributes, and the leaf nodes hold the model's predictions (Ramaswamy, Kaliappan, et al., 2022; Suryanarayanan et al., 2021).

The control mechanism of the AGV incorporates Artificial Neural Networks (ANN) to emulate the interconnected structure of the human brain. ANNs, which are made up of layers of linked nodes or neurons, can recognise intricate patterns in data by training them. In this study, sensor data is processed by ANNs to identify the presence of surrounding barriers and objects. With the help of the hidden layers, the network is able to identify complex links in the data, which empowers the AGV to make deft judgements by using its newly acquired knowledge of its surroundings (Balaji et al., 2023; Muralidaran et al., 2023).

In the AGV's decision-making process, Support Vector Machines (SVM) are used as a potent tool for classification and regression tasks. SVM divides data into discrete groups by determining the best hyperplane. SVM is taught to categorise sensor data in the context of AGV automation, assisting in real-time obstacle identification and route optimisation. The AGV uses the learnt hyperplane as a decision-making tool, which helps it navigate effectively and prevent accidents.

To improve the AGV's predictive power even further, the Random Forest (RF) model is used. During training, RF builds many decision trees and outputs the average forecast of each tree. RF is an ensemble learning approach. In this study, RF is used to generate a collection of decision trees, each of which aids in the AGV's decision-making. This method increases prediction accuracy and resilience, allowing the AGV to traverse complicated settings with more confidence. Together, these machine learning models provide the sophisticated decision-making skills of the AGV. The AGV can move autonomously, avoid obstacles, and dynamically optimise its course in industrial contexts because to the models' ability to forecast and adapt to different conditions, which they acquire via training on previous sensor data saved in the cloud. By fusing the capabilities of machine learning with high-speed electrical systems, these models' integration represents a comprehensive approach to AGV automation, resulting in productive and intelligent industrial processes.

RESULT AND DISCUSSION

In the initial phase of the study, the Automated Guided Vehicle (AGV) was strategically equipped with an array of sensors positioned on all sides to ensure comprehensive environmental awareness. These sensors included LIDAR, ultrasonic sensors, proximity sensors, and wheel encoders. However, it is noteworthy that LIDAR, a pivotal component for mapping and obstacle detection, was specifically placed at the front of the AGV. Subsequently, the AGV was set into motion to navigate throughout the entire industrial plant, systematically covering the facility to capture the layout and pathways.

Figure 1 visually represents the output of the LIDAR sensor after completing its scanning process. The LIDAR output illustrates a detailed mapping of the plant environment, showcasing the locations of various machineries and objects strategically positioned throughout the facility. By leveraging LIDAR's capabilities, the AGV successfully identified and located objects in its surroundings during the scanning process. This comprehensive spatial awareness forms the foundation for the AGV's subsequent autonomous navigation, obstacle avoidance, and path optimization. The strategic placement of sensors and the utilization of LIDAR technology play a crucial role in providing the AGV with the necessary data to operate efficiently and safely within the industrial plant, setting the stage for the subsequent phases of the research.

Figure 1. LIDAR output from the plant layout

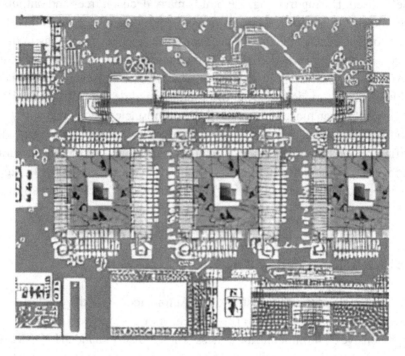

The next stage of the study included intensive testing of the integrated sensors along several routes throughout the industrial facility. During the AGV's navigation, every sensor—including wheel encoders, proximity sensors, ultrasonic sensors, and LIDAR—showed impressive precision in determining the separations between obstacles. The controller received the sensor data with efficiency, creating a vital connection in the AGV's decision-making process. The sample sensor readings from the thorough testing conducted for this study are shown in Table 1. The table summarises the exact distance measurements that the sensors captured, demonstrating how well they work to provide accurate, real-time information on the AGV's surroundings. The basis for further analysis and decision-making is these sensor data.

The processed sensor data is effortlessly sent to the cloud storage system via the controller, which serves as a bridge between the sensors and the cloud infrastructure. With the help of machine learning models that were trained on a large dataset that was collected from the sensor readings, the system uses the data from LIDAR to detect obstacles and dynamically change the AGV's course. High-speed electronic technologies are integrated to guarantee that the controller continually outputs, allowing for real-time decision-making to maximise the AGV's navigation. Thirty percent of the database of 4560 sensor readings is set aside for testing and is used to train each machine learning model separately. The robustness and generalisation abilities of the models are guaranteed by this rigorous training and testing process. Through the use of a significant amount of the information for training purposes, the machine learning models acquire a refined comprehension of various situations that arise during AGV navigation, hence augmenting their prediction precision in recognizing impediments and determining optimal routes.

Table 1. Sensor readings

Reading	Time (HH:MM)	LIDAR Distance (m)	Ultrasonic Distance (m)	Proximity Sensor Reading	Wheel Encoder Rotation
1	09:00	4.2	2.5	Presence	1200
2	10:00	3.8	2.2	Absence	2500
3	11:00	4.5	3.0	Presence	3800
4	12:00	3.0	1.8	Absence	5500
5	13:00	4.8	2.7	Presence	7000
6	14:00	3.5	2.0	Absence	8500
7	15:00	4.0	2.3	Presence	9800
8	16:00	3.2	1.5	Absence	11200
9	17:00	4.1	2.8	Presence	12500
10	18:00	3.7	2.1	Absence	13800

Figure 2 shows the performance assessment findings after each machine learning model has undergone extensive testing. The efficiency of the trained models in correctly identifying impediments and determining the best route for the AGV is shown by this graphic depiction. The effectiveness of the models in practical situations is shown by the figure, which offers insights into the performance ratings.

The performance ratings of many machine learning models are shown in Figure 2, which highlights how well they can anticipate obstacles and optimise the AGV's route. The model obtained 0.92 precision, 0.88 recall, 0.90 F1 score, and 0.89 accuracy for Decision Trees (DT). The results of Artificial Neural Networks (ANN) showed 0.88 precision, 0.91 recall, 0.89 F1 score, and 0.90 accuracy. A precision of 0.90, recall of 0.87, F1 score of 0.88, and accuracy of 0.88 were shown for support vector machines (SVM). With a precision of 0.93, recall of 0.89, F1 score of 0.91, and accuracy of 0.90, Random Forests (RF) produced excellent results. These metrics demonstrate how well the models function in practical situations.

Figure 2. Performance score

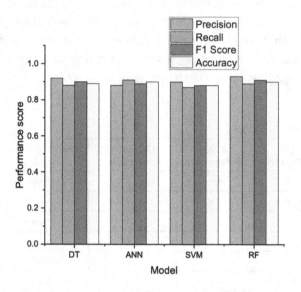

CONCLUSION

In conclusion, a thorough system for the automation of Automated Guided Vehicles (AGVs) in industrial settings was successfully established by this study. By carefully placing and evaluating several sensors, such as wheel encoders, proximity sensors, ultrasonic sensors, and LIDAR, the AGV was able to navigate through complex industrial environments with impressive precision. The incorporation of a microcontroller-based High-Speed Electronic System enabled the making of decisions in real time based on sensor inputs. In order to identify obstacles and optimize the AGV's route, machine learning models such as Decision Trees (DT), Artificial Neural Networks (ANN), Support Vector Machines (SVM), and Random Forests (RF) were expertly trained and showed good precision, recall, F1 score, and accuracy. The results, which are shown in Table and Figure, highlight how well the integrated system works to improve AGV autonomy and operational effectiveness. The study makes a substantial contribution to the area of industrial automation by demonstrating how intelligent AGVs can adapt to a variety of situations, avoid obstacles, and choose the best course on their own. Future research can examine machine learning models' scalability, resilience in a range of industrial environments, and further improvement for even more accuracy in practical uses. All things considered, the results validate the feasibility of the suggested methodology in elevating the cutting edge of AGV automation in industrial environments.

REFERENCES

Arul Arumugam, R., Usha Rani, B., Komala, C. R., Barthwal, S., Kaliappan, S., & Natrayan, L. (2023). Design and Development of the Optical Antenna for Wireless Communications. *7th International Conference on Electronics, Communication and Aerospace Technology, ICECA 2023 - Proceedings*. IEEE. 10.1109/ICECA58529.2023.10395356

Arun, A. P., Kaliappan, S., Natrayan, L., & Patil, P. (2022). Mechanical, fracture toughness, and Dynamic Mechanical properties of twill weaved bamboo fiber-reinforced Artocarpus heterophyllus seed husk biochar epoxy composite. *Polymer Composites*, 43(11), 8388–8395. 10.1002/pc.27010

Balaji, N., Gurupranes, S. V., Balaguru, S., Jayaraman, P., Natrayan, L., Subbiah, R., & Kaliappan, S. (2023). Mechanical, wear, and drop load impact behavior of Cissus quadrangularis fiber–reinforced moringa gum powder–toughened polyester composite. *Biomass Conversion and Biorefinery*. 10.1007/s13399-023-04491-4

Balaji, N., Natrayan, L., Kaliappan, S., Patil, P. P., & Sivakumar, N. S. (2022). Annealed peanut shell biochar as potential reinforcement for aloe vera fiber-epoxy biocomposite: Mechanical, thermal conductivity, and dielectric properties. *Biomass Conversion and Biorefinery*. 10.1007/s13399-022-02650-7

Chehelgerdi, M., Chehelgerdi, M., Allela, O. Q. B., Pecho, R. D. C., Jayasankar, N., Rao, D. P., Thamaraikani, T., Vasanthan, M., Viktor, P., Lakshmaiya, N., Saadh, M. J., Amajd, A., Abo-Zaid, M. A., Castillo-Acobo, R. Y., Ismail, A. H., Amin, A. H., & Akhavan-Sigari, R. (2023). Progressing nanotechnology to improve targeted cancer treatment: Overcoming hurdles in its clinical implementation. *Molecular Cancer*, 22(1), 169. 10.1186/s12943-023-01865-037814270

Chinta, N. D., Karthikeyan, K. R., Natrayan, L., & Kaliappan, S. (2023). Pressure Induced Variations in Mode II Behaviour of Uni-Directional Kenaf Reinforced Polymers. *International Journal of Vehicle Structures and Systems*, 15(7). 10.4273/ijvss.15.7.19

Dhaygude, A. D., Ameta, G. K., Khan, I. R., Singh, P. P., Maaliw, R. R.III, Lakshmaiya, N., Shabaz, M., Khan, M. A., Hussein, H. S., & Alshazly, H. (2024). Knowledge-based deep learning system for classifying Alzheimer's disease for multi-task learning. *CAAI Transactions on Intelligence Technology*, cit2.12291. 10.1049/cit2.12291

Dumka, P., Mishra, D. R., Singh, B., Chauhan, R., Siddiqui, M. H. I., Natrayan, L., & Shah, M. A. (2024). Enhancing solar still performance with Plexiglas and jute cloth additions: Experimental study. *Sustainable Environment Research*, 34(1), 3. 10.1186/s42834-024-00208-y

Hemalatha, K., James, C., Natrayan, L., & Swamynadh, V. (2020). Analysis of RCC T-beam and prestressed concrete box girder bridges super structure under different span conditions. *Materials Today: Proceedings*, 37(Part 2), 1507–1516. 10.1016/j.matpr.2020.07.119

Josphineleela, R., Kaliapp, S., Natrayan, L., & Garg, A. (2023). Big Data Security through Privacy - Preserving Data Mining (PPDM): A Decentralization Approach. *Proceedings of the 2023 2nd International Conference on Electronics and Renewable Systems, ICEARS 2023*. IEEE. 10.1109/ICEARS56392.2023.10085646

Josphineleela, R., Kaliappan, S., Natrayan, L., & Bhatt, U. M. (2023). Intelligent Virtual Laboratory Development and Implementation using the RASA Framework. *Proceedings - 7th International Conference on Computing Methodologies and Communication, ICCMC 2023*. IEEE. 10.1109/ICCMC56507.2023.10083701

Kaliappan, S., Mothilal, T., Natrayan, L., Pravin, P., & Olkeba, T. T. (2023). Mechanical Characterization of Friction-Stir-Welded Aluminum AA7010 Alloy with TiC Nanofiber. *Advances in Materials Science and Engineering*, 2023, 1–7. 10.1155/2023/1466963

Kaliappan, S., & Natrayan, L. (2024). Impact of Kenaf Fiber and Inorganic Nano-fillers on Mechanical Properties of Epoxy-Based Nanocomposites for Sustainable Automotive Applications. *SAE Technical Papers*. 10.4271/2023-01-5115

Kaliappan, S., Natrayan, L., & Garg, N. (2023). Checking and Supervisory System for Calculation of Industrial Constraints using Embedded System. *Proceedings of the 4th International Conference on Smart Electronics and Communication, ICOSEC 2023*. IEEE. 10.1109/ICOSEC58147.2023.10275952

Kaliappan, S., Natrayan, L., Mohammed Ali, H., & Kumar, P. (2024). Thermal and Mechanical Properties of Abutilon indicum Fiber-Based Polyester Composites under Alkali Treatment for Automotive Sector. *SAE Technical Papers*. 10.4271/2024-01-5031

Kaliappan, S., Natrayan, L., & Rajput, A. (2023). Sentiment Analysis of News Headlines Based on Sentiment Lexicon and Deep Learning. *Proceedings of the 4th International Conference on Smart Electronics and Communication, ICOSEC 2023*. IEEE. 10.1109/ICOSEC58147.2023.10276102

Kaliappan, S., Velumayil, R., Natrayan, L., & Pravin, P. (2023). Mechanical, DMA, and fatigue behavior of Vitis vinifera stalk cellulose Bambusa vulgaris fiber epoxy composites. *Polymer Composites*, 44(4), 2115–2121. 10.1002/pc.27228

Kanimozhi, G., Natrayan, L., Angalaeswari, S., & Paramasivam, P. (2022). An Effective Charger for Plug-In Hybrid Electric Vehicles (PHEV) with an Enhanced PFC Rectifier and ZVS-ZCS DC/DC High-Frequency Converter. *Journal of Advanced Transportation*, 2022, 1–14. 10.1155/2022/7840102

Karthick, M., Meikandan, M., Kaliappan, S., Karthick, M., Sekar, S., Patil, P. P., Raja, S., Natrayan, L., & Paramasivam, P. (2022). Experimental Investigation on Mechanical Properties of Glass Fiber Hybridized Natural Fiber Reinforced Penta-Layered Hybrid Polymer Composite. *International Journal of Chemical Engineering*, 2022, 1–9. 10.1155/2022/1864446

Lakshmaiya, N., Kaliappan, S., Patil, P. P., Ganesan, V., Dhanraj, J. A., Sirisamphanwong, C., Wongwuttanasatian, T., Chowdhury, S., Channumsin, S., Channumsin, M., & Techato, K. (2022). Influence of Oil Palm Nano Filler on Interlaminar Shear and Dynamic Mechanical Properties of Flax/Epoxy-Based Hybrid Nanocomposites under Cryogenic Condition. *Coatings*, 12(11), 1675. 10.3390/coatings12111675

Lakshmaiya, N., Surakasi, R., Nadh, V. S., Srinivas, C., Kaliappan, S., Ganesan, V., Paramasivam, P., & Dhanasekaran, S. (2023). Tanning Wastewater Sterilization in the Dark and Sunlight Using Psidium guajava Leaf-Derived Copper Oxide Nanoparticles and Their Characteristics. *ACS Omega*, 8(42), 39680–39689. 10.1021/acsomega.3c0558837901496

Muralidaran, V. M., Natrayan, L., Kaliappan, S., & Patil, P. P. (2023). Grape stalk cellulose toughened plain weaved bamboo fiber-reinforced epoxy composite: Load bearing and time-dependent behavior. *Biomass Conversion and Biorefinery*. 10.1007/s13399-022-03702-8

Muthiya, S. J., Natrayan, L., Kaliappan, S., Patil, P. P., Naveena, B. E., Dhanraj, J. A., Subramaniam, M., & Paramasivam, P. (2022). Experimental investigation to utilize adsorption and absorption technique to reduce CO_2 emissions in diesel engine exhaust using amine solutions. *Adsorption Science and Technology*, 2022, 9621423. 10.1155/2022/9621423

Muthiya, S. J., Natrayan, L., Yuvaraj, L., Subramaniam, M., Dhanraj, J. A., & Mammo, W. D. (2022). Development of Active CO_2 Emission Control for Diesel Engine Exhaust Using Amine-Based Adsorption and Absorption Technique. *Adsorption Science and Technology*, 2022, 8803585. 10.1155/2022/8803585

Nadh, V. S., Krishna, C., Natrayan, L., Kumar, K., Nitesh, K. J. N. S., Raja, G. B., & Paramasivam, P. (2021). Structural Behavior of Nanocoated Oil Palm Shell as Coarse Aggregate in Lightweight Concrete. *Journal of Nanomaterials*, 2021, 1–7. 10.1155/2021/4741296

Natrayan, L., Ali, H. M., Kaliappan, S., & Kumar, G. R. (2023). Data Mining and AI for Early Diagnosis and Treatment Optimization in Autoimmune Encephalitis. *3rd IEEE International Conference on ICT in Business Industry and Government, ICTBIG 2023.* IEEE. 10.1109/ICTBIG59752.2023.10456042

Natrayan, L., Ameen, F., Chinta, N. D., Teja, N. B., Muthu, G., Kaliappan, S., Ali, S., & Vadiveloo, A. (2024). Antibacterial and dynamical behaviour of silicon nanoparticles influenced sustainable waste flax fibre-reinforced epoxy composite for biomedical application. *Green Processing and Synthesis*, 13(1), 20230214. 10.1515/gps-2023-0214

Natrayan, L., Balaji, S., Bharathiraja, G., Kaliappan, S., Veeman, D., & Mammo, W. D. (2021). Experimental Investigation on Mechanical Properties of TiAlN Thin Films Deposited by RF Magnetron Sputtering. *Journal of Nanomaterials*, 2021, 1–7. 10.1155/2021/5943486

Natrayan, L., Chinta, N. D., Gogulamudi, B., Nadh, V. S., Muthu, G., Kaliappan, S., & Srinivas, C. (2024). Investigation on mechanical properties of the green synthesis bamboo fiber/eggshell/coconut shell powder-based hybrid biocomposites under NaOH conditions. *Green Processing and Synthesis*, 13(1), 20230185. 10.1515/gps-2023-0185

Natrayan, L., Chinta, N. D., Teja, N. B., Muthu, G., Kaliappan, S., Kirubanandan, S., & Paramasivam, P. (2024). Evaluating mechanical, thermal, and water absorption properties of biocomposites with Opuntia cladode fiber and palm flower biochar for industrial applications. *Discover Applied Sciences*, 6(2), 30. 10.1007/s42452-024-05660-4

Natrayan, L., Janardhan, G., Nadh, V. S., Srinivas, C., Kaliappan, S., & Velmurugan, G. (2024). Eco-friendly zinc oxide nanoparticles from Moringa oleifera leaf extract for photocatalytic and antibacterial applications. *Clean Technologies and Environmental Policy*. 10.1007/s10098-024-02814-1

Natrayan, L., & Kaliappan, S. (2023). Mechanical Assessment of Carbon-Luffa Hybrid Composites for Automotive Applications. *SAE Technical Papers*. 10.4271/2023-01-5070

Natrayan, L., Kaliappan, S., Saravanan, A., Vickram, A. S., Pravin, P., Abbas, M., Ahamed Saleel, C., Alwetaishi, M., & Saleem, M. S. M. (2023). Recyclability and catalytic characteristics of copper oxide nanoparticles derived from bougainvillea plant flower extract for biomedical application. *Green Processing and Synthesis*, 12(1), 20230030. 10.1515/gps-2023-0030

Natrayan, L., & Kumar, M. S. (2019). Influence of silicon carbide on tribological behaviour of AA2024/Al2O3/SiC/Gr hybrid metal matrix squeeze cast composite using Taguchi technique. *Materials Research Express*, 6(12), 1265f9. 10.1088/2053-1591/ab676d

Natrayan, L., & Kumar, M. S. (2020). Optimization of wear behaviour on AA6061/Al2O3/SiC metal matrix composite using squeeze casting technique-Statistical analysis. *Materials Today: Proceedings*, 27, 306–310. 10.1016/j.matpr.2019.11.038

Natrayan, L., & Merneedi, A. (2020). Experimental investigation on wear behaviour of bio-waste reinforced fusion fiber composite laminate under various conditions. *Materials Today: Proceedings*, 37(Part 2), 1486–1490. 10.1016/j.matpr.2020.07.108

Natrayan, L., Merneedi, A., Veeman, D., Kaliappan, S., Raju, P. S., Subbiah, R., & Kumar, S. V. (2021). Evaluating the Mechanical and Tribological Properties of DLC Nanocoated Aluminium 5051 Using RF Sputtering. *Journal of Nanomaterials*, 2021, 1–7. 10.1155/2021/8428822

Natrayan, L., Niveditha, V. R., Nadh, V. S., Srinivas, C., Dhanraj, J. A., & Saravanan, A. (2024). Application of response surface and artificial neural network optimization approaches for exploring methylene blue adsorption using luffa fiber treated with sodium chlorite. *Journal of Water Process Engineering*, 58, 104778. 10.1016/j.jwpe.2024.104778

Natrayan, L., Sakthi Shunmuga Sundaram, P., & Elumalai, J. (2019). Analyzing the uterine physiological with mmg signals using svm. *International Journal of Pharmaceutical Research*, 11(2). 10.31838/ijpr/2019.11.02.009

Natrayan, L., Senthil Kumar, M., & Chaudhari, M. (2020). Optimization of squeeze casting process parameters to investigate the mechanical properties of AA6061/Al 2 O 3/SiC hybrid metal matrix composites by Taguchi and Anova approach. In *Advances in Intelligent Systems and Computing* (*Vol. 949*). Springer. 10.1007/978-981-13-8196-6_35

Natrayan, L., Senthil Kumar, M., & Palanikumar, K. (2018). Optimization of squeeze cast process parameters on mechanical properties of Al2O3/SiC reinforced hybrid metal matrix composites using taguchi technique. *Materials Research Express*, 5(6), 066516. 10.1088/2053-1591/aac873

Natrayan, L., Sivaprakash, V., & Santhosh, M. S. (2018). Mechanical, microstructure and wear behavior of the material aa6061 reinforced sic with different leaf ashes using advanced stir casting method. *International Journal of Engineering and Advanced Technology*, 8.

Niveditha, V. R., & Rajakumar, P. S. (2020). Pervasive computing in the context of COVID-19 prediction with AI-based algorithms. *International Journal of Pervasive Computing and Communications*, 16(5). 10.1108/IJPCC-07-2020-0082

Palaniyappan, S., Veeman, D., Sivakumar, N. K., & Natrayan, L. (2022). Development and optimization of lattice structure on the walnut shell reinforced PLA composite for the tensile strength and dimensional error properties. *Structures*, 45, 163–178. 10.1016/j.istruc.2022.09.023

Ponnusamy, M., Natrayan, L., Kaliappan, S., Velmurugan, G., & Thanappan, S. (2022). Effectiveness of Nanosilica on Enhancing the Mechanical and Microstructure Properties of Kenaf/Carbon Fiber-Reinforced Epoxy-Based Nanocomposites. *Adsorption Science and Technology*, 2022, 4268314. 10.1155/2022/4268314

Pragadish, N., Kaliappan, S., Subramanian, M., Natrayan, L., Satish Prakash, K., Subbiah, R., & Kumar, T. C. A. (2023). Optimization of cardanol oil dielectric-activated EDM process parameters in machining of silicon steel. *Biomass Conversion and Biorefinery*, 13(15), 14087–14096. 10.1007/s13399-021-02268-1

Ragumadhavan, R., Sateesh Kumar, D., Charyulu Rompicharla, L. N., Dhondiya, S. A., Kaliappan, S., & Natrayan, L. (2023). Design and Development of Light Communication Systems Using Modulation Techniques. *7th International Conference on Electronics, Communication and Aerospace Technology, ICECA 2023 - Proceedings*. IEEE. 10.1109/ICECA58529.2023.10395831

Ramaswamy, R., Gurupranes, S. V., Kaliappan, S., Natrayan, L., & Patil, P. P. (2022). Characterization of prickly pear short fiber and red onion peel biocarbon nanosheets toughened epoxy composites. *Polymer Composites*, 43(8), 4899–4908. 10.1002/pc.26735

Ramaswamy, R., Kaliappan, S., Natrayan, L., & Patil, P. P. (2022). Pear cactus fiber with onion sheath biocarbon nanosheet toughened epoxy composite: Mechanical, thermal, and electrical properties. *Biomass Conversion and Biorefinery*. 10.1007/s13399-022-03335-x

Ramesh, C., Vijayakumar, M., Alshahrani, S., Navaneethakrishnan, G., Palanisamy, R., Natrayan, L., Saleel, C. A., Afzal, A., Shaik, S., & Panchal, H. (2022). Performance enhancement of selective layer coated on solar absorber panel with reflector for water heater by response surface method: A case study. *Case Studies in Thermal Engineering*, 36, 102093. 10.1016/j.csite.2022.102093

Saadh, M. J., Almoyad, M. A. A., Arellano, M. T. C., Maaliw, R. R.III, Castillo-Acobo, R. Y., Jalal, S. S., Gandla, K., Obaid, M., Abdulwahed, A. J., Ibrahem, A. A., Sârbu, I., Juyal, A., Lakshmaiya, N., & Akhavan-Sigari, R. (2023). Long non-coding RNAs: Controversial roles in drug resistance of solid tumors mediated by autophagy. *Cancer Chemotherapy and Pharmacology*, 92(6), 439–453. 10.1007/s00280-023-04582-z37768333

Saadh, M. J., Rasulova, I., Almoyad, M. A. A., Kiasari, B. A., Ali, R. T., Rasheed, T., Faisal, A., Hussain, F., Jawad, M. J., Hani, T., Sârbu, I., Lakshmaiya, N., & Ciongradi, C. I. (2024). Recent progress and the emerging role of lncRNAs in cancer drug resistance; focusing on signaling pathways. *Pathology, Research and Practice*, 253, 154999. 10.1016/j.prp.2023.15499938118218

Saadh, M. J., Rasulova, I., Khalil, M., Farahim, F., Sârbu, I., Ciongradi, C. I., Omar, T. M., Alhili, A., Jawad, M. J., Hani, T., Ali, T., & Lakshmaiya, N. (2024). Natural killer cell-mediated immune surveillance in cancer: Role of tumor microenvironment. *Pathology, Research and Practice*, 254, 155120. 10.1016/j.prp.2024.15512038280274

Saravanan, K. G., Kaliappan, S., Natrayan, L., & Patil, P. P. (2023). Effect of cassava tuber nanocellulose and satin weaved bamboo fiber addition on mechanical, wear, hydrophobic, and thermal behavior of unsaturated polyester resin composites. *Biomass Conversion and Biorefinery*. 10.1007/s13399-023-04495-0

Sathish, T., Natrayan, L., Prasad Jones Christydass, S., Sivananthan, S., Kamalakannan, R., Vijayan, V., & Paramasivam, P. (2022). Experimental Investigation on Tribological Behaviour of AA6066: HSS-Cu Hybrid Composite in Dry Sliding Condition. *Advances in Materials Science and Engineering*, 2022, 1–9. 10.1155/2022/9349847

Sathish, T., Palani, K., Natrayan, L., Merneedi, A., de Poures, M. V., & Singaravelu, D. K. (2021). Synthesis and characterization of polypropylene/ramie fiber with hemp fiber and coir fiber natural biopolymer composite for biomedical application. *International Journal of Polymer Science*, 2021, 1–8. 10.1155/2021/2462873

Selvi, S., Mohanraj, M., Duraipandy, P., Kaliappan, S., Natrayan, L., & Vinayagam, N. (2023). Optimization of Solar Panel Orientation for Maximum Energy Efficiency. *Proceedings of the 4th International Conference on Smart Electronics and Communication, ICOSEC 2023*. IEEE. 10.1109/ICOSEC58147.2023.10276287

Sendrayaperumal, A., Mahapatra, S., Parida, S. S., Surana, K., Balamurugan, P., Natrayan, L., & Paramasivam, P. (2021). Energy Auditing for Efficient Planning and Implementation in Commercial and Residential Buildings. *Advances in Civil Engineering*, 2021, 1–10. 10.1155/2021/1908568

Singh, M. (2017). An experimental investigation on mechanical behaviour of siCp reinforced Al 6061 MMC using squeeze casting process. *International Journal of Mechanical and Production Engineering Research and Development*, 7(6). 10.24247/ijmperddec201774

Sivakumar, V., Kaliappan, S., Natrayan, L., & Patil, P. P. (2023). Effects of Silane-Treated High-Content Cellulose Okra Fibre and Tamarind Kernel Powder on Mechanical, Thermal Stability and Water Absorption Behaviour of Epoxy Composites. *Silicon*, 15(10), 4439–4447. 10.1007/s12633-023-02370-1

Suman, T., Kaliappan, S., Natrayan, L., & Dobhal, D. C. (2023a). IoT based Social Device Network with Cloud Computing Architecture. *Proceedings of the 2023 2nd International Conference on Electronics and Renewable Systems, ICEARS 2023*. IEEE. 10.1109/ICEARS56392.2023.10085574

Suman, T., Kaliappan, S., Natrayan, L., & Dobhal, D. C. (2023b). IoT based Social Device Network with Cloud Computing Architecture. *Proceedings of the 2023 2nd International Conference on Electronics and Renewable Systems, ICEARS 2023*. IEEE. 10.1109/ICEARS56392.2023.10085574

Sureshkumar, P., Jagadeesha, T., Natrayan, L., Ravichandran, M., Veeman, D., & Muthu, S. M. (2022). Electrochemical corrosion and tribological behaviour of AA6063/Si3N4/Cu composite processed using single-pass ECA route with 120° die angle. *Journal of Materials Research and Technology*, 16, 715–733. 10.1016/j.jmrt.2021.12.020

Suryanarayanan, R., Sridhar, V. G., Natrayan, L., Kaliappan, S., Merneedi, A., Sathish, T., & Yeshitla, A. (2021). Improvement on Mechanical Properties of Submerged Friction Stir Joining of Dissimilar Tailor Welded Aluminum Blanks. *Advances in Materials Science and Engineering*, 2021, 1–6. 10.1155/2021/3355692

Vaishali, K. R., Rammohan, S. R., Natrayan, L., Usha, D., & Niveditha, V. R. (2021). Guided container selection for data streaming through neural learning in cloud. *International Journal of Systems Assurance Engineering and Management*. 10.1007/s13198-021-01124-9

Vasanthi, P., Selvan, S. S., Natrayan, L., & Thanappan, S. (2023). Experimental studies on the effect of nano silica modified novel concrete CFST columns. *Materials Research Express*, 10(8), 085303. 10.1088/2053-1591/aced82

Velmurugan, G., & Natrayan, L. (2023). Experimental investigations of moisture diffusion and mechanical properties of interply rearrangement of glass/Kevlar-based hybrid composites under cryogenic environment. *Journal of Materials Research and Technology*, 23, 4513–4526. 10.1016/j.jmrt.2023.02.089

Velumayil, R., Gnanakumar, G., Natrayan, L., Chinta, N. D., & Kaliappan, S. (2023). Bifunctional Aluminum Oxide/Carbon Fiber/Epoxy Nanocomposites Preparation and Evaluation. *International Journal of Vehicle Structures and Systems*, 15(7). 10.4273/ijvss.15.7.18

Venkatesh, R., Manivannan, S., Kaliappan, S., Socrates, S., Sekar, S., Patil, P. P., Natrayan, L., & Bayu, M. B. (2022). Influence of Different Frequency Pulse on Weld Bead Phase Ratio in Gas Tungsten Arc Welding by Ferritic Stainless Steel AISI-409L. *Journal of Nanomaterials*, 2022, 1–11. 10.1155/2022/9530499

Vijayakumar, M. D., Surendhar, G. J., Natrayan, L., Patil, P. P., Ram, P. M. B., & Paramasivam, P. (2022). Evolution and Recent Scenario of Nanotechnology in Agriculture and Food Industries. *Journal of Nanomaterials*, 2022, 1–17. 10.1155/2022/1280411

Viswakethu, C., Pichappan, R., Perumal, P., & Lakshmaiya, N. (2024). An experimental and response-surface-based optimization approach towards production of producer gas in a circulating fluidized bed gasifier using blends of renewable fibre-based biomass mixtures. *Sustainable Energy & Fuels*, 8(5), 975–986. 10.1039/D3SE00551H

Yogeshwaran, S., Natrayan, L., Udhayakumar, G., Godwin, G., & Yuvaraj, L. (2020). Effect of waste tyre particles reinforcement on mechanical properties of jute and abaca fiber - Epoxy hybrid composites with pre-treatment. *Materials Today: Proceedings*, 37(Part 2), 1377–1380. 10.1016/j.matpr.2020.06.584

Chapter 15
Enhancement of System Performance Using PeSche Scheduling Algorithm on Multiprocessors

M. Sreenath

Infosys Ltd., Bangalore, India

P. A. Vijaya

BNM Institute of Technology, India

ABSTRACT

The scheduling techniques have been investigated by the job execution process in a system in order to maximize multiprocessor utilization. DPM (dynamic power management) and DVFS (dynamic voltage and frequency scaling) are two general strategies for lowering energy use. PeSche (performance enhanced scheduling) is a proposed scheduling algorithm that has been designed for an optimal solution. CodeBlocks were used to run the extensive simulations. In terms of computing performance (average waiting time and average turnaround time), the PeSche scheduling algorithm outperformed recently reported scheduling algorithms such as SJF, RR, FCFS, Priority, and SJF-LJF. PeSche scheduling algorithm gives better results by assigning the priority in terms of energy time ratio, programming running time, total energy and total time than existed algorithms. In comparison to minimum energy schedule (MES) and slack utilization for reduced energy (SURE), PeSche used less energy.

DOI: 10.4018/979-8-3693-3314-3.ch015

INTRODUCTION

The Present technology has been changing day to day by providing more options to satisfy the user requirements with better performance in terms of finishing a number of things in the allotted amount of time. A real time environment incorporated with the closed-loop system followed quick response with high accuracy. Hardware and firmware come together to form an embedded system, that completes the predetermined task. A critical phase in the execution of an application's early stage is the assignment of the tasks within the system. The system may leads to get a catastrophe atmosphere, if tasks are not properly allocated and executed. Time restrictions are one of the key observations in various scheduling jobs. Minimal computation task time is preferable for better performance in a system to speed up the operation. Multiprocessor based system is authoritative to handle the intricate applications like avionics while considering the less execution time and low power consumption. In multiprocessor based system, most scheduling algorithms are not satisfying the requirements to provide full optimal solution.

Through the use of task parameters including start (s_j), process (p_j), releasing (r_j) times, deadline (d_j), due date (d_j^-), task completion $(C_j = s_j + p_j)$, Lateness $(L_j = C_j + d_j)$, flow time $(F_j = C_j - r_j)$, wait period $(W_j = s_j - r_j)$, and tardiness $(D_j = \max C_j - d_j, 0)$ are all related terms (Ji et al., 2019). The performance of a system has been where "j" stands for the relevant task-related data. When calculating the system's efficiency, throughput a word used to describe the quantity of jobs the system completes in a predetermined amount of time. Time taken by the processor, when it is in a ready state for execution of corresponding to the task called response time. A process scheduler assigns distinct processes to the CPU according to specific scheduling algorithms. Scheduling algorithm decide the process of execution in a system for allocating the priorities to all tasks to achieve maximum utilization of processor. Standard structure is used to construct traditional real time scheduling methods for satisfying the requirements with less execution time, power consumption and high performance. Real time control is increasingly necessary for different applications, includes aviation, industrial, and data processing systems. The study's main goal is to determine the best way to use all CPUs on multi-processor based system to reduce power consumption and thus low heat dissipation. To accomplish the same on avionics system, list programming and McNaughton is implemented to obtain optimum solution. The amount of CPU time allotted to programmes and threads is determined by a scheduling mechanism. Each planning method's goal is to fulfil a specific set of requirements. Ideally, the scheduler should be scalable as the amount of tasks rises.

Modern battery-powered devices energy usage has become one of the most crucial design considerations in the near past. This presents an extra issue in a multi-processor environment. The key development criteria and goal is to lower system operating costs through low energy consumption, an extended battery life, and less heat dissipation. When the system's resource consumption is subpar, it can occasionally lead to decreased performance levels since more energy is needed to complete tasks. The amount of CPUs and cores affects how much energy the system uses while performing activities. If the system executes a more no of tasks, may face different difficulties to maintain a good performance. Embedded technology forms a humanless real time environment for getting efficient and better results (Jinchao, 2021). This environment support closed loop system to get responses with high accuracy (Strohbach, 2004). Amalgamate of firmware and hardware defines an embedded system to perform a predefined task. Scheduling algorithm is a technique in which decides how much time is allocate to the threads & processes. A scheduler is a machine that keeps track of and manages schedules. Real time scheduling techniques are used for a range of applications and operations (Jiang, 2019). Scheduling algorithms are mostly used to reduce famine and Non-deterministic Polynomial (NP) complete problems (Öztop, 2018). Scheduling algorithms as classified as static and dynamic. Dynamic scheduling algorithms are based on planning and best efforts.

These algorithms are mainly utilized for the platform of Multiprocessors (Naela, 2022) to achieve better response than the normal conditions. However, this platform provides optimum solutions to NP complete problem. The system performance can further be enhanced (Bhuiyan, 2018) by selecting the appropriate scheduling algorithm. Scheduling toolboxes are used to schedule the tasks on processors. Toolbox task parameters & optimization criterion offered appropriate resources for configuration and define the scheduling problem using routines. At any time, the energy consumption dynamically managed by the Energy aware scheduling algorithm (Yong Chen, 2022). In computing, multitasking (Ji, M, 2019) is the hierarchy execution of various tasks over a span of moment and hinders the implementation & execution of basic program tasks. This pre-emption technique works based on priority assigned to the tasks available in each segment by sharing common resources to all. In context switching, the current task address of main program is saved in stack memory before it suspends temporarily the execution of main program when interrupt occurs. If there are many interruptions at once, the processor responds to them in order of the priorities it has given them. The processor will continue to run the main program's remaining code when interrupt service routine program execution is complete (Bose, 2019). This approach has been developed for multi core processors to cover all requirements like low power consumption, execution speed, tardiness task exemption, completion time, long battery life etc.

The two run-time solutions that are utilised to improve the system are DVS and DPM (Chasapis & Qin, 2019). Now a days, battery based system models are becoming a major important considerations in design. Reduce all jobs execution time as much as possible, including tardy tasks, amalgamate scheduling algorithms are used to distribute processor time to available tasks in a system (C. Maia, 2013). This improves system's efficiency by calculating the relevant speed of resources, based on the time slots allocated with real time scheduling algorithms. Speed of the processors or controllers is high initially and gradually decreases until deadlines are met, which further helps in saving the power. Actually, user expects low power consumption and high performance from any type of system. By using the system's available CPUs to their full potential, a system's efficiency can be raised. When using battery-based systems, the use of energy is a crucial design measure. On multicore or processors based system has some difficulties to satisfy the above parameters. Optimization & search problems like constrained and unconstrained may be solved using genetic algorithms (Sahoo, 2019).

The process of biological evolution is known as natural selection, and a method based on natural selection known as a genetic algorithm can be utilised to tackle both limited and unconstrained optimization problems (Wei, 2020). Multiple times, a group of original solutions is modified by the evolutionary algorithms. The creation of dynamic provisioning for optimization and exploration issues, genetic algorithms are frequently used. Systems with many processors behave differently than those with a single processor. In a multiprocessor based system, scheduling algorithm is a two dimensional issue that involves local job scheduling within each processor as well as allocating input load to available processors. Additionally, compared to a single processor, multiprocessor systems use varying amounts of energy (Tang, 2020). A multiprocessor system makes it feasible for tasks to be transferred from one to another processor, for example, and to communicate with one another to share resources and manage memory. When compared with single-processor systems, these factors cause multiprocessor-based systems to consume more energy. As a result, we're concentrating on multiprocessor system design, development, and operation (Deng, 2021). The primary purpose of these systems is to maximize total throughput of a flow of interconnected activities while minimizing task implementation computation time. Several strategies for managing energy utilization in a multiprocessor system are explored, including scheduling jobs so that they are completed within the time limitations (Mehalaine, 2020).

On a multi-core machine, polynomial non-deterministic hard problem identified while arrange the tasks for proper execution by scheduling strategy. In order to schedule jobs more effectively and efficiently, this study uses a genetic algorithm (S. Chang, 2022). The goal of task scheduling is for jobs to be completed as rapidly as possible while using as little energy as possible. When many objectives must be optimized at the same time, collaborative measures-based decision-making is required. Multi-objective optimization ideas were used to construct the genetic approach. The process of finding one or more optimal solutions to an optimization problem with several objectives is known as multi-objective optimization. The current work makes use of two homogenous cores and amount of memory are found in a multicore systems to reduce energy consumption and minimize schedule length during simultaneous optimization (C. Lin, 2022).

DESCRIPTION OF THE MODEL

The best method to reduce waiting times is to prepare in advance with SJF. The ideal situation is when every process is accessible at the same time. Non-pre-emptive not all SJF processes are placed in the waiting list at time 0, as well as some jobs arrive later, due to the various arrival times of SJF processes (Paul, 2019). This results in the starvation issue, where a quicker operation must wait a very long time for such current, longer process to finish. With pre-emptive SJF Scheduling, tasks are added to a waiting list as they arrive, the running process is stopped, and the shorter task is carried out first. Non-pre-emptive scheduling is used by the Scheduling approach LJF (Longest Job First) (Kumar, 2016). This approach relies on the process burst times. As according their burst times, the processes are grouped in decreasing priority in the queue. This strategy is based on operation with the largest burst length is treated first, as the name implies. The algorithm's pre-emptive version is called Longest Remaining Time First (LRTF) (Burkimsher, 2013).

Starting with the processes arrival time, sort them in increasing order. Select the process that has the longest Burst Time among those that have so far arrived. Check to see if any other processes arrive before this one finishes. Repeat the previous two stages until all of the processes have been completed. The activity that arrived first is given priority by FCFS if the burst times of two methods are equal (Chandran, 2021). For a particular set of processes, this algorithm produces significantly high average waiting and turn-around time. A brief process might not ever be carried out, as well as the system will keep running the longer operations in its place. As a result, the system becomes less effective and uses less energy. SJF algorithm redistributes tasks so that the next procedure to be carried out is the one with the smallest burst time. It is used to reduce the typical duration it takes for subsequent activities to finish. The preventive version, abbreviated SRTF, is used (Santra, 2014). When a piece of work is submitted, the burst time determines where it will be in the queue. By favouring the execution of activities with shorter burst periods over those that have longer burst time, SJF reduces waiting times on average. The main benefit of utilising this strategy is that it lengthens turnaround and average waiting times, which increases system efficiency. If there are processes in the ready list with faster execution times, while few processes are being handled, large burst times are apt to be disregarded. The shortcoming of this method is that it cannot manage operations with long execution periods. Network & process schedulers employ round-robin (RR) as one of their approaches to manage all processes equally and without regard to priority by allocating equal amounts of time slice to each activity in a predefined sequence (equal priority). The scheduler removes the activity off the CPU once the time quota has been reached, making the round-robin technique a preventative strategy (Singh, 2010).

Context switching that isn't desirable, a slow reaction time, a long average time, limited throughput, and a short turnaround time, leads to get catastrophic effect and it does not support real time execution also. The programming technique is known as "shortest job first" for the pre-emptive jobs to reduce the undesirable context switching and controlled other parameters like, average time, throughput (Prakash, 2020). In multitasking, most preferably chosen Round Robin (RR) algorithm to meet the desired requirements in terms of real time execution. Improved Round Robin (IRR) scheduling algorithm performs well and overcome the drawbacks of RR like high context switching, desired throughput and average waiting time (Nayak, 2012). Cloud environment setup playing a major role for business operations. Dynamic Priority Scheduling Algorithm (DPSA) implemented for satisfying the requirements to the consumers and service providers. The DPSA is better optimal and efficient than the first come first serve algorithm (Lee, Z, 2011). In essence, how quickly activities are completed determines how well a system performs and how efficient it is. The provision of the specified needs, such as short execution times and rapid reaction times, was greatly aided by the quality of services (QoS). A new Hybrid-SJF-LJF (HSLJF) scheduling algorithm was developed by combining the Longest Job and Shortest Job First scheduling algorithms. On this proposed algorithm, tasks are arranged in ascending order for better execution and throughput (Alworafi, 2019).

In an embedded system, Dynamic Power Management (DPM) approach is used for reducing the power dissipation when the CMOS gates are randomly switched on processor. Introduced three algorithms for the above task in terms of reducing the power dissipation, i.e. Energy-Aware Earliest Deadline First (EAEDF), Enhanced Energy-Aware Earliest Deadline First (EEA-EDF) and Slack Utilization for Reduced Energy (SURE). Despite the fact that the EAEDF and EEAEDF methods are merely extensions of the EDF, the SURE algorithm adds a slack utilization technique based on shared devices, task groups, and power requirements to reduce power dissipation (G. Xie, 2017). In order to decrease the energy usage, multiprocessor-based integrative structures with constant energy usage have a successful history. The CPU experiences a latency while switching from a low-energy state to an operational one. By including additional jobs to the model, can extend the optimal time. To limit the amount of pre-emption, this method used mixed integer linear programming (Legout, 2013). Identify idle servers in data centres and freeze power utilization to reduce power consumption using the Green Scheduling Algorithm in conjunction with a neural network predictor. To reduce power usage, a neural network predictor is utilized to estimate load requirements based on previous activities and switches off unused servers and restarts them as needed. This approach given better power consumption results than the existed approaches (Duy, 2010). The figure predicts the recommended methodology.

The most crucial factor taken into account when calculating design metrics is energy consumption. The DVFS method is used in the area of energy consumption. Shorter schedule length Efficient Scheduling Algorithm based on relative average work assignments is proposed (Song, 2017). Cost optimization is a crucial design factor in heterogeneous network embedded systems when it comes to delivering high-quality services in terms of quick response times and good dependability. A proposed processor-merging method is used to conserve energy, together with a slack time reclamation approach to turn off optimal processors (energy inefficient). Scaling back the workload levels and processor frequency using the DVFS approach helped cut down on energy consumption (Hu, B, 2021). Define and assign the necessary variables first, like the quantity of processors and burst duration. After that, organize the jobs in ascending order and then switch them out based on the conditions being met and process timeframes. The aforementioned process and conditions were used to compute the overall turnaround and waiting time.

LITERATURE REVIEW

First, do the Shortest Job First (SJF) The best way to cut down on waiting time is to plan ahead. When all of the processes are available at the same instance, it is ideal. Non-pre-emptive Because SJF processes have different arrival timings, not all processes are available in the ready queue at time 0, and some jobs arrive later (Butangen, 2020). This leads to the Starvation dilemma, in which a shorter process must wait a long time for the present lengthier process to complete. Jobs are put into a ready queue as they come, the existing process is prevented from execution, and the shorter job is executed first in Pre-emptive Shortest Job First Scheduling. The CPU scheduling algorithm LJF (Longest Job First) is a non-pre-emptive scheduling algorithm (Kumar, M., 2016). This method is based on the burst time of the processes. The processes are placed in the ready queue in descending order according to their burst times. This approach is based on the fact that, as the name says, the process with the longest burst length is addressed first. Longest Remaining Time First (LRTF) is the algorithm's pre-emptive version (Burkimsher, 2013).

Sort the processes first by their Arrival Time in ascending order. Choose the process with the longest Burst Time out of all those that have arrived up to that point. Check to see if any other processes arrive before this one finishes. Repeat the previous two stages until all of the processes have been completed. If the burst time of two processes is the same, FCFS prioritises the process that arrived first (AL-Bakhrani, 2020). For a particular set of processes, this algorithm produces significantly high avg. waiting and turn-around time. It's possible that a brief process will never be executed, and the system will continue to run the lengthier processes. It lowers the processing speed, lowering the system's efficiency and usage. The shortest job first (SJF) algorithm is a technique that reorders jobs so that the process with the least burst time is selected for execution next. It's used to cut down on the average time it takes for other operations to complete. Shortest Remaining Time First is the pre-emptive version (SRTF) (Santra, 2014). When a work is submitted, it is placed in the queue according to its burst time. SJF reduces the avg. waiting time by prioritising the service of processes with shorter burst times over those with longer burst times. The main benefit of utilising this method is that it improves the system's efficiency by increasing avg. waiting and turn-around time. If processes with lower execution times are in the ready list, processes with long burst times are likely to be ignored while small processes are served. This algorithm's weakness is its inability to handle processes with extended execution times.

Round-robin (RR) is one of the techniques used by process and network schedulers to assign equal chunks of time slices (quantum) to each process in a circular sequence, managing all processes without priority. The scheduler removes the process from the CPU after the time quota expires, making the round-robin method a pre-emptive algorithm (Singh, 2010).

- Completion Time: The amount of time it takes for a process to finish its execution.
- Turnaround Time (TAT): The amount of time between completion and arrival.
- TAT = Completion Time – Arrival Time
- Waiting Time (WT): The time between the turnaround and burst times.
- Turn Around Time - Burst Time = WT

Context switching that isn't desirable, a slow reaction time, a long average time, limited throughput, and a short turnaround time, leads to get catastrophic effect and it does not support real time execution also. Shortest job first algorithm used for scheduling the preemptive tasks to reduce the undesirable context switching and controlled other parameters like, average time, throughput (Hamayun, 2015). In multitasking, most preferably chosen Round Robin (RR) algorithm to meet the desired requirements in terms of real time execution. Improved Round Robin (IRR) scheduling algorithm performs well and overcome the drawbacks of RR like high context switching, desired throughput, average waiting time (Nayak, 2012). Cloud environment setup playing a major role for business operations. Dynamic Priority Scheduling Algorithm (DPSA) implemented for satisfying the requirements to the consumers and service providers. The DPSA is better optimal and efficient than the first come first serve algorithm (Lee, Z, 2011). Basically, execution time of the tasks decides the performance and efficiency of a system. Quality of Services (QoS) played a major role for providing the desired requirements like less execution time, quick response time, etc. Shortest Job First (SJF) and Longest Job First (LJF) scheduling algorithms were combined into a new Hybrid-SJF-LJF (HSLJF) scheduling method. On this proposed algorithm, tasks are arranged in ascending order for better execution and throughput (Alworafi, 2019).

In an embedded system, Dynamic Power Management (DPM) approach is used for reducing the power dissipation when the CMOS gates are randomly switched on processor. Introduced three algorithms for the above task in terms of reducing the power dissipation, i.e. Slack Utilization for Reduced Energy (SURE), Enhanced Energy-Aware EDF (EEA-EDF), and Energy-Aware EDF (EA-EDF). The first two methods are merely extensions of the Earliest Deadline First (EDF), but the SURE algorithm uses a slack utilization technique to reduce power dissipation based on shared devices, task sets, and power requirements (Krishnapura, 2004). On multiprocessors, low power states used properly in embedded real time systems for reducing the power consumption as static. When a processor is in a low-power mode, it takes time, or a transition delay, to return to an active state. Increase the optimal time by adding more tasks to the model in this method. To limit the amount of preemptions, this method used mixed integer linear programming (Legout, 2013). Identify idle servers in data centers and freeze power utilization to reduce power consumption using the Green Scheduling Algorithm in conjunction with a neural network predictor. To reduce power usage, a neural network predictor is utilized to estimate load requirements based on previous activities and switches off unused servers and restarts them as needed. This approach given better power consumption results than the existed approaches (Duy, 2010).

Energy consumption is the most important considered parameter on design metrics. For energy usage, the Dynamic Voltage and Frequency Scaling (DVFS) approach is applied. Proposed Efficient Scheduling Algorithm with shorter schedule length based on relative average assignments for the tasks (Song, 2017). When providing good quality service in terms of quick reaction time and good dependability, cost optimization is a key design criterion in heterogeneous distributed embedded systems. To save energy, a proposed processor-merging technique is employed, as well as a slack time reclamation algorithm to turn off ideal processors (energy inefficient).

The DVFS technique was used to reduce energy usage by scaling down the job levels and frequency of the processors (Hu, B, 2021).

OBJECTIVES OF THE WORK

The fundamental goal is to reduce the maximum time required to complete all jobs by using scheduling algorithms to allocate or allocate processor time to all activities in a system. The performance of a system can be enhanced as a result. Energy can be conserved while several operations with various characteristics are operating by implementing the load-balancing strategy among resources to achieve efficient use. Two general methods for conserving energy are DPM and DVFS. The PeSche (Performance enhanced Scheduling) method has been put forth in a novel approach. Whenever the work load is not evenly distributed and inactive processors are not used for execution of tasks, the system speed decreases since a single CPU can only handle so many tasks at once. As a result, tasks are stolen from the master processor and transferred to idle processors. Work stealing is a cost-effective method of distributing dynamic load balancing among multiple processors. Work stealing will improve Parallel application performance without affecting the schedulability of other activities. Amalgamate scheduling techniques share or allot processor time to all jobs in a system to reduce both the overall work completion time and energy consumption. Performance of a system will consequently be enhanced.

SIMULATION RESULTS AND DISCUSSIONS

A process scheduler uses particular scheduling methods to assign different programmes to the CPU. Some of the most common process scheduling approaches include First Come, First Served (FCFS), Priority Scheduling and Shortest Job Next (SJN). The method that controls how much CPU time is given to processes and threads is known as a scheduling algorithm. Any scheduling algorithm's goal is to meet a set of criteria. The scheduler should ideally be able to scale as the number of jobs grows.

```
=================================================
===============
Enter the choice to execute specific functionalities
1.Execute all schedule algorithms
2.Execute all scheduling tasks related functionalities
3.Exit
1
```

Enter time quantum:2
Enter no.of process:2
Enter burst time of process in msec 1:8
Enter burst time of process in msec 2:5

Table 1. FCFS algorithm

Process	Burst Time (msec)	Waiting time (msec)	Turnaround time (msec)
p1	8.000000	0.000000	8.000000
p2	5.000000	8.000000	13.000000

Avg_WT: 4.000000
Avg_TAT: 10.500000

Table 2. SJF algorithm

Process	Burst Time (msec)	Waiting time (msec)	Turnaround time (msec)
p1	5.000000	0.000000	5.000000
p2	8.000000	5.000000	13.000000

Avg_WT: 2.500000
Avg_TAT: 9.000000

Table 3. RR algorithm

Process	Burst Time (msec)	Waiting time (msec)	Turnaround time (msec)
p1	8.000000	0.000000	8.000000
p2	5.000000	-2.000000	3.000000

Avg_WT: -1.000000
Avg_TAT: 5.500000

Table 4. Priority algorithm

Process	Priority	Burst Time (msec)	Waiting time (msec)	Turnaround time (msec)
p	2	8.000000	0.000000	8.000000
p	1	5.000000	8.000000	5.000000

Avg_WT: 4.000000
Avg_TAT: 6.500000

Table 5. Modified SJF-LJF algorithm

Process	Burst Time (msec)	Waiting time (msec)	Turnaround time (msec)
P0	5.000000	0.000000	5.000000
P1	8.000000	5.000000	13.000000

Avg_WT: 2.500000
Avg_TAT: 9.000000

Table 6. Performance enhanced algorithm

Process	Burst Time (msec)	Waiting time (msec)	Turnaround time (msec)
P0	5.000000	0.000000	5.000000
P1	8.000000	5.000000	6.000000

Avg_WT: 2.500000
Avg_TAT: 5.500000

Table 7. Name of algorithm

S.No	Name of the algorithm	Avg_WT	Avg_TAT
1	FCFS	4	6.5
2	SJF	2.5	9
3	RR	-1	5.5
4	Priority	4	6.5
5	SJF-LJF	2.5	9
6	PeSche	2.5	5.5

An algorithm for non-preemptive scheduling is called longest job first (LJF). This approach is based on the processes burst times. Depending on their burst times, or in descending order of burst times, the prepared queue is updated with the processes. The traits were noted Shortest Job First- Longest Job First (SJF-LJF) like Average waiting time (Avg_WT) and Average turnaround time (Avg_TAT) based on burst time and processors used for execution, and Table 5 shows the related result. This algorithm is based, as its name implies, on the principle that the operation with the longest burst time is handled first. FCFS is used to break ties when two methods share the same burst time; the activity that came first is handled first. The corresponding results verified in Table 1. Preemptive scheduling is used in this approach to treat each stage equally. There is a quantum, or running time, interval for each process to maintain a queue and each technique is subject to quantum. A task is relegated to the rear of the line once it has finished its quantum, at which point a new mechanism is initiated. Servers and desktop computers both use the round robin scheduling method. The time quantum's size affects how well the RR Algorithm performs. Observed the characteristics of RR like Average waiting and turnaround time based on burst time and processors used for execution, and Table 3 shows the related result. Table 2, which shows the SJF relevant result, demonstrates the queuing and turnaround time restrictions. In Table 1, the proper result of the priority algorithm is displayed.

It has also been found that the suggested algorithm tends to have longer waiting, turn around, and burst times. It could be improved in the future to use any other legal application. Priority driven scheduling is the most used preemptive scheduling technique and added a ground-breaking algorithm to the suggested method. Many real time applications benefit from it, including those where a job's priority whether something is CPU-bound in quasi platforms determines how it works. Planning tools with static tables must be redistributed in order to meet deadlines and guarantee that safety-critical activities get the attention they require. The capability of static schedules is evaluated using static table-driven techniques. A plan that is the result of the planning process is used to identify when a job may begin to be carried out utilizing dynamic planning-based approaches.

It has historically been the goal of Dynamic Power Management (DPM) strategies in integrated practical cases to reduce the power consumption dynamically that happens whenever a CMOS gate in a Processor changes. On received little attention, the power used by I/O devices and other subsystems as well as processor leakage power. However, non-real time devices have seen a significant amount of research attention with I/O-based DPM approaches. These methods, which switch I/O devices to reduced power modes based on a number of regulations, cannot be applied due to the erratic design of the rules, actual events. Reduced power consumption while retaining temporal accuracy is thus the goal of conserving energy in embedded practical applications. Propose three scheduling methods with increasing complexity to solve this issue. Given their simplicity and the low the price of changing energy states, these strategies offer significant energy reductions. But generally speaking, SURE is more advantageous the more energy is required to change power levels. The power efficiency provided by the SURE approach decrease as the price of shifting power modes rises, notably when compared to Energy-Aware EDF (EA-EDF) and EEA-EDF. The problem of finding a processes contribute that consumes the lowest amount of power from the I/O devices. Instead of choosing the best alternative, the main objective was to automate processes that can be employed remotely and reduce the energy consumption of numerous shared machines.

By creating the whole tree of anticipatory strategies for a certain job set and choosing the technique that used the lowest amount of energy, the Minimum Energy Schedule (MES) and Slack Utilization for Reduced Energy (SURE) for a task list were evaluated. This was accomplished by using a Depth-First-Search approach, which involved creating a tree of H levels and scanning the tree at each time-tick. Every level takes pre-emptive plans into account, thus for the sake of argument, think of CPU idle as a work with indefinite deadline and implementation length. No subsequent jobs at that position in the hierarchy are considered if a job is late without additional branching, the following job in the same level if a job has not yet been released. Simply said, this indicates that at any given time, only consider scheduling ready jobs. Every level computes the energy. The least energy value for the specified task set once all schedules have been completed. This approach has an O $((n + 1)^{H-1})$ complexity, where the task set's there are n overall jobs, and H is the duration of the excitable phase.

Table 8. Comparison SURE with the MES

H	MAKESPAN/PERFORMANCE TIME		POWER/ENERGY CONSUMPTION (J)	
	Strategy of MES	Strategy of SURE	Strategy of MES	Strategy of SURE
≤ 10	< 1 Sec	< 1 Sec	74	78
≤ 20	> 30 Min	< 1 Sec	121	123
≤ 30	> 30 Min	< 1 Sec	116	120
≤ 40	> 30 Min	< 1 Sec	176	180
≤ 50	> 30 Min	< 1 Sec	138	138
≤ 60	> 1 Day	< 1 Sec	164	164

Conducted studies for H with task temporal parameters and DRS that varied from 10 to 60 time units. Table 5.6 displays the worst-case values for the Minimum Energy method's execution time and comparing the provided task's minimum energy value to the SURE algorithm. Since it was taking many days to do some task sets, halted when H > 60. As per new approach higher orders of the hyper period, Table 5.6 demonstrates that the SURE schedule's energy savings are greater than 90% of the ideal option. Furthermore, SURE strategy can be computed in several orders of magnitude less time than the MES schedule.

A process scheduler uses particular scheduling methods to assign different programmes to the CPU. Priority Scheduling, Shortest Job Next, and FCFS are some of the most popular process scheduling techniques. The method that controls how much CPU time is given to processes and threads is known as a strategy for planning. Every proposed method seeks to fulfil a set of conditions. The organiser should ideally be able to scale as the number of jobs grows.

===
===============

Enter the choice to execute specific functionalities
1. Execute all schedule algorithms
2. Execute all scheduling tasks related functionalities
3. Exit

1
Enter time quantum: 2
Enter the number of process: 2
Enter the burst time of process in msec 1: 8
Enter the burst time of process in msec 2: 5

Table 9. WT and TAT of different scheduling algorithms

Name of the algorithm	Processor Name	Burst Time (msec)	Waiting Time (msec)	Turnaround Time (msec)
FCFS	P1	8.000000	0.000000	8.000000
	P2	5.000000	8.000000	13.000000
SJF	P1	5.000000	0.000000	5.000000
	P2	8.000000	5.000000	13.000000
RR	P1	8.000000	0.000000	8.000000
	P2	5.000000	-2.000000	3.000000
PA	P1(2)	8.000000	0.000000	8.000000
	P2(1)	5.000000	8.000000	5.000000
SJF-LJF	P1	5.000000	0.000000	5.000000
	P2	8.000000	5.000000	13.00000
PeSche	P1	5.000000	0.000000	5.000000
	P2	8.000000	5.000000	6.000000

The specific steps involved in putting the performance-enhanced scheduling method shown in Figure 2.1 into practice. Observed the parameters of average waiting and turnaround time dependent on burst time and processors used for execution. The relevant result can be verified in Table 5.7 and Table 5.8.

Table 10. Avg_WT and Avg_TAT of different scheduling algorithms

Algorithm	Avg_WT	Avg_TAT
FCFS	4	10.5
SJF	2.5	9
RR	-1	5.5
Priority	4	6.5
SJF-LJF	2.5	9
PeSche	2.5	5.5

Enter the choice to execute specific functionalities
1. Execute all schedule algorithms
2. Execute all scheduling tasks related functionalities

3. Exit
    2
    Assigning Priority
    21 14 14 13 10 13 9 8 7 4
    Sorted Priority Array looks like this:
    4 7 8 9 10 13 13 14 14 21
    priority_index
    0 2 1 3 5 4 6 7 8 9
    cloud_task
    0 0 0 0 0 0 0 0 0 0
    T_re
    5 5 5 5 5 5 5 5 5 5
    T_L_min
    5 5 4 3 2 4 3 2 2 2
    w
    7 6 5 5 3 5 5 4 3 4
    Task 1 was executed in 3 with an endtime of 5
    Task 3 was executed in 3 with an endtime of 9
    Task 2 was executed in 4 with an endtime of 10
    Task 4 was executed in 2 with an endtime of 10
    Task 6 was executed in 1 with an endtime of 12
    Task 5 was executed in 3 with an endtime of 11
    Task 7 was executed in 3 with an endtime of 14
    Task 8 was executed in 2 with an endtime of 16
    Task 9 was executed in 3 with an endtime of 16
    Task 10 was executed in 3 with an endtime of 18
    Total Energy = 122(Joules)
    Total Time = 18(msec)
    Initial Scheduling Result Seq =
    2 2 3 1 0 2 2 1 2 2

Table 11. Total energy (Joules) of PeSche Algorithm

Total_energy (Joules)			
91	**96**	**102**	**87**
92	96	102	91
105	109	117	102
99	102	104	97
102	107	111	100

continued on following page

Table 11. Continued

Total_energy (Joules)			
91	**96**	**102**	**87**
99	102	102	99
98	100	102	95
100	102	102	99
99	100	102	99
101	102	102	99

Table 12. Total time (msec) of PeSche algorithm

Total_time (msec)			
20	**18**	**16**	**16**
17	16	16	16
18	16	16	16
18	16	16	16
16	16	16	16
16	16	16	16
20	17	16	17
16	16	16	16
19	17	16	19
21	18	16	19

Table 13. Energy time ratio of PeSche algorithm: Iteration 1

Energy Time Ratio			
4.55	**5.33333**	**6.375**	**5.4375**
5.41176	6	6.375	5.6875
5.83333	6.8125	7.3125	6.375
5.5	6.375	6.5	6.0625
6.375	6.6875	6.9375	6.25
6.1875	6.375	6.375	6.1875
4.9	5.88235	6.375	5.58824
6.25	6.375	6.375	6.1875
5.21053	5.88235	6.375	5.21053
4.80952	5.66667	6.375	5.21053

Min Ratio = 4.55 was present at i,j = 0 0

Table 14. Energy time ratio of pesche algorithm: Iteration 2

Energy Time Ratio			
4.35	**5.11111**	**6.125**	**4.9375**
3.66667	4.05	4.35	3.6
4.27273	4.9	5.3	4.35
3.81818	4.35	4.45	3.9
4.35	4.6	4.8	4.05
4.2	4.35	4.35	4
3.45833	4.04762	4.35	3.61905
3.86364	4.35	4.35	3.80952
3.65217	4.04762	4.35	3.47826
3.44	3.95455	4.35	3.80952

Min Ratio in loop = 3.44, xMin = 9, yMin = 0, E_total = 86 J, T_Total = 25 msec

Table 15. (c) Energy time ratio of PeSche algorithm: Iteration 3

Energy Time Ratio			
3.44	**3.95652**	**4.61905**	**3.71429**
2.92308	3.2	3.44	2.84
3.44444	3.88	4.2	3.44
3.07407	3.44	3.52	3.08
3.44	3.64	3.8	3.2
3.32	3.44	3.44	3.16
2.82759	3.23077	3.44	2.88462
3.11111	3.44	3.44	3.03846
2.96429	3.23077	3.44	2.82143
3.44	3.95455	4.35	3.80952

Min Ratio in loop = 2.821, xMin = 8, yMin = 3, E_total = 79 J, T_Total = 28 msec

Table 16. (d) Energy time ratio of PeSche algorithm: Iteration 4

Energy Time Ratio			
2.82143	**3.23077**	**3.75**	**2.95833**
2.46429	2.60714	2.82143	2.28571
3.07143	3.21429	3.5	2.82143
2.71429	2.82143	2.89286	2.5
2.82143	3.11111	3.38462	2.80769

continued on following page

Table 16. Continued

Energy Time Ratio			
2.82143	**3.23077**	**3.75**	**2.95833**
2.71429	2.82143	2.82143	2.57143
2.58621	2.75	2.82143	2.42857
2.75	2.82143	2.82143	2.57143
2.96429	3.23077	3.44	2.82143
2.82143	3.2	3.47826	3.04167

Min Ratio in loop = 2.285, xMin = 1, yMin = 3, E_total = 64 J, T_Total = 28 msec

Table 17. Energy time ratio of PeSche algorithm: Iteration 5

Energy Time Ratio			
2.28571	**2.65385**	**3.125**	**2.33333**
2.46429	2.60714	2.82143	2.28571
2.53571	2.67857	2.96429	2.28571
2.17857	2.28571	2.35714	1.96429
2.28571	2.55556	2.80769	2.23077
2.17857	2.28571	2.28571	2.03571
2.06897	2.21429	2.28571	1.89286
2.21429	2.28571	2.28571	2.03571
2.42857	2.65385	2.84	2.28571
2.28571	2.6	2.82609	2.41667

Min Ratio in loop = 1.892, xMin = 6, yMin = 3, E_total = 53 J, T_Total = 28 msec

Table 18. Energy time ratio of PeSche algorithm: Iteration 6

Energy Time Ratio			
1.89286	**2.23077**	**2.66667**	**1.875**
2.07143	2.21429	2.42857	1.89286
2.06897	2.28571	2.57143	1.89286
1.78571	1.89286	1.96429	1.57143
1.89286	2.14815	2.38462	1.80769
1.78571	1.89286	1.89286	1.64286
2.06897	2.21429	2.28571	1.89286
1.82143	1.89286	1.89286	1.64286
2.03571	2.23077	2.30769	1.89286

continued on following page

Table 18. Continued

Energy Time Ratio			
1.89286	**2.23077**	**2.66667**	**1.875**
1.89286	2.16	2.34783	1.95833

Min Ratio in loop = 1.571, xMin = 3, yMin = 3, E_total = 44 J, T_Total = 28 msec

Table 19. Energy time ratio of PeSche algorithm: Iteration 7

Energy Time Ratio			
1.57143	**1.88462**	**2.29167**	**1.5**
1.75	1.89286	2.10714	1.57143
1.75862	1.96429	2.25	1.57143
1.78571	1.89286	1.96429	1.57143
1.57143	1.81481	2.03846	1.46154
1.46429	1.57143	1.57143	1.32143
1.75862	1.89286	1.96429	1.57143
1.5	1.57143	1.57143	1.32143
1.71429	1.88462	1.96154	1.57143
1.57143	1.8	1.95652	1.58333

Min Ratio in loop = 1.321, xMin = 5, yMin = 3, E_total = 37 J, T_Total = 28 msec

Table 20. Energy time ratio of PeSche algorithm: Iteration 8

Energy Time Ratio			
1.32143	**1.61538**	**2**	**1.20833**
1.5	1.64286	1.85714	1.32143
1.51724	1.71429	2	1.32143
1.53571	1.64286	1.71429	1.32143
1.32143	1.55556	1.76923	1.19231
1.46429	1.57143	1.57143	1.32143
1.51724	1.64286	1.71429	1.32143
1.25	1.32143	1.32143	1.07143
1.46429	1.61538	1.69231	1.32143
1.32143	1.52	1.65217	1.29167

Min Ratio in loop = 1.071, xMin = 7, yMin = 3, E_total = 30 J, T_Total = 28 msec

Table 21. (i) Energy time ratio of PeSche algorithm: Iteration 9

Energy Time Ratio			
1.07143	**1.34615**	**1.70833**	**0.916667**
1.25	1.39286	1.60714	1.07143
1.27586	1.46429	1.75	1.07143
1.28571	1.39286	1.46429	1.07143
1.07143	1.2963	1.5	0.923077
1.21429	1.32143	1.32143	1.07143
1.27586	1.39286	1.46429	1.07143
1.25	1.32143	1.32143	1.07143
1.21429	1.34615	1.42308	1.07143
1.07143	1.24	1.34783	1

Min Ratio in loop = 0.916, xMin = 0, yMin = 3, E_total = 22 J, T_Total = 24 msec

Program Running Time: 1057ms

Tables 5.9 and 5.10, respectively, provide evidence of the PeSche algorithm's total energy (Joules) and total time (msec). Results from iterations 1 to 9 of the PeSche algorithm's energy time ratio can be seen in Tables 5.11 (a) to 5.11 (i). Table 6.6 compares the PeSche minimum energy approach to the SURE algorithm and displays the task's worst-case completion time and minimal energy value.

Table 22. Comparative analysis of algorithms in terms of energy consumption

H	MAKESPAN/PERFORMANCE TIME			POWER/ENERGY CONSUMPTION (J)		
	Strategy of MES	Strategy of SURE	Strategy of PeSche	Strategy of MES	Strategy of SURE	Strategy of PeSche
≤ 10	< 1 Sec	< 1 Sec	< 0.2777 Sec	74	78	22
≤ 20	> 30 Min	< 1 Sec	< 0.3889 Sec	121	123	36
≤ 30	> 30 Min	< 1 Sec	< 0.5112 Sec	116	120	34
≤ 40	> 30 Min	< 1 Sec	< 0.6724 Sec	176	180	52
≤ 50	> 30 Min	< 1 Sec	< 0.8272 Sec	138	138	41
≤ 60	> 1 Day	< 1 Sec	< 0.9889 Sec	164	164	49

H was stopped when it reached 60 since some job sets were taking a long time to finish. Table 5.12 demonstrates that the energy savings with the PeSche exceed 90% of the optimal solution as closer to higher orders of the hyper period. More notably, compared to the SURE schedule, the PeSche schedule can be generated in several orders of magnitude less time. CodeBlocks 20.03 (MinGW-W64-builds-4.3.5) is employed in the simulation of suggested approach. C++ was used to build the code's functionality. In embedded real time systems, DPM methods are employed to control power dissipation. SURE (Slack Utilization for Reduced Energy) is a preemptive method that employs a slack utilization technique to reduce power consumption based on shared devices, task sets, and power requirements. SURE provides more energy savings than the Energy-Aware EDF (EA-EDF), and Enhanced Energy-Aware EDF (EEA-EDF) algorithms. To find H levels for each time tick, the depth-first-search method was utilized. The SURE algorithm saved more energy than previous algorithms. As shown in Table 5.12, the Minimum Energy Schedule (MES) algorithm was implemented using the Brute force method to create a tree of schedules for the given job set with less energy than SURE.

In embedded real-time systems, DPM methods are employed to control power dissipation. SURE (Slack Utilization for Reduced Energy) is a pre-emptive method that employs a slack utilisation technique to reduce power consumption based on shared devices, task sets, and power requirements. SURE provides more energy savings than the EEA-EDF and EA-EDF algorithms. To find H levels for each time tick, the depth-first-search method was utilised. The SURE algorithm saved more energy than previous algorithms. As shown in figure 5.1

Figure+5.1+Energy+consumption+of+different+algorithms.tiff, the Minimum Energy Schedule (MES) algorithm was implemented using the Brute force method to create a tree of schedules for the given job set with less energy than SURE. CodeBlocks 20.03 (MinGW-W64-builds-4.3.5) is employed in the simulation of the proposed algorithm. The code was written in the C++ programming language.

CONCLUSION AND FUTURE SCOPE

The proposed PeSche (Performance improved Scheduling) method is implemented together with the process, burst, waiting, and turnaround time on an embedded real-time system. Two processors are used to run the performance improved Scheduling algorithm. PeSche scheduling algorithm outperformed SJF, RR, FCFS, Priority, and SJF-LJF in terms of energy-time ratio, running time, total energy, and total time. As seen in figure 5.1, PeSche consumed less energy than MES and SURE. The proposed approach could be tweaked in the future to execute jobs faster and hence improve performance by allocating time slots to available CPUs. The complete number of processors has been efficiently employed as a result of this method.

COMPLIANCE WITH ETHICAL STANDARDS

The scheduling techniques have been investigated by the job execution process in a system in order to maximize multiprocessor utilization. As a result, the study aimed to develop a new real-time scheduling technique to increase the number of tasks execution on multiprocessor platform. Proposed system will overcome the drawbacks of above said. Energy consumption is the most important considered parameter on design metrics. DPM (Dynamic Power Management) and DVFS (Dynamic Voltage and Frequency Scaling) are two general strategies for lowering energy use. When there is an imbalance in the work load and idle CPUs are identified while executing the tasks, the system's response time is slowed. PeSche (Performance enhanced Scheduling) is a proposed scheduling algorithm that has been designed for an optimal solution. In future, the proposed algorithm may be adjusted to execute the tasks faster and hence enhance the performance by assigning the time slots to the available processors. Hence this approach emphasis effectively employed by extending the number of processors.

There is no scope of Research involving Human Participants and/or Animals and Informed consent.

REFERENCES

Al-Bakhrani, A., Hagar, A., Hamoud, A. A., & Kawathekar, S. (2020). Comparative Analysis of Cpu Scheduling Algorithms: Simulation And Its Applications. *International Journal of Advanced Science and Technology*, 29(3), 483–494.

Alworafi, M. A., Dhari, A., El-Booz, S. A., Nasr, A. A., Arpitha, A., & Mallappa, S. (2019). An enhanced task scheduling in cloud computing based on hybrid approach. In *Data Analytics and Learning* (pp. 11–25). Springer. 10.1007/978-981-13-2514-4_2

Bhuiyan, A., Guo, Z., Saifullah, A., Guan, N., & Xiong, H. (2018). Energy efficient real time scheduling of DAG tasks. *ACM Transactions on Embedded Computing Systems*, 17(5), 84. 10.1145/3241049

Bose, A., Biswas, T., & Kuila, P. (2019). *A Novel Genetic Algorithm Based Scheduling for Multi-core Systems in Smart Innovations in Communication and Computational Sciences*. Springer., 10.1007/978-981-13-2414-7_5

Burkimsher, A., Bate, I., & Indrusiak, L. S. (2013). Scheduling HPC workflows for responsiveness and fairness with networking delays and inaccurate estimates of execution times. *European Conference on Parallel Processing*. Springer. 10.1007/978-3-642-40047-6_15

Burkimsher, A., Bate, I., & Indrusiak, L. S. (2013, August). Scheduling HPC workflows for responsiveness and fairness with networking delays and inaccurate estimates of execution times. In *European Conference on Parallel Processing* (pp. 126-137). Springer. 10.1007/978-3-642-40047-6_15

Butangen, A. K. G., Velasco, C. E., Codmos, J. C. B., Bayani, E. F., & Baquirin, R. B. (2020, January). Utilizing Dynamic Mean Quantum Time Round Robin to Optimize the Shortest Job First Scheduling Algorithm. In *Proceedings of 2020 the 6th International Conference on Computing and Data Engineering* (pp. 14-18). ACM. 10.1145/3379247.3379296

Chandran, J., & Viswanatham, V. M. (2021). Evaluating the effectiveness of community detection algorithms for influence maximization in social networks. *2021 International Conference on Advances in Electrical, Computing, Communication and Sustainable Technologies (ICAECT)*. IEEE. 10.1109/ICAECT49130.2021.9392387

Chang, S., Bi, R., Sun, J., Liu, W., Yu, Q., Deng, Q., & Gu, Z. (2022, November). Toward Minimum WCRT Bound for DAG Tasks Under Prioritized List Scheduling Algorithms. *IEEE Transactions on Computer-Aided Design of Integrated Circuits and Systems*, 41(11), 3874–3885. 10.1109/TCAD.2022.3197532

Chasapis, D., Moretó, M., Schulz, M., Rountree, B., & Casas, M. (2019). Power efficient job scheduling by predicting the impact of processor manufacturing variability. *Proceedings of the ACM International Conference on Supercomputing.* ACM. 10.1145/3330345.3330372

Chen, J., & Han, P. (2021). Yifan Liu Xiaoyan Du. Scheduling independent tasks in cloud environment based on modified differential evolution. *Concurrency and Computation.* 10.1002/cpe.6256

Chen, Y. (2022). A local search 4/3-approximation algorithm for the minimum 3-path partition problem. *Journal of Combinatorial Optimization, 44*, 3595-3610. 10.1007/s10878-022-00915-5

Deng, Z., Cao, D., Shen, H., Yan, Z., & Huang, H. (2021). Reliability-aware task scheduling for energy efficiency on heterogeneous multiprocessor systems. *The Journal of Supercomputing, 77*(10), 1–39. 10.1007/s11227-021-03764-x

Duy, T. V. T., Sato, Y., & Inoguchi, Y. (2010). *Performance evaluation of a green scheduling algorithm for energy savings in cloud computing in 2010 IEEE international symposium on parallel & distributed processing, workshops and Phd forum (IPDPSW).* IEEE. 10.1109/IPDPSW.2010.5470908

Duy, T. V. T., Sato, Y., & Inoguchi, Y. (2010, April). Performance evaluation of a green scheduling algorithm for energy savings in cloud computing. In *2010 IEEE international symposium on parallel & distributed processing, workshops and Phd forum (IPDPSW)* (pp. 1-8). IEEE. 10.1109/IPDPSW.2010.5470908

Hamayun, M., & Khurshid, H. (2015). An optimized shortest job first scheduling algorithm for CPU scheduling. *Journal of Applied Environmental and Biological Sciences*, 5(12), 42–46.

He, Q., Jiang, X., Guan, N., & Guo, Z. (2019). *Intra-Task Priority Assignment in Real time Scheduling of DAG Tasks on Multi-cores.* IEEE Transactions on Parallel and Distributed Systems. 10.1109/TPDS.2019.2910525

Hu, B., Cao, Z., & Zhou, M. (2021). Energy-minimized scheduling of real time parallel workflows on heterogeneous distributed computing systems. *IEEE Transactions on Services Computing.* 10.1109/TSC.2021.3054754

Ji, M., Zhang, W., Liao, L., Cheng, T. C. E., & Tan, Y. (2019). *Multitasking parallel-machine scheduling with machinedependent slack due-window assignment. International Journal of Production Research.* Taylor & Francis. 10.1080/00207543.2018.1497312

Krishnapura, R., Goddard, S., & Qadi, A. A. (2004). A dynamic real-time scheduling algorithm for reduced energy consumption. *CSE Technical reports, 72*.

Kumar, M., & Sharma, S. C. (2016). Priority Aware Longest Job First (PA-LJF) algorithm for utilization of the resource in cloud environment in 3rd *International Conference on Computing for Sustainable Glmessobal Development (INDIACom)*. IEEE.

Lee, Z., Wang, Y., & Zhou, W. (2011, August). A dynamic priority scheduling algorithm on service request scheduling in cloud computing. In *Proceedings of 2011 International Conference on Electronic & Mechanical Engineering and Information Technology* (Vol. 9, pp. 4665-4669). IEEE. 10.1109/EMEIT.2011.6024076

Legout, V., Jan, M., & Pautet, L. (2013, October). A scheduling algorithm to reduce the static energy consumption of multiprocessor real-time systems. In *Proceedings of the 21st International Conference on Real-Time Networks and Systems* (pp. 99-108). ACM. 10.1145/2516821.2516839

Lin, C.-C., Shi, J., Ueter, N., Günzel, M., Reineke, J., & Chen, J.-J. (2022). Type-aware Federated Scheduling for Typed DAG Tasks on Heterogeneous Multicore Platforms. *IEEE Transactions on Computers*. 10.1109/TC.2022.3202748

Maia, C., Nogueira, L., & Pinho, L. M. (2013). Scheduling parallel real time tasks using a fixed-priority work-stealing algorithm on multiprocessors. *2013 8thIEEE International Symposium on Industrial Embedded Systems* (SIES), (pp. 89-92). IEEE. 10.1109/SIES.2013.6601477

Mehalaine, R., & Boutekkouk, F. (2020). *Energy Consumption Reduction in Real Time Multiprocessor Embedded Systems with Uncertain Data in Computer Science*. Springer, Cham. 10.1007/978-3-030-51971-1_4

Nayak, D., Malla, S. K., & Debadarshini, D. (2012). Improved round robin scheduling using dynamic time quantum. *International Journal of Computer Applications*, 38(5), 34–38. 10.5120/4607-6816

Öztop, H., Tasgetiren, M. F., Eliiyi, D. T., & Pan, Q. K. (2018). Green Permutation Flowshop Scheduling: A Trade-off-Between Energy Consumption and Total Flow Time. *International Conference on Intelligent Computing*. Springer. 10.1007/978-3-319-95957-3_79

Paul, T., Hossain, R., & Samsuddoha, M. (2019). Improved round robin scheduling algorithm with progressive time quantum. *International Journal of Computer Applications*, 178(49), 30–36. 10.5120/ijca2019919419

Prakash, K. B. (2020). *A Critical Review on Federated Cloud Consumer Perspective of Maximum Resource Utilization for Optimal Price Using EM Algorithm*. Soft Computing for Problem Solving., 10.1007/978-981-15-0184-5_15

Qin, Y., Zeng, G., Kurachi, R., Li, Y., Matsubara, Y., & Takada, H. (2019). Energy-Efficient Intra-Task DVFS Scheduling Using Linear Programming Formulation. *IEEE Access : Practical Innovations, Open Solutions*, 7, 30536–30547. 10.1109/ACCESS.2019.2902353

Rizvi, N. (2022). A Workflow Scheduling Approach with Modified Fuzzy Adaptive Genetic Algorithm in IaaS Clouds, IEEE Transactions on Services Computing, May, SCI, DOI: 10.1109/TSC.2022.3174112

Sahoo, R. M., & Padhy, S. K. (2019). Improved Crow Search Optimization for Multiprocessor Task Scheduling: A Novel Approach. *International Conference on Application of Robotics in Industry using Advanced Mechanisms*, (pp. 1- 13). Springer, Cham. 10.1007/978-3-030-30271-9_1

Santra, S., Dey, H., Majumdar, S., & Jha, G. S. (2014, July). New simulation toolkit for comparison of scheduling algorithm on cloud computing. In *2014 International Conference on Control, Instrumentation, Communication and Computational Technologies (ICCICCT)* (pp. 466-469). IEEE. .2014.699300710.1109/ICCICCT.2014.6993007

Singh, A., Goyal, P., & Batra, S. (2010). An optimized round robin scheduling algorithm for CPU scheduling. *International Journal on Computer Science and Engineering*, 2(7), 2383–2385. 10.1145/3484824.3484917

Song, J., Xie, G., Li, R., & Chen, X. (2017). *An efficient scheduling algorithm for energy consumption constrained parallel applications on heterogeneous distributed systems*. IEEE., 10.1109/ISPA/IUCC.2017.00015

Strohbach, M., Gellersen, H. W., Kortuem, G., & Kray, C. (2004). Cooperative artefacts: Assessing real world situations with embedded technology. In *International Conference on Ubiquitous Computing,* (pp. 250-267). Springer. 10.1007/978-3-540-30119-6_15

Tang, Q., Zhu, L. H., Lian, J., Zhou, L., & Wei, J. B. (2020). An efficient multi-functional duplication-based scheduling framework for multiprocessor systems. *The Journal of Supercomputing*, 76(11), 1–26. 10.1007/s11227-020-03208-y

Wei, H., Bao, H., & Ruan, X. (2020). Genetic algorithm-driven discovery of unexpected thermal conductivity enhancement by disorder. *Nano Energy*, 71, 104619. 10.1016/j.nanoen.2020.104619

Xie, G., Zeng, G., Xiao, X., Li, R., & Li, K. (2017, December 1). Energy-Efficient Scheduling Algorithms for Real time Parallel Applications on Heterogeneous Distributed Embedded Systems. *IEEE Transactions on Parallel and Distributed Systems*, 28(12), 3426–3442. 10.1109/TPDS.2017.2730876

Chapter 16
Enhancing Operational Cost Savings in Electric Utilities on Global Optimization in Power System Planning and Operation

M. D. Rajkamal
Velammal Institute of Technology, India

H. Mohammed Ali
SRM Institute of Science and Technology, Ramapuram, India

A. Krishnakumari
Hindustan Institute of Technology and Science, Padur, India

M. Saravanan
Hindustan Institute of Technology and Science, Padur, India

Manikandan I.
KCG College of Technology, Karapakkam, India

Ramya M.
Lovely Professional University, Punjab, India

ABSTRACT

Operational cost savings in electric utilities using the application of genetic algorithms in power system planning and operation characterize an innovative approach that involves computational intelligence to optimize complex decision-making processes in power grid functioning. Electric utilities involve various challenges which involve managing power generation, transmission and distribution that are necessary to meet the ever-growing demand for electricity with the reduction in operational

DOI: 10.4018/979-8-3693-3314-3.ch016

costs. These challenges are overcome using the aid of a genetic algorithm. In the field of power system planning, the genetic algorithms are engaged to optimize the configuration and expansion of generation, transmission and distribution.

INTRODUCTION

A power system is a complex network planned to generate, transmit, distribute and employ electrical energy efficiently (Josphineleela, Kaliapp, et al., 2023). It establishes a serious infrastructure that provides the necessary energy to power homes, businesses, industries and various technological devices (Natrayan & Kaliappan, 2023). The power system includes three main components such as generation, transmission and distribution (Kaliappan, Natrayan, & Garg, 2023). Generation involves the conversion of various energy sources into electrical power. These sources can range from traditional fossil fuels like coal, natural gas and oil to renewable resources such as solar, wind, hydro, and geothermal (Natrayan, Kaliappan, & Pundir, 2023). Power plants, whether conventional or renewable play a fundamental role in transforming these energy sources into electricity (Kaliappan, Natrayan, & Rajput, 2023). Transmission is the phase where high-voltage electrical energy is transported over long distances from power plants to distribution centres and eventually to end-users (Suman et al., 2023). This process minimizes energy losses and ensures that electricity reaches distant locations efficiently (Chinta et al., 2023).

High-voltage transmission lines, transformers and substations are key elements in this part of the power system. Distribution involves the delivery of electricity from distribution centres to consumers (Kaliappan, Mothilal, et al., 2023). Local distribution networks, consisting of medium and low-voltage lines, transformers and substations. Smart grids helps in incorporating advanced technologies like sensors and communication systems and tends to enhance the efficiency and reliability of distribution networks (Velumayil et al., 2023). The power system is considered by its interconnected nature where various components work together effortlessly to meet the ever-growing demand for electricity (Selvi et al., 2023). It requires careful planning, monitoring and maintenance to safeguard a stable and reliable supply of power (Ragumadhavan et al., 2023). Power system engineers and operators service sophisticated tools and technologies to manage the grid balance generation and demand and respond to disturbances or faults (Natrayan, Kaliappan, Saravanan, et al., 2023). Artificial Intelligence (AI) plays an essential role in modern power systems which helps in the transformation . One of the important key contributions of AI in the power sector is optimizing energy generation and consumption. This helps in improving the overall efficiency of the system. (Lakshmaiya, 2023i; Natrayan & De Poures, 2023a) AI algorithms can analyze massive quantities of information from diverse sources including weather patterns, energy demand forecasts and equipment health monitoring (Lakshmaiya & Murugan, 2023d; Rajasekaran & Natrayan, 2023b). This is used to make precise forecasts and optimize the operation of power plants. This leads to enhanced resource utilization with reduced downtime and improved grid reliability (Lakshmaiya & Murugan, 2023c; Rajasekaran & Natrayan, 2023a). In power grid management, the AI technologies allow intelligent control and automation helping operators make real-time decisions for maintaining grid stability (Lakshmaiya & Murugan, 2023a; Natrayan & Richard, 2023a). Advanced machine learning models can expect potential issues such as equipment failures or fluctuations in demand and take active actions to inhibit disturbances. AI-driven projecting maintenance is also vital for identifying equipment degradation before it leads to costly failures (Kiruba Sandou et al., 2023; Lakshmaiya, 2023h; Sukumaran et al., 2023). Thus improving the overall reliability of the power infrastructure. AI enables the integration of renewable energy sources into the power grid. The recurrent and adjustable nature of renewable energy, such as solar and wind, poses challenges for grid stability (Arul Arumugam et al., 2023; Sasi et al., 2023). AI algorithms can forecast renewable energy generation patterns and dynamically adjust the grid operation to accommodate these fluctuations (Prabagar et al., 2023). This helps in attaining a more sustainable and resilient power system by maximizing the utilization of clean energy sources (Mehta et al., 2023). AI enables the development of smart grids and smart meters allowing consumers to actively contribute in energy management. AI algorithms analyze consumption patterns, preferences and historical information to optimize energy usage which helps to decrease waste and lower costs for end-users (Konduri et al., 2023).

AI contributes to the operation of power systems by providing real-time monitoring, control and decision-making support (Siddiqui et al., 2023). Advanced machine learning algorithms uninterruptedly analyze data from sensors, smart grids and other sources to detect anomalies, predict equipment failures and optimize the dispatch of generation resources (Biradar et al., 2023; M. Vijayakumar et al., 2023). AI-driven predictive maintenance helps utilities recognise potential issues before they escalate, minimizing downtime and improving overall system reliability. AI plays a crucial role in enhancing grid flexibility and resilience (Mahat et al., 2023). Smart grid technologies tends to facilitate the integration of renewable energy sources by efficiently managing the inconsistency and unpredictability associated with solar and wind power (Anjankar et al., 2023; Sai et al., 2023). AI algorithms can predict renewable energy output, optimize energy storage systems, and dynamically adjust grid parameters to accommodate fluctuations in supply and demand (Natrayan & Richard, 2023b). This results in a more stable and adaptive power grid capable of handling the challenges posed by the increasing penetration of renewable energy (Lakshmaiya, 2023g; Lakshmaiya & Murugan, 2023e, 2023b). AI contributes to the development of demand response programs and energy efficiency initiatives. By analyzing consumer behavior and preferences, AI can assist in designing personalized energy management strategies, encouraging users to shift their consumption patterns during peak demand periods or adopt energy-efficient practices (Lakshmaiya, 2023f; Natrayan & De Poures, 2023b). Demand response systems empowered by AI can efficiently balance supply and demand by incentivizing consumers to adjust their energy consumption during peak periods (Kaushal et al., 2023). AI revolutionizes the power sector by enhancing operational efficiency, grid reliability, and sustainability. Its applications range from predictive maintenance and grid optimization to the integration of renewable energy sources and demand-side management. As technology continues to advance, the role of AI in the power system is expected to grow, ushering in a new era of intelligent and resilient energy infrastructure.

EXISTING SYSTEM

The existing system involves a fuzzy logic system for the improvement of operational cost savings in power utilities which involves various drawbacks as listed below.

- Fuzzy logic systems can be complex to design and implement. Developing a comprehensive fuzzy logic system for global optimization in power systems requires a deep understanding of both the power system domain and fuzzy logic principles.
- Fuzzy logic systems are often used to handle uncertainty in data and system dynamics. However, the modeling of uncertainty itself introduces a degree of subjectivity and the fuzzy rules might not always accurately arrest the true system behavior.
- Fuzzy logic systems can lack transparency and interpretability. Understanding the decision-making process and the impact of different fuzzy rules on the overall system can be challenging, which may lead to difficulties in gaining trust and acceptance from stakeholders.
- The performance of a fuzzy logic system is highly reliant on the quality and quantity of input data. Inaccurate or insufficient data can lead to suboptimal results and compromise the effectiveness of the optimization process.
- Fuzzy logic systems may not adapt well to rapid changes or extreme conditions in the power system. Sudden disruptions, such as extreme weather events or equipment failures, may challenge the ability of the fuzzy logic system to provide optimal solutions in real-time.

To overcome the drawbacks, the proposed system is implemented using a genetic algorithm.

PROPOSED METHODOLOGY

The proposed methodology involves a genetic algorithm for enhancing operational cost savings in electric utilities in power systems. This is implemented through various stages. The information about the power system, generation units, demand, and operational constraints are analyzed and gathered for further analysis (Velmurugan & Natrayan, 2023). They are used for load forecasting and demand prediction. Then the schedules are planned for electricity generation to meet the predicted demand efficiently (Lakshmaiya et al., 2022; Natrayan et al., 2021). The efficient power transfer are done through optimization techniques. Here genetic algorithm are used for the identification of optimal solutions for power system planning and operation (Lakshmaiya et al., 2022; Ponnusamy et al., 2022). The output of the genetic algorithm helps in obtaining plans with system configurations in power system. Continuous monitoring of the power system are done for efficient functioning (Natrayan et al., 2019; M. D. et al. Vijayakumar, 2022). The performance of the system are analyzed using various metrics such as cost savings, reliability, and other appropriate metrics (Balaji et al., 2022). Feedback and adjustments are done for improving future iterations. The decision support system helps in obtaining information recommendations based on the optimization results. Figure 1 represents various stages in the proposed system (M. et al., Singh, 2017).

Figure 1. Proposed system

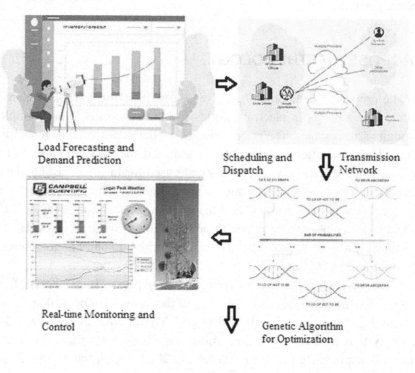

Performance Evaluation and Analysis

IMPROVED OPERATIONAL COST IN ELECTRIC UTILITIES IN POWER SYSTEM

Objective Function for Demonstrating the Goal of Minimizing Operational Costs

Power system planning and operation are critical components of the energy sector that aim to ensure the reliable, economical, and sustainable supply of electrical power to meet the ever-growing demands of society (Pragadish et al., 2023). The objectives of power system planning encompass a comprehensive and forward-looking approach to anticipate, accommodate, and manage the complex dynamics within the electricity grid (Natrayan & Kumar, 2019; Niveditha VR. & Rajakumar PS., 2020). Firstly, a key goal is to guarantee the reliability of the power system. This involves assessing the capacity and adequacy of generation, transmission, and distribution infrastructure to meet the forecasted demand while considering contingencies such as equipment failures or unforeseen events (Natrayan et al., 2020). Reliability is vital to maintaining a stable and secure supply of electricity, preventing blackouts or disruptions that could have severe economic and social consequences (Yogeshwaran et al., 2020).

Economic efficiency is another critical objective in power system planning. This entails optimizing the allocation of resources and minimizing costs across the entire energy value chain, from generation to consumption (Natrayan, Senthil Kumar, et al., 2018; Natrayan & Merneedi, 2020). Planners must balance investments in new infrastructure, such as power plants and transmission lines, against the operational costs of running the system. The aim is to achieve the most cost-effective and sustainable mix of energy sources while meeting environmental and regulatory standards (Muthiya, Natrayan, Kaliappan, et al., 2022; Natrayan, Sivaprakash, et al., 2018). This involves considering factors like fuel prices, technology advancements, and environmental impacts to make informed decisions that benefit both consumers and the overall economy (Natrayan & Kumar, 2020; Sathish et al., 2021). Environmental sustainability is increasingly becoming a central objective in power system planning and operation. As the world grapples with climate change and environmental concerns, there is a growing emphasis on integrating renewable energy sources and reducing greenhouse gas emissions (Muthiya, Natrayan, Yuvaraj, et al., 2022; Palaniyappan et al., 2022). Planners strive to design systems that promote the use of clean and sustainable energy, balancing the need for economic viability with environmental stewardship. This often involves integrating technologies such as wind, solar, and hydropower into the grid and implementing policies to incentivize the transition to low-carbon energy sources (Sendrayaperumal et al., 2021). The power system planning aims to foster adaptability and resilience in the face of evolving technological, economic, and regulatory landscapes. Rapid advancements in energy storage, smart grid technologies, and decentralized generation require planners to anticipate and respond to these changes (Ramesh et al., 2022; Sathish et al., 2022). Additionally, the increasing complexity of interconnected grids and the integration of diverse energy resources necessitate robust planning processes that can accommodate uncertainty and variability (Sureshkumar et al., 2022).

Identification of Decision Variables

The operational cost of a power system is significantly influenced by various decision variables, particularly those related to generation schedules and power flow distribution (Hemalatha et al., 2020; Nadh et al., 2021; Venkatesh et al., 2022). Generation schedules play a pivotal role in determining when and how much power is generated by each power plant within the system (Loganathan et al., 2023). These schedules are influenced by factors such as fuel costs, availability of renewable resources, maintenance schedules, and demand forecasts (Josphineleela, Lekha, et al., 2023; Reddy et al., 2023). The decision on which power plants to dispatch and at what capacity is crucial in minimizing operational costs while ensuring a reliable power supply (Josphineleela, Kaliapp, et al., 2023; Suman et al., 2023). The power flow distribution across the transmission network is another critical set of decision variables affecting operational costs (Balamurugan et al., 2023; Lakshmaiya, 2023e). Power flow distribution refers to how electrical power is distributed and transmitted through the network to meet demand at various locations (Lakshmaiya, 2023j, 2023d, 2023a). The decision variables associated with power flow distribution include the choice of transmission paths, line capacities, and voltage levels (Lakshmaiya, 2023b). Optimal power flow solutions involve balancing generation and demand across the entire network to minimize transmission losses and ensure efficient energy delivery (Natrayan, 2023). The decision variables related to the integration of renewable energy sources also impact operational costs (Chehelgerdi et al., 2023a; Lakshmaiya, 2023c). The intermittent nature of renewable resources, such as solar and wind, introduces additional complexity in generation scheduling (Chennai Viswanathan et al., 2023; Saadh et al., 2023). Decisions regarding the integration of energy storage systems, demand response programs, and advanced grid management technologies play a crucial role in optimizing the utilization of renewable energy sources and minimizing operational costs (Thakre et al., 2023; Ugle et al., 2023).

Formulation of Constraints With Encoding Schemes

The formulation of constraints is a critical aspect that plays a pivotal role in ensuring the stable and reliable operation of the electrical grid. Constraints are conditions or limitations that must be satisfied to prevent undesirable outcomes such as equipment overloading, voltage instability, or violations of operational limits. Encoding schemes are employed to represent these constraints in a mathematical format suitable for computational analysis and optimization algorithms. One fundamental constraint in power systems pertains to the thermal limits of transmission lines and power transformers. These limits are defined by the maximum allowable current and temperature that the equipment can withstand without risk of damage. Encoding these constraints involves expressing the power flow equations, which describe the relationship between active and reactive power, within the physical constraints of the equipment. This ensures that the power flowing through each component does not exceed its thermal capacity (Chehelgerdi et al., 2023b; Kanimozhi et al., 2022). Voltage stability is another critical constraint in power systems, as maintaining acceptable voltage levels is essential for the proper functioning of electrical devices and equipment (Karthick et al., 2022; Vaishali et al., 2021). Encoding voltage constraints involves formulating equations that represent the balance between active and reactive power, considering the voltage limits at various nodes within the network (Anita et al., 2024). Voltage stability constraints are crucial in preventing voltage collapse and ensuring that the system operates within acceptable voltage limits (Velmurugan et al., 2022).

Network connectivity constraints are also integral in power system modeling. These constraints capture the physical topology of the grid and the allowable flow of power between different nodes (Kaliappan & Natrayan, 2024c, 2024b). Encoding these constraints involves representing the network as a set of equations that reflect the Kirchhoff's laws, ensuring that power injected into the system at one point is equal to the sum of the power flows at interconnected nodes (Kaliappan & Natrayan, 2024a; Natrayan, Ashok, et al., 2024; Natrayan, Kaliappan, et al., 2024). Incorporating renewable energy sources introduces additional constraints related to their intermittent nature and dependency on environmental conditions (Kaliappan & Natrayan, 2024d; Malladi et al., 2024; Pandian et al., 2024). Encoding these constraints involves modeling the variability and uncertainty of renewable generation, incorporating forecast errors, and safeguarding the balance between generation and demand (Kaliappan, Natrayan, et al., 2024; Natrayan, Janardhan, et al., 2024).

Selection, Mutation, and Crossover

Genetic algorithms (GAs) have proven to be powerful optimization techniques in addressing complex problems, and their application to power system planning and operation has become increasingly prevalent, particularly in the pursuit of operational cost savings (Natrayan, Ameen, et al., 2024; P. Singh et al., 2024). The three fundamental genetic operators—selection, mutation, and crossover play pivotal roles in shaping the evolutionary process of solutions within the algorithm ultimately enhancing the efficiency and effectiveness of power system optimization as shown in figure 2 (Kumar et al., 2024; Natrayan, Chinta, Gogulamudi, et al., 2024). The selection process in a genetic algorithm is analogous to the principles of natural selection. Fit individuals, or solutions in the population, are more likely to be chosen for reproduction, mirroring the survival of the fittest in biological evolution. In the realm of power system planning, this translates to prioritizing solutions that exhibit superior operational cost characteristics, such as reduced fuel consumption or minimized maintenance expenses (Kaliappan, Paranthaman, et al., 2024). Through the iterative application of selection, the genetic algorithm converges towards increasingly optimal solutions, refining the pool of potential candidates over successive generations (Natrayan, Chinta, Teja, et al., 2024).

Mutation serves as a mechanism for introducing diversity into the population. In genetic algorithms for power system optimization, mutation corresponds to small, random changes in the genetic makeup of individual solutions (Ramaswamy et al., 2022). This stochastic perturbation prevents premature convergence to suboptimal solutions and explores a broader solution space. In the context of operational cost savings, mutation could manifest as incremental adjustments to parameters governing power generation and distribution, ensuring a more comprehensive exploration of the solution landscape.

Figure 2. Genetic algorithm

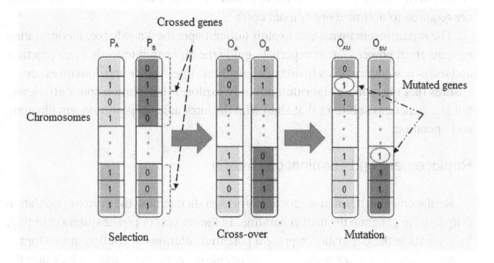

Crossover, also known as recombination, emulates genetic recombination in biological organisms. In the context of power system optimization, crossover involves combining genetic information from two parent solutions to create offspring. This exchange of traits enables the propagation of promising features while potentially eliminating less desirable ones. In the pursuit of operational cost savings, crossover mechanisms can be tailored to integrate cost-efficient strategies from different parent solutions, fostering the emergence of offspring with superior economic performance.

Repair Mechanisms

The repair mechanisms within genetic algorithms play a pivotal role in addressing constraints and ensuring feasible solutions. These mechanisms are designed to rectify infeasible or violated solutions generated during the optimization process, ensuring that the solutions adhere to the intricate constraints inherent in power system planning and operation. Constraints in this domain could include transmission line capacities, voltage limits, and generation capacity constraints, among others. Repair mechanisms within genetic algorithms can be tailored to prioritize solutions that not only meet the system's constraints but also exhibit characteristics conducive to minimizing operational costs. This involves the intelligent manipulation of variables such as generation schedules, transmission line loading, and reactive power generation, while simultaneously considering the economic implications of these adjustments. The repair mechanisms can be designed to dynamically adapt to changing conditions, allowing the genetic algorithm to respond effectively to fluctuations in demand, fuel prices, or unforeseen contingencies. This adaptability is crucial in the dynamic environment of power systems, where real-time adjustments are required to optimize operational costs.

The repair mechanisms can exploit domain-specific knowledge, incorporating insights from power system experts to guide the algorithm towards more practical and realistic solutions. This fusion of algorithmic intelligence and domain expertise ensures that the genetic algorithm not only explores the solution space efficiently but also generates solutions that align with the intricacies of power system planning and operation.

Replacement and Termination Criteria

Replacement criteria in a genetic algorithm dictate how the current population is updated to generate the next generation. In the context of power system planning, individuals in the population represent potential solutions or configurations for the system. Common replacement strategies include generational replacement, where the entire current population is replaced by the offspring, and steady-state replacement, where only a portion of the population is replaced. The choice of replacement criteria significantly influences the diversity and convergence of the population, impacting the algorithm's ability to explore the solution space effectively.

Termination criteria are equally pivotal in ensuring that the genetic algorithm converges to a satisfactory solution without unnecessary computational burden. In the context of operational cost savings in power systems, termination criteria may be based on achieving a predefined cost threshold, a specified number of generations, or reaching a plateau where further iterations do not yield significant improvements. Setting appropriate termination criteria is essential to strike a balance between obtaining an optimal solution and avoiding excessive computational expenses.

Analysis of the Final Solution Using Post-Processing

The sensitivity analysis can be performed during post-processing to assess the robustness of the obtained solutions under different scenarios and uncertainties. This helps in identifying potential weaknesses and improving the overall reliability of the power system. Moreover, the post-processing phase may involve incorporating additional information or adjusting parameters based on real-time data, ensuring that the solutions remain adaptable to dynamic changes in the power system environment. The post-processing may focus on refining the economic dispatch solutions obtained from the genetic algorithm. This involves optimizing the scheduling of power generation units, considering factors like fuel costs, environmental constraints, and demand variations. The post-processing step may also include the integration of demand response strategies or renewable energy sources to further enhance the cost-effectiveness of the power system operation.

Validation and Testing Analysis

Validation is a crucial step that involves assessing the performance of the genetic algorithm against known benchmarks or historical data. In the context of operational cost savings, the validation process aims to verify whether the algorithm produces results that align with established best practices or reference scenarios. This often involves comparing the outcomes generated by the genetic algorithm with real-world data or simulations based on conventional planning methods. Rigorous validation ensures that the algorithm accurately represents the complexities of the power system and effectively addresses the objectives of minimizing operational costs. Testing analysis, on the other hand, focuses on evaluating the robustness and adaptability of the genetic algorithm under various scenarios and conditions. Power systems are inherently dynamic, subject to fluctuations in demand, supply, and unforeseen events. The testing phase involves subjecting the algorithm to a diverse set of scenarios, including different load profiles, generation patterns, and potential disturbances. This process helps assess the algorithm's ability to deliver consistently optimal solutions and its resilience in the face of uncertainties.

Table 1. Deployment phase

Deployment Phase	Monitoring Parameters	Optimization Strategies
Real-world employment	Energy generation and allocation accuracy	Periodic model rehabilitation
Performance tracing	Prediction of errors and cost saving factors	Adjusting GA parameters in power system
Maintenance	Sensor accuracy and reliability	Fine-tune DL models
User Feedback	User satisfaction	Incorporate user feedback

Table 1 represents the deployment aspects with various monitoring parameters. The genetic algorithm's performance may be analyzed in terms of convergence speed, solution quality, and computational efficiency. Convergence speed refers to how quickly the algorithm reaches an optimal solution, while solution quality assesses the effectiveness of the obtained solutions in minimizing operational costs. Computational efficiency is crucial, particularly in large-scale power systems, where the algorithm must handle complex optimization problems within acceptable time frames.

COMPARATIVE ANALYSIS

The performance analysis of the proposed system is done using Matlab Simulink through considering various parameters such as accuracy, recall and precision. The proposed system is compared with the existing system for assessment of the performance analysis through certain metrics as shown in Figure 3.

Figure 3. Comparative analysis

The comparative analysis shows that the proposed system results in higher performance metrics resulting in planning and operation in the power system.

CONCLUSION

In conclusion, the pursuit of enhancing operational cost savings in electric utilities through global optimization in power system planning and operation represents a critical and transformative approach in the contemporary energy landscape. The increasing complexity and interconnectedness of power systems on a global scale necessitate sophisticated optimization strategies to maximize efficiency and minimize operational costs. By adopting advanced global optimization techniques, electric utilities can achieve a more streamlined and resilient power infrastructure that not only meets the growing electricity demand but also does so sustainably and cost-effectively. The implementation of global optimization techniques empowers electric utilities to make informed decisions based on real-time data, predictive analytics, and scenario analysis. This enhances their ability to anticipate and respond to fluctuations in demand, supply, and market conditions. The optimization process considers various factors, including fuel costs, environmental regulations, and technological advancements, ensuring that the power system remains resilient and adaptable to changing circumstances. As a result, electric utilities can achieve a more agile and responsive operational framework, reducing the risk of disruptions and ensuring reliable energy delivery. The integration of global optimization in power system planning enables utilities to holistically assess and optimize the entire energy value chain. This includes optimizing the generation mix, transmission and distribution infrastructure and demand-side management strategies. Such comprehensive optimization not only results in immediate cost savings but also contributes to long-term sustainability by reducing environmental impacts and promoting the integration of renewable energy sources. The dynamic nature of power systems, coupled with the increasing penetration of renewable energy, demands a proactive and adaptive approach to planning and operation, which global optimization facilitates. the financial implications of operational cost savings are substantial. Electric utilities, by optimizing their operations globally, can allocate resources efficiently, leading to reduced capital and operational expenses. The savings generated can then be reinvested in infrastructure upgrades, research and development, and the implementation of innovative technologies. This not only bolsters the economic viability of the utilities but also fosters a culture of continuous improvement and innovation within the industry.

REFERENCES

Anita, S., Rodrigues, P., Nagabhooshanam, N., Londhe, G. V., Salunkhe, S. S., Kumar, P. D., L, N., & Bhima Raju, P. S. D. (2024, February 06). L, N., & Bhima Raju, P. S. D. (2024). Energy Trading and Optimum Scheduling for Microgrids Using Multiple Agents Based DL Approach. *Electric Power Components and Systems*, 1–19. 10.1080/15325008.2023.2300329

Anjankar, P., Lakade, S., Padalkar, A., Nichal, S., Devarajan, Y., Lakshmaiya, N., & Subbaiyan, N. (2023). Experimental investigation on the effect of liquid phase and vapor phase separation over performance of falling film evaporator. *Environmental Quality Management*, 33(1), 61–69. 10.1002/tqem.21952

Arul Arumugam, R., Usha Rani, B., Komala, C. R., Barthwal, S., Kaliappan, S., & Natrayan, L. (2023). Design and Development of the Optical Antenna for Wireless Communications. *7th International Conference on Electronics, Communication and Aerospace Technology, ICECA 2023 - Proceedings*. IEEE. 10.1109/ICECA58529.2023.10395356

Balaji, N., Natrayan, L., Kaliappan, S., Patil, P. P., & Sivakumar, N. S. (2022). Annealed peanut shell biochar as potential reinforcement for aloe vera fiber-epoxy biocomposite: Mechanical, thermal conductivity, and dielectric properties. *Biomass Conversion and Biorefinery*. 10.1007/s13399-022-02650-7

Balamurugan, P., Agarwal, P., Khajuria, D., Mahapatra, D., Angalaeswari, S., Natrayan, L., & Mammo, W. D. (2023). State-Flow Control Based Multistage Constant-Current Battery Charger for Electric Two-Wheeler. *Journal of Advanced Transportation*, 2023, 1–11. 10.1155/2023/4554582

Biradar, V. S., Al-Jiboory, A. K., Sahu, G., Tilak Babu, S. B. G., Mahender, K., & Natrayan, L. (2023). Intelligent Control Systems for Industrial Automation and Robotics. *2023 10th IEEE Uttar Pradesh Section International Conference on Electrical, Electronics and Computer Engineering, UPCON 2023*. IEEE. 10.1109/UPCON59197.2023.10434927

Chehelgerdi, M., Chehelgerdi, M., Allela, O. Q. B., Pecho, R. D. C., Jayasankar, N., Rao, D. P., Thamaraikani, T., Vasanthan, M., Viktor, P., Lakshmaiya, N., Saadh, M. J., Amajd, A., Abo-Zaid, M. A., Castillo-Acobo, R. Y., Ismail, A. H., Amin, A. H., & Akhavan-Sigari, R. (2023a). Progressing nanotechnology to improve targeted cancer treatment: Overcoming hurdles in its clinical implementation. *Molecular Cancer*, 22(1), 169. 10.1186/s12943-023-01865-037814270

Chehelgerdi, M., Chehelgerdi, M., Allela, O. Q. B., Pecho, R. D. C., Jayasankar, N., Rao, D. P., Thamaraikani, T., Vasanthan, M., Viktor, P., Lakshmaiya, N., Saadh, M. J., Amajd, A., Abo-Zaid, M. A., Castillo-Acobo, R. Y., Ismail, A. H., Amin, A. H., & Akhavan-Sigari, R. (2023b). Progressing nanotechnology to improve targeted cancer treatment: Overcoming hurdles in its clinical implementation. *Molecular Cancer*, 22(1), 169. 10.1186/s12943-023-01865-037814270

Chennai Viswanathan, P., Venkatesh, S. N., Dhanasekaran, S., Mahanta, T. K., Sugumaran, V., Lakshmaiya, N., Paramasivam, P., & Nanjagoundenpalayam Ramasamy, S. (2023). Deep Learning for Enhanced Fault Diagnosis of Monoblock Centrifugal Pumps: Spectrogram-Based Analysis. *Machines*, 11(9), 874. 10.3390/machines11090874

Chinta, N. D., Karthikeyan, K. R., Natrayan, L., & Kaliappan, S. (2023). Pressure Induced Variations in Mode II Behaviour of Uni-Directional Kenaf Reinforced Polymers. *International Journal of Vehicle Structures and Systems*, 15(7). 10.4273/ijvss.15.7.19

Hemalatha, K., James, C., Natrayan, L., & Swamynadh, V. (2020). Analysis of RCC T-beam and prestressed concrete box girder bridges super structure under different span conditions. *Materials Today: Proceedings*, 37(Part 2), 1507–1516. 10.1016/j.matpr.2020.07.119

Josphineleela, R., Kaliapp, S., Natrayan, L., & Garg, A. (2023). Big Data Security through Privacy - Preserving Data Mining (PPDM): A Decentralization Approach. *Proceedings of the 2023 2nd International Conference on Electronics and Renewable Systems, ICEARS 2023*. IEEE. 10.1109/ICEARS56392.2023.10085646

Josphineleela, R., Lekha, D., Natrayan, L., & Purohit, K. C. (2023). Biometric Aided Intelligent Security System Built using Internet of Things. *Proceedings of the 2023 2nd International Conference on Electronics and Renewable Systems, ICEARS 2023*. IEEE. 10.1109/ICEARS56392.2023.10085572

Kaliappan, S., Mothilal, T., Natrayan, L., Pravin, P., & Olkeba, T. T. (2023). Mechanical Characterization of Friction-Stir-Welded Aluminum AA7010 Alloy with TiC Nanofiber. *Advances in Materials Science and Engineering*, 2023, 1–7. 10.1155/2023/1466963

Kaliappan, S., & Natrayan, L. (2024a). Enhancement of Mechanical and Thermal Characteristics of Automobile Parts using Flax/Epoxy-Graphene Nanofiller Composites. *SAE Technical Papers*. 10.4271/2023-01-5116

Kaliappan, S., & Natrayan, L. (2024b). Impact of Kenaf Fiber and Inorganic Nano-fillers on Mechanical Properties of Epoxy-Based Nanocomposites for Sustainable Automotive Applications. *SAE Technical Papers*. 10.4271/2023-01-5115

Kaliappan, S., & Natrayan, L. (2024c). Polypropylene Composite Materials with Natural Fiber Reinforcement: An Acoustic and Mechanical Analysis for Automotive Implementations. *SAE Technical Papers*. 10.4271/2023-01-5130

Kaliappan, S., & Natrayan, L. (2024d). Revolutionizing Automotive Materials through Enhanced Mechanical Properties of Epoxy Hybrid Bio-Composites with Hemp, Kenaf, and Coconut Powder. *SAE Technical Papers*. 10.4271/2023-01-5185

Kaliappan, S., Natrayan, L., & Garg, N. (2023). Checking and Supervisory System for Calculation of Industrial Constraints using Embedded System. *Proceedings of the 4th International Conference on Smart Electronics and Communication, ICOSEC 2023*. IEEE. 10.1109/ICOSEC58147.2023.10275952

Kaliappan, S., Natrayan, L., Mohammed Ali, H., & Kumar, P. (2024). Thermal and Mechanical Properties of Abutilon indicum Fiber-Based Polyester Composites under Alkali Treatment for Automotive Sector. *SAE Technical Papers*. 10.4271/2024-01-5031

Kaliappan, S., Natrayan, L., & Rajput, A. (2023). Sentiment Analysis of News Headlines Based on Sentiment Lexicon and Deep Learning. *Proceedings of the 4th International Conference on Smart Electronics and Communication, ICOSEC 2023*. IEEE. 10.1109/ICOSEC58147.2023.10276102

Kaliappan, S., Paranthaman, V., Natrayan, L., Kumar, B. V., & Muthukannan, M. (2024). Leveraging Machine Learning Algorithm for Predicting Personality Traits on Twitter. *Proceedings of the 14th International Conference on Cloud Computing, Data Science and Engineering, Confluence 2024*. 10.1109/Confluence60223.2024.10463468

Kanimozhi, G., Natrayan, L., Angalaeswari, S., & Paramasivam, P. (2022). An Effective Charger for Plug-In Hybrid Electric Vehicles (PHEV) with an Enhanced PFC Rectifier and ZVS-ZCS DC/DC High-Frequency Converter. *Journal of Advanced Transportation*, 2022, 1–14. 10.1155/2022/7840102

Karthick, M., Meikandan, M., Kaliappan, S., Karthick, M., Sekar, S., Patil, P. P., Raja, S., Natrayan, L., & Paramasivam, P. (2022). Experimental Investigation on Mechanical Properties of Glass Fiber Hybridized Natural Fiber Reinforced Penta-Layered Hybrid Polymer Composite. *International Journal of Chemical Engineering*, 2022, 1–9. 10.1155/2022/1864446

Kaushal, R. K., Arvind, R., Giri, K. K. B., Sindhu, M., Natrayan, L., & Ronald, B. (2023). Deep Learning Based Segmentation Approach for Automatic Lane Detection in Autonomous Vehicle. *International Conference on Self Sustainable Artificial Intelligence Systems, ICSSAS 2023 - Proceedings*. IEEE. 10.1109/ICS-SAS57918.2023.10331835

Kiruba Sandou, D., Sunad Kumara, A. N., Choudhary, B. K., & Gurpur, S., Sar-ishma, Natrayan, L., & Sivaramkumar, M. (2023). Design and Implementation of Neuro-Fuzzy Control Approach for Robot's Trajectory Tracking. *7th International Conference on Electronics, Communication and Aerospace Technology, ICECA 2023 - Proceedings*. IEEE. 10.1109/ICECA58529.2023.10395675

Konduri, S., Walke, S., Kumar, A., Pavithra, G., Bhagirath Jadhav, A., & Natrayan, L. (2023). Reinforcement Learning for Multi-Robot Coordination and Cooperation in Manufacturing. *2023 10th IEEE Uttar Pradesh Section International Conference on Electrical, Electronics and Computer Engineering, UPCON 2023*. IEEE. 10.1109/UPCON59197.2023.10434651

Kumar, J. V. S. P., Kaliappan, S., Natrayan, L., Raturi, A., Seikh, A. H., Iqbal, A., & Mohanavel, V. (2024). Isolation of biosilica from biomass waste Setaria italica husks and its reinforcement effect on banana fiber-epoxy composite. *Biomass Conversion and Biorefinery*. 10.1007/s13399-024-05334-6

Lakshmaiya, N. (2023b). Experimental analysis on heat transfer cube shape of two vertical surfaces during melting condition. *Proceedings of SPIE- The International Society for Optical Engineering, 12616*. SPIE. doi:10.1117/12.267555210.1117/12.2675552

Lakshmaiya, N. (2023c). Experimental analysis on heat transfer cube shape of two vertical surfaces during melting condition. *Proceedings of SPIE- The International Society for Optical Engineering, 12616*. SPIE. doi:10.1117/12.267555210.1117/12.2675552

Lakshmaiya, N. (2023d). Experimental investigation on computational volumetric heat in real time neural pathways. *Proceedings of SPIE- The International Society for Optical Engineering, 12616*. SPIE. doi:10.1117/12.267555510.1117/12.2675555

Lakshmaiya, N. (2023e). Investigation on ultraviolet radiation of flow pattern and particles transportation in vanishing raindrops. *Proceedings of SPIE- The International Society for Optical Engineering, 12616*. SPIE. doi:10.1117/12.267555610.1117/12.2675556

Lakshmaiya, N. (2023f). Mechanical evaluation of coir/kenaf/jute laminated hybrid composites designed for geotechnical uses. *Proceedings of SPIE- The International Society for Optical Engineering, 12936.* SPIE. doi:10.1117/12.301171010.1117/12.3011710

Lakshmaiya, N. (2023g). Organic material nuts flour greens laminate preparation and mechanical characteristics of natural materials. *Proceedings of SPIE- The International Society for Optical Engineering, 12936.* SPIE. doi:10.1117/12.3011712 10.1117/12.3011712

Lakshmaiya, N. (2023h). Polylactic acid/hydroxyapatite/yttria-stabilized zircon synthetic nanocomposite scaffolding compression and flexural characteristics. *Proceedings of SPIE- The International Society for Optical Engineering, 12936.* SPIE. doi:10.1117/12.301171510.1117/12.3011715

Lakshmaiya, N. (2023i). Preparation and evaluation of bamboo laminated cannabis paper physico - mechanical characteristics. *Proceedings of SPIE- The International Society for Optical Engineering, 12936.* SPIE. doi:10.1117/12.301171610.1117/12.3011716

Lakshmaiya, N. (2023j). Simulating laminar induced heat capacity and heat transmission convection using Al2O3 nanofluid. *Proceedings of SPIE- The International Society for Optical Engineering, 12616.* SPIE. doi:10.1117/12.267555710.1117/12.2675557

Lakshmaiya, N., Kaliappan, S., Patil, P. P., Ganesan, V., Dhanraj, J. A., Sirisamphanwong, C., Wongwuttanasatian, T., Chowdhury, S., Channumsin, S., Channumsin, M., & Techato, K. (2022). Influence of Oil Palm Nano Filler on Interlaminar Shear and Dynamic Mechanical Properties of Flax/Epoxy-Based Hybrid Nanocomposites under Cryogenic Condition. *Coatings*, 12(11), 1675. 10.3390/coatings12111675

Loganathan, A. S., Ramachandran, V., Perumal, A. S., Dhanasekaran, S., Lakshmaiya, N., & Paramasivam, P. (2023). Framework of Transactive Energy Market Strategies for Lucrative Peer-to-Peer Energy Transactions. *Energies*, 16(1), 6. 10.3390/en16010006

Mahat, D., Niranjan, K., Naidu, C. S. K. V. R., Babu, S. B. G. T., Kumar, M. S., & Natrayan, L. (2023). AI-Driven Optimization of Supply Chain and Logistics in Mechanical Engineering. *2023 10th IEEE Uttar Pradesh Section International Conference on Electrical, Electronics and Computer Engineering, UPCON 2023.* IEEE. 10.1109/UPCON59197.2023.10434905

Malladi, A., Kaliappan, S., Natrayan, L., & Mahesh, V. (2024). Effectiveness of Thermal and Mechanical Properties of Jute Fibers under Different Chemical Treatment for Automotive Interior Trim. *SAE Technical Papers*. 10.4271/2024-01-5008

Mehta, A. K., Lanjewar, P., Murthy, D. S., Ghildiyal, P., Faldu, R., & Natrayan, L. (2023). AI & Lean Management Principles Based Pharmaceutical Manufacturing Processes. *2023 10th IEEE Uttar Pradesh Section International Conference on Electrical, Electronics and Computer Engineering, UPCON 2023*. IEEE. 10.1109/UPCON59197.2023.10434834

Muthiya, S. J., Natrayan, L., Kaliappan, S., Patil, P. P., Naveena, B. E., Dhanraj, J. A., Subramaniam, M., & Paramasivam, P. (2022). Experimental investigation to utilize adsorption and absorption technique to reduce CO_2 emissions in diesel engine exhaust using amine solutions. *Adsorption Science and Technology*, 2022, 9621423. 10.1155/2022/9621423

Muthiya, S. J., Natrayan, L., Yuvaraj, L., Subramaniam, M., Dhanraj, J. A., & Mammo, W. D. (2022). Development of Active CO_2 Emission Control for Diesel Engine Exhaust Using Amine-Based Adsorption and Absorption Technique. *Adsorption Science and Technology*, 2022, 8803585. 10.1155/2022/8803585

Nadh, V. S., Krishna, C., Natrayan, L., Kumar, K., Nitesh, K. J. N. S., Raja, G. B., & Paramasivam, P. (2021). Structural Behavior of Nanocoated Oil Palm Shell as Coarse Aggregate in Lightweight Concrete. *Journal of Nanomaterials*, 2021, 1–7. 10.1155/2021/4741296

Natrayan, L. (2023). Humidity Impact on the Material Characteristics of a Sisal Laminate: The Role of the Rapid Vibrational Method. *International Journal of Vehicle Structures and Systems*, 15(7). 10.4273/ijvss.15.7.17

Natrayan, L., Ameen, F., Chinta, N. D., Teja, N. B., Muthu, G., Kaliappan, S., Ali, S., & Vadiveloo, A. (2024). Antibacterial and dynamical behaviour of silicon nanoparticles influenced sustainable waste flax fibre-reinforced epoxy composite for biomedical application. *Green Processing and Synthesis*, 13(1), 20230214. 10.1515/gps-2023-0214

Natrayan, L., Ashok, S. K., Kaliappan, S., & Kumar, P. (2024). Effect of Stacking Sequence on Mechanical Properties of Bamboo/Bagasse Composite Fiber for Automobile Seat Cushions and Upholstery Application. *SAE Technical Papers*. 10.4271/2024-01-5013

Natrayan, L., Chinta, N. D., Gogulamudi, B., Nadh, V. S., Muthu, G., Kaliappan, S., & Srinivas, C. (2024). Investigation on mechanical properties of the green synthesis bamboo fiber/eggshell/coconut shell powder-based hybrid biocomposites under NaOH conditions. *Green Processing and Synthesis*, 13(1), 20230185. 10.1515/gps-2023-0185

Natrayan, L., Chinta, N. D., Teja, N. B., Muthu, G., Kaliappan, S., Kirubanandan, S., & Paramasivam, P. (2024). Evaluating mechanical, thermal, and water absorption properties of biocomposites with Opuntia cladode fiber and palm flower biochar for industrial applications. *Discover Applied Sciences*, 6(2), 30. 10.1007/s42452-024-05660-4

Natrayan, L., & De Poures, M. V. (2023a). Experimental investigations of heat ageing with chemical modification of hemp fiber elastic characteristics. *Proceedings of SPIE- The International Society for Optical Engineering, 12936*. SPIE. 10.1117/12.3011708

Natrayan, L., & De Poures, M. V. (2023b). Influence of gasoline on high speed evaporation gasoline sprays: a large-eddy model of sprayer a with different fuels. *Proceedings of SPIE- The International Society for Optical Engineering, 12936*. SPIE. 10.1117/12.3011709

Natrayan, L., Janardhan, G., Nadh, V. S., Srinivas, C., Kaliappan, S., & Velmurugan, G. (2024). Eco-friendly zinc oxide nanoparticles from Moringa oleifera leaf extract for photocatalytic and antibacterial applications. *Clean Technologies and Environmental Policy*. 10.1007/s10098-024-02814-1

Natrayan, L., & Kaliappan, S. (2023). Mechanical Assessment of Carbon-Luffa Hybrid Composites for Automotive Applications. *SAE Technical Papers*. 10.4271/2023-01-5070

Natrayan, L., Kaliappan, S., Balaji, N., & Mahesh, V. (2024). Dynamic Mechanical and Thermal Properties of Polymer-Coated Jute Fibers for Enhanced Automotive Parts. *SAE Technical Papers*. 10.4271/2024-01-5019

Natrayan, L., Kaliappan, S., & Pundir, S. (2023). Control and Monitoring of a Quadcopter in Border Areas Using Embedded System. *Proceedings of the 4th International Conference on Smart Electronics and Communication, ICOSEC 2023*. IEEE. 10.1109/ICOSEC58147.2023.10276196

Natrayan, L., Kaliappan, S., Saravanan, A., Vickram, A. S., Pravin, P., Abbas, M., Ahamed Saleel, C., Alwetaishi, M., & Saleem, M. S. M. (2023). Recyclability and catalytic characteristics of copper oxide nanoparticles derived from bougainvillea plant flower extract for biomedical application. *Green Processing and Synthesis*, 12(1), 20230030. 10.1515/gps-2023-0030

Natrayan, L., & Kumar, M. S. (2019). Influence of silicon carbide on tribological behaviour of AA2024/Al2O3/SiC/Gr hybrid metal matrix squeeze cast composite using Taguchi technique. *Materials Research Express*, 6(12), 1265f9. 10.1088/2053-1591/ab676d

Natrayan, L., & Kumar, M. S. (2020). Optimization of wear behaviour on AA6061/Al2O3/SiC metal matrix composite using squeeze casting technique-Statistical analysis. *Materials Today: Proceedings*, 27, 306–310. 10.1016/j.matpr.2019.11.038

Natrayan, L., & Merneedi, A. (2020). Experimental investigation on wear behaviour of bio-waste reinforced fusion fiber composite laminate under various conditions. *Materials Today: Proceedings*, 37(Part 2), 1486–1490. 10.1016/j.matpr.2020.07.108

Natrayan, L., Merneedi, A., Veeman, D., Kaliappan, S., Raju, P. S., Subbiah, R., & Kumar, S. V. (2021). Evaluating the Mechanical and Tribological Properties of DLC Nanocoated Aluminium 5051 Using RF Sputtering. *Journal of Nanomaterials*, 2021, 1–7. 10.1155/2021/8428822

Natrayan, L., & Richard, T. (2023a). Experimental investigations of bagasse ash strands featuring variable surface influence on polypropylene based polymer composites. *Proceedings of SPIE- The International Society for Optical Engineering, 12936*. SPIE.10.1117/12.3011691

Natrayan, L., & Richard, T. (2023b). Organo modified nanocomposites terephthalic acid polymers temperature and microstructural characteristics. *Proceedings of SPIE- The International Society for Optical Engineering, 12936*. SPIE. 10.1117/12.3011863

Natrayan, L., Sakthi Shunmuga Sundaram, P., & Elumalai, J. (2019). Analyzing the uterine physiological with mmg signals using svm. *International Journal of Pharmaceutical Research*, 11(2). 10.31838/ijpr/2019.11.02.009

Natrayan, L., Senthil Kumar, M., & Chaudhari, M. (2020). Optimization of squeeze casting process parameters to investigate the mechanical properties of AA6061/Al 2 O 3/SiC hybrid metal matrix composites by Taguchi and Anova approach. In *Advances in Intelligent Systems and Computing (Vol. 949)*. Springer. 10.1007/978-981-13-8196-6_35

Natrayan, L., Senthil Kumar, M., & Palanikumar, K. (2018). Optimization of squeeze cast process parameters on mechanical properties of Al2O3/SiC reinforced hybrid metal matrix composites using taguchi technique. *Materials Research Express*, 5(6), 066516. 10.1088/2053-1591/aac873

Natrayan, L., Sivaprakash, V., & Santhosh, M. S. (2018). Mechanical, microstructure and wear behavior of the material aa6061 reinforced sic with different leaf ashes using advanced stir casting method. *International Journal of Engineering and Advanced Technology*, 8.

Niveditha, V. R., & Rajakumar, P. S. (2020). Pervasive computing in the context of COVID-19 prediction with AI-based algorithms. *International Journal of Pervasive Computing and Communications*, 16(5). 10.1108/IJPCC-07-2020-0082

Palaniyappan, S., Veeman, D., Sivakumar, N. K., & Natrayan, L. (2022). Development and optimization of lattice structure on the walnut shell reinforced PLA composite for the tensile strength and dimensional error properties. *Structures*, 45, 163–178. 10.1016/j.istruc.2022.09.023

Pandian, A., Kaliappan, S., Natrayan, L., & Reddy, V. (2024). Analyzing the Moisture and Chemical Retention Behavior of Flax Fiber-Ceramic Hybrid Composites for Automotive Underbody Shields. *SAE Technical Papers*. 10.4271/2024-01-5006

Ponnusamy, M., Natrayan, L., Kaliappan, S., Velmurugan, G., & Thanappan, S. (2022). Effectiveness of Nanosilica on Enhancing the Mechanical and Microstructure Properties of Kenaf/Carbon Fiber-Reinforced Epoxy-Based Nanocomposites. *Adsorption Science and Technology*, 2022, 4268314. 10.1155/2022/4268314

Prabagar, S., Al-Jiboory, A. K., Nair, P. S., Mandal, P., Garse, K. M., & Natrayan, L. (2023). Artificial Intelligence-Based Control Strategies for Unmanned Aerial Vehicles. *2023 10th IEEE Uttar Pradesh Section International Conference on Electrical, Electronics and Computer Engineering, UPCON 2023*. IEEE. 10.1109/UPCON59197.2023.10434918

Pragadish, N., Kaliappan, S., Subramanian, M., Natrayan, L., Satish Prakash, K., Subbiah, R., & Kumar, T. C. A. (2023). Optimization of cardanol oil dielectric-activated EDM process parameters in machining of silicon steel. *Biomass Conversion and Biorefinery*, 13(15), 14087–14096. 10.1007/s13399-021-02268-1

Ragumadhavan, R., Sateesh Kumar, D., Charyulu Rompicharla, L. N., Dhondiya, S. A., Kaliappan, S., & Natrayan, L. (2023). Design and Development of Light Communication Systems Using Modulation Techniques. *7th International Conference on Electronics, Communication and Aerospace Technology, ICECA 2023 - Proceedings*. IEEE. 10.1109/ICECA58529.2023.10395831

Rajasekaran, S., & Natrayan, L. (2023a). Estimation of corrective and preventive action on trend end plug-based machining activities using manual and failure mode with effects analysis. *Proceedings of SPIE- The International Society for Optical Engineering, 12936.* SPIE. 10.1117/12.3011698

Rajasekaran, S., & Natrayan, L. (2023b). Evaluation of occurrence number and communication based on FMEA operations in product development. *Proceedings of SPIE- The International Society for Optical Engineering, 12936.* 10.1117/12.3011702

Ramaswamy, R., Kaliappan, S., Natrayan, L., & Patil, P. P. (2022). Pear cactus fiber with onion sheath biocarbon nanosheet toughened epoxy composite: Mechanical, thermal, and electrical properties. *Biomass Conversion and Biorefinery.* 10.1007/s13399-022-03335-x

Ramesh, C., Vijayakumar, M., Alshahrani, S., Navaneethakrishnan, G., Palanisamy, R., Natrayan, L., Saleel, C. A., Afzal, A., Shaik, S., & Panchal, H. (2022). Performance enhancement of selective layer coated on solar absorber panel with reflector for water heater by response surface method: A case study. *Case Studies in Thermal Engineering*, 36, 102093. 10.1016/j.csite.2022.102093

Reddy, P. N., Umaeswari, P., Natrayan, L., & Choudhary, A. (2023). Development of Programmed Autonomous Electric Heavy Vehicle: An Application of IoT. *Proceedings of the 2023 2nd International Conference on Electronics and Renewable Systems, ICEARS 2023.* IEEE. 10.1109/ICEARS56392.2023.10085492

Saadh, M. J., Almoyad, M. A. A., Arellano, M. T. C., Maaliw, R. R. III, Castillo-Acobo, R. Y., Jalal, S. S., Gandla, K., Obaid, M., Abdulwahed, A. J., Ibrahem, A. A., Sârbu, I., Juyal, A., Lakshmaiya, N., & Akhavan-Sigari, R. (2023). Long non-coding RNAs: Controversial roles in drug resistance of solid tumors mediated by autophagy. *Cancer Chemotherapy and Pharmacology*, 92(6), 439–453. 10.1007/s00280-023-04582-z37768333

Sai, S. A., Venkatesh, S. N., Dhanasekaran, S., Balaji, P. A., Sugumaran, V., Lakshmaiya, N., & Paramasivam, P. (2023). Transfer Learning Based Fault Detection for Suspension System Using Vibrational Analysis and Radar Plots. *Machines*, 11(8), 778. 10.3390/machines11080778

Sasi, J. P., Nidhi Pandagre, K., Royappa, A., Walke, S., Pavithra, G., & Natrayan, L. (2023). Deep Learning Techniques for Autonomous Navigation of Underwater Robots. *2023 10th IEEE Uttar Pradesh Section International Conference on Electrical, Electronics and Computer Engineering, UPCON 2023.* IEEE. 10.1109/UPCON59197.2023.10434865

Sathish, T., Natrayan, L., Prasad Jones Christydass, S., Sivananthan, S., Kamalakannan, R., Vijayan, V., & Paramasivam, P. (2022). Experimental Investigation on Tribological Behaviour of AA6066: HSS-Cu Hybrid Composite in Dry Sliding Condition. *Advances in Materials Science and Engineering*, 2022, 1–9. 10.1155/2022/9349847

Sathish, T., Palani, K., Natrayan, L., Merneedi, A., de Poures, M. V., & Singaravelu, D. K. (2021). Synthesis and characterization of polypropylene/ramie fiber with hemp fiber and coir fiber natural biopolymer composite for biomedical application. *International Journal of Polymer Science*, 2021, 1–8. 10.1155/2021/2462873

Selvi, S., Mohanraj, M., Duraipandy, P., Kaliappan, S., Natrayan, L., & Vinayagam, N. (2023). Optimization of Solar Panel Orientation for Maximum Energy Efficiency. *Proceedings of the 4th International Conference on Smart Electronics and Communication, ICOSEC 2023*. IEEE. 10.1109/ICOSEC58147.2023.10276287

Sendrayaperumal, A., Mahapatra, S., Parida, S. S., Surana, K., Balamurugan, P., Natrayan, L., & Paramasivam, P. (2021). Energy Auditing for Efficient Planning and Implementation in Commercial and Residential Buildings. *Advances in Civil Engineering*, 2021, 1–10. 10.1155/2021/1908568

Siddiqui, E., Siddique, M., Safeer Pasha, M., Boyapati, P., Pavithra, G., & Natrayan, L. (2023). AI and ML for Enhancing Crop Yield and Resource Efficiency in Agriculture. *2023 10th IEEE Uttar Pradesh Section International Conference on Electrical, Electronics and Computer Engineering, UPCON 2023*. IEEE. 10.1109/UPCON59197.2023.10434493

Singh, M. (2017). An experimental investigation on mechanical behaviour of siCp reinforced Al 6061 MMC using squeeze casting process. *International Journal of Mechanical and Production Engineering Research and Development*, 7(6). 10.24247/ijmperddec201774

Singh, P., Mahor, V., Lakshmaiya, N., Shanker, K., Kaliappan, S., Muthukannan, M., & Rajendran, G. (2024). Prediction of Groundwater Contamination in an Open Landfill Area Using a Novel Hybrid Clustering Based AI Model. *Environment Protection Engineering*, 50(1). 10.37190/epe240106

Sukumaran, C., Indhumathi, K., Balamurugan, P., Ambilwade, R. P., Sunthari, P. M., & Natrayan, L. (2023). The Role of AI in Biochips for Early Disease Detection. *Proceedings - International Conference on Technological Advancements in Computational Sciences, ICTACS 2023*. 10.1109/ICTACS59847.2023.10390419

Suman, T., Kaliappan, S., Natrayan, L., & Dobhal, D. C. (2023). IoT based Social Device Network with Cloud Computing Architecture. *Proceedings of the 2023 2nd International Conference on Electronics and Renewable Systems, ICEARS 2023*. IEEE. 10.1109/ICEARS56392.2023.10085574

Sureshkumar, P., Jagadeesha, T., Natrayan, L., Ravichandran, M., Veeman, D., & Muthu, S. M. (2022). Electrochemical corrosion and tribological behaviour of AA6063/Si_3N_4/Cu(NO_3)$_2$ composite processed using single-pass ECAP$_A$ route with 120° die angle. *Journal of Materials Research and Technology*, 16. 10.1016/j.jmrt.2021.12.020

Thakre, S., Pandhare, A., Malwe, P. D., Gupta, N., Kothare, C., Magade, P. B., Patel, A., Meena, R. S., Veza, I., Natrayan, L., & Panchal, H. (2023). Heat transfer and pressure drop analysis of a microchannel heat sink using nanofluids for energy applications. *Kerntechnik*, 88(5), 543–555. 10.1515/kern-2023-0034

Ugle, V. V., Arulprakasajothi, M., Padmanabhan, S., Devarajan, Y., Lakshmaiya, N., & Subbaiyan, N. (2023). Investigation of heat transport characteristics of titanium dioxide nanofluids with corrugated tube. *Environmental Quality Management*, 33(2), 127–138. 10.1002/tqem.21999

Vaishali, K. R., Rammohan, S. R., Natrayan, L., Usha, D., & Niveditha, V. R. (2021). Guided container selection for data streaming through neural learning in cloud. *International Journal of Systems Assurance Engineering and Management*. 10.1007/s13198-021-01124-9

Velmurugan, G., & Natrayan, L. (2023). Experimental investigations of moisture diffusion and mechanical properties of interply rearrangement of glass/Kevlar-based hybrid composites under cryogenic environment. *Journal of Materials Research and Technology*, 23, 4513–4526. 10.1016/j.jmrt.2023.02.089

Velmurugan, G., Siva Shankar, V., Natrayan, L., Sekar, S., Patil, P. P., Kumar, M. S., & Thanappan, S. (2022). Multiresponse Optimization of Mechanical and Physical Adsorption Properties of Activated Natural Fibers Hybrid Composites. *Adsorption Science and Technology*, 2022, 1384738. 10.1155/2022/1384738

Velumayil, R., Gnanakumar, G., Natrayan, L., Chinta, N. D., & Kaliappan, S. (2023). Bifunctional Aluminum Oxide/Carbon Fiber/Epoxy Nanocomposites Preparation and Evaluation. *International Journal of Vehicle Structures and Systems*, 15(7). 10.4273/ijvss.15.7.18

Venkatesh, R., Manivannan, S., Kaliappan, S., Socrates, S., Sekar, S., Patil, P. P., Natrayan, L., & Bayu, M. B. (2022). Influence of Different Frequency Pulse on Weld Bead Phase Ratio in Gas Tungsten Arc Welding by Ferritic Stainless Steel AISI-409L. *Journal of Nanomaterials*, 2022, 1–11. 10.1155/2022/9530499

Vijayakumar, M., & Shreeraj Nair, P. G Tilak Babu, S. B., Mahender, K., Venkateswaran, T. S., & Natrayan, L. (2023). Intelligent Systems For Predictive Maintenance In Industrial IoT. *2023 10th IEEE Uttar Pradesh Section International Conference on Electrical, Electronics and Computer Engineering, UPCON 2023.* IEEE. 10.1109/UPCON59197.2023.10434814

Vijayakumar, M. D., Surendhar, G. J., Natrayan, L., Patil, P. P., Ram, P. M. B., & Paramasivam, P. (2022). Evolution and Recent Scenario of Nanotechnology in Agriculture and Food Industries. *Journal of Nanomaterials*, 2022, 1–17. 10.1155/2022/1280411

Yogeshwaran, S., Natrayan, L., Udhayakumar, G., Godwin, G., & Yuvaraj, L. (2020). Effect of waste tyre particles reinforcement on mechanical properties of jute and abaca fiber - Epoxy hybrid composites with pre-treatment. *Materials Today: Proceedings*, 37(Part 2), 1377–1380. 10.1016/j.matpr.2020.06.584

Chapter 17
Enhancing Photovoltaic System Performance Using PSO for Maximum Power Point Tracking and DC–Bus Voltage Regulation in Grid–Connected PV Systems

Socrates S.

Velammal Institute of Technology, Chennai, India

M. Saravanan

Hindustan Institute of Technology and Science, Padur, India

K. K. Manivannan

KCG College of Technology, Chennai, India

M. Shanmugapriya

KCG College of Technology, Karapakkam, India

A. Krishnakumari

Hindustan Institute of Technology and Science, Padur, India

M. D. Raj Kamal

Velammal Institute of Technology, Chennai, India

ABSTRACT

This research presents an integrated approach to enhance the performance of grid-connected photovoltaic (PV) systems by combining sensor-based orientation with

DOI: 10.4018/979-8-3693-3314-3.ch017

the practical swarm optimization (PSO) algorithm for maximum power point tracking (MPPT) and a proportional-integral (PI) controller for DC voltage regulation. Solar positioning and infrared sensors provide real-time data, guiding the dynamic movement of the solar panel. The PSO algorithm optimizes motor movements for efficient MPPT, ensuring the panel aligns with the optimal sun position throughout the day. Simultaneously, the PI controller regulates the DC bus voltage, contributing to system stability and grid compliance. Experimental results reveal increased power output, demonstrating the synergistic impact of the integrated system. This approach not only maximizes energy capture but also improves system reliability.

INTRODUCTION

Grid-connected photovoltaic (PV) systems are gaining popularity as a feasible and long-term alternative for generating clean energy (Pragadish et al., 2023). As the demand for renewable energy sources increases, it is critical to optimise the performance of grid-connected PV systems in order to maximise efficiency and production (Niveditha VR. & Rajakumar PS., 2020). In recent years, sensor-based orientation and intelligent control algorithms have emerged as viable approaches to improving system performance (Natrayan & Merneedi, 2020). The purpose of this literature review is to investigate and analyse existing research on the optimisation of grid-connected PV systems through sensor-based orientation and intelligent control algorithms (Natrayan, Senthil Kumar, et al., 2018; Natrayan, Sivaprakash, et al., 2018). Sensor-based orientation is crucial for increasing the energy capture of PV systems. Several sensors, including sun trackers and inclination sensors, have been used to precisely align the PV panels with the incident solar energy (Natrayan & Kumar, 2020; Sathish et al., 2021). Sensor-based orientation ensures that the panels receive optimal solar irradiance throughout the day by constantly tracking the sun's location and altering the panel orientation accordingly (Palaniyappan et al., 2022; Vaishali et al., 2021). This increases the overall energy generation of the system and maximises the use of the available solar resource (Chehelgerdi et al., 2023).

Furthermore, intelligent control solutions have demonstrated promising results in improving the operation and performance of grid-connected PV systems (Ramesh et al., 2022; Sathish et al., 2022; Sendrayaperumal et al., 2021). These strategies combine advanced control algorithms, machine learning techniques, and data-driven approaches. Intelligent control systems can use real-time data from sensors and other sources to dynamically modify system characteristics such as power output, voltage regulation, and reactive power control (Hemalatha et al., 2020; Sureshkumar et al., 2022; Venkatesh et al., 2022). This allows the PV system to perform at its full capability despite changing environmental conditions and load demands. Furthermore, intelligent control strategies can improve fault detection, diagnostics, and predictive maintenance, ensuring the system's dependability and lifetime (Kanimozhi et al., 2022; Karthick et al., 2022; Nadh et al., 2021).

Several studies have looked into the advantages and disadvantages of sensor-based orientation and intelligent control algorithms in grid-connected PV systems. Experimental studies have shown that sensor-based orientation has a favourable impact on energy yield, with much higher power output than fixed-tilt or manually adjusted systems (Natrayan, Balaji, et al., 2021; Velmurugan & Natrayan, 2023). Furthermore, simulation-based research have investigated the usefulness of intelligent control algorithms in optimising PV system performance, taking into account weather conditions, shading effects, and system dynamics (Lakshmaiya et al., 2022; Natrayan et al., 2019; Natrayan, Merneedi, et al., 2021; M. D. et al. Vijayakumar, 2022). Furthermore, economic analysis and feasibility studies have been undertaken to assess the cost-effectiveness and ROI of integrating sensor-based orientation and intelligent control algorithms in grid-connected PV systems (Natrayan & Kumar, 2019; Singh, 2017). These assessments take into account initial investment costs, energy savings, system reliability, and maintenance requirements (Natrayan et al., 2020). The findings show that the long-term benefits, such as higher energy output and enhanced system efficiency, surpass the initial expenditures, making these optimisation measures financially viable and appealing to PV system owners and operators (Reddy et al., 2023).

Despite the multiple benefits of sensor-based orientation and intelligent control systems, there remain obstacles and constraints to overcome (Loganathan et al., 2023). These include the complexities of control algorithms, the need for precise sensor measurements, potential system integration challenges, and the need for ongoing monitoring and maintenance (Josphineleela, Lekha, et al., 2023). Additionally, the scalability and application of these solutions to diverse PV system sizes, geographical locations, and environmental circumstances need to be researched further (Balamurugan et al., 2023; Josphineleela, Kaliapp, et al., 2023; Suman et al., 2023). Sensor-based orientation and intelligent control algorithms have tremendous potential for improving the performance of grid-connected PV systems (Kaliappan, Mothilal, Natrayan, et al., 2023; Kaushal et al., 2023; Lakshmaiya, 2023j). The combination of precise sensor-based orientation and adaptive control algorithms allows the system to adapt to changing conditions, maximise energy capture, and increase overall system efficiency (Lakshmaiya, 2023b; Natrayan, Kaliappan, & Pundir, 2023). However, additional research and development are needed to solve the issues of implementation, scalability, and economic feasibility (Lakshmaiya, 2023a, 2023d). Grid-connected PV systems can play a larger part in addressing the growing demand for renewable energy and contributing to a better future if these optimisation tactics are advanced (Natrayan & Richard, 2023b).

NEED FOR OPTIMISATION AND VOLTAGE REGULATION

Ensuring the proper orientation of solar panels is crucial in harvesting the most energy potential from photovoltaic (PV) systems (Chinta et al., 2023; Natrayan, 2023; Velumayil et al., 2023). Solar panels perform most effectively when directly facing sunshine, gathering the greatest possible solar energy (Lakshmaiya, 2023c; Saadh et al., 2023; Ugle et al., 2023). By applying sophisticated optimization methods, such as the Practical Swarm Optimization algorithm for Maximum Power Point Tracking (MPPT), the system dynamically changes the panel's orientation (Konduri et al., 2023; Mahat et al., 2023; Siddiqui et al., 2023). This adaptive technique examines real-time environmental factors, including sunshine intensity and direction, ensuring that the solar panel continually works around the Maximum Power Point (MPP) (Mehta et al., 2023; Prabagar et al., 2023; Sasi et al., 2023). The accuracy in panel orientation, assisted by advanced algorithms and sensor inputs, is vital for reaching peak energy production and increasing the overall efficiency of the PV system (Ragumadhavan et al., 2023).

The management of the DC-bus voltage is a vital component in the smooth integration of grid-connected PV systems. Fluctuations in DC voltage may impair the stability, efficiency, and power quality of the system (Arul Arumugam et al., 2023; Kiruba Sandou et al., 2023; Lakshmaiya, 2023h). The deployment of a Proportional-Integral (PI) controller is important for keeping the DC-bus voltage within a set range. This closed-loop control system continually checks the actual measured voltage and compares it with a reference voltage setpoint (Sukumaran et al., 2023). The PI controller dynamically changes the inverter's duty cycle, ensuring that the DC-bus voltage stays steady (Natrayan & Richard, 2023a). This stability is not only necessary for optimum inverter performance but also aligns with grid standards, minimising voltage-related difficulties and assuring the dependability of the total PV system (Lakshmaiya & Murugan, 2023a, 2023c, 2023e). By managing the DC-bus voltage, the system mitigates possible dangers, boosts power quality, and contributes to the long-term sustainability of grid-connected solar power plants (Rajasekaran & Natrayan, 2023a, 2023b). In essence, the optimization and exact orientation of solar panels, together with the management of DC-bus voltage, jointly contribute to the efficiency, reliability, and performance of grid-connected PV systems (Lakshmaiya, 2023i; Lakshmaiya & Murugan, 2023d; Natrayan & De Poures, 2023a). These techniques not only increase energy absorption but also link the system with industry norms, permitting a smooth integration of solar electricity into the larger electrical grid (Lakshmaiya & Murugan, 2023b; Selvi et al., 2023).

METHODOLOGY

In this research study, the performance of the photovoltaic (PV) system is enhanced by the combination of two separate methodologies. The first technique includes the employment of multiple sensors, including sun positioning sensors and infrared (IR) sensors. These sensors capture critical data relating to the solar panel's orientation, allowing the system to dynamically alter its placement for optimum energy production (Lakshmaiya, 2023e, 2023f, 2023g). The controller, functioning as the central intelligence hub, interprets information received from various sensors and orchestrates the exact orientation of the solar panel (Kaliappan, Natrayan, & Garg, 2023; Natrayan, Kaliappan, Saravanan, et al., 2023; Natrayan & Kaliappan, 2023). To effectuate this movement, two 12V DC motors, strategically positioned underneath the solar panel, are utilised to rotate and align the panel with the best solar position. The sensor-based technique is crucial in gathering real-time environmental factors such as sunlight intensity and direction. Solar positioning sensors offer information on the sun's azimuth and elevation angles, allowing the system to identify the sun's exact location in the sky (Biradar et al., 2023; Kaliappan, Natrayan, & Rajput, 2023; Natrayan & De Poures, 2023b). Additionally, IR sensors give significant data relating to temperature swings, allowing for modifications that maximise the panel's performance under diverse thermal circumstances (Chennai Viswanathan et al., 2023; Sai et al., 2023; M. Vijayakumar et al., 2023). The integration of these sensors produces a thorough feedback loop, giving the control system with the essential inputs for precise and dynamic solar panel placement (Thakre et al., 2023).

The rotation of the solar panel is done by the activation of two 12V DC motors. These motors are strategically positioned underneath the solar panel to provide the regulated movement necessary for maximum energy collection (Kaliappan et al., 2024; Kaliappan & Natrayan, 2024d). The exact location of the solar panel is a vital aspect in obtaining optimal power production. By integrating the rotating capabilities of the DC motors into the system design, the solar panel may be dynamically shifted to face the sun most efficiently throughout the day (Malladi et al., 2024; Natrayan, Ashok, et al., 2024; Pandian et al., 2024). This movement guarantees that the solar panel runs at or near the Maximum Power Point (MPP), enhancing total energy generation (Natrayan, Kaliappan, et al., 2024).

To further optimise the optimization process, the technique uses the Practical Swarm Optimization algorithm for Maximum Power Point Tracking (MPPT). This system employs swarm intelligence to dynamically change the operating point of the solar panel, ensuring that it constantly works at the MPP despite different environmental circumstances (Kaliappan & Natrayan, 2024c, 2024b, 2024a). The Practical Swarm Optimization method provides an intelligent and adaptable approach to monitoring the MPP, including elements like as shade, temperature variations, and changes in sun irradiation (Kaliappan, Velumayil, Natrayan, et al., 2023; Lakshmaiya et al., 2023; Sivakumar et al., 2023). By utilising the collective intelligence of the swarm, the programme repeatedly refines the direction of the solar panel for increased energy collection (Arockiasamy et al., 2023; Muralidaran et al., 2023; Ramaswamy et al., 2022).

In parallel, the second technique focuses on DC-bus voltage control, a vital feature of grid-connected PV systems. The DC-bus voltage is regulated using a Proportional-Integral (PI) controller. This controller functions by continually comparing the actual observed DC voltage with a predetermined reference voltage setpoint. The error signal created from this comparison is processed using proportional and integral terms, leading the adjustment of the inverter's duty cycle to keep the DC-bus voltage within the intended range. The PI controller, a well-established control approach, becomes important in assuring the stability and efficiency of the PV system. Through the closed-loop control system, the PI controller dynamically reacts to variances in the DC-bus voltage, aiming to minimise mistakes and maintain a regulated voltage level. This control is critical for optimum inverter performance, compliance with grid requirements, and avoidance of possible harm to system components. The entire architecture of the research are shown in figure 1.

Figure 1. Working of the proposed system

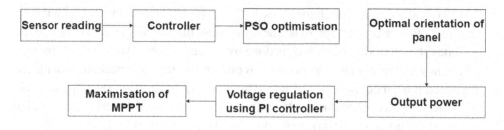

PARTICLE SWARM OPTIMIZATION

Particle Swarm Optimization (PSO) stands as a strong method in the area of optimization, finding practical applications in boosting the performance of photovoltaic (PV) systems. In the context of solar power, PSO is mainly applied for the optimization of the Maximum Power Point Tracking (MPPT) procedure. The MPPT algorithm serves a critical role in ensuring that a solar panel works at its Maximum Power Point (MPP), where it provides the maximum potential power output. PSO takes inspiration from the collective behavior of swarms, such as flocks of birds or schools of fish. In the context of PV systems, the "particles" in PSO represent possible solutions within the solution space, each with a given set of parameters. These particles iteratively modify their locations depending on their own experiences and the experiences of their neighbors, collectively converging towards an ideal solution.

In the application of PSO to MPPT, each particle in the swarm corresponds to a possible MPP candidate. The programme actively explores the solution space, modifying the parameters to reflect changes in sun irradiance, temperature, and other environmental conditions. This adaptable aspect of PSO is especially advantageous in cases when the working conditions of the solar panel alter, for as owing to changes in cloud cover or shade. One significant benefit of PSO is in its capacity to tackle complicated, non-linear optimization problems. The algorithm thrives in dynamically changing surroundings, making it well-suited for the fundamentally fluctuating circumstances of solar energy production. As the swarm collectively seeks the optimum solution, PSO reacts to changes in the environment, continually improving the search for the MPP. By adding PSO into the MPPT process, researchers and engineers may boost the overall efficiency of PV systems. The algorithm's flexibility, efficiency in exploring solution spaces, and capacity to manage dynamic situations lead to increased energy collection, eventually increasing the output of solar panels and boosting the practicality and sustainability of solar energy as a renewable power source.

PI CONTROLLER FOR VOLTAGE REGULATION

As part of a closed-loop system, the PI controller continually measures and compares the actual DC voltage to a setpoint reference value. Following this comparison, the error signal is handled using integral and proportional terms, which affect how the duty cycle of the inverter is adjusted. While the integral term corrects long-term faults and ensures accurate regulation over time, the proportional term reacts quickly to variations from the reference voltage. The PI controller's capacity to adjust to changing load levels and environmental variables is what makes it so useful in PV systems. In order to maintain the intended DC-bus voltage, the PI controller dynamically adjusts the inverter's operation when solar irradiation varies and grid needs change. This stability adds to the dependability and compliance of grid-connected PV systems by optimising energy conversion and protecting the system from any problems. The PI controller is crucial to accomplishing the operational objectives of the study because of its strong performance and capacity to strike a balance between responsiveness and stability.

RESULT AND DISCUSSION

In order to assess how integrating several sensors with an MPPT algorithm might improve the performance of a photovoltaic (PV) system, a thorough experimental setup has been built in this study. Infrared (IR), tilt, and sun positioning sensors are all included in the system, and they all help to collect data in real time throughout the day. A comprehensive log of the sensor data the system collected from dawn to dusk is shown in Table 1. The system can accurately follow the movement of the sun to the vital information that solar positioning sensors offer on the azimuth and elevation angles of the sun. Infrared sensors record temperature differences simultaneously, allowing the system to adjust to changing external circumstances. The tilt sensor readings provide information on the solar panel's inclination, which helps with the best orientation changes.

Table 1. Sensor reading

Time	Solar Positioning (Azimuth) [degrees]	Solar Positioning (Elevation) [degrees]	IR Sensor Reading [°C]	Tilt Sensor Reading [degrees]
08:00	120	45	28.5	25
09:00	150	60	30.2	30
10:00	180	75	31.8	35
11:00	210	60	32.5	40
12:00	240	45	33.2	45
13:00	270	30	34.0	50
14:00	300	45	32.8	45
15:00	330	60	31.5	40
16:00	0	75	29.7	35
17:00	30	60	28.5	30

Over the course of a day, the study performs a thorough analysis to determine the effect of the integrated sensor system on the PV system's performance. Table 2 displays the power output of the solar panel, which is recorded. In addition to displaying the power output while the sensor system is operating, this table also compares the results with another panel that measures performance in the absence of the sensor system.

The power outputs from the solar panel with and without the integrated sensor system are shown in Table 2. This comparison study offers insightful information about the efficiency advantages made possible by the MPPT algorithm and sensor-based orientation. The independent panel is used for baseline measurements in the absence of the sensor system and provides a point of comparison for assessing the effect of the system on total energy collection. These trial results add to a comprehensive knowledge of how well the suggested method performs the PV system and maximises power generation. The information gathered from sensor readings and comparative power evaluations forms the basis for evaluating the usefulness of the deployed technology and its possible consequences for further developments in solar energy harvesting systems.

The PSO technique, which is renowned for its ability to locate ideal solutions in intricate search spaces, is used to ascertain the exact motions of the motors accountable for the orientation of the solar panel. The PSO algorithm provides precise parameters that control the motors' rotation at every instant, ensuring that the solar panel is oriented in relation to the sun at its best angle. This clever programme considers the intrinsic properties of the solar panel system, ambient factors, and real-time sensor data. The PSO algorithm makes use of the swarm's collective intelligence to dynamically adjust the motor movements to changing conditions. This improves the photovoltaic system's overall efficiency by ensuring that the solar panel is consistently aligned with the Maximum Power Point (MPP) for maximum energy capture.

Table 2. Comparison of Power Before and After Orientation System

Time	Power Output with Sensor System [W]	Power Output without Sensor System [W]
08:00	1500	1200
09:00	1800	1400
10:00	2200	1800
11:00	2000	1600
12:00	2500	2000
13:00	2800	2300
14:00	2400	1900
15:00	2000	1500
16:00	1800	1400
17:00	1600	1200

In this research, a Proportional-Integral (PI) controller for DC voltage regulation is used to carefully maintain the stability and efficiency of the grid-connected photovoltaic (PV) system. One crucial characteristic for optimum inverter performance and grid compliance is the direct current (DC) bus voltage, which the PI control method is skilled at continually monitoring and regulating. The PI controller operates as a closed-loop system in which a predetermined reference voltage setpoint and the actual measured DC voltage are compared. An error signal is produced by this comparison and is subsequently handled by both proportional (P) and integral

(I) terms. While the integral term tackles and removes long-term mistakes, the proportional term reacts to sudden departures from the reference voltage. The PI controller may offer a responsive and subtle adjustment of the DC bus voltage thanks to its dual-term technique.

The duty cycle of the inverter's switching components is affected by the PI controller's change. The inverter controls how much DC power is supplied into the grid by varying the duty cycle, which keeps the DC bus voltage within the intended range. This procedure is essential for preventing overvoltage or undervoltage situations, protecting the PV system's integrity, and adhering to strict grid regulations. Stability and improved power quality are further benefits of the PV system's smooth integration of the PI control approach. The PI controller's adaptive feature enables it to react quickly to variations in temperature, sun irradiance, and other environmental factors. This flexibility is especially important for maintaining a steady and controlled DC voltage in the face of changing operating circumstances.

A comparison of the photovoltaic (PV) system's power production before and after DC voltage regulation using a proportional-integral (PI) controller is shown in Figure 2. The power output without DC regulation is shown in the left column, which illustrates how well the system functions in its default configuration. On the other hand, the power output is shown in the right column, where the DC voltage is actively regulated by the PI controller. The power production at different times of the day is represented by the figures in each row. This table shows how well the PI controller works to improve the stability and efficiency of the PV system by controlling the DC bus voltage.

Figure 2. Power Output Before and After DC Regulation

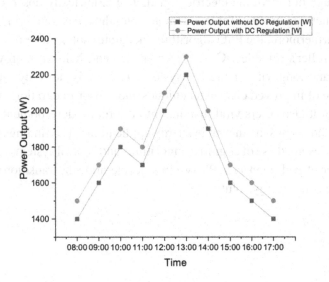

The total performance of the photovoltaic (PV) system is much improved by combining the sensor-based orientation system with the Proportional-Integral (PI) controller for DC voltage regulation and the Practical Swarm Optimisation (PSO) algorithm. To maximise energy collection, the sensor system makes sure that the solar panels are oriented precisely throughout the day. Simultaneously, the PSO algorithm modifies motor motions dynamically to achieve effective Maximum Power Point Tracking (MPPT). By contributing to steady DC voltage, the PI controller complies with grid requirements. In grid-connected PV systems, this combination strategy produces a synergistic boost that shows promise for maximising energy production, enhancing system dependability, and guaranteeing grid compliance.

CONCLUSION

In conclusion, this study revealed the effectiveness of a multimodal approach to improving the performance of grid-connected photovoltaic (PV) systems. The combination of sensor-based orientation, which uses solar positioning and infrared sensors, and the Practical Swarm Optimisation (PSO) algorithm for Maximum Power Point Tracking (MPPT), has proven effective in dynamically altering the solar panel's orientation for best energy acquisition. Simultaneously, the Proportional-Integral (PI) controller successfully regulated the DC bus voltage, assuring stability and grid compliance. The combination of these two methods has resulted in a synergistic effect, optimising energy output, increasing system reliability, and allowing for smooth integration with the electrical grid. The empirically observed increase in power production, shown in Table 2, demonstrates the effectiveness of this integrated method. Furthermore, the PSO algorithm's accurate motor movements, along with the PI controller's reliable DC voltage management, help to improve the overall efficiency and longevity of the PV system. This study not only emphasises the significance of improved control techniques and sensor integration in solar energy systems, but it also offers vital insights into the future development of smart and adaptive technologies in renewable energy applications. The findings pave the door for more widespread use of cognitive algorithms and control systems to optimise the performance of grid-connected PV systems, accelerating the transition to sustainable and reliable solar energy solutions.

REFERENCES

Arockiasamy, F. S., Muthukrishnan, M., Iyyadurai, J., Kaliappan, S., Lakshmaiya, N., Djearamane, S., Tey, L.-H., Wong, L. S., Kayarohanam, S., Obaid, S. A., Alfarraj, S., & Sivakumar, S. (2023). Tribological characterization of sponge gourd outer skin fiber-reinforced epoxy composite with Tamarindus indica seed filler addition using the Box-Behnken method. *E-Polymers*, 23(1), 20230052. 10.1515/epoly-2023-0052

Arul Arumugam, R., Usha Rani, B., Komala, C. R., Barthwal, S., Kaliappan, S., & Natrayan, L. (2023). Design and Development of the Optical Antenna for Wireless Communications. *7th International Conference on Electronics, Communication and Aerospace Technology, ICECA 2023 - Proceedings*. 10.1109/ICECA58529.2023.10395356

Balamurugan, P., Agarwal, P., Khajuria, D., Mahapatra, D., Angalaeswari, S., Natrayan, L., & Mammo, W. D. (2023). State-Flow Control Based Multistage Constant-Current Battery Charger for Electric Two-Wheeler. *Journal of Advanced Transportation*, 2023, 1–11. 10.1155/2023/4554582

Biradar, V. S., Al-Jiboory, A. K., Sahu, G., Tilak Babu, S. B. G., Mahender, K., & Natrayan, L. (2023). Intelligent Control Systems for Industrial Automation and Robotics. *2023 10th IEEE Uttar Pradesh Section International Conference on Electrical, Electronics and Computer Engineering, UPCON 2023*. IEEE. 10.1109/UPCON59197.2023.10434927

Chehelgerdi, M., Chehelgerdi, M., Allela, O. Q. B., Pecho, R. D. C., Jayasankar, N., Rao, D. P., Thamaraikani, T., Vasanthan, M., Viktor, P., Lakshmaiya, N., Saadh, M. J., Amajd, A., Abo-Zaid, M. A., Castillo-Acobo, R. Y., Ismail, A. H., Amin, A. H., & Akhavan-Sigari, R. (2023). Progressing nanotechnology to improve targeted cancer treatment: Overcoming hurdles in its clinical implementation. *Molecular Cancer*, 22(1), 169. 10.1186/s12943-023-01865-037814270

Chennai Viswanathan, P., Venkatesh, S. N., Dhanasekaran, S., Mahanta, T. K., Sugumaran, V., Lakshmaiya, N., Paramasivam, P., & Nanjagoundenpalayam Ramasamy, S. (2023). Deep Learning for Enhanced Fault Diagnosis of Monoblock Centrifugal Pumps: Spectrogram-Based Analysis. *Machines*, 11(9), 874. 10.3390/machines11090874

Chinta, N. D., Karthikeyan, K. R., Natrayan, L., & Kaliappan, S. (2023). Pressure Induced Variations in Mode II Behaviour of Uni-Directional Kenaf Reinforced Polymers. *International Journal of Vehicle Structures and Systems*, 15(7). 10.4273/ijvss.15.7.19

Hemalatha, K., James, C., Natrayan, L., & Swamynadh, V. (2020). Analysis of RCC T-beam and prestressed concrete box girder bridges super structure under different span conditions. *Materials Today: Proceedings*, 37(Part 2), 1507–1516. 10.1016/j.matpr.2020.07.119

Josphineleela, R., Kaliapp, S., Natrayan, L., & Garg, A. (2023). Big Data Security through Privacy - Preserving Data Mining (PPDM): A Decentralization Approach. *Proceedings of the 2023 2nd International Conference on Electronics and Renewable Systems, ICEARS 2023*. IEEE. 10.1109/ICEARS56392.2023.10085646

Josphineleela, R., Lekha, D., Natrayan, L., & Purohit, K. C. (2023). Biometric Aided Intelligent Security System Built using Internet of Things. *Proceedings of the 2023 2nd International Conference on Electronics and Renewable Systems, ICEARS 2023*. IEEE. 10.1109/ICEARS56392.2023.10085572

Kaliappan, S., Mothilal, T., Natrayan, L., Pravin, P., & Olkeba, T. T. (2023). Mechanical Characterization of Friction-Stir-Welded Aluminum AA7010 Alloy with TiC Nanofiber. *Advances in Materials Science and Engineering*, 2023, 1–7. 10.1155/2023/1466963

Kaliappan, S., & Natrayan, L. (2024a). Enhancement of Mechanical and Thermal Characteristics of Automobile Parts using Flax/Epoxy-Graphene Nanofiller Composites. *SAE Technical Papers*. 10.4271/2023-01-5116

Kaliappan, S., & Natrayan, L. (2024b). Impact of Kenaf Fiber and Inorganic Nanofillers on Mechanical Properties of Epoxy-Based Nanocomposites for Sustainable Automotive Applications. *SAE Technical Papers*. 10.4271/2023-01-5115

Kaliappan, S., & Natrayan, L. (2024c). Polypropylene Composite Materials with Natural Fiber Reinforcement: An Acoustic and Mechanical Analysis for Automotive Implementations. *SAE Technical Papers*. 10.4271/2023-01-5130

Kaliappan, S., & Natrayan, L. (2024d). Revolutionizing Automotive Materials through Enhanced Mechanical Properties of Epoxy Hybrid Bio-Composites with Hemp, Kenaf, and Coconut Powder. *SAE Technical Papers*. 10.4271/2023-01-5185

Kaliappan, S., Natrayan, L., & Garg, N. (2023). Checking and Supervisory System for Calculation of Industrial Constraints using Embedded System. *Proceedings of the 4th International Conference on Smart Electronics and Communication, ICOSEC 2023*. IEEE. 10.1109/ICOSEC58147.2023.10275952

Kaliappan, S., Natrayan, L., Mohammed Ali, H., & Kumar, P. (2024). Thermal and Mechanical Properties of Abutilon indicum Fiber-Based Polyester Composites under Alkali Treatment for Automotive Sector. *SAE Technical Papers*. 10.4271/2024-01-5031

Kaliappan, S., Natrayan, L., & Rajput, A. (2023). Sentiment Analysis of News Headlines Based on Sentiment Lexicon and Deep Learning. *Proceedings of the 4th International Conference on Smart Electronics and Communication, ICOSEC 2023*. IEEE. 10.1109/ICOSEC58147.2023.10276102

Kaliappan, S., Velumayil, R., Natrayan, L., & Pravin, P. (2023). Mechanical, DMA, and fatigue behavior of Vitis vinifera stalk cellulose Bambusa vulgaris fiber epoxy composites. *Polymer Composites*, 44(4), 2115–2121. 10.1002/pc.27228

Kanimozhi, G., Natrayan, L., Angalaeswari, S., & Paramasivam, P. (2022). An Effective Charger for Plug-In Hybrid Electric Vehicles (PHEV) with an Enhanced PFC Rectifier and ZVS-ZCS DC/DC High-Frequency Converter. *Journal of Advanced Transportation*, 2022, 1–14. 10.1155/2022/7840102

Karthick, M., Meikandan, M., Kaliappan, S., Karthick, M., Sekar, S., Patil, P. P., Raja, S., Natrayan, L., & Paramasivam, P. (2022). Experimental Investigation on Mechanical Properties of Glass Fiber Hybridized Natural Fiber Reinforced Penta-Layered Hybrid Polymer Composite. *International Journal of Chemical Engineering*, 2022, 1–9. 10.1155/2022/1864446

Kaushal, R. K., Arvind, R., Giri, K. K. B., Sindhu, M., Natrayan, L., & Ronald, B. (2023). Deep Learning Based Segmentation Approach for Automatic Lane Detection in Autonomous Vehicle. *International Conference on Self Sustainable Artificial Intelligence Systems, ICSSAS 2023 - Proceedings*. IEEE. 10.1109/ICSSAS57918.2023.10331835

Kiruba Sandou, D., Sunad Kumara, A. N., Choudhary, B. K., & Gurpur, S., Sarishma, Natrayan, L., & Sivaramkumar, M. (2023). Design and Implementation of Neuro-Fuzzy Control Approach for Robot's Trajectory Tracking. *7th International Conference on Electronics, Communication and Aerospace Technology, ICECA 2023 - Proceedings*. IEEE. 10.1109/ICECA58529.2023.10395675

Konduri, S., Walke, S., Kumar, A., Pavithra, G., Bhagirath Jadhav, A., & Natrayan, L. (2023). Reinforcement Learning for Multi-Robot Coordination and Cooperation in Manufacturing. *2023 10th IEEE Uttar Pradesh Section International Conference on Electrical, Electronics and Computer Engineering, UPCON 2023*. IEEE. 10.1109/UPCON59197.2023.10434651

Lakshmaiya, N. (2023b). Experimental analysis on heat transfer cube shape of two vertical surfaces during melting condition. *Proceedings of SPIE- The International Society for Optical Engineering, 12616.* SPIE. doi:10.1117/12.267555210.1 117/12.2675552

Lakshmaiya, N. (2023c). Experimental analysis on heat transfer cube shape of two vertical surfaces during melting condition. *Proceedings of SPIE- The International Society for Optical Engineering, 12616.* SPIE. doi:10.1117/12.267555210.1 117/12.2675552

Lakshmaiya, N. (2023d). Experimental investigation on computational volumetric heat in real time neural pathways. *Proceedings of SPIE- The International Society for Optical Engineering, 12616.* SPIE. doi:10.1117/12.267555510.1117/12.2675555

Lakshmaiya, N. (2023e). Investigation on ultraviolet radiation of flow pattern and particles transportation in vanishing raindrops. *Proceedings of SPIE- The International Society for Optical Engineering, 12616.* SPIE. doi:10.1117/12.267555610. 1117/12.2675556

Lakshmaiya, N. (2023f). Mechanical evaluation of coir/kenaf/jute laminated hybrid composites designed for geotechnical uses. *Proceedings of SPIE- The International Society for Optical Engineering, 12936.* SPIE. doi:10.1117/12.301171010.1 117/12.3011710

Lakshmaiya, N. (2023g). Organic material nuts flour greens laminate preparation and mechanical characteristics of natural materials. *Proceedings of SPIE- The International Society for Optical Engineering, 12936.* SPIE. doi:10.1117/12.30117 1210.1117/12.3011712

Lakshmaiya, N. (2023h). Polylactic acid/hydroxyapatite/yttria-stabilized zircon synthetic nanocomposite scaffolding compression and flexural characteristics. *Proceedings of SPIE- The International Society for Optical Engineering, 12936.* SPIE. doi:10.1117/12.301171510.1117/12.3011715

Lakshmaiya, N. (2023i). Preparation and evaluation of bamboo laminated cannabis paper physico - mechanical characteristics. *Proceedings of SPIE- The International Society for Optical Engineering, 12936.* SPIE. doi:10.1117/12.301171610.1 117/12.3011716

Lakshmaiya, N. (2023j). Simulating laminar induced heat capacity and heat transmission convection using Al2O3 nanofluid. *Proceedings of SPIE- The International Society for Optical Engineering, 12616.* SPIE. doi:10.1117/12.267555710. 1117/12.2675557

Lakshmaiya, N., Kaliappan, S., Patil, P. P., Ganesan, V., Dhanraj, J. A., Sirisamphan-wong, C., Wongwuttanasatian, T., Chowdhury, S., Channumsin, S., Channumsin, M., & Techato, K. (2022). Influence of Oil Palm Nano Filler on Interlaminar Shear and Dynamic Mechanical Properties of Flax/Epoxy-Based Hybrid Nanocomposites under Cryogenic Condition. *Coatings*, 12(11), 1675. 10.3390/coatings12111675

Lakshmaiya, N., Surakasi, R., Nadh, V. S., Srinivas, C., Kaliappan, S., Ganesan, V., Paramasivam, P., & Dhanasekaran, S. (2023). Tanning Wastewater Steriliza-tion in the Dark and Sunlight Using Psidium guajava Leaf-Derived Copper Oxide Nanoparticles and Their Characteristics. *ACS Omega*, 8(42), 39680–39689. 10.1021/acsomega.3c0558837901496

Loganathan, A. S., Ramachandran, V., Perumal, A. S., Dhanasekaran, S., Laksh-maiya, N., & Paramasivam, P. (2023). Framework of Transactive Energy Market Strategies for Lucrative Peer-to-Peer Energy Transactions. *Energies*, 16(1), 6. 10.3390/en16010006

Mahat, D., Niranjan, K., Naidu, C. S. K. V. R., Babu, S. B. G. T., Kumar, M. S., & Natrayan, L. (2023). AI-Driven Optimization of Supply Chain and Logistics in Mechanical Engineering. *2023 10th IEEE Uttar Pradesh Section International Conference on Electrical, Electronics and Computer Engineering, UPCON 2023*. IEEE. 10.1109/UPCON59197.2023.10434905

Malladi, A., Kaliappan, S., Natrayan, L., & Mahesh, V. (2024). Effectiveness of Thermal and Mechanical Properties of Jute Fibers under Different Chemical Treat-ment for Automotive Interior Trim. *SAE Technical Papers*. 10.4271/2024-01-5008

Mehta, A. K., Lanjewar, P., Murthy, D. S., Ghildiyal, P., Faldu, R., & Natrayan, L. (2023). AI & Lean Management Principles Based Pharmaceutical Manufactur-ing Processes. *2023 10th IEEE Uttar Pradesh Section International Conference on Electrical, Electronics and Computer Engineering, UPCON 2023*. IEEE. 10.1109/UPCON59197.2023.10434834

Muralidaran, V. M., Natrayan, L., Kaliappan, S., & Patil, P. P. (2023). Grape stalk cellulose toughened plain weaved bamboo fiber-reinforced epoxy composite: Load bearing and time-dependent behavior. *Biomass Conversion and Biorefinery*. 10.1007/s13399-022-03702-8

Nadh, V. S., Krishna, C., Natrayan, L., Kumar, K., Nitesh, K. J. N. S., Raja, G. B., & Paramasivam, P. (2021). Structural Behavior of Nanocoated Oil Palm Shell as Coarse Aggregate in Lightweight Concrete. *Journal of Nanomaterials*, 2021, 1–7. 10.1155/2021/4741296

Natrayan, L. (2023). Humidity Impact on the Material Characteristics of a Sisal Laminate: The Role of the Rapid Vibrational Method. *International Journal of Vehicle Structures and Systems*, 15(7). 10.4273/ijvss.15.7.17

Natrayan, L., Ashok, S. K., Kaliappan, S., & Kumar, P. (2024). Effect of Stacking Sequence on Mechanical Properties of Bamboo/Bagasse Composite Fiber for Automobile Seat Cushions and Upholstery Application. *SAE Technical Papers*. 10.4271/2024-01-5013

Natrayan, L., Balaji, S., Bharathiraja, G., Kaliappan, S., Veeman, D., & Mammo, W. D. (2021). Experimental Investigation on Mechanical Properties of TiAlN Thin Films Deposited by RF Magnetron Sputtering. *Journal of Nanomaterials*, 2021, 1–7. 10.1155/2021/5943486

Natrayan, L., & De Poures, M. V. (2023a). Experimental investigations of heat ageing with chemical modification of hemp fiber elastic characteristics. *Proceedings of SPIE- The International Society for Optical Engineering, 12936*. SPIE. 10.1117/12.3011708

Natrayan, L., & De Poures, M. V. (2023b). Influence of gasoline on high speed evaporation gasoline sprays: a large-eddy model of sprayer a with different fuels. *Proceedings of SPIE- The International Society for Optical Engineering, 12936*. SPIE. 10.1117/12.3011709

Natrayan, L., & Kaliappan, S. (2023). Mechanical Assessment of Carbon-Luffa Hybrid Composites for Automotive Applications. *SAE Technical Papers*. 10.4271/2023-01-5070

Natrayan, L., Kaliappan, S., Balaji, N., & Mahesh, V. (2024). Dynamic Mechanical and Thermal Properties of Polymer-Coated Jute Fibers for Enhanced Automotive Parts. *SAE Technical Papers*. 10.4271/2024-01-5019

Natrayan, L., Kaliappan, S., & Pundir, S. (2023). Control and Monitoring of a Quadcopter in Border Areas Using Embedded System. *Proceedings of the 4th International Conference on Smart Electronics and Communication, ICOSEC 2023*. IEEE. 10.1109/ICOSEC58147.2023.10276196

Natrayan, L., Kaliappan, S., Saravanan, A., Vickram, A. S., Pravin, P., Abbas, M., Ahamed Saleel, C., Alwetaishi, M., & Saleem, M. S. M. (2023). Recyclability and catalytic characteristics of copper oxide nanoparticles derived from bougainvillea plant flower extract for biomedical application. *Green Processing and Synthesis*, 12(1), 20230030. 10.1515/gps-2023-0030

Natrayan, L., & Kumar, M. S. (2019). Influence of silicon carbide on tribological behaviour of AA2024/Al2O3/SiC/Gr hybrid metal matrix squeeze cast composite using Taguchi technique. *Materials Research Express*, 6(12), 1265f9. 10.1088/2053-1591/ab676d

Natrayan, L., & Kumar, M. S. (2020). Optimization of wear behaviour on AA6061/Al2O3/SiC metal matrix composite using squeeze casting technique-Statistical analysis. *Materials Today: Proceedings*, 27, 306–310. 10.1016/j.matpr.2019.11.038

Natrayan, L., & Merneedi, A. (2020). Experimental investigation on wear behaviour of bio-waste reinforced fusion fiber composite laminate under various conditions. *Materials Today: Proceedings*, 37(Part 2), 1486–1490. 10.1016/j.matpr.2020.07.108

Natrayan, L., Merneedi, A., Veeman, D., Kaliappan, S., Raju, P. S., Subbiah, R., & Kumar, S. V. (2021). Evaluating the Mechanical and Tribological Properties of DLC Nanocoated Aluminium 5051 Using RF Sputtering. *Journal of Nanomaterials*, 2021, 1–7. 10.1155/2021/8428822

Natrayan, L., & Richard, T. (2023a). Experimental investigations of bagasse ash strands featuring variable surface influence on polypropylene based polymer composites. *Proceedings of SPIE- The International Society for Optical Engineering, 12936*. SPIE. 10.1117/12.3011691

Natrayan, L., & Richard, T. (2023b). Organo modified nanocomposites terephthalic acid polymers temperature and microstructural characteristics. *Proceedings of SPIE- The International Society for Optical Engineering, 12936*. SPIE.10.1117/12.3011863

Natrayan, L., Sakthi Shunmuga Sundaram, P., & Elumalai, J. (2019). Analyzing the uterine physiological with mmg signals using svm. *International Journal of Pharmaceutical Research*, 11(2). 10.31838/ijpr/2019.11.02.009

Natrayan, L., Senthil Kumar, M., & Chaudhari, M. (2020). Optimization of squeeze casting process parameters to investigate the mechanical properties of AA6061/Al2O3/SiC hybrid metal matrix composites by Taguchi and Anova approach. In *Advances in Intelligent Systems and Computing* (*Vol. 949*). 10.1007/978-981-13-8196-6_35

Natrayan, L., Senthil Kumar, M., & Palanikumar, K. (2018). Optimization of squeeze cast process parameters on mechanical properties of Al2O3/SiC reinforced hybrid metal matrix composites using taguchi technique. *Materials Research Express*, 5(6), 066516. 10.1088/2053-1591/aac873

Natrayan, L., Sivaprakash, V., & Santhosh, M. S. (2018). Mechanical, microstructure and wear behavior of the material aa6061 reinforced sic with different leaf ashes using advanced stir casting method. *International Journal of Engineering and Advanced Technology*, 8.

Niveditha, V. R., & Rajakumar, P. S. (2020). Pervasive computing in the context of COVID-19 prediction with AI-based algorithms. *International Journal of Pervasive Computing and Communications*, 16(5). 10.1108/IJPCC-07-2020-0082

Palaniyappan, S., Veeman, D., Sivakumar, N. K., & Natrayan, L. (2022). Development and optimization of lattice structure on the walnut shell reinforced PLA composite for the tensile strength and dimensional error properties. *Structures*, 45, 163–178. 10.1016/j.istruc.2022.09.023

Pandian, A., Kaliappan, S., Natrayan, L., & Reddy, V. (2024). Analyzing the Moisture and Chemical Retention Behavior of Flax Fiber-Ceramic Hybrid Composites for Automotive Underbody Shields. *SAE Technical Papers*. 10.4271/2024-01-5006

Prabagar, S., Al-Jiboory, A. K., Nair, P. S., Mandal, P., Garse, K. M., & Natrayan, L. (2023). Artificial Intelligence-Based Control Strategies for Unmanned Aerial Vehicles. *2023 10th IEEE Uttar Pradesh Section International Conference on Electrical, Electronics and Computer Engineering, UPCON 2023*. IEEE. 10.1109/UPCON59197.2023.10434918

Pragadish, N., Kaliappan, S., Subramanian, M., Natrayan, L., Satish Prakash, K., Subbiah, R., & Kumar, T. C. A. (2023). Optimization of cardanol oil dielectric-activated EDM process parameters in machining of silicon steel. *Biomass Conversion and Biorefinery*, 13(15), 14087–14096. 10.1007/s13399-021-02268-1

Ragumadhavan, R., Sateesh Kumar, D., Charyulu Rompicharla, L. N., Dhondiya, S. A., Kaliappan, S., & Natrayan, L. (2023). Design and Development of Light Communication Systems Using Modulation Techniques. *7th International Conference on Electronics, Communication and Aerospace Technology, ICECA 2023 - Proceedings*. IEEE. 10.1109/ICECA58529.2023.10395831

Rajasekaran, S., & Natrayan, L. (2023a). Estimation of corrective and preventive action on trend end plug-based machining activities using manual and failure mode with effects analysis. *Proceedings of SPIE- The International Society for Optical Engineering, 12936*. IEEE. 10.1117/12.3011698

Rajasekaran, S., & Natrayan, L. (2023b). Evaluation of occurrence number and communication based on FMEA operations in product development. *Proceedings of SPIE- The International Society for Optical Engineering, 12936*. SPIE. 10.1117/12.3011702

Ramaswamy, R., Gurupranes, S. V., Kaliappan, S., Natrayan, L., & Patil, P. P. (2022). Characterization of prickly pear short fiber and red onion peel biocarbon nanosheets toughened epoxy composites. *Polymer Composites*, 43(8), 4899–4908. 10.1002/pc.26735

Ramesh, C., Vijayakumar, M., Alshahrani, S., Navaneethakrishnan, G., Palanisamy, R., Natrayan, L., Saleel, C. A., Afzal, A., Shaik, S., & Panchal, H. (2022). Performance enhancement of selective layer coated on solar absorber panel with reflector for water heater by response surface method: A case study. *Case Studies in Thermal Engineering*, 36, 102093. 10.1016/j.csite.2022.102093

Reddy, P. N., Umaeswari, P., Natrayan, L., & Choudhary, A. (2023). Development of Programmed Autonomous Electric Heavy Vehicle: An Application of IoT. *Proceedings of the 2023 2nd International Conference on Electronics and Renewable Systems, ICEARS 2023*. SPIE. 10.1109/ICEARS56392.2023.10085492

Saadh, M. J., Almoyad, M. A. A., Arellano, M. T. C., Maaliw, R. R. III, Castillo-Acobo, R. Y., Jalal, S. S., Gandla, K., Obaid, M., Abdulwahed, A. J., Ibrahem, A. A., Sârbu, I., Juyal, A., Lakshmaiya, N., & Akhavan-Sigari, R. (2023). Long non-coding RNAs: Controversial roles in drug resistance of solid tumors mediated by autophagy. *Cancer Chemotherapy and Pharmacology*, 92(6), 439–453. 10.1007/s00280-023-04582-z37768333

Sai, S. A., Venkatesh, S. N., Dhanasekaran, S., Balaji, P. A., Sugumaran, V., Lakshmaiya, N., & Paramasivam, P. (2023). Transfer Learning Based Fault Detection for Suspension System Using Vibrational Analysis and Radar Plots. *Machines*, 11(8), 778. 10.3390/machines11080778

Sasi, J. P., Nidhi Pandagre, K., Royappa, A., Walke, S., Pavithra, G., & Natrayan, L. (2023). Deep Learning Techniques for Autonomous Navigation of Underwater Robots. *2023 10th IEEE Uttar Pradesh Section International Conference on Electrical, Electronics and Computer Engineering, UPCON 2023*. SPIE. 10.1109/UPCON59197.2023.10434865

Sathish, T., Natrayan, L., Prasad Jones Christydass, S., Sivananthan, S., Kamalakannan, R., Vijayan, V., & Paramasivam, P. (2022). Experimental Investigation on Tribological Behaviour of AA6066: HSS-Cu Hybrid Composite in Dry Sliding Condition. *Advances in Materials Science and Engineering*, 2022, 1–9. 10.1155/2022/9349847

Sathish, T., Palani, K., Natrayan, L., Merneedi, A., de Poures, M. V., & Singaravelu, D. K. (2021). Synthesis and characterization of polypropylene/ramie fiber with hemp fiber and coir fiber natural biopolymer composite for biomedical application. *International Journal of Polymer Science*, 2021, 1–8. 10.1155/2021/2462873

Selvi, S., Mohanraj, M., Duraipandy, P., Kaliappan, S., Natrayan, L., & Vinayagam, N. (2023). Optimization of Solar Panel Orientation for Maximum Energy Efficiency. *Proceedings of the 4th International Conference on Smart Electronics and Communication, ICOSEC 2023*. IEEE. 10.1109/ICOSEC58147.2023.10276287

Sendrayaperumal, A., Mahapatra, S., Parida, S. S., Surana, K., Balamurugan, P., Natrayan, L., & Paramasivam, P. (2021). Energy Auditing for Efficient Planning and Implementation in Commercial and Residential Buildings. *Advances in Civil Engineering*, 2021, 1–10. 10.1155/2021/1908568

Siddiqui, E., Siddique, M., Safeer Pasha, M., Boyapati, P., Pavithra, G., & Natrayan, L. (2023). AI and ML for Enhancing Crop Yield and Resource Efficiency in Agriculture. *2023 10th IEEE Uttar Pradesh Section International Conference on Electrical, Electronics and Computer Engineering, UPCON 2023*. IEEE. 10.1109/UPCON59197.2023.10434493

Singh, M. (2017). An experimental investigation on mechanical behaviour of siCp reinforced Al 6061 MMC using squeeze casting process. *International Journal of Mechanical and Production Engineering Research and Development*, 7(6). 10.24247/ijmperddec201774

Sivakumar, V., Kaliappan, S., Natrayan, L., & Patil, P. P. (2023). Effects of Silane-Treated High-Content Cellulose Okra Fibre and Tamarind Kernel Powder on Mechanical, Thermal Stability and Water Absorption Behaviour of Epoxy Composites. *Silicon*, 15(10), 4439–4447. 10.1007/s12633-023-02370-1

Sukumaran, C., Indhumathi, K., Balamurugan, P., Ambilwade, R. P., Sunthari, P. M., & Natrayan, L. (2023). The Role of AI in Biochips for Early Disease Detection. *Proceedings - International Conference on Technological Advancements in Computational Sciences, ICTACS 2023*. IEEE. 10.1109/ICTACS59847.2023.10390419

Suman, T., Kaliappan, S., Natrayan, L., & Dobhal, D. C. (2023). IoT based Social Device Network with Cloud Computing Architecture. *Proceedings of the 2023 2nd International Conference on Electronics and Renewable Systems, ICEARS 2023*. IEEE. 10.1109/ICEARS56392.2023.10085574

Sureshkumar, P., Jagadeesha, T., Natrayan, L., Ravichandran, M., Veeman, D., & Muthu, S. M. (2022). Electrochemical corrosion and tribological behaviour of AA6063/Si$_3$N$_4$/Cu(NO$_3$)$_2$ composite processed using single-pass ECAP$_A$ route with 120° die angle. *Journal of Materials Research and Technology*, 16. 10.1016/j.jmrt.2021.12.020

Thakre, S., Pandhare, A., Malwe, P. D., Gupta, N., Kothare, C., Magade, P. B., Patel, A., Meena, R. S., Veza, I., Natrayan, L., & Panchal, H. (2023). Heat transfer and pressure drop analysis of a microchannel heat sink using nanofluids for energy applications. *Kerntechnik*, 88(5), 543–555. 10.1515/kern-2023-0034

Ugle, V. V., Arulprakasajothi, M., Padmanabhan, S., Devarajan, Y., Lakshmaiya, N., & Subbaiyan, N. (2023). Investigation of heat transport characteristics of titanium dioxide nanofluids with corrugated tube. *Environmental Quality Management*, 33(2), 127–138. 10.1002/tqem.21999

Vaishali, K. R., Rammohan, S. R., Natrayan, L., Usha, D., & Niveditha, V. R. (2021). Guided container selection for data streaming through neural learning in cloud. *International Journal of Systems Assurance Engineering and Management*. 10.1007/s13198-021-01124-9

Velmurugan, G., & Natrayan, L. (2023). Experimental investigations of moisture diffusion and mechanical properties of interply rearrangement of glass/Kevlar-based hybrid composites under cryogenic environment. *Journal of Materials Research and Technology*, 23, 4513–4526. 10.1016/j.jmrt.2023.02.089

Velumayil, R., Gnanakumar, G., Natrayan, L., Chinta, N. D., & Kaliappan, S. (2023). Bifunctional Aluminum Oxide/Carbon Fiber/Epoxy Nanocomposites Preparation and Evaluation. *International Journal of Vehicle Structures and Systems*, 15(7). 10.4273/ijvss.15.7.18

Venkatesh, R., Manivannan, S., Kaliappan, S., Socrates, S., Sekar, S., Patil, P. P., Natrayan, L., & Bayu, M. B. (2022). Influence of Different Frequency Pulse on Weld Bead Phase Ratio in Gas Tungsten Arc Welding by Ferritic Stainless Steel AISI-409L. *Journal of Nanomaterials*, 2022, 1–11. 10.1155/2022/9530499

Vijayakumar, M., & Shreeraj Nair, P. G Tilak Babu, S. B., Mahender, K., Venkateswaran, T. S., & Natrayan, L. (2023). Intelligent Systems For Predictive Maintenance In Industrial IoT. *2023 10th IEEE Uttar Pradesh Section International Conference on Electrical, Electronics and Computer Engineering, UPCON 2023*. IEEE. 10.1109/UPCON59197.2023.10434814

Vijayakumar, M. D., Surendhar, G. J., Natrayan, L., Patil, P. P., Ram, P. M. B., & Paramasivam, P. (2022). Evolution and Recent Scenario of Nanotechnology in Agriculture and Food Industries. *Journal of Nanomaterials*, 2022, 1–17. 10.1155/2022/1280411

Compilation of References

(2021). Gopal. V., M. Alphin, and R. Bharanidaran. Design of Compliant Mechanism Microgripper Utilizing the Hoekens Straight Line Mechanism (2021). *Journal of Testing and Evaluation*, 49(3), 1599–1612.

Abas, M., Habib, T., Noor, S., & Khan, K. M. (2022). Comparative study of I-optimal design and definitive screening design for developing prediction models and optimization of average surface roughness of PLA printed parts using fused deposition modeling. *International Journal of Advanced Manufacturing Technology*. Advance online publication. 10.1007/s00170-022-10784-1

Abas, M., Habib, T., Noor, S., Salah, B., & Zimon, D. (2022). Parametric Investigation and Optimization to Study the Effect of Process Parameters on the Dimensional Deviation of Fused Deposition Modeling of 3D Printed Parts. *Polymers*, 14(17), 3667. 10.3390/polym1417366736080740

Abas, M., Habib, T., Noor, S., Zimon, D., & Woźniak, J. (2023). Application of multi-criteria decision-making methods in the selection of additive manufacturing materials for solid ankle foot orthoses. *Journal of Engineering Design*, 34(8), 616–643. 10.1080/09544828.2023.2247859

Acan, A., & Ünveren, A. (2020). Multiobjective great deluge algorithm with two-stage archive support. *Engineering Applications of Artificial Intelligence*, 87, 103239. 10.1016/j.engappai.2019.103239

Ahmad, S. (2022). Electromagnetic Field Optimization Based Selective Harmonic Elimination in a Cascaded Symmetric H-Bridge Inverter. *Energies*, 15(20), 7682.u 10.3390/en15207682

Al-Bakhrani, A., Hagar, A., Hamoud, A. A., & Kawathekar, S. (2020). Comparative Analysis of Cpu Scheduling Algorithms: Simulation And Its Applications. *International Journal of Advanced Science and Technology*, 29(3), 483–494.

Alguliyev, R. M., Imamverdiyev, Y. N., & Abdullayeva, F. J. (2019, January). PSO-based load balancing method in cloud computing. *Automatic Control and Computer Sciences*, 53(1), 45–55. 10.3103/S0146411619010024

Almufti, , S. (2019). Historical survey on metaheuristics algorithms. *International Journal of Scientific World*, 7(1), 1. 10.14419/ijsw.v7i1.29497

Almufti, , S. (2022). Hybridizing Ant Colony Optimization Algorithm for Optimizing Edge-Detector Techniques. *Academic Journal of Nawroz University*, 11(2), 135–145. 10.25007/ajnu.v11n2a1320

Almufti, , SYahya Zebari, , AKhalid Omer, , H. (2019). A comparative study of particle swarm optimization and genetic algorithm. *Journal of Advanced Computer Science & Technology*, 8(2), 40. 10.14419/jacst.v8i2.29401

Almufti, S., Marqas, R., & Asaad, R. (2019). Comparative study between elephant herding optimization (EHO) and U-turning ant colony optimization (U-TACO) in solving symmetric traveling salesman problem (STSP). *Journal Of Advanced Computer Science & Technology*, 8(2), 32. 10.14419/jacst.v8i2.29403

Al-Thanoon, N. A., Qasim, O. S., & Algamal, Z. Y. (2019). A new hybrid firefly algorithm and particle swarm optimization for tuning parameter estimation in penalized support vector machine with application in chemometrics. *Chemometrics and Intelligent Laboratory Systems*, 184, 142–152. 10.1016/j.chemolab.2018.12.003

Alworafi, M. A., Dhari, A., El-Booz, S. A., Nasr, A. A., Arpitha, A., & Mallappa, S. (2019). An enhanced task scheduling in cloud computing based on hybrid approach. In *Data Analytics and Learning* (pp. 11–25). Springer. 10.1007/978-981-13-2514-4_2

Anita, S., Rodrigues, P., Nagabhooshanam, N., Londhe, G. V., Salunkhe, S. S., Kumar, P. D., L, N., & Bhima Raju, P. S. D. (2024, February 06). L, N., & Bhima Raju, P. S. D. (2024). Energy Trading and Optimum Scheduling for Microgrids Using Multiple Agents Based DL Approach. *Electric Power Components and Systems*, 1–19. 10.1080/15325008.2023.2300329

Anjankar, P., Lakade, S., Padalkar, A., Nichal, S., Devarajan, Y., Lakshmaiya, N., & Subbaiyan, N. (2023). Experimental investigation on the effect of liquid phase and vapor phase separation over performance of falling film evaporator. *Environmental Quality Management*, 33(1), 61–69. 10.1002/tqem.21952

Arockiasamy, F. S., Muthukrishnan, M., Iyyadurai, J., Kaliappan, S., Lakshmaiya, N., Djearamane, S., Tey, L.-H., Wong, L. S., Kayarohanam, S., Obaid, S. A., Alfarraj, S., & Sivakumar, S. (2023). Tribological characterization of sponge gourd outer skin fiber-reinforced epoxy composite with Tamarindus indica seed filler addition using the Box-Behnken method. *E-Polymers*, 23(1), 20230052. 10.1515/epoly-2023-0052

Arul Arumugam, R., Usha Rani, B., Komala, C. R., Barthwal, S., Kaliappan, S., & Natrayan, L. (2023). Design and Development of the Optical Antenna for Wireless Communications. *7th International Conference on Electronics, Communication and Aerospace Technology, ICECA 2023 - Proceedings*. IEEE. 10.1109/ICECA58529.2023.10395356

Arun, A. P., Kaliappan, S., Natrayan, L., & Patil, P. (2022). Mechanical, fracture toughness, and Dynamic Mechanical properties of twill weaved bamboo fiber-reinforced Artocarpus heterophyllus seed husk biochar epoxy composite. *Polymer Composites*, 43(11), 8388–8395. 10.1002/pc.27010

ASTM E23; Standard Test Methods for Notched Bar Impact Testing of Metallic Materials. (n.d.). ASTM International: West Conshohocken, PA. https://www.astm.org/standards/e23

Compilation of References

Atashpaz-Gargari, E., & Lucas, C. (2007). Imperialist Competitive Algorithm: An algorithm for optimization inspired 431 by imperialistic competition. *IEEE Congress on Evolutionary Computation.* IEEE. 10.1109/CEC.2007.4425083

Ba, J. L., Kiros, J. R., & Hinton, G. E. (2016). *Layer normalization.* arXiv:1607.06450.

Baker, J., & Heyman, J. (1969). *Plastic Design of Frames 1 Fundamentals.* Cambridge University Press. 10.1017/CBO9780511586514

Baker, S. J. F., Horne, M. R., & Heyman, J. (1961). *The Steel Skeleton.* English Language Book Society.

Balaji, N., Gurupranes, S. V., Balaguru, S., Jayaraman, P., Natrayan, L., Subbiah, R., & Kaliappan, S. (2023). Mechanical, wear, and drop load impact behavior of Cissus quadrangularis fiber–reinforced moringa gum powder–toughened polyester composite. *Biomass Conversion and Biorefinery.* 10.1007/s13399-023-04491-4

Balaji, N., Natrayan, L., Kaliappan, S., Patil, P. P., & Sivakumar, N. S. (2022). Annealed peanut shell biochar as potential reinforcement for aloe vera fiber-epoxy biocomposite: Mechanical, thermal conductivity, and dielectric properties. *Biomass Conversion and Biorefinery.* 10.1007/s13399-022-02650-7

Balamurugan, P., Agarwal, P., Khajuria, D., Mahapatra, D., Angalaeswari, S., Natrayan, L., & Mammo, W. D. (2023). State-Flow Control Based Multistage Constant-Current Battery Charger for Electric Two-Wheeler. *Journal of Advanced Transportation*, 2023, 1–11. 10.1155/2023/4554582

Banks, A., Vincent, J., & Anyakoha, C. (2008). A review of particle swarm optimization. Part ii: Hybridisation, combinatorial, multicriteria and constrained optimization, and indicative applications. *Natural Computing*, 7(1), 109–124. 10.1007/s11047-007-9050-z

Battaglia, P., Pascanu, R., & Lai, M (2020). *Interaction networks for learning about objects, relations and physics.* Advances in neural information processing systems, Barcelona0.

Battaglia, P. W., Hamrick, J. B., & Bapst, V. (2018). *Relational inductive biases, deep learning, and graph networks.* arXiv:1806.01261.

Bender, J., & Koschier, D. (2015). Divergence-free smoothed particle hydrodynamics. In: *Proceedings of the 2015 ACM SIG-GRAPH/Eurographics Symposium on Computer Anima-tion.* California:ACM.10.1145/2786784.2786796

Bhuiyan, A., Guo, Z., Saifullah, A., Guan, N., & Xiong, H. (2018). Energy efficient real time scheduling of DAG tasks. *ACM Transactions on Embedded Computing Systems*, 17(5), 84. 10.1145/3241049

Biradar, V. S., Al-Jiboory, A. K., Sahu, G., Tilak Babu, S. B. G., Mahender, K., & Natrayan, L. (2023). Intelligent Control Systems for Industrial Automation and Robotics. *2023 10th IEEE Uttar Pradesh Section International Conference on Electrical, Electronics and Computer Engineering, UPCON 2023.* IEEE. 10.1109/UPCON59197.2023.10434927

Bose, A., Biswas, T., & Kuila, P. (2019). *A Novel Genetic Algorithm Based Scheduling for Multi-core Systems in Smart Innovations in Communication and Computational Sciences.* Springer., 10.1007/978-981-13-2414-7_5

Burkimsher, A., Bate, I., & Indrusiak, L. S. (2013). Scheduling HPC workflows for responsiveness and fairness with networking delays and inaccurate estimates of execution times. *European Conference on Parallel Processing.* Springer. 10.1007/978-3-642-40047-6_15

Butangen, A. K. G., Velasco, C. E., Codmos, J. C. B., Bayani, E. F., & Baquirin, R. B. (2020, January). Utilizing Dynamic Mean Quantum Time Round Robin to Optimize the Shortest Job First Scheduling Algorithm. In *Proceedings of 2020 the 6th International Conference on Computing and Data Engineering* (pp. 14-18). ACM. 10.1145/3379247.3379296

Cabrero, J. Beaudonnet, Anne-Laure., Boussant, Roux, Yves, Leon, Marcel., Levy, Benjamin, Gilbert, Robert. (2021). Shot-peening powder. *Patent No: 11951592.*

Chandran, J., & Viswanatham, V. M. (2021). Evaluating the effectiveness of community detection algorithms for influence maximization in social networks. *2021 International Conference on Advances in Electrical, Computing, Communication and Sustainable Technologies (ICAECT).* IEEE. 10.1109/ICAECT49130.2021.9392387

Chang, S., Bi, R., Sun, J., Liu, W., Yu, Q., Deng, Q., & Gu, Z. (2022, November). Toward Minimum WCRT Bound for DAG Tasks Under Prioritized List Scheduling Algorithms. *IEEE Transactions on Computer-Aided Design of Integrated Circuits and Systems*, 41(11), 3874–3885. 10.1109/TCAD.2022.3197532

Charnes, A., & Greenberg, H. J. (1951). Plastic collapse and linear programming-preliminary report. *Bulletin of the American Mathematical Society*, 57(6), 480.

Chasapis, D., Moretó, M., Schulz, M., Rountree, B., & Casas, M. (2019). Power efficient job scheduling by predicting the impact of processor manufacturing variability. *Proceedings of the ACM International Conference on Supercomputing.* ACM. 10.1145/3330345.3330372

Chavarat, Jarungvittayakon., Anak, Khantachawana., Paphon, Sa-ngasoongsong. (2023). The Effect of Particle Type and Size on CoCr Surface Properties by Fine-Particle Shot Peening. *Applied Sciences (Basel, Switzerland)*, 13(9).

Chehelgerdi, M., Chehelgerdi, M., Allela, O. Q. B., Pecho, R. D. C., Jayasankar, N., Rao, D. P., Thamaraikani, T., Vasanthan, M., Viktor, P., Lakshmaiya, N., Saadh, M. J., Amajd, A., Abo-Zaid, M. A., Castillo-Acobo, R. Y., Ismail, A. H., Amin, A. H., & Akhavan-Sigari, R. (2023). Progressing nanotechnology to improve targeted cancer treatment: Overcoming hurdles in its clinical implementation. *Molecular Cancer*, 22(1), 169. Advance online publication. 10.1186/s12943-023-01865-037814270

Chen, Y. (2022). A local search 4/3-approximation algorithm for the minimum 3-path partition problem. *Journal of Combinatorial Optimization, 44*, 3595-3610. 10.1007/s10878-022-00915-5

Compilation of References

Chen, J., & Han, P. (2021). Yifan Liu Xiaoyan Du. Scheduling independent tasks in cloud environment based on modified differential evolution. *Concurrency and Computation.* 10.1002/cpe.6256

Chennai Viswanathan, P., Venkatesh, S. N., Dhanasekaran, S., Mahanta, T. K., Sugumaran, V., Lakshmaiya, N., Paramasivam, P., & Nanjagoundenpalayam Ramasamy, S. (2023). Deep Learning for Enhanced Fault Diagnosis of Monoblock Centrifugal Pumps: Spectrogram-Based Analysis. *Machines*, 11(9), 874. Advance online publication. 10.3390/machines11090874

Chen, W.-F., & Zhang, H. (1991). *Structural Plasticity: Theory, Problems, and CAE Software*, 2. Springer. 10.1007/978-1-4612-2984-1

Chinchanikar, S., Shinde, S., Shaikh, A., Gaikwad, V., & Ambhore, N. H. (2023). *Multi-objective Optimization of FDM Using Hybrid Genetic Algorithm-Based Multi-criteria Decision-Making (MCDM) Techniques. Journal of The Institution of Engineers.* Series D., 10.1007/s40033-023-00459-w

Chinta, N. D., Karthikeyan, K. R., Natrayan, L., & Kaliappan, S. (2023). Pressure Induced Variations in Mode II Behaviour of Uni-Directional Kenaf Reinforced Polymers. *International Journal of Vehicle Structures and Systems*, 15(7). Advance online publication. 10.4273/ijvss.15.7.19

College, P. S. G. (2011). *Design Data Book for engineers.* Kalaikathirachchaagam.

Cuturi, M. Sinkhorn Distances: Lightspeed computation of optimal transportation distances. 2013, arXiv:1306.0895.

Deeks, A. J. (1996). Automatic computation of plastic collapse loads for frames. *Computers & Structures*, 60(3), 391–402. 10.1016/0045-7949(95)00394-0

Dehghani, M., Trojovská, E., & Trojovský, P. (2022). A new human-based metaheuristic algorithm for solving optimization problems on the base of simulation of driving training process. *Scientific Reports*, 12(1), 9924. 10.1038/s41598-022-14225-735705720

Deng, Z., Cao, D., Shen, H., Yan, Z., & Huang, H. (2021). Reliability-aware task scheduling for energy efficiency on heterogeneous multiprocessor systems. *The Journal of Supercomputing*, 77(10), 1–39. 10.1007/s11227-021-03764-x

Dev, S., & Srivastava, R. (2020). Experimental investigation and optimization of FDM process parameters for material and mechanical strength. *Materials Today: Proceedings*, 26, 1995–1999. 10.1016/j.matpr.2020.02.435

Dey, A., Hoffman, D., & Yodo, N. (2020). Optimizing multiple process parameters in fused deposition modeling with particle swarm optimization. [IJIDeM]. *International Journal on Interactive Design and Manufacturing*, 14(2), 393–405. 10.1007/s12008-019-00637-9

Dhaygude, A. D., Ameta, G. K., Khan, I. R., Singh, P. P., Maaliw, R. R.III, Lakshmaiya, N., Shabaz, M., Khan, M. A., Hussein, H. S., & Alshazly, H. (2024). Knowledge-based deep learning system for classifying Alzheimer's disease for multi-task learning. *CAAI Transactions on Intelligence Technology*, cit2.12291. 10.1049/cit2.12291

Dhiman, G., & Kumar, V. (2017). Spotted hyena optimizer: A novel bio-inspired based meta-heuristic technique for engineering applications. *Advances in Engineering Software*, 114, 48–70. 10.1016/j.advengsoft.2017.05.014

Dixit, N., & Jain, P. K. (2023). Multi-objective Strength Optimization of Fused Filament Fabricated Complex Flexible Parts Using Grey Relational Analysis. *Iranian Journal of Science and Technology. Transaction of Mechanical Engineering*, 47(4), 1–11. 10.1007/s40997-022-00589-8

Dumka, P., Mishra, D. R., Singh, B., Chauhan, R., Siddiqui, M. H. I., Natrayan, L., & Shah, M. A. (2024). Enhancing solar still performance with Plexiglas and jute cloth additions: Experimental study. *Sustainable Environment Research*, 34(1), 3. 10.1186/s42834-024-00208-y

Duy, T. V. T., Sato, Y., & Inoguchi, Y. (2010). *Performance evaluation of a green scheduling algorithm for energy savings in cloud computing in 2010 IEEE international symposium on parallel & distributed processing, workshops and Phd forum (IPDPSW)*. IEEE. 10.1109/IPD-PSW.2010.5470908

Enemuoh, E. U., & Asante-Okyere, S. (2023). Impact of feature selection on neural network prediction of fused deposition modelling (FDM) print part properties. *International Journal on Interactive Design and Manufacturing (IJIDeM)*. 10.1007/s12008-023-01598-w

Fountas, N. A., Zaoutsos, S., Chaidas, D., Kechagias, J. D., & Vaxevanidis, N. M. (2023). Statistical modelling and optimization of mechanical properties for PLA and PLA/Wood FDM materials. *Materials Today: Proceedings*. IEEE.

Fuchs, H. O. (1974). *Shot peening stress profiles*. Publication. Metal Improvement Company Inc.

Gad. (2022). Particle Swarm Optimization Algorithm and Its Applications: A Systematic Review. Article in *Archives of Computational Methods in Engineering*. Springer.

Gakias, C., Maliaris, G., & Savaidis, G. (2022). Investigation of the Shot Size Effect on Residual Stresses through a 2D FEM Model of the Shot Peening Process. *Metals*, 12(6), 956. 10.3390/met12060956

Gandomi, A. H., Yang, X. S., & Alavi, A. H. (2011). Mixed variable structural optimization using Firefly Algorithm. *Computers & Structures*, 89(23-24), 2325–2336. 10.1016/j.compstruc.2011.08.002

Gilmer, J., Schoenholz, S. S., & Riley, P. F. (2017). Neural message passing for quantum chemistry. In: *Proceedings of the 34th International Conference on Machine Learning*. JMLR..

Gopal, V., & Raja, D. M. R. (2021). Mechanical Behaviour of Al7075 Hybrid Composites Developed through Squeeze Casting. *International Journal of Vehicle Structures and Systems*, 13(3), 314–318. 10.4273/ijvss.13.3.14

Gorman, M.R. (1981). *Automated generation for limit analysis of frames*. Academic Press.

Compilation of References

Greco, A., Cannizzaro, F., & Pluchino, A. (2019). Automatic evaluation of plastic collapse conditions for planar frames with vertical irregularities. *Engineering with Computers*, 35(1), 57–73. 10.1007/s00366-018-0583-9

Gretton, A., Borgwardt, K. M., & Rasch, M. J. (2012). A kernel two-sample test. *Journal of Machine Learning Research*, 13(Mar), 723–773.

Hamayun, M., & Khurshid, H. (2015). An optimized shortest job first scheduling algorithm for CPU scheduling. *Journal of Applied Environmental and Biological Sciences*, 5(12), 42–46.

Haverty, D., & Kennedy, B. (2009). *Shot Peening: A Powerful Surface Coating Tool for Biomedical Implants*. The Shot Peener, Electronics, Inc.

Hemalatha, K., James, C., Natrayan, L., & Swamynadh, V. (2020). Analysis of RCC T-beam and prestressed concrete box girder bridges super structure under different span conditions. *Materials Today: Proceedings*, 37(Part 2), 1507–1516. Advance online publication. 10.1016/j.matpr.2020.07.119

He, Q., Jiang, X., Guan, N., & Guo, Z. (2019). *Intra-Task Priority Assignment in Real time Scheduling of DAG Tasks on Multi-cores*. IEEE Transactions on Parallel and Distributed Systems. 10.1109/TPDS.2019.2910525

Heyman, J. (1960). On the minimum-weight design of a simple portal frame. *International Journal of Mechanical Sciences*, 1(1), 121–134. 10.1016/0020-7403(60)90034-5

Holl, P., Koltun, V., & Thuerey, N. (2020). Learning to control pdes with differentiable physics. arXiv:2001.07457.

Horne, M. R. (1953). Determination of the shape of fixed ended beams for maximum economy according to the plastic theory. In *International Association of Bridge and Structural Engineering*. Fourth Congress.

Hu Y, Fang Y, & Ge Z. (2018). A moving least squares material point method with displacement discontinuity and two-way rigid body coupling. *ACM Trans. Graph.*, 37(4).

Hu, B., Cao, Z., & Zhou, M. (2021). Energy-minimized scheduling of real time parallel workflows on heterogeneous distributed computing systems. *IEEE Transactions on Services Computing*. 10.1109/TSC.2021.3054754

Hu, Y., Anderson, L., & Li, T. M., (2019). Difftaichi: Differentiable programming for physical simulation. arXiv:1910.00935.

Iruthayarajan, M. W., & Baskar, S. (2010). Covariance matrix adaptation evolution strategy based design of centralized PID controller. *Expert Systems with Applications*, 37(8), 5775–5781. 10.1016/j.eswa.2010.02.031

Jan, Z., Abas, M., Khan, I., Qazi, M. I., & Jan, Q. M. U. (2023). Design and Analysis of Wrist Hand Orthosis for Carpal Tunnel Syndrome Using Additive Manufacturing. *Journal of Engineering Research*. https://doi.org/10.1016/j.jer.2023.12.001

Jennings, P.A. (1983). *Adapting the Simplex Method to Plastic Design*. Academic Press.

Ji, M., Zhang, W., Liao, L., Cheng, T. C. E., & Tan, Y. (2019). *Multitasking parallel-machine scheduling with machinedependent slack due-window assignment. International Journal of Production Research*. Taylor & Francis. 10.1080/00207543.2018.1497312

John, J., Devjani, D., Ali, S., Abdallah, S., & Pervaiz, S. (2023). Optimization of 3D printed polylactic acid structures with different infill patterns using Taguchi-grey relational analysis. *Advanced Industrial and Engineering Polymer Research*, 6(1), 62–78. 10.1016/j.aiepr.2022.06.002

Joseph Edward Shigley (2014). *Theory of machines and mechanism*. Tata McGraw Hill Education pvt.

Josphineleela, R., Kaliappan, S., Natrayan, L., & Bhatt, U. M. (2023). Intelligent Virtual Laboratory Development and Implementation using the RASA Framework. *Proceedings - 7th International Conference on Computing Methodologies and Communication, ICCMC 2023*. IEEE. 10.1109/ICCMC56507.2023.10083701

Josphineleela, R., Kaliapp, S., Natrayan, L., & Garg, A. (2023). Big Data Security through Privacy - Preserving Data Mining (PPDM): A Decentralization Approach. *Proceedings of the 2023 2nd International Conference on Electronics and Renewable Systems, ICEARS 2023*. IEEE. 10.1109/ICEARS56392.2023.10085646

Josphineleela, R., Lekha, D., Natrayan, L., & Purohit, K. C. (2023). Biometric Aided Intelligent Security System Built using Internet of Things. *Proceedings of the 2023 2nd International Conference on Electronics and Renewable Systems, ICEARS 2023*. IEEE. 10.1109/ICEARS56392.2023.10085572

Kaliappan, S., & Natrayan, L. (2024a). Enhancement of Mechanical and Thermal Characteristics of Automobile Parts using Flax/Epoxy-Graphene Nanofiller Composites. *SAE Technical Papers*. 10.4271/2023-01-5116

Kaliappan, S., & Natrayan, L. (2024b). Impact of Kenaf Fiber and Inorganic Nanofillers on Mechanical Properties of Epoxy-Based Nanocomposites for Sustainable Automotive Applications. *SAE Technical Papers*. 10.4271/2023-01-5115

Kaliappan, S., & Natrayan, L. (2024c). Polypropylene Composite Materials with Natural Fiber Reinforcement: An Acoustic and Mechanical Analysis for Automotive Implementations. *SAE Technical Papers*. 10.4271/2023-01-5130

Kaliappan, S., & Natrayan, L. (2024d). Revolutionizing Automotive Materials through Enhanced Mechanical Properties of Epoxy Hybrid Bio-Composites with Hemp, Kenaf, and Coconut Powder. *SAE Technical Papers*. 10.4271/2023-01-5185

Kaliappan, S., Natrayan, L., Mohammed Ali, H., & Kumar, P. (2024). Thermal and Mechanical Properties of Abutilon indicum Fiber-Based Polyester Composites under Alkali Treatment for Automotive Sector. *SAE Technical Papers*. 10.4271/2024-01-5031

Compilation of References

Kaliappan, S., Mothilal, T., Natrayan, L., Pravin, P., & Olkeba, T. T. (2023). Mechanical Characterization of Friction-Stir-Welded Aluminum AA7010 Alloy with TiC Nanofiber. *Advances in Materials Science and Engineering*, 2023, 1–7. 10.1155/2023/1466963

Kaliappan, S., Natrayan, L., & Garg, N. (2023a). Checking and Supervisory System for Calculation of Industrial Constraints using Embedded System. *Proceedings of the 4th International Conference on Smart Electronics and Communication, ICOSEC 2023*. IEEE. 10.1109/ICOSEC58147.2023.10275952

Kaliappan, S., Natrayan, L., & Rajput, A. (2023). Sentiment Analysis of News Headlines Based on Sentiment Lexicon and Deep Learning. *Proceedings of the 4th International Conference on Smart Electronics and Communication, ICOSEC 2023*. IEEE. 10.1109/ICOSEC58147.2023.10276102

Kaliappan, S., Paranthaman, V., Natrayan, L., Kumar, B. V., & Muthukannan, M. (2024). Leveraging Machine Learning Algorithm for Predicting Personality Traits on Twitter. *Proceedings of the 14th International Conference on Cloud Computing, Data Science and Engineering, Confluence 2024*. IEEE. 10.1109/Confluence60223.2024.10463468

Kaliappan, S., Velumayil, R., Natrayan, L., & Pravin, P. (2023). Mechanical, DMA, and fatigue behavior of Vitis vinifera stalk cellulose Bambusa vulgaris fiber epoxy composites. *Polymer Composites*, 44(4), 2115–2121. 10.1002/pc.27228

Kanimozhi, G., Natrayan, L., Angalaeswari, S., & Paramasivam, P. (2022). An Effective Charger for Plug-In Hybrid Electric Vehicles (PHEV) with an Enhanced PFC Rectifier and ZVS-ZCS DC/DC High-Frequency Converter. *Journal of Advanced Transportation*, 2022, 1–14. 10.1155/2022/7840102

Karthick, M., Meikandan, M., Kaliappan, S., Karthick, M., Sekar, S., Patil, P. P., Raja, S., Natrayan, L., & Paramasivam, P. (2022). Experimental Investigation on Mechanical Properties of Glass Fiber Hybridized Natural Fiber Reinforced Penta-Layered Hybrid Polymer Composite. *International Journal of Chemical Engineering*, 2022, 1–9. 10.1155/2022/1864446

Kaushal, R. K., Arvind, R., Giri, K. K. B., Sindhu, M., Natrayan, L., & Ronald, B. (2023). Deep Learning Based Segmentation Approach for Automatic Lane Detection in Autonomous Vehicle. *International Conference on Self Sustainable Artificial Intelligence Systems, ICSSAS 2023 - Proceedings*. IEEE. 10.1109/ICSSAS57918.2023.10331835

Kaveh, A. & Dadras Eslamlou, A. (2020). Water strider algorithm: A new metaheuristic and applications. *Structures, 25*, 520–41.

Kaveh, A. & Seddighian, M.R. (2020). Simultaneously multi-material layout, and connectivity optimization of truss structures via an Enriched Firefly Algorithm. *Structures, 27*, 2217–31.

Kaveh, A. (1976). Improved cycle bases for the flexibility analysis of structures. *Computer Methods in Applied Mechanics and Engineering*, 9(3), 267–272. 10.1016/0045-7825(76)90031-1

Kaveh, A., Bakhshpoori, T., & Kalateh-Ahani, M. (2013). Optimum plastic analysis of planar frames using ant colony system and charged system search algorithms. *Scientia Iranica*, 20(3), 414–421.

Kaveh, A., & Ghafari, M. H. (2015). Plastic analysis of planar frames using CBO and ECBO algorithms. *Int J Optim Civil Eng*, 5(4), 479–492.

Kaveh, A., & Jahanshahi, M. (2008). Plastic limit analysis of frames using ant colony systems. *Computers & Structures*, 86(11–12), 1152–1163. 10.1016/j.compstruc.2008.01.001

Kaveh, A., & Khanlari, K. (2004). Collapse load factor of planar frames using a modified genetic algorithm. *Communications in Numerical Methods in Engineering*, 20(12), 911–925. 10.1002/cnm.716

Kaveh, A., & Rahami, H. (2006). Analysis, design and optimization of structures using force method and genetic algorithm. *International Journal for Numerical Methods in Engineering*, 65(10), 1570–1584. 10.1002/nme.1506

Kaveh, A., Seddighian, M. R., & Ghanadpour, E. (2019). Upper and lower bounds for the collapse load factor of rectangular grids using FEM. *Int J Optim Civil Eng*, 9(3), 543–554.

Kaveh, A., Seddighian, M. R., & Ghanadpour, E. (2020). Black Hole Mechanics Optimization: A novel meta-heuristic algorithm. *Asian J Civil Eng.*, 21(7), 1129–1149. 10.1007/s42107-020-00282-8

Kaveh, A., & Zolghadr, A. (2013). Topology optimization of trusses considering static and dynamic constraints using the CSS. *Applied Soft Computing*, 13(5), 2727–2734. 10.1016/j.asoc.2012.11.014

Kaveh, A., & Zolghadr, A. (2016). A novel meta-heuristic algorithm: Tug of war optimization. *Int J Optim Civil Eng*, 6(4), 469–492.

Kennedy, J., & Eberhart, R. (1995). Particle swarm optimization. *Proceedings of ICNN'95- international conference on neural networks*. IEEE.

Khadwilard, A., Chansombat, S., Thepphakorn, T., Chainate, W., & Pongcharoen, P. (2012). Application of firefly algorithm and its parameter setting for job shop scheduling. *Indust Technol*, 8(1), 49–58.

Khan, I., Farooq, U., Tariq, M., Abas, M., Ahmad, S., Shakeel, M., Riaz, A. A., & Hira, F. (2023). Investigation of Effects of Processing Parameters on the Impact Strength and microstructure of thick Tri-Material based Layered Composite Fabricated via Extrusion based Additive Manufacturing. *Journal of Engineering Research*. https://doi.org/https://doi.org/10.1016/j.jer.2023.08.007

Khan, I., Tariq, M., Abas, M., Shakeel, M., Hira, F., Al Rashid, A., & Koç, M. (2023). Parametric investigation and optimisation of mechanical properties of thick tri-material based composite of PLA-PETG-ABS 3D-printed using fused filament fabrication. *Composites Part C: Open Access*, 12, 100392. https://doi.org/10.1016/j.jcomc.2023.100392

Kingma, D. P., & Ba, J. Adam: A method for stochastic optimization. 2014, arXiv:1412.6980.

Kirk, D. (2009). *Non-Uniformity of Shot Peening Coverage*. Electronics, Inc.

Compilation of References

Kiruba Sandou, D., Sunad Kumara, A. N., Choudhary, B. K., & Gurpur, S., Sarishma, Natrayan, L., & Sivaramkumar, M. (2023). Design and Implementation of Neuro-Fuzzy Control Approach for Robot's Trajectory Tracking. *7th International Conference on Electronics, Communication and Aerospace Technology, ICECA 2023* - Proceedings. doi:10.1109/ICECA58529.2023.10395675

Kiruba Sandou, D., Sunad Kumara, A. N., Choudhary, B. K., & Gurpur, S., Sarishma, Natrayan, L., & Sivaramkumar, M. (2023). Design and Implementation of Neuro-Fuzzy Control Approach for Robot's Trajectory Tracking. *7th International Conference on Electronics, Communication and Aerospace Technology, ICECA 2023 - Proceedings*. IEEE. 10.1109/ICECA58529.2023.10395675

Konduri, S., Walke, S., Kumar, A., Pavithra, G., Bhagirath Jadhav, A., & Natrayan, L. (2023). Reinforcement Learning for Multi-Robot Coordination and Cooperation in Manufacturing. *2023 10th IEEE Uttar Pradesh Section International Conference on Electrical, Electronics and Computer Engineering, UPCON 2023*. IEEE. 10.1109/UPCON59197.2023.10434651

Konduri, S., Walke, S., Kumar, A., Pavithra, G., Bhagirath Jadhav, A., & Natrayan, L. (2023). Reinforcement Learning for Multi-Robot Coordination and Cooperation in Manufacturing. *2023 10th IEEE Uttar Pradesh Section International Conference on Electrical, Electronics and Computer Engineering, UPCON 2023*. IEEE. doi:10.1109/UPCON59197.2023.10434651

Krishnapura, R., Goddard, S., & Qadi, A. A. (2004). A dynamic real-time scheduling algorithm for reduced energy consumption. *CSE Technical reports, 72.*

Kumar, M., & Sharma, S. C. (2016). Priority Aware Longest Job First (PA-LJF) algorithm for utilization of the resource in cloud environment in 3rd *International Conference on Computing for Sustainable Glmessobal Development (INDIACom)*. IEEE.

Kumar, J. V. S. P., Kaliappan, S., Natrayan, L., Raturi, A., Seikh, A. H., Iqbal, A., & Mohanavel, V. (2024). Isolation of biosilica from biomass waste Setaria italica husks and its reinforcement effect on banana fiber-epoxy composite. *Biomass Conversion and Biorefinery.* 10.1007/s13399-024-05334-6

Lakshmaiya, N. (2023a). Effectiveness of mixed convection flow following pressure vessel gas evacuation. *Proceedings of SPIE- The International Society for Optical Engineering, 12616.* SPIE. 10.1117/12.2675550

Lakshmaiya, N. (2023b). Experimental analysis on heat transfer cube shape of two vertical surfaces during melting condition. *Proceedings of SPIE- The International Society for Optical Engineering, 12616.* SPIE. 10.1117/12.2675552

Lakshmaiya, N. (2023d). Experimental investigation on computational volumetric heat in real time neural pathways. *Proceedings of SPIE- The International Society for Optical Engineering, 12616.* SPIE. 10.1117/12.2675555

Lakshmaiya, N. (2023e). Investigation on ultraviolet radiation of flow pattern and particles transportation in vanishing raindrops. *Proceedings of SPIE- The International Society for Optical Engineering, 12616.* SPIE. 10.1117/12.2675556

Lakshmaiya, N. (2023f). Mechanical evaluation of coir/kenaf/jute laminated hybrid composites designed for geotechnical uses. *Proceedings of SPIE- The International Society for Optical Engineering, 12936*. SPIE. 10.1117/12.3011710

Lakshmaiya, N. (2023g). Organic material nuts flour greens laminate preparation and mechanical characteristics of natural materials. *Proceedings of SPIE- The International Society for Optical Engineering, 12936*. SPIE. 10.1117/12.3011712

Lakshmaiya, N. (2023h). Polylactic acid/hydroxyapatite/yttria-stabilized zircon synthetic nanocomposite scaffolding compression and flexural characteristics. *Proceedings of SPIE- The International Society for Optical Engineering, 12936*. SPIE. 10.1117/12.3011715

Lakshmaiya, N. (2023i). Preparation and evaluation of bamboo laminated cannabis paper physico - mechanical characteristics. *Proceedings of SPIE- The International Society for Optical Engineering, 12936*. SPIE. 10.1117/12.3011716

Lakshmaiya, N. (2023j). Simulating laminar induced heat capacity and heat transmission convection using Al2O3 nanofluid. *Proceedings of SPIE- The International Society for Optical Engineering, 12616*. SPIE. 10.1117/12.2675557

Lakshmaiya, N., & Murugan, V. S. (2023a). Bolstering EVA photovoltaic devices enclosing sheets with esterified cellulose nanofibers improves the mechanical and barrier characteristics. *Proceedings of SPIE- The International Society for Optical Engineering, 12936*. SPIE. 10.1117/12.3011858

Lakshmaiya, N., & Murugan, V. S. (2023b). Effects of machining parameters on surface quality of composites reinforced with natural fibers. *Proceedings of SPIE- The International Society for Optical Engineering, 12936*. SPIE. 10.1117/12.3011869

Lakshmaiya, N., & Murugan, V. S. (2023c). Experimental investigation of removal of sulphur di-oxide from exhaust gas by using semi-dry flue gas desulfurization (FGD). *Proceedings of SPIE- The International Society for Optical Engineering, 12936*. SPIE. 10.1117/12.3011865

Lakshmaiya, N., & Murugan, V. S. (2023d). Experimental investigations of thermal solutions to increase heat transfer rate by utilizing the effects of pitch ratio and length. *Proceedings of SPIE- The International Society for Optical Engineering, 12936*. SPIE. 10.1117/12.3011873

Lakshmaiya, N., & Murugan, V. S. (2023e). Improvement of the interfaces and mechanical characteristics of kenaf/kraft paper natural fibre reinforced composite materials. *Proceedings of SPIE- The International Society for Optical Engineering, 12936*. SPIE. 10.1117/12.3011859

Lakshmaiya, N., Kaliappan, S., Patil, P. P., Ganesan, V., Dhanraj, J. A., Sirisamphanwong, C., Wongwuttanasatian, T., Chowdhury, S., Channumsin, S., Channumsin, M., & Techato, K. (2022). Influence of Oil Palm Nano Filler on Interlaminar Shear and Dynamic Mechanical Properties of Flax/Epoxy-Based Hybrid Nanocomposites under Cryogenic Condition. *Coatings*, 12(11), 1675. 10.3390/coatings12111675

Compilation of References

Lakshmaiya, N., Surakasi, R., Nadh, V. S., Srinivas, C., Kaliappan, S., Ganesan, V., Paramasivam, P., & Dhanasekaran, S. (2023). Tanning Wastewater Sterilization in the Dark and Sunlight Using Psidium guajava Leaf-Derived Copper Oxide Nanoparticles and Their Characteristics. *ACS Omega*, 8(42), 39680–39689. 10.1021/acsomega.3c0558837901496

Lee, Z., Wang, Y., & Zhou, W. (2011, August). A dynamic priority scheduling algorithm on service request scheduling in cloud computing. In *Proceedings of 2011 International Conference on Electronic & Mechanical Engineering and Information Technology* (Vol. 9, pp. 4665-4669). IEEE. 10.1109/EMEIT.2011.6024076

Legout, V., Jan, M., & Pautet, L. (2013, October). A scheduling algorithm to reduce the static energy consumption of multiprocessor real-time systems. In *Proceedings of the 21st International Conference on Real-Time Networks and Systems* (pp. 99-108). ACM. 10.1145/2516821.2516839

Li, G., & Wu, Z. (2019, April). Ant colony optimization task scheduling algorithm for SWIM based on load balancing. *Future Internet*, 11(4), 90. 10.3390/fi11040090

Lin, C.-C., Shi, J., Ueter, N., Günzel, M., Reineke, J., & Chen, J.-J. (2022). Type-aware Federated Scheduling for Typed DAG Tasks on Heterogeneous Multicore Platforms. *IEEE Transactions on Computers*. 10.1109/TC.2022.3202748

Li, Y., Wu, J., & Tedrake, R. (2018). Learning particle dynamics for manipulating rigid bodies, deformable objects, and fluids. arXiv:1810.01566.

Li, Y., Wu, J., & Zhu, J. Y. (2019). Propagation networks for model-based control under partial observation. In: *International Conference on Robotics and Automation (ICRA)*. Montreal: IEEE. 10.1109/ICRA.2019.8793509

Loganathan, A. S., Ramachandran, V., Perumal, A. S., Dhanasekaran, S., Lakshmaiya, N., & Paramasivam, P. (2023). Framework of Transactive Energy Market Strategies for Lucrative Peer-to-Peer Energy Transactions. *Energies*, 16(1), 6. 10.3390/en16010006

Maguluri, N., Suresh, G., & Rao, K. V. (2023). Assessing the effect of FDM processing parameters on mechanical properties of PLA parts using Taguchi method. *Journal of Thermoplastic Composite Materials*, 36(4), 1472–1488. 10.1177/08927057211053036

Mahat, D., Niranjan, K., Naidu, C. S. K. V. R., Babu, S. B. G. T., Kumar, M. S., & Natrayan, L. (2023). AI-Driven Optimization of Supply Chain and Logistics in Mechanical Engineering. *2023 10th IEEE Uttar Pradesh Section International Conference on Electrical, Electronics and Computer Engineering, UPCON 2023*. IEEE. 10.1109/UPCON59197.2023.10434905

Maia, C., Nogueira, L., & Pinho, L. M. (2013). Scheduling parallel real time tasks using a fixed-priority work-stealing algorithm on multiprocessors. *2013 8thIEEE International Symposium on Industrial Embedded Systems* (SIES), (pp. 89-92). IEEE. 10.1109/SIES.2013.6601477

Malladi, A., Kaliappan, S., Natrayan, L., & Mahesh, V. (2024). Effectiveness of Thermal and Mechanical Properties of Jute Fibers under Different Chemical Treatment for Automotive Interior Trim. *SAE Technical Papers*. 10.4271/2024-01-5008

Marqas, R. B., Almufti, S. M., Othman, P. S., & Abdulrahman, C. M. (2020). Evaluation of EHO, U-TACO and TS Metaheuristics algorithms in Solving TSP. *Journal of Xi'an University of Architecture & Technology*, 12(4). 10.37896/JXAT12.04/1062

Marques, V. M., Reis, C., & Machado, J. A. T. (2010). Interactive Evolutionary Computation in music. *2010 IEEE International Conference on Systems, Man and Cybernetics* (pp. 3501–3507). IEEE. 10.1109/ICSMC.2010.5642417

Mehalaine, R., & Boutekkouk, F. (2020). *Energy Consumption Reduction in Real Time Multiprocessor Embedded Systems with Uncertain Data in Computer Science*. Springer, Cham. 10.1007/978-3-030-51971-1_4

Mehta, A. K., Lanjewar, P., Murthy, D. S., Ghildiyal, P., Faldu, R., & Natrayan, L. (2023). AI & Lean Management Principles Based Pharmaceutical Manufacturing Processes. *2023 10th IEEE Uttar Pradesh Section International Conference on Electrical, Electronics and Computer Engineering, UPCON 2023*. IEEE. 10.1109/UPCON59197.2023.10434834

Mellal, M. A., Laifaoui, C., Ghezal, F., & Williams, E. J. (2022). Multi-objective factors optimization in fused deposition modelling with particle swarm optimization and differential evolution. [IJIDeM]. *International Journal on Interactive Design and Manufacturing*, 16(4), 1669–1674. 10.1007/s12008-022-00868-3

Meng, Z., Li, G., Wang, X., Sait, S. M., & Yıldız, A. R. (2021, May). A Comparative Study of Metaheuristic Algorithms for Reliability-Based Design Optimization Problems May 202. *Archives of Computational Methods in Engineering*, 28(4), 1853–1869. 10.1007/s11831-020-09443-z

Metals handbook. (1975). ASM Metals Park.

Mokhtar-zadeh, A., & Kaveh, A. (1999). Optimal plastic analysis and design of frames: Graph theoretical methods. *Computers & Structures*, 73(1–5), 485–496. 10.1016/S0045-7949(98)00250-8

Monaghan, J. J. (1992). Smoothed particle hydrodynamics. *Annual Review of Astronomy and Astrophysics*, 30(1), 543–574. 10.1146/annurev.aa.30.090192.002551

Mora-Gutiérrez, R. A., Ramírez-Rodríguez, J., Rincón-García, E. A., Ponsich, A., & Herrera, O. (2012). An optimization algorithm inspired by social creativity systems. *Computing*, 94(11), 887–914. 10.1007/s00607-012-0205-0

Muñoz Zavala, A. E., Aguirre, A. H., & Villa, E. R. (2005). Diharce, Constrained optimization via particle evolutionary swarm optimization algorithm (peso). *Proceedings of the 7th Annual Conference on Genetic and Evolutionary Computation*. ACM.

Muralidaran, V. M., Natrayan, L., Kaliappan, S., & Patil, P. P. (2023). Grape stalk cellulose toughened plain weaved bamboo fiber-reinforced epoxy composite: Load bearing and time-dependent behavior. *Biomass Conversion and Biorefinery*. 10.1007/s13399-022-03702-8

Compilation of References

Muthiya, S. J., Natrayan, L., Kaliappan, S., Patil, P. P., Naveena, B. E., Dhanraj, J. A., Subramaniam, M., & Paramasivam, P. (2022). Experimental investigation to utilize adsorption and absorption technique to reduce CO2 emissions in diesel engine exhaust using amine solutions. *Adsorption Science and Technology*, 2022, 9621423. 10.1155/2022/9621423

Muthiya, S. J., Natrayan, L., Yuvaraj, L., Subramaniam, M., Dhanraj, J. A., & Mammo, W. D. (2022). Development of Active CO_2 Emission Control for Diesel Engine Exhaust Using Amine-Based Adsorption and Absorption Technique. *Adsorption Science and Technology*, 2022, 8803585. 10.1155/2022/8803585

Nadh, V. S., Krishna, C., Natrayan, L., Kumar, K., Nitesh, K. J. N. S., Raja, G. B., & Paramasivam, P. (2021). Structural Behavior of Nanocoated Oil Palm Shell as Coarse Aggregate in Lightweight Concrete. *Journal of Nanomaterials*, 2021, 1–7. 10.1155/2021/4741296

Natrayan, L., & De Poures, M. V. (2023a). Experimental investigations of heat ageing with chemical modification of hemp fiber elastic characteristics. *Proceedings of SPIE- The International Society for Optical Engineering, 12936*. SPIE. 10.1117/12.3011708

Natrayan, L., & De Poures, M. V. (2023b). Influence of gasoline on high speed evaporation gasoline sprays: a large-eddy model of sprayer a with different fuels. *Proceedings of SPIE- The International Society for Optical Engineering, 12936*. SPIE. 10.1117/12.3011709

Natrayan, L., & Kaliappan, S. (2023). Mechanical Assessment of Carbon-Luffa Hybrid Composites for Automotive Applications. *SAE Technical Papers*. 10.4271/2023-01-5070

Natrayan, L., & Richard, T. (2023a). Experimental investigations of bagasse ash strands featuring variable surface influence on polypropylene based polymer composites. *Proceedings of SPIE- The International Society for Optical Engineering, 12936*. SPIE. 10.1117/12.3011691

Natrayan, L., & Richard, T. (2023b). Organo modified nanocomposites terephthalic acid polymers temperature and microstructural characteristics. *Proceedings of SPIE- The International Society for Optical Engineering, 12936*. SPIE. 10.1117/12.3011863

Natrayan, L., Ashok, S. K., Kaliappan, S., & Kumar, P. (2024). Effect of Stacking Sequence on Mechanical Properties of Bamboo/Bagasse Composite Fiber for Automobile Seat Cushions and Upholstery Application. *SAE Technical Papers*. 10.4271/2024-01-5013

Natrayan, L., Kaliappan, S., Balaji, N., & Mahesh, V. (2024). Dynamic Mechanical and Thermal Properties of Polymer-Coated Jute Fibers for Enhanced Automotive Parts. *SAE Technical Papers*. 10.4271/2024-01-5019

Natrayan, L., Senthil Kumar, M., & Chaudhari, M. (2020). Optimization of squeeze casting process parameters to investigate the mechanical properties of AA6061/Al 2 O 3/SiC hybrid metal matrix composites by Taguchi and Anova approach. In *Advances in Intelligent Systems and Computing (Vol. 949)*. Springer. 10.1007/978-981-13-8196-6_35

Natrayan, L. (2023). Humidity Impact on the Material Characteristics of a Sisal Laminate: The Role of the Rapid Vibrational Method. *International Journal of Vehicle Structures and Systems*, 15(7). Advance online publication. 10.4273/ijvss.15.7.17

Natrayan, L., Ali, H. M., Kaliappan, S., & Kumar, G. R. (2023). Data Mining and AI for Early Diagnosis and Treatment Optimization in Autoimmune Encephalitis. *3rd IEEE International Conference on ICT in Business Industry and Government, ICTBIG 2023*. IEEE. 10.1109/ICT-BIG59752.2023.10456042

Natrayan, L., Ameen, F., Chinta, N. D., Teja, N. B., Muthu, G., Kaliappan, S., Ali, S., & Vadiveloo, A. (2024). Antibacterial and dynamical behaviour of silicon nanoparticles influenced sustainable waste flax fibre-reinforced epoxy composite for biomedical application. *Green Processing and Synthesis*, 13(1), 20230214. 10.1515/gps-2023-0214

Natrayan, L., Balaji, S., Bharathiraja, G., Kaliappan, S., Veeman, D., & Mammo, W. D. (2021). Experimental Investigation on Mechanical Properties of TiAlN Thin Films Deposited by RF Magnetron Sputtering. *Journal of Nanomaterials*, 2021, 1–7. 10.1155/2021/5943486

Natrayan, L., Chinta, N. D., Gogulamudi, B., Nadh, V. S., Muthu, G., Kaliappan, S., & Srinivas, C. (2024). Investigation on mechanical properties of the green synthesis bamboo fiber/eggshell/coconut shell powder-based hybrid biocomposites under NaOH conditions. *Green Processing and Synthesis*, 13(1), 20230185. 10.1515/gps-2023-0185

Natrayan, L., Chinta, N. D., Teja, N. B., Muthu, G., Kaliappan, S., Kirubanandan, S., & Paramasiv-am, P. (2024). Evaluating mechanical, thermal, and water absorption properties of biocomposites with Opuntia cladode fiber and palm flower biochar for industrial applications. *Discover Applied Sciences*, 6(2), 30. 10.1007/s42452-024-05660-4

Natrayan, L., Janardhan, G., Nadh, V. S., Srinivas, C., Kaliappan, S., & Velmurugan, G. (2024). Eco-friendly zinc oxide nanoparticles from Moringa oleifera leaf extract for photocat-alytic and antibacterial applications. *Clean Technologies and Environmental Policy*. 10.1007/s10098-024-02814-1

Natrayan, L., Jayakrishna, M., Shanker, K., Muthu, G., Kaliappan, S., & Velmurugan, G. (2024). Green synthesis of silver nanoparticles using lawsonia inermis for enhanced degradation of organic pollutants in wastewater treatment. *Global NEST Journal*, 26(3). 10.30955/gnj.005463

Natrayan, L., Kaliappan, S., & Pundir, S. (2023). Control and Monitoring of a Quadcopter in Border Areas Using Embedded System. *Proceedings of the 4th International Conference on Smart Electronics and Communication, ICOSEC 2023*. IEEE. 10.1109/ICOSEC58147.2023.10276196

Natrayan, L., Kaliappan, S., Saravanan, A., Vickram, A. S., Pravin, P., Abbas, M., Ahamed Saleel, C., Alwetaishi, M., & Saleem, M. S. M. (2023). Recyclability and catalytic characteristics of copper oxide nanoparticles derived from bougainvillea plant flower extract for biomedical application. *Green Processing and Synthesis*, 12(1), 20230030. 10.1515/gps-2023-0030

Compilation of References

Natrayan, L., & Kumar, M. S. (2019). Influence of silicon carbide on tribological behaviour of AA2024/Al2O3/SiC/Gr hybrid metal matrix squeeze cast composite using Taguchi technique. *Materials Research Express*, 6(12), 1265f9. 10.1088/2053-1591/ab676d

Natrayan, L., & Kumar, M. S. (2020). Optimization of wear behaviour on AA6061/Al2O3/SiC metal matrix composite using squeeze casting technique-Statistical analysis. *Materials Today: Proceedings*, 27, 306–310. 10.1016/j.matpr.2019.11.038

Natrayan, L., & Merneedi, A. (2020). Experimental investigation on wear behaviour of bio-waste reinforced fusion fiber composite laminate under various conditions. *Materials Today: Proceedings*, 37(Part 2), 1486–1490. 10.1016/j.matpr.2020.07.108

Natrayan, L., Merneedi, A., Veeman, D., Kaliappan, S., Raju, P. S., Subbiah, R., & Kumar, S. V. (2021). Evaluating the Mechanical and Tribological Properties of DLC Nanocoated Aluminium 5051 Using RF Sputtering. *Journal of Nanomaterials*, 2021, 1–7. 10.1155/2021/8428822

Natrayan, L., Niveditha, V. R., Nadh, V. S., Srinivas, C., Dhanraj, J. A., & Saravanan, A. (2024). Application of response surface and artificial neural network optimization approaches for exploring methylene blue adsorption using luffa fiber treated with sodium chlorite. *Journal of Water Process Engineering*, 58, 104778. 10.1016/j.jwpe.2024.104778

Natrayan, L., Sakthi Shunmuga Sundaram, P., & Elumalai, J. (2019). Analyzing the uterine physiological with mmg signals using svm. *International Journal of Pharmaceutical Research*, 11(2). 10.31838/ijpr/2019.11.02.009

Natrayan, L., Senthil Kumar, M., & Palanikumar, K. (2018). Optimization of squeeze cast process parameters on mechanical properties of Al2O3/SiC reinforced hybrid metal matrix composites using taguchi technique. *Materials Research Express*, 5(6), 066516. 10.1088/2053-1591/aac873

Natrayan, L., Sivaprakash, V., & Santhosh, M. S. (2018). Mechanical, microstructure and wear behavior of the material aa6061 reinforced sic with different leaf ashes using advanced stir casting method. *International Journal of Engineering and Advanced Technology*, 8.

Nayak, D., Malla, S. K., & Debadarshini, D. (2012). Improved round robin scheduling using dynamic time quantum. *International Journal of Computer Applications*, 38(5), 34–38. 10.5120/4607-6816

Neal, B. G., & Symonds, P. S. (1950). The calculation of collapse loads for framed structures. (Includes appendix). *Journal of the Institution of Civil Engineers*, 35(1), 21–40. 10.1680/IJO-TI.1950.12815

Neal, B. G., & Symonds, P. S. (1952a). The calculation of plastic loads for plane frames. In *International Association for Bridge and Structural Engineering*. Fourth Congress.

Neal, B. G., & Symonds, P. S. (1952b). The rapid calculation of the plastic collapse load for a framed structure. *Proceedings - Institution of Civil Engineers*, 1(2), 58–71. 10.1680/ipeds.1952.12270

Niveditha, V. R., & Rajakumar, P. S. (2020). Pervasive computing in the context of COVID-19 prediction with AI-based algorithms. *International Journal of Pervasive Computing and Communications*, 16(5). Advance online publication. 10.1108/IJPCC-07-2020-0082

Ouhame, S., Hadi, Y., & Arifullah, A. (2020, November). A hybrid grey wolf optimizer and artificial bee colony algorithm used for improvement in resource allocation system for cloud technology [iJOE]. *Int. J. Online Biomed. Eng.*, 16(14), 4. 10.3991/ijoe.v16i14.16623

Öztop, H., Tasgetiren, M. F., Eliiyi, D. T., & Pan, Q. K. (2018). Green Permutation Flowshop Scheduling: A Trade-off-Between Energy Consumption and Total Flow Time. *International Conference on Intelligent Computing.* Springer. 10.1007/978-3-319-95957-3_79

Palaniyappan, S., Veeman, D., Sivakumar, N. K., & Natrayan, L. (2022). Development and optimization of lattice structure on the walnut shell reinforced PLA composite for the tensile strength and dimensional error properties. *Structures*, 45, 163–178. 10.1016/j.istruc.2022.09.023

Palizi, S., & Saedi Daryan, A. (2020). Plastic analysis of braced frames by application of meta-heuristic optimization algorithms. *International Journal of Steel Structures*, 20(4), 1135–1150. 10.1007/s13296-020-00347-z

Pan, H. (2023). Effect of Shot Peening Strengths on Microstructure and Mechanical Properties of 316L Stainless Steel Prepared by 3D Printing. *Advanced Engineering Materials, 25* (11).

Pandian, A., Kaliappan, S., Natrayan, L., & Reddy, V. (2024). Analyzing the Moisture and Chemical Retention Behavior of Flax Fiber-Ceramic Hybrid Composites for Automotive Underbody Shields. *SAE Technical Papers*. 10.4271/2024-01-5006

Patel, R., Jani, S., & Joshi, A. (2023). Review on multi-objective optimization of FDM process parameters for composite materials. [IJIDeM]. *International Journal on Interactive Design and Manufacturing*, 17(5), 2115–2125. 10.1007/s12008-022-01111-9

Paul, T., Hossain, R., & Samsuddoha, M. (2019). Improved round robin scheduling algorithm with progressive time quantum. *International Journal of Computer Applications*, 178(49), 30–36. 10.5120/ijca2019919419

Pellegrino, S. & Calladine, C.R. (1991). *Structural computation of an assembly of rigid links, frictionless joints, and elastic springs.* Academic Press.

Ponnusamy, M., Natrayan, L., Kaliappan, S., Velmurugan, G., & Thanappan, S. (2022). Effectiveness of Nanosilica on Enhancing the Mechanical and Microstructure Properties of Kenaf/Carbon Fiber-Reinforced Epoxy-Based Nanocomposites. *Adsorption Science and Technology*, 2022, 4268314. 10.1155/2022/4268314

Prabagar, S., Al-Jiboory, A. K., Nair, P. S., Mandal, P., Garse, K. M., & Natrayan, L. (2023). Artificial Intelligence-Based Control Strategies for Unmanned Aerial Vehicles. *2023 10th IEEE Uttar Pradesh Section International Conference on Electrical, Electronics and Computer Engineering, UPCON 2023.* IEEE. 10.1109/UPCON59197.2023.10434918

Pragadish, N., Kaliappan, S., Subramanian, M., Natrayan, L., Satish Prakash, K., Subbiah, R., & Kumar, T. C. A. (2023). Optimization of cardanol oil dielectric-activated EDM process parameters in machining of silicon steel. *Biomass Conversion and Biorefinery*, 13(15), 14087–14096. Advance online publication. 10.1007/s13399-021-02268-1

Compilation of References

Prakash, K. B. (2020). *A Critical Review on Federated Cloud Consumer Perspective of Maximum Resource Utilization for Optimal Price Using EM Algorithm.* Soft Computing for Problem Solving., 10.1007/978-981-15-0184-5_15

Qin, Y., Zeng, G., Kurachi, R., Li, Y., Matsubara, Y., & Takada, H. (2019). Energy-Efficient Intra-Task DVFS Scheduling Using Linear Programming Formulation. *IEEE Access : Practical Innovations, Open Solutions*, 7, 30536–30547. 10.1109/ACCESS.2019.2902353

Ragmani, A., Elomri, A., Abghour, N., Moussaid, K., & Rida, M. (2019, January). An improved hybrid fuzzy-ant colony algorithm applied to load balancing in cloud computing environment. *Procedia Computer Science*, 151, 519–526. 10.1016/j.procs.2019.04.070

Ragumadhavan, R., Sateesh Kumar, D., Charyulu Rompicharla, L. N., Dhondiya, S. A., Kaliappan, S., & Natrayan, L. (2023). Design and Development of Light Communication Systems Using Modulation Techniques. *7th International Conference on Electronics, Communication and Aerospace Technology, ICECA 2023 - Proceedings.* IEEE. 10.1109/ICECA58529.2023.10395831

Rajan, K., Samykano, M., Kadirgama, K., Harun, W. S. W., & Rahman, M. M. (2022). Fused deposition modeling: Process, materials, parameters, properties, and applications. *International Journal of Advanced Manufacturing Technology*, 120(3), 1531–1570. 10.1007/s00170-022-08860-7

Rajasekaran, S., & Natrayan, L. (2023a). Estimation of corrective and preventive action on trend end plug-based machining activities using manual and failure mode with effects analysis. *Proceedings of SPIE- The International Society for Optical Engineering, 12936.* SPIE. 10.1117/12.3011698

Rajasekaran, S., & Natrayan, L. (2023b). Evaluation of occurrence number and communication based on FMEA operations in product development. *Proceedings of SPIE- The International Society for Optical Engineering, 12936.* SPIE. 10.1117/12.3011702

Raju, M., Gupta, M. K., Bhanot, N., & Sharma, V. S. (2019). A hybrid PSO–BFO evolutionary algorithm for optimization of fused deposition modelling process parameters. *Journal of Intelligent Manufacturing*, 30(7), 2743–2758. 10.1007/s10845-018-1420-0

Ramaswamy, R., Gurupranes, S. V., Kaliappan, S., Natrayan, L., & Patil, P. P. (2022). Characterization of prickly pear short fiber and red onion peel biocarbon nanosheets toughened epoxy composites. *Polymer Composites*, 43(8), 4899–4908. 10.1002/pc.26735

Ramaswamy, R., Kaliappan, S., Natrayan, L., & Patil, P. P. (2022). Pear cactus fiber with onion sheath biocarbon nanosheet toughened epoxy composite: Mechanical, thermal, and electrical properties. *Biomass Conversion and Biorefinery*. 10.1007/s13399-022-03335-x

Ramesh, C., Vijayakumar, M., Alshahrani, S., Navaneethakrishnan, G., Palanisamy, R., Natrayan, L., Saleel, C. A., Afzal, A., Shaik, S., & Panchal, H. (2022). Performance enhancement of selective layer coated on solar absorber panel with reflector for water heater by response surface method: A case study. *Case Studies in Thermal Engineering*, 36, 102093. 10.1016/j.csite.2022.102093

Rao, R. V., Savsani, V. J., & Vakharia, D. P. (2011). Teaching–learning-based optimization: A novel method for constrained mechanical design optimization problems. *Computer Aided Design*, 43(3), 303–315. 10.1016/j.cad.2010.12.015

Rasheed, A., Hussain, M., Ullah, S., Ahmad, Z., Kakakhail, H., Riaz, A. A., Khan, I., Ahmad, S., Akram, W., Eldin, S. M., & Khan, I. (2023). Experimental investigation and Taguchi optimization of FDM process parameters for the enhancement of tensile properties of Bi-layered printed PLA-ABS. *Materials Research Express*, 10(9), 95307. 10.1088/2053-1591/acf1e7

Reddy, P. N., Umaeswari, P., Natrayan, L., & Choudhary, A. (2023). Development of Programmed Autonomous Electric Heavy Vehicle: An Application of IoT. *Proceedings of the 2023 2nd International Conference on Electronics and Renewable Systems, ICEARS 2023.* IEEE. 10.1109/ICEARS56392.2023.10085492

Rizvi, N. (2022). A Workflow Scheduling Approach with Modified Fuzzy Adaptive Genetic Algorithm in IaaS Clouds, IEEE Transactions on Services Computing, May, SCI, DOI: 10.1109/TSC.2022.3174112

Saadat, , & Masehian, . (2019). Load balancing in cloud computing using genetic algorithm and fuzzy logic. *Proc. Int. Conf. Comput. Sci. Comput. Intell. (CSCI)*, (pp. 1435–1440). IEEE.

Saadh, M. J., Almoyad, M. A. A., Arellano, M. T. C., Maaliw, R. R.III, Castillo-Acobo, R. Y., Jalal, S. S., Gandla, K., Obaid, M., Abdulwahed, A. J., Ibrahem, A. A., Sârbu, I., Juyal, A., Lakshmaiya, N., & Akhavan-Sigari, R. (2023). Long non-coding RNAs: Controversial roles in drug resistance of solid tumors mediated by autophagy. *Cancer Chemotherapy and Pharmacology*, 92(6), 439–453. 10.1007/s00280-023-04582-z37768333

Saadh, M. J., Rasulova, I., Almoyad, M. A. A., Kiasari, B. A., Ali, R. T., Rasheed, T., Faisal, A., Hussain, F., Jawad, M. J., Hani, T., Sârbu, I., Lakshmaiya, N., & Ciongradi, C. I. (2024). Recent progress and the emerging role of lncRNAs in cancer drug resistance; focusing on signaling pathways. *Pathology, Research and Practice*, 253, 154999. 10.1016/j.prp.2023.15499938118218

Saadh, M. J., Rasulova, I., Khalil, M., Farahim, F., Sârbu, I., Ciongradi, C. I., Omar, T. M., Alhili, A., Jawad, M. J., Hani, T., Ali, T., & Lakshmaiya, N. (2024). Natural killer cell-mediated immune surveillance in cancer: Role of tumor microenvironment. *Pathology, Research and Practice*, 254, 155120. 10.1016/j.prp.2024.15512038280274

Saad, M. S., Mohd Nor, A., Zakaria, M. Z., Baharudin, M. E., & Yusoff, W. S. (2021). Modelling and evolutionary computation optimization on FDM process for flexural strength using integrated approach RSM and PSO. *Progress in Additive Manufacturing*, 6(1), 143–154. 10.1007/s40964-020-00157-z

Saad, M. S., Nor, A. M., Baharudin, M. E., Zakaria, M. Z., & Aiman, A. F. (2019). Optimization of surface roughness in FDM 3D printer using response surface methodology, particle swarm optimization, and symbiotic organism search algorithms. *International Journal of Advanced Manufacturing Technology*, 105(12), 5121–5137. 10.1007/s00170-019-04568-3

Compilation of References

Sahoo, R. M., & Padhy, S. K. (2019). Improved Crow Search Optimization for Multiprocessor Task Scheduling: A Novel Approach. *International Conference on Application of Robotics in Industry using Advanced Mechanisms*, (pp. 1- 13). Springer, Cham. 10.1007/978-3-030-30271-9_1

Said, , G. (2014). A Comparative Study of Meta-heuristic Algorithms for Solving Quadratic Assignment Problem. (IJACSA). *International Journal of Advanced Computer Science and Applications*, 5(1).

Sai, S. A., Venkatesh, S. N., Dhanasekaran, S., Balaji, P. A., Sugumaran, V., Lakshmaiya, N., & Paramasivam, P. (2023). Transfer Learning Based Fault Detection for Suspension System Using Vibrational Analysis and Radar Plots. *Machines*, 11(8), 778. Advance online publication. 10.3390/machines11080778

Salunkhe, S., Jatti, D. V. S., Tamboli, S., Shaikh, S., Solke, N., Gulia, V., Jatti, V. S., Khedkar, N. K., Pagac, M., & Abouel Nasr, E. (2023). Optimization of Tensile Strength in 3D Printed PLA Parts via Meta-heuristic Approaches: A Comparative Study. *Frontiers in Materials*, 10, 1336837.

Sanchez-Gonzalez, A., Bapst, V., & Cranmer, K. (2019). Hamiltonian graph networks with ode integrators. arXiv:1909.12790.

Sanchez-Gonzalez, A., Godwin, J., & Pfaff, T. (2020). Learning to simulate complex physics with graph networks. arXiv:2002.09405.

Sanchez-Gonzalez, A., Heess, N., & Springenberg, J. T. (2018). Graph networks as learnable physics engines for inference and control. arXiv:1806.01242.

Santra, S., Dey, H., Majumdar, S., & Jha, G. S. (2014, July). New simulation toolkit for comparison of scheduling algorithm on cloud computing. In *2014 International Conference on Control, Instrumentation, Communication and Computational Technologies (ICCICCT)* (pp. 466-469). IEEE. .2014.699300710.1109/ICCICCT.2014.6993007

Saravanan, K. G., Kaliappan, S., Natrayan, L., & Patil, P. P. (2023). Effect of cassava tuber nanocellulose and satin weaved bamboo fiber addition on mechanical, wear, hydrophobic, and thermal behavior of unsaturated polyester resin composites. *Biomass Conversion and Biorefinery*. 10.1007/s13399-023-04495-0

Sarhania, M. (2020). *Initialization of metaheuristics: comprehensive review, critical analysis, and research directions.* Institute of Information Systems, University of Hamburg.

Sasi, J. P., Nidhi Pandagre, K., Royappa, A., Walke, S., Pavithra, G., & Natrayan, L. (2023). Deep Learning Techniques for Autonomous Navigation of Underwater Robots. *2023 10th IEEE Uttar Pradesh Section International Conference on Electrical, Electronics and Computer Engineering, UPCON 2023*. IEEE. 10.1109/UPCON59197.2023.10434865

Sathish, T., Natrayan, L., Prasad Jones Christydass, S., Sivananthan, S., Kamalakannan, R., Vijayan, V., & Paramasivam, P. (2022). Experimental Investigation on Tribological Behaviour of AA6066: HSS-Cu Hybrid Composite in Dry Sliding Condition. *Advances in Materials Science and Engineering*, 2022, 1–9. 10.1155/2022/9349847

Sathish, T., Palani, K., Natrayan, L., Merneedi, A., de Poures, M. V., & Singaravelu, D. K. (2021). Synthesis and characterization of polypropylene/ramie fiber with hemp fiber and coir fiber natural biopolymer composite for biomedical application. *International Journal of Polymer Science*, 2021, 1–8. 10.1155/2021/2462873

Scarselli, F., Gori, M., & Tsoi, A. C. (2008). The graph neural network model. *IEEE Transactions on Neural Networks*, 20(1), 61–80. 10.1109/TNN.2008.200560519068426

Selvi, S., Mohanraj, M., Duraipandy, P., Kaliappan, S., Natrayan, L., & Vinayagam, N. (2023). Optimization of Solar Panel Orientation for Maximum Energy Efficiency. *Proceedings of the 4th International Conference on Smart Electronics and Communication, ICOSEC 2023*. IEEE. 10.1109/ICOSEC58147.2023.10276287

Sendrayaperumal, A., Mahapatra, S., Parida, S. S., Surana, K., Balamurugan, P., Natrayan, L., & Paramasivam, P. (2021). Energy Auditing for Efficient Planning and Implementation in Commercial and Residential Buildings. *Advances in Civil Engineering*, 2021, 1–10. 10.1155/2021/1908568

Shami, T. M., El-Saleh, A. A., Alswaitti, M., Al-Tashi, Q., Summakieh, M. A., & Mirjalili, S. (2022). Particle swarm optimization: A comprehensive survey. *IEEE Access*: *Practical Innovations, Open Solutions*, 10, 10031–10061. 10.1109/ACCESS.2022.3142859

Shirmohammadi, M., Goushchi, S. J., & Keshtiban, P. M. (2021). Optimization of 3D printing process parameters to minimize surface roughness with hybrid artificial neural network model and particle swarm algorithm. *Progress in Additive Manufacturing*, 6(2), 199–215. 10.1007/s40964-021-00166-6

Siddiqui, E., Siddique, M., Safeer Pasha, M., Boyapati, P., Pavithra, G., & Natrayan, L. (2023). AI and ML for Enhancing Crop Yield and Resource Efficiency in Agriculture. *2023 10th IEEE Uttar Pradesh Section International Conference on Electrical, Electronics and Computer Engineering, UPCON 2023*. IEEE. 10.1109/UPCON59197.2023.10434493

Singh, A., Goyal, P., & Batra, S. (2010). An optimized round robin scheduling algorithm for CPU scheduling. *International Journal on Computer Science and Engineering*, 2(7), 2383–2385. 10.1145/3484824.3484917

Singh, M. (2017). An experimental investigation on mechanical behaviour of siCp reinforced Al 6061 MMC using squeeze casting process. *International Journal of Mechanical and Production Engineering Research and Development*, 7(6). 10.24247/ijmperddec201774

Singh, P., Mahor, V., Lakshmaiya, N., Shanker, K., Kaliappan, S., Muthukannan, M., & Rajendran, G. (2024). Prediction of Groundwater Contamination in an Open Landfill Area Using a Novel Hybrid Clustering Based AI Model. *Environment Protection Engineering*, 50(1). 10.37190/epe240106

Sivakumar, V., Kaliappan, S., Natrayan, L., & Patil, P. P. (2023). Effects of Silane-Treated High-Content Cellulose Okra Fibre and Tamarind Kernel Powder on Mechanical, Thermal Stability and Water Absorption Behaviour of Epoxy Composites. *Silicon*, 15(10), 4439–4447. 10.1007/s12633-023-02370-1

Compilation of References

Smail, B., & Laid, S. M. (2021). Second-order analysis of plane steel structures using Rankine-Merchant-Wood approach. *Asian J Civil Eng*, 22(4), 701–711. 10.1007/s42107-020-00341-0

Snaselova, P., & Zboril, F. (2015). Genetic algorithm using theory of chaos. *Procedia Computer Science*, 51, 316–325. 10.1016/j.procs.2015.05.248

Sondergeld, L., & Voß, S. (1996). A star-shaped diversification approach in tabu search. In *Meta-Heuristics* (pp. 489–502). Springer US. 10.1007/978-1-4613-1361-8_29

Song, J., Xie, G., Li, R., & Chen, X. (2017). *An efficient scheduling algorithm for energy consumption constrained parallel applications on heterogeneous distributed systems*. IEEE., 10.1109/ISPA/IUCC.2017.00015

Strohbach, M., Gellersen, H. W., Kortuem, G., & Kray, C. (2004). Cooperative artefacts: Assessing real world situations with embedded technology. In *International Conference on Ubiquitous Computing*, (pp. 250-267). Springer. 10.1007/978-3-540-30119-6_15

Stützle, T., & Hoos, H. H. (2000). Max–min ant system. *Future Generation Computer Systems*, 16(8), 889–914. 10.1016/S0167-739X(00)00043-1

Sukumaran, C., Indhumathi, K., Balamurugan, P., Ambilwade, R. P., Sunthari, P. M., & Natrayan, L. (2023). The Role of AI in Biochips for Early Disease Detection. *Proceedings - International Conference on Technological Advancements in Computational Sciences, ICTACS 2023*. IEEE. 10.1109/ICTACS59847.2023.10390419

Sulsky, D., Zhou, S. J., & Schreyer, H. L. (1995). Application of a particle-in-cell method to solid mechanics. *Computer Physics Communications*, 87(1-2), 236–252. 10.1016/0010-4655(94)00170-7

Suman, T., Kaliappan, S., Natrayan, L., & Dobhal, D. C. (2023). IoT based Social Device Network with Cloud Computing Architecture. *Proceedings of the 2023 2nd International Conference on Electronics and Renewable Systems, ICEARS 2023*. IEEE. 10.1109/ICEARS56392.2023.10085574

Sureshkumar, P., Jagadeesha, T., Natrayan, L., Ravichandran, M., Veeman, D., & Muthu, S. M. (2022). Electrochemical corrosion and tribological behaviour of AA6063/Si_3N_4/Cu(NO$_3$)$_2$ composite processed using single-pass ECAP$_A$ route with 120° die angle. *Journal of Materials Research and Technology*, 16. 10.1016/j.jmrt.2021.12.020

Suryanarayanan, R., Sridhar, V. G., Natrayan, L., Kaliappan, S., Merneedi, A., Sathish, T., & Yeshitla, A. (2021). Improvement on Mechanical Properties of Submerged Friction Stir Joining of Dissimilar Tailor Welded Aluminum Blanks. *Advances in Materials Science and Engineering*, 2021, 1–6. 10.1155/2021/3355692

Tang, Q., Zhu, L. H., Lian, J., Zhou, L., & Wei, J. B. (2020). An efficient multi-functional duplication-based scheduling framework for multiprocessor systems. *The Journal of Supercomputing*, 76(11), 1–26. 10.1007/s11227-020-03208-y

Thakre, S., Pandhare, A., Malwe, P. D., Gupta, N., Kothare, C., Magade, P. B., Patel, A., Meena, R. S., Veza, I., Natrayan, L., & Panchal, H. (2023). Heat transfer and pressure drop analysis of a microchannel heat sink using nanofluids for energy applications. *Kerntechnik*, 88(5), 543–555. 10.1515/kern-2023-0034

Thierauf, G. (1978). A method for optimal limit design of structures with alternative loads. *Computer Methods in Applied Mechanics and Engineering*, 16(2), 135–149. 10.1016/0045-7825(78)90039-7

Ugle, V. V., Arulprakasajothi, M., Padmanabhan, S., Devarajan, Y., Lakshmaiya, N., & Subbaiyan, N. (2023). Investigation of heat transport characteristics of titanium dioxide nanofluids with corrugated tube. *Environmental Quality Management*, 33(2), 127–138. 10.1002/tqem.21999

Ullah, M., Wahab, A., Khan, S. U., Naeem, M,. ur Rehman, K., Ali, H., Ullah, A., Khan, A., Khan, N. R., Rizg, W. Y., Hosny, K. M., Alissa, M., Badr, M. Y., & Alkhalidi, H. M. (2023). 3D printing technology: A new approach for the fabrication of personalized and customized pharmaceuticals. *European Polymer Journal, 195*, 112240. https://doi.org/10.1016/j.eurpolymj.2023.112240

Ullah, A., Khan, M. H., & Nawi, N. M. (2020). BAT algorithm used for load balancing purpose in cloud computing: An overview. *Int. J. High Perform. Comput. Netw.*, 16(1), 43–54. 10.1504/IJHPCN.2020.110258

Vaishali, K. R., Rammohan, S. R., Natrayan, L., Usha, D., & Niveditha, V. R. (2021). Guided container selection for data streaming through neural learning in cloud. *International Journal of Systems Assurance Engineering and Management.* 10.1007/s13198-021-01124-9

Vasanthi, P., Selvan, S. S., Natrayan, L., & Thanappan, S. (2023). Experimental studies on the effect of nano silica modified novel concrete CFST columns. *Materials Research Express*, 10(8), 085303. 10.1088/2053-1591/aced82

Velmurugan, G., & Natrayan, L. (2023). Experimental investigations of moisture diffusion and mechanical properties of interply rearrangement of glass/Kevlar-based hybrid composites under cryogenic environment. *Journal of Materials Research and Technology*, 23, 4513–4526. 10.1016/j.jmrt.2023.02.089

Velmurugan, G., Siva Shankar, V., Natrayan, L., Sekar, S., Patil, P. P., Kumar, M. S., & Thanappan, S. (2022). Multiresponse Optimization of Mechanical and Physical Adsorption Properties of Activated Natural Fibers Hybrid Composites. *Adsorption Science and Technology*, 2022, 1384738. 10.1155/2022/1384738

Velumayil, R., Gnanakumar, G., Natrayan, L., Chinta, N. D., & Kaliappan, S. (2023). Bifunctional Aluminum Oxide/Carbon Fiber/Epoxy Nanocomposites Preparation and Evaluation. *International Journal of Vehicle Structures and Systems*, 15(7). 10.4273/ijvss.15.7.18

Venkatesan, A., & Gopal, V. (2017). Enhancing Wear Resistance & Fatigue Strength of Mild Steel & Aluminium Alloys Using Detonation Spray Coating. *International Journal of Engineering Research in Mechanical and Civil Engineering*, 4(2).

Compilation of References

Venkatesh, R., Manivannan, S., Kaliappan, S., Socrates, S., Sekar, S., Patil, P. P., Natrayan, L., & Bayu, M. B. (2022). Influence of Different Frequency Pulse on Weld Bead Phase Ratio in Gas Tungsten Arc Welding by Ferritic Stainless Steel AISI-409L. *Journal of Nanomaterials*, 2022, 1–11. 10.1155/2022/9530499

Vijayakumar, M., & Shreeraj Nair, P. G., Tilak Babu, S. B., Mahender, K., Venkateswaran, T. S., & Natrayan, L. (2023). Intelligent Systems For Predictive Maintenance In Industrial IoT. *2023 10th IEEE Uttar Pradesh Section International Conference on Electrical, Electronics and Computer Engineering, UPCON 2023*. IEEE. 10.1109/UPCON59197.2023.10434814

Vijayakumar, M. D., Surendhar, G. J., Natrayan, L., Patil, P. P., Ram, P. M. B., & Paramasivam, P. (2022). Evolution and Recent Scenario of Nanotechnology in Agriculture and Food Industries. *Journal of Nanomaterials*, 2022, 1–17. 10.1155/2022/1280411

Villani, C. (2003). *Topics in optimal transportation* (1st ed.). American Mathematical Soc. 10.1090/gsm/058

Viswakethu, C., Pichappan, R., Perumal, P., & Lakshmaiya, N. (2024). An experimental and response-surface-based optimization approach towards production of producer gas in a circulating fluidized bed gasifier using blends of renewable fibre-based biomass mixtures. *Sustainable Energy & Fuels*, 8(5), 975–986. 10.1039/D3SE00551H

Waseem, M., Habib, T., Ghani, U., Abas, M., Jan, Q. M. U., & Khan, M. A. Z. (2022). Optimisation of tensile and compressive behaviour of PLA 3D printed parts using categorical response surface methodology. *International Journal of Industrial and Systems Engineering*, 41(4), 417–437. 10.1504/IJISE.2022.124997

Waseem, M., Salah, B., Habib, T., Saleem, W., Abas, M., Khan, R., Ghani, U., & Siddiqi, M. U. R. (2020). Multi-Response Optimization of Tensile Creep Behavior of PLA 3D Printed Parts Using Categorical Response Surface Methodology. *Polymers*, 12(12), 2962. 10.3390/polym1212296233322445

Watwood, V. B. (1979). Mechanism generation for limit analysis of frames. *Journal of the Structural Division*, 105(1), 1–15. 10.1061/JSDEAG.0005071

Wei, H., Bao, H., & Ruan, X. (2020). Genetic algorithm-driven discovery of unexpected thermal conductivity enhancement by disorder. *Nano Energy*, 71, 104619. 10.1016/j.nanoen.2020.104619

Xie, G., Zeng, G., Xiao, X., Li, R., & Li, K. (2017, December 1). Energy-Efficient Scheduling Algorithms for Real time Parallel Applications on Heterogeneous Distributed Embedded Systems. *IEEE Transactions on Parallel and Distributed Systems*, 28(12), 3426–3442. 10.1109/TPDS.2017.2730876

Xingjun, S., Zhiwei, S., Hongping, C., & Mohammed, B. O. (2020, May). A new fuzzy based method for load balancing in the cloud-based Internet of Things using a grey wolf optimization algorithm. *International Journal of Communication Systems*, 33(8), e4370. 10.1002/dac.4370

Yang, S. & Slowik, A. (2020). *Firefly algorithm, in Swarm Intelligence Algorithms*. CRC Press.

Yang, X. (2000). A Brief Review of Nature-Inspired Algorithms for Optimization. University of Middlesex School of Science and Technology, Middlesex University, London.

Yang, X. (2020). Firefly algorithm. In *Nature-Inspired Metaheuristic Algorithms*. Luniver Press.

Yang, Y., Dai, X., Yang, B., Zou, P., Gao, F., Duan, J., & Wang, C. (2023). Optimization of poly-lactic acid 3D printing parameters based on support vector regression and cuckoo search. *Polymer Engineering and Science*, 63(10), 3243–3253. doi.org/10.1002/pen.26440. 10.1002/pen.26440

Yodo, N., & Dey, A. (2023). Multiobjective process parameter optimization in fused filament fabrication with nature-inspired algorithms. In A. Kumar, R. K. Mittal, & A. B. T.-A. In Haleem, A. M. (Ed.), *Additive Manufacturing Materials and Technologies* (pp. 349–359). Elsevier. doi.org/10.1016/B978-0-323-91834-3.00026-0

Yogeshwaran, S., Natrayan, L., Udhayakumar, G., Godwin, G., & Yuvaraj, L. (2020). Effect of waste tyre particles reinforcement on mechanical properties of jute and abaca fiber - Epoxy hybrid composites with pre-treatment. *Materials Today: Proceedings*, 37(Part 2), 1377–1380. 10.1016/j.matpr.2020.06.584

About the Contributors

S. Kaliappan is Professor in the Department of Mechatronics Engineering at KCG College of Technology, Chennai-97, where he has been a faculty member since 2023. He completed his Ph.D. at College of Engineering Gundy, Anna University, Chennai, his postgraduate studies in Internal Combustion Engineering at College of Engineering Gundy, Anna University, Chennai, and his undergraduate studies at R.V.S College of Engineering & Technology, Dindigul. He is in teaching profession for more than 25 years. He is recognized supervisor in Anna University in the Department of Mechanical Engineering in the research area Thermal Engineering, Heat Transfer, CFD, Composite Materials. He has served as technical committee head for varous conferences and workshop and worked as the reviewers and Editorial Board Member for several National and International Journals. He published more than 200 research articles in various national and international journals and conferences, organized nearly 20 STTPs, FDPs, Conferences and other technical events. He holds 15 international Australian Patent Grants, 14 published Indian Patents and 1 Indian patent granted which signifies his academic credentials. He also authored 20 books which is being used by the first year to final year students. He is Life member in Indian Society for Technical Education (LMISTE), International Association of Engineers (IAENG), a fellow member in Universal Association of Mechanical and Aeronautical Engineers (UAMAE), Institute of Research Engineers and Doctors (theIRED), and also member in Society of Automotive Engineers (SAEINDIA). He got Best Academician Award for the year 2023 from Scientific International Publishing House. He got Young Researcher Award in InSc awards-2021 for his research work, which is published in the Journal of Applied Fluid Mechanics. He is a Member of the Doctoral Committee in Saveetha University.

Mothilal Thulasiraman is currently working as Professor and Head in the Department of Automobile in KCG College of Technology, earned Bachelor Degree in Mechanical Engineering from Madras University followed by Master's Degree in Internal Combustion Engineering from Anna University and completed Ph.D. in Thermal science. Having 23 years of teaching, good at thermal related subjects, Research interest lie in thermal Engineering, CFD, composite material, Materials Engineering, Heat Transfer etc, published more than 40 journals,6 patents granted, Throughout the career received numerous accolades like best paper presentation award several times, domain awards in NPTEL, delivered lecture in various engineering college, Life member in Indian Society for Technical Education (LMISTE), International Association of Engineers (IAENG), Institute of Research Engineers and Doctors (theIRED), and also member in Society of Automotive Engineers (SAEINDIA).Recognized research supervisor in Anna University in the Department of Mechanical Engineering, organised several events, workshop, conference etc

***

Muhammad Abas is working as a lecturer at Industrial Engineering Department UET Peshawar, Pakistan. He did his PhD in Industrial Engineering from same university. His area of research is additive manufacturing and machine learning.

G. Drakshaveni is currently working as a Assistant Professor in the Department of Information science and Engineering at B M S Institute of Technology and Management, Yelahanka, Bangalore. I stood second place in My M.tech. Completed My PhD from Visvesvaraya Technological University (VTU), Belagavi, India. I have more than 21 years of experience in Teaching. I also worked in M S Ramaiah College for 5 year.I was appointed as the member of BoE, VTU, Belagavi,BoE(ISE & MCA) BMSIT. I have published papers both in National, International journals. I received Best Paper Incentive from BMSIT&M on 26.11.2020 for the paper titled "ultrasound and thermal image enhancement technique using convolution neural network". I was a reviewer for Sixth International Conference on "Emerging Research in Computing, information, communication and applications"(ERRICA-2020 held during September 25.9.2020 to 28.9.2020 at NMIT, Bangalore, India. Major research areas are Medical Image Processing, Data Base Management, Software testing, I has received a Best paper Award for the paper titled "Embedding data in JPEG & BMP image using LSB & cryptography algorithm" in International conference Global Paradigm shifts AVANT-GRADE-2014 Organized by Bangalore university Teacher's council of commerce & management and Seshadripuram first grade college, Bangalore, 19th March 2014, and also received best paper award for the paper titled "Color Segmentation using Digital image processing" national conference on "Computing for community services" organized by 27th CSI Karnataka students convention" & Reva Institute of technology & management, Bangalore 27th and 28th March 2013, and also received best projects awards for the project titled "Information Hidding using steganography system approach" has received Best Project conducted by Dept. of MCA, BMSIT June 2014 Received FIRST PLACE in Project contest, Project titled "A Utility for scraping and parsing data in webpages" has received Best Project conducted by Dept. of MCA, BMSIT 18th June 2015 Received SECOND PLACE in Project contest and project titled "Multifunction Smart-Bot Using Arduino" have received Best Project on OPEN DAY conducted by Dept. of MCA, BMSIT 2019 FIRST PLACE and received APPRECIATION FOR ACHIEVING 100% RESULTS IN THE SUBJECTS HANDLED II Sem MCA – Data structure using C – July 2011, II Sem MCA – Data structure using C – July 2012, III Sem MCA – Data Base Management system – Jan 2011, III Sem MCA – Data Base Management system – Jan 2013, V Sem MCA – Software Testing – Jan 2011, IV Sem MCA- software Testing – August 2019,V Sem MCA –Dot net Programming- Jan 2019 she attended workshop in Attended Workshop On "Social Media Strategy "organized by GoogleDigital Garages at Virgin Money Sheffield Lounge,66 Fargate, S1 2HE Sheffield, United Kingdom on held on 20th June 2018 • Attended workshop on "Python "organized by Python Sheffield at Union St,18-20 Union Street, S1 2JP Sheffield, United Kingdom held on 26th June 2018 • Attended workshop on "Agile Toolkits supporting Rapid Delivery/Game Storming "organized by Agile Sheffield at Electric Works, Sheffield Digital Campus sheffield S1 2BJ, Sheffield, United Kingdom, on held on 28th June 2018 • Attended conference on "Developing Outstanding Mentoring across the SHU Partnership" at Charles Street Building, Sheffield Hallam University, City CampusS1 2ND Sheffield, United Kingdom on 29th June, 2018. • Attended workshop on "DOT NET "organized by DOTNETSHEFFIELD at Sheffield Hallam University, Owen Building 942, City Campus, Howard Street, Sheffield, S11WB, Sheffield, United Kingdom held on 3rd July,2018.

Ziaullah Jan is MS student at Faculty of Mechanical Engineering GIK Institute Topi, Pakistan. He did his BSc in Industrial Engineering from Department of Industrial Engineering, UET Peshawar, Pakistan. His area of research is additive manufacturing of Electromagnetic Metamaterials and printed electronics.

K. Arthi, working as Associate Professor in SRM University, has more than 13 years of teaching and research experience. She has earned her M.E. and Ph.D. in Computer Science Engineering from College of Engineering, Anna University, Chennai in 2005 and 2015 respectively. Specializing in IoT and Machine Learning, she has published more than 25 articles in reputed journals and holds two patents in her area of specialization. She has professional membership in ACM and ISTE, through which she has organised multiple events.

Imran Khan is working as a lecturer at the Department of Mechanical Engineering, UET Peshawar, Pakistan. He did his MS in Mechanical Engineering from GIK Institute Topi, Pakistan. His area of research is additive manufacturing, friction stir welding, and friction stir processing.

About the Contributors

M. Muthukannan is a Professor in the faculty of Engineering at the Kalasalingam Academy of Research and Education (A deemed to be University), India. He has published number of research papers in peer-reviewed International and National journals. He has also several conference presentations to his credit. He has plenty of experience in guiding research scholar for their PhD degrees.

Sreenath M received B.Tech degree from JNTU Hyderabad and M.Tech degree from JNTU Anantapuramu. Received Ph.D in the Dept. of ECE., at BNMIT, Bangalore under VTU, Belagavi. Currently working as Assistant Professor in the Department of E.C.E., Vidyanikethan Engineering College, Tirupati., Andhra Pradesh, India. Areas of interests are embedded Real Time systems, Microprocessors & Microcontrollers and Control Systems.

M. Subramanian is an Assistant Professor in the Department of Mechanical Engineering at St. Joseph's College of Engineering. He received his Undergraduate degree, and his master's degree from Anna University, Chennai, Tamil Nadu, India, in 2008, 2011. His areas of research are: development, Corrosion Science, Machining Science, and material Characterization. He has published more than 15 research articles in reputed international journals and conferences proceedings.

Ramya Maranan is an accomplished researcher working in the Lovely Professional University, Punjab, India. With a passion for pushing the boundaries of knowledge and driving innovation, Ramya plays a vital role in advancing the research activities of the institution. Ramya's work primarily revolves around conducting research and development activities within their area of specialization. They are involved in designing and executing experiments, collecting and analyzing data, and disseminating their findings through scholarly publications. Ramya's dedication to research demonstrates its commitment to advancing scientific understanding and promoting technological advancements. Their work has the potential to create a positive impact on society and contribute to the overall academic and scientific community.

Mohamed Ibrahim A is a distinguished academic and researcher in the field of Electrical Engineering. He completed his Bachelor of Engineering in Electrical and Electronics Engineering from Sri Krishna College of Technology, Coimbatore. He pursued his Master of Engineering in Power Systems Engineering at the Government College of Technology, Coimbatore and subsequently earned his Ph.D. in Electrical Engineering from Anna University, Chennai. Dr. Ibrahim's research primarily focuses on Optical Power Flow using Flexible AC Transmission Systems devices and soft computing techniques. His innovative work in these areas has led to significant advancements and has been widely recognized in the academic community. He has authored 9 research papers in prestigious international journals, presented 12 papers at international conferences and national conferences.

Priyanka N. is currently working as an assistant professor at the Vellore Institute of Technology, Vellore. She did her Ph.D. at Anna University, Chennai. She did her Master's degree in software engineering at Anna University, Chennai. Her areas of interest include software-defined networks, next-generation wireless networks, the Internet of Things, and network security.

P.A.Vijaya received Ph.D degree from IISc, Bangalore, M.Tech degree from IISc, Bangalore, PGDCA from Mysore University and MBA(Information Technology) from SMUDE. Worked as Professor and Head in the Department of E.C.E., BNMIT, Bangalore, India. Areas of interests are Operating Systems, Embedded Systems, Real time systems, RTOS and Distributed Systems

C. K. Arvinda Pandian, B.E., M.E., Ph.D., is serving as Assistant Professor (Senior Grade) in the Department of Automobile Engineering, School of Mechanical Sciences, B. S. Abdur Rahman Crescent Institute of Science & Technology, Chennai, India. He is having more than twelve years of experience in academic and research. He has published more than 15 articles in SCI/Scopus indexed /WOS journals. He has three conference publications. He has one granted patent, published three patents, and filed two patents to his credit. He has authored four book chapters. His research interests include Polymer & Bio-Polymer Composites, 3D Printing, Piezocomposites, and Natural Fibers.

R. Renuga Devi received her Ph.D Degree in the Department of Information and Communication Engineering, Anna University. Her research interest includes wireless sensor network, mobile computing, Machine learning and Internet of Things. She published more than 20 papers in International journals and Conferences . Currently, She is working as Associate professor in the department of Computer science and Engineering, R.M.K Engineering College. She has around 16 years of teaching experience in Engineering colleges. She is a life member of IAENG and ISTE.

S. Radha was born at Namakkal, India. She completed her B.E. and M.E. in Computer Science and Engineering from Mahendra Engineering College, Salem, and Ph.D in Anna University, Chennai. Currently she is working as an Associate Professor & Head in the Department of Information Technology in Vivekanandha College of Engineering for Women, Tiruchengode and has published papers in many international & national journals and patents. She is having 18 years of teaching experience and her research interest include Cloud Computing, Machine Learning, Networking Data Mining and Internet of Things.

M. Sabarimuthu is a faculty member in the Department of Electrical and Electronics Engineering at Kongu Engineering College, situated in Perundurai, Tamil Nadu 638060, India.

Bathrinath Sankaranarayanan's areas of interests are Industrial Engineering, Production Scheduling and Optimization, Supply Chain Management, Industrial Safety. He obtained his Post Doctoral Fellowship in University of Southern Denmark. He has several publications in the area of Industrial Engineering.

J. Shobana received Ph.D. in Computer Science and Engineering. Working as an Assistant Professor in the department of Data Science and Business systems, SRM Institute of Science and Technology has been serving the Education Profession for the past 17 years. Her area of interest is Text Mining,Natural Language Processing, Artificial Intelligence and Machine Learning.

Index

Ensure Quality Research is Introduced to the Academic Community

Become a Reviewer for IGI Global Authored Book Projects

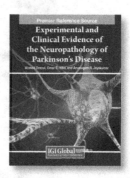
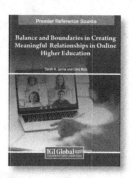

The overall success of an authored book project is dependent on quality and timely manuscript evaluations.

Applications and Inquiries may be sent to:
development@igi-global.com

Applicants must have a doctorate (or equivalent degree) as well as publishing, research, and reviewing experience. Authored Book Evaluators are appointed for one-year terms and are expected to complete at least three evaluations per term. Upon successful completion of this term, evaluators can be considered for an additional term.

If you have a colleague that may be interested in this opportunity, we encourage you to share this information with them.

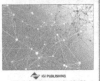

Printed in the United States
by Baker & Taylor Publisher Services